Hypothesis-Driven Simulation Studies

Fabian Lorig

Hypothesis-Driven Simulation Studies

Assistance for the Systematic Design
and Conducting of Computer
Simulation Experiments

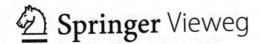

Springer Vieweg

Fabian Lorig
FB IV, Wirtschaftsinformatik
Universität Trier
Trier, Germany

Dissertation at Trier University, FB IV, Chair of Business Information Systems I, 2018

Diese Arbeit erhielt den Förderpreis 2019 des Freundeskreises Trierer Universität e.V. für herausragende Dissertationen.

ISBN 978-3-658-27587-7   ISBN 978-3-658-27588-4   (eBook)
https://doi.org/10.1007/978-3-658-27588-4

Springer Vieweg

This Springer Vieweg imprint is published by the registered company Springer Fachmedien Wiesbaden GmbH part of Springer Nature.
The registered company address is: Abraham-Lincoln-Str. 46, 65189 Wiesbaden, Germany

Till dig.

Preface and Acknowledgements

This dissertation proposes an approach that facilitates the conducting of "Hypothesis-Driven Simulation Studies". It has been written in fulfillment of the requirements for the degree of *Doctor of Natural Sciences* (Dr. rer. nat.) at Faculty IV (Business Administration, Economics, Mathematics, Computer Science, Business Informatics) of Trier University, Germany. From 2014 to 2019, during the writing of this thesis, I have worked as research assistant at the chair for *Business Information Systems I* of *Prof. Dr.-Ing. Ingo J. Timm*, who also was my doctoral supervisor. The research of the chair mainly focuses on the design of intelligent assistance systems by means of distributed artificial intelligence and computer simulation techniques.

Even though the circumstances under which I finished my master's studies and started to work as part of the research group were devastating and uncertain, I received friendly and loving support and encouragement from a number of great persons, to whom I would like to express my sincerest gratitude. At first I would like to thank my doctoral supervisor *Ingo Timm*, who first introduced me to computer simulation, got me enthusiastic about its systematic scientific use, and generously provided me with an inspiring and unrestricted research environment. In the course of the following years, the efforts and investments in various research initiatives paid off and we had the pleasure of watching the group grow and to welcome a number of new great colleagues. I am grateful for the support, exchange, experiences, and encouragement *Jan Ole Berndt, Tjorben Bogon, Sarah Gessinger, Sebastian Görg, Bernhard Heß, Axel Kalenborn, Lukas Reuter, Stephanie Rodermund,* and *Ralf Schepers* provided me with. With respect to the subject of thesis, my special thanks go to *Colja Becker* for his valued contributions as part of his master's thesis and for many fruitful discussions that led to the development of the *FITS* language.

Some services and implementations that are introduced in this work also emerged from the collaboration with students as part of theses, research projects, and independent studies they completed during their studies. My thanks go especially to *Kilian Brachtendorf, Anne Hammes, Marie-Elisabeth Godefroid, Paul Kugener, Moritz Künzl, Rania Nabhan, Marc Schmidt,*

Christopher and Nicolas Schulz, Lukas Tapp, Dennis Thiery, Patrick Weil, and *Felix Zolitschka.*

With regard to the final phase of the work, I would also like to thank *Prof. Dr. Paul Davidsson* from the IoTaP research center at Malmö University, who has kindly agreed to join the dissertation committee as external reviewer and who came to Trier shortly before Christmas to make the oral defense possible on 2019-12-19. *Tack så mycket!* Likewise, I am thankful to *Prof. Dr. Ralph Bergmann* for taking the role as chairman of the dissertation committee.

Zuletzt geht mein herzlichster Dank an meine Familie und engsten Freunde, die mich auch über diese Arbeit hinaus stets bedingungslos und verständnisvoll unterstützt haben. Dies sind neben meinen liebevollen Eltern *Gabi und Roland* auch meine Schwester *Katrin* und meine Patentante *Andrea mit Jörg.* Aber auch meinen großartigen Freunden *Benni, Christina, Daniel* und *Fabian,* die mich teilweise schon mein Leben lang begleiten, und vorallem meiner lieben *Tess* möchte ich für ihren Zuspruch und ihre Zuwendung ganz besonders danken.

Trier, Summer 2019

Fabian Lorig

Contents

III   Application and Evaluation   **261**

7   Case Study: Supply Chain Management   **263**

8   Conclusions and Outlook   **341**

List of Figures

List of Tables

Abstract

Computer simulation has become established in a two-fold way: As a tool for planning, analyzing, and optimizing complex systems but also as a method for the scientific instigation of theories and thus for the generation of knowledge. Generated results often serve as a basis for investment decisions, e.g., road construction and factory planning, or provide evidence for scientific theory-building processes. To ensure the generation of credible and reproducible results, it is indispensable to conduct systematic and methodologically sound simulation studies. A variety of procedure models exist that structure and predetermine the process of a study. As a result, experimenters are often required to repetitively but thoroughly carry out a large number of experiments. Moreover, the process is not sufficiently specified and many important design decisions still have to be made by the experimenter, which might result in an unintentional bias of the results.

To facilitate the conducting of simulation studies and to improve both replicability and reproducibility of the generated results, this thesis proposes a procedure model for carrying out *Hypothesis-Driven Simulation Studies*, an approach that assists the experimenter during the design, execution, and analysis of simulation experiments. In contrast to existing approaches, a formally specified hypothesis becomes the key element of the study so that each step of the study can be adapted and executed to directly contribute to the verification of the hypothesis. To this end, the *FITS* language is presented, which enables the specification of hypotheses as assumptions regarding the influence specific input values have on the observable behavior of the model. The proposed procedure model systematically designs relevant simulation experiments, runs, and iterations that must be executed to provide evidence for the verification of the hypothesis. Generated outputs are then aggregated for each defined performance measure to allow for the application of statistical hypothesis testing approaches. Hence, the proposed assistance only requires the experimenter to provide an executable simulation model and a corresponding hypothesis to conduct a sound simulation study. With respect to the implementation of the proposed assistance system, this thesis presents an abstract architecture and provides formal specifications of all required services.

To evaluate the concept of Hypothesis-Driven Simulation Studies, two case studies are presented from the manufacturing domain. The introduced approach is applied to a NetLogo simulation model of a four-tiered supply chain. Two scenarios as well as corresponding assumptions about the model behavior are presented to investigate conditions for the occurrence of the bullwhip effect. Starting from the formal specification of the hypothesis, each step of a Hypothesis-Driven Simulation Study is presented in detail, with specific design decisions outlined, and generated intermediate data as well as final results illustrated. With respect to the comparability of the results, a conventional simulation study is conducted which serves as reference data. The approach that is proposed in this thesis is beneficial for both practitioners and scientists. The presented assistance system allows for a more effortless and simplified execution of simulation experiments while the efficient generation of credible results is ensured.

Keywords: Automation of Simulation, Hypothesis Testing, Simulation Studies, Epistemology of Simulation, Assistance System.

Part I

Introduction and Background

1 Introduction

In various research disciplines, scientific advances rely on the application of computer simulation[1]. The use of simulation opens innovative opportunities for analyzing and understanding systems by extending existing domain-specific approaches or by providing alternative techniques for investigating systems. Some shortcomings of conventional approaches include limited access, exposure to risk, or the non-existence of the investigated system as well as economic reasons such as the cost-benefit ratio (Banks, 2014). This often restricts or even prevents the application of empirical or analytical methods as well as the possibility of conducting experiments for investigating the behavior of the system in question. To address this issue, modeling and simulation techniques allow for the creation of artificial systems that imitate the actions and behavior of real-world systems over time (Zeigler et al., 2000). Simulated systems provide a wide range of scientific opportunities as they can serve as a subject for experimentation in place of real-world systems and allow for the investigation of *what-if* questions on the behavior of such systems. This facilitates a more economic and risk-free conducting of scientific experiments as well as ex ante investigations of system developments or modifications.

Especially in information systems research, simulation has become established as a means for planning, analyzing, and optimizing complex systems (Hudert et al., 2010). This is associated with a general trend from descriptive research, with the aim of developing theories for explaining systems or phenomena, to a more comprehensive *design science* perspective where information systems (*artifacts*) are designed and used for solving problems. Yet, the use of simulation is not limited to information systems research as other domains also recognized the benefits of the experimental analysis of artificial systems. Examples include but are not limited to sociology and economics (Gilbert and Troitzsch, 2005), production and manufacturing logistics (Rabe et al., 2008), as well as traffic and transport logistics (Davidsson et al., 2005). Across these disciplines, simulation is used for

---

[1] For reasons of readability, the terms *computer simulation* and *simulation* are used synonymously in this thesis. The used terminology is introduced in Section 2.2.1.

© Springer Fachmedien Wiesbaden GmbH, part of Springer Nature 2019
F. Lorig, *Hypothesis-Driven Simulation Studies*,

different tasks such as optimization, input-output analysis, investigation of mechanisms, or advancement of knowledge (Axelrod, 1997). Moreover, the temporal perspective of simulation analysis is not limited so that it can be applied to understand past phenomena as well as be used for the prediction of future developments. In either case, many potential applications of simulation are related to decision support. To this end, the investigation of the model's *behavior* is of relevance, i.e., how specific circumstances or changes of circumstances (inputs) affect the observable behavior of the model (outputs). By investigating a system's behavior under different circumstances, detailed information regarding the mechanics of a system can be gathered and considered during the decision-making process.

Especially in terms of decision support but also for the acquisition and validation of knowledge, the methodologically sound and reproducible application of simulation is essential (Tolk et al., 2013b). Only if the results generated by means of simulation are replicable are they of epistemological relevance in accordance with the scientific method and provide a reliable decision-making basis. The systematic application of simulation is subject to *simulation studies*. They aim at answering questions or analyzing assumptions regarding the behavior of a model. Such questions or assumptions are often phrased as *if-then* statements (*phenomenological hypotheses*). For instance, a potential phenomenological hypothesis about the behavior of a manufacturing model is: *If the number of machines in a production line increases, the average cycle time of the manufactured products decreases.* In this statement, an inversely proportional relationship is assumed between the inputs of a model (number of machines) and the measured performance (average cycle time).

To investigate and verify such hypotheses by means of simulation, studies must comprise two aspects: model building and experimentation (Law, 2008). The resulting process is extensive and requires advanced expertise of different aspects of simulation (Bley et al., 2000). This includes specialized domain knowledge with regard to model building as well as sophisticated simulation engineering skills for designing, executing, and evaluating relevant experiments. In addition to this, the difficulty of simulation studies increases as the complexity of the modeled systems or the number of parameters that potentially influence the model's behavior increases.

To facilitate the conducting of simulation studies, a large number of frameworks, toolkits, and libraries was developed (Byrne et al., 2010; Himmelspach, 2007). While some of these applications contribute to specific scientific disciplines and domains, others can be utilized across different areas of application. Most of these tools provide valuable assistance as they simplify the creation of simulation models or the conducting of experiments. Common steps of simulation studies that are assisted by frameworks include the systematic coverage of the model's parameter space (Better et al., 2007), estimation of necessary replications (Hoad et al., 2007), or assessing the statistical significance of the results (Steiger and Wilson, 2002).

1.1 Problem Statement

Even though a variety of assistance functionalities exists, conducting sound and credible studies is not trivial and using the aforementioned systems and models is no silver bullet. The process of simulation studies is extensive and most tools do not cover the entire process of the study or are not fully suitable for the intended purpose. Often, the assistance provided is limited to single steps of the study or requires individual and application-specific adaptions. Accordingly, to conduct simulation studies and for answering research hypotheses on the behavior of a model, a model-specific identification, customization, and combination of suitable means is required. As a result, important design decisions that affect the course of the study as well as the generated results are primarily made by the researcher. This might result in the occurrence of *experimenter bias* (*observer-expectancy effect*), where researchers unintentionally influence the quality or credibility of the study's outcome (Tolk, 2017a). According to this effect, it needs to be assumed that the experimenters' expectations in terms of the model's performance, e.g., the subjective opinion on a model's suitability or quality, influence the study and consequently bias the results. Furthermore, decisions that are insufficiently documented or made methodologically ungrounded might also affect the reliability and reproducibility of the results (Uhrmacher et al., 2016).

To prevent experimenter bias and to ensure the quality and reproducibility of scientific studies, other research areas such as medicine or aviation defined standardized and systematic procedure models as well as guidelines. During the development of new aircraft such as planes or helicopters, *RTCA DO-160* document provides recommendations for the certification process (SC-135, 2014). It defines performance standards as well as environmental conditions that must be satisfied during the conducting of tests. Likewise, *clinical trials* define a methodological frame for the experimental testing and approval of medical treatments (Simon, 1989). The goal of these well-defined studies is to prove the efficacy of new medical treatments, e.g., drugs or vaccines, before release. The procedure is structured in phases that pursue different goals and include an increasing number of test subjects. Through this, both the effect and therapeutic efficacy of a new treatment are ensured. In summary, in aviation as well as in pharmaceutics, controlled conditions are defined in order to ensure the generation of comparable and reproducable results.

These approaches are similar to procedure models in simulation which give advice on the conducting of simulation studies (Banks, 2014; Law, 2014). Procedure models define a step-wise and systematic process for the conducting of simulation studies where the researcher is advised on essential steps for the execution of sound and successful simulation studies. However, methodological differences can be identified. Even though most procedure models describe similar steps and address related demands, the instructions or guidelines provided by these models are too vague to ensure the generation of reproducible results. Specific instructions on how each step of the simulation study must be performed to answer the initial research question are rarely provided (Timm and Lorig, 2015). Moreover, a lack of systematization in the formulation of hypotheses as well as the alignment of the study's process with respect to testing hypotheses can be identified (Lorig et al., 2017a).

Epistemological shortcomings are not limited to underspecified procedure models but also result from unavailable models, missing documentation, and insufficient statistical validation of the outcomes (Dalle, 2012). This results in a lack of justification of the derived results. To close this gap and to improve reproducibility, the assistance of the entire life-cycle of simulation studies is proposed (Teran-Somohano et al., 2014). This comprises the systematic design, execution, and evaluation of relevant simulation experiments. To achieve this, existing frameworks, services, and assistance functionalities must be logically linked in accordance with existing procedure models. Furthermore, the entire process of a simulation study must be aligned with the overall research hypothesis whose verification is the study's goal. To support and facilitate this comprehensive process, a demand arises for the provision of an assistance system that facilitates the automated evaluation of hypotheses using simulation experiments. Especially with respect to the automation of simulation, the "loop" between experiment design, data collection, hypothesis formation and revision, as well as new experiments needs to be closed (Waltz and Buchanan, 2009, p. 43). To this end, additional standards for the use of simulation in scientific research are required so that simulation can last as an "epistemological engine" (Tolk et al., 2013b, p. 1154). In summary, a twofold problem can be identified: On the one hand, a theoretical problem arises from a lack of systematization of simulation studies for answering research hypotheses on the behavior of a model. On the other hand, a practical problem can be identified in terms of a lack of assistance for the design and automated conducting of simulation experiments.

1.2 Research Questions and Objectives

To address these issues, the aim of this thesis is the systematization of simulation studies with respect to the replicable and reproducible verification of research hypotheses on the behavior of a simulation model. This thesis proposes a process for *Hypothesis-Driven Simulation Studies*, which aligns procedure models for simulation studies with a specified research hypothesis. Through this, assistance is provided for the systematic design, conducting, and evaluation of simulation experiments that are relevant for answering the specified hypothesis.

The presented problem indicates that current approaches are not capable of systematically assisting the verification of hypotheses by means of simulation experiments. Addressing this gap results in different research questions that must be answered first. Most of these research questions are related to different aspects and phases of simulation studies. They are contextualized and related by the following superior research question that structures the entire work.

How can assistance be provided for answering
phenomenological hypotheses by systematically designing
and conducting simulation experiments?

The stated research question aims at developing a methodology which allows for systematically answering research hypothesis on the behavior of a simulation model based on simulation experiments. The research question is formulated with respect to improving both the replicability and reproducibility of simulation studies and to mitigate experimenter bias. It is driven by the endeavor to facilitate and further establish the efficient utilization of simulation as an epistemological method in information systems research. The presented research question consists of four aspects: assistance, hypothesis testing, experimental design, and systematization. Each of these aspects is covered by more specific research questions. Additionally, a fifth research question arises regarding the status quo of assisting and automating simulation.

In summary, the resulting research questions that are addressed by this thesis are:

1. What is the current status quo in the application, assistance, and automation of simulation?

2. How can both specification and testing of phenomenological hypotheses be assisted?

3. How can relevant simulation experiments be derived and designed from hypotheses?

4. What is a suitable methodology for the conducting of Hypothesis-Driven Simulation Studies?

5. How must existing methods, frameworks, and tools be logically linked to provide assistance for the systematic testing of hypotheses in simulation studies?

As a first step towards a simulation-based assistance for answering research hypotheses, the hypothesis itself must be integrated into the procedure of simulation studies. For this purpose, a machine-readable and unambiguous formal specification of the hypothesis is required. Research efforts related to this question require the identification of essential components as well as the development of a formal specification language.

Subsequently, relevant simulation experiments must be derived from the hypothesis that is specified by the developed language. In case the model consists of a large number of input factors, the investigated parameter space must be limited with due consideration of a potential loss of information. This requires an approach for the identification of input factors that are of importance for the model's performance measure, which is specified in the hypothesis. Furthermore, a data basis must be created so that statistical hypothesis testing approaches can be applied.

The research problem stated in this thesis is not a challenge that is caused by a lack of adequate tools or frameworks. Instead, the issue can be attributed to missing or inadequate methods for the suitable and targeted linkage of existing approaches and techniques. Accordingly, the fourth research question aims at logically linking existing functionalities to assist the simulation-based verification of hypotheses in simulation studies.

Finally, a corresponding methodology must be developed that provides a systematic theoretical framework for the concept of Hypothesis-Driven Simulation Studies. To this end, existing methods and best practices must be aligned with procedure models of simulation studies. An integrated framework is required which defines a procedure for the systematic design and conducting of experiments with respect to answering a specific hypothesis. The methodology must focus on aspects of assistance and reproducibility so that the conducting of Hypothesis-Driven Simulation Studies is facilitated.

1.3 Contribution

In this thesis, a design science approach is pursued to accomplish the presented goals and to answer the stated research questions. To this end, the main question is addressed by answering the five resulting research questions. Unlike the behavioral science paradigm, design science research aims at the design, development, and application of innovative artifacts to improve the understanding of a specific problem or to provide a solution to it (Hevner et al., 2004). To facilitate the problem solving process, the community agreed on guidelines that respective research projects should follow. This includes the relevance of the investigated problem, the thorough application of rigorous evaluation methods, and the statement of verifiable contributions. In this regard, simulation is suggested as an experimental method for design evaluation. The European information systems research community also proposed principles for the conducting design-oriented research and described a process that related initiatives should follow (Österle et al., 2011). The process consists of four phases: *analysis, design, evaluation*, and *diffusion* and resembles the aforementioned guidelines.

The contribution of this thesis can be specified in terms of the design science paradigm. Hevner et al. (2004) distinguished between three potential types of contributions while at least one of them must be fulfilled by a research project: *design artifacts, foundations*, or *methodologies*. Different aspects of the approach presented in this thesis can be attributed to each of the three types. First, the presented assistance corresponds to the type of contribution referred to as *design artifact*. The problem the assistance addresses is that the reliability of current simulation approaches strongly depends on the knowledge of the user. Due to a lack of assistance, important design decisions must be made by the user which might result in experimenter bias and decreased reproducibility. By providing assistance that covers the entire process of a study, from the formulation of the hypothesis to the interpretation of the results, the conducting of methodologically sound and reproducible Hypothesis-Driven Simulation Studies is enabled and facilitated. Second, to allow for both formulation and testing of hypotheses on the behavior of a model, a formal specification language is proposed. In terms of the presented types of contributions, the introduced modeling formalism must be considered to be scientific *foundations* for the verification of hypotheses on the behavior of simulation models. By identifying relevant components of formalized research hypotheses, the design-science knowledge base is extended by this contribution to the spectrum of methods. Third, the theoretical framework for conducting Hypothesis-Driven Simulation Studies that is proposed in this work counts as a *methodology* considering the typology of contributions. It facilitates the use of simulation as an evaluation method in scientific projects as it structures the entire process with due regard to soundness and reproducibility, two major evaluation criteria. Through this, simulation is further established as a scientific method and the credibility of simulation-based results is enhanced.

By providing assistance for the design and conducting of simulation experiments, the contributions of this thesis can be summarized as follows:

- The process of formulating and testing phenomenological hypotheses on simulation models is simplified,

- the conducting of reproducible and methodologically sound simulation studies is assisted and facilitated, and

- a contribution is made to further establish simulation as an epistemological method in information systems research.

With respect to the diffusion of the presented contributions, different aspects of this thesis were presented at relevant conferences and published in respective proceedings. They can be found in established literature databases such as ACM or DBLP and are publicly accessible via the Internet. The three most relevant publications that present contributions from this thesis are:

Lorig, F., Lebherz D. S., Berndt, J. O., & Timm, I. J. (2017). Hypothesis-Driven Experiment Design in Computer Simulation Studies. In: E. H. Page, G. Wainer, J. Tufarolo, V. Chan, A. D'Ambrogio, G. Zacharewicz, and N. Mustafee (Eds.): Proceedings of the 2017 Winter Simulation Conference, IEEE.

Lorig, F., Becker, C. A., & Timm, I. J. (2017). Formal Specification of Hypotheses for Assisting Computer Simulation Studies. In: Proceedings of the Symposium on Theory of Modeling & Simulation (part of the SpringSim conference). Society for Computer Simulation International.

Timm, I. J. and Lorig, F. (2015). A Survey on Methodological Aspects of Computer Simulation as Research Technique. In: L. Yilmaz, W. K. V. Chan, I. Moon, T. M. K. Roeder, C. Macal, and M. D. Rossetti (Eds.): Proceedings of the 2015 Winter Simulation Conference, IEEE.

1.4 Outline

With respect to the presented objectives and for answering the related research questions, this thesis consists of three parts (cf. Figure 1.1). The structure refers to the phases of design science research as proposed by Österle et al. (2011). In this regard, the diffusion phase is taken account of by writing and publishing this thesis as well as related scientific contributions such as conference papers.

The first part of this thesis provides an overview of relevant methods and current approaches for the assistance and automation of simulation. Relevant related work is divided and presented in two distinct chapters. While Chapter 2 introduces fundamental methods of simulation, Chapter 3 presents recent advances that address the assistance and automation of individual components of simulation studies or that guide the entire study. The second part executes a requirements analysis and proposes a concept for the conducting and assistance of Hypothesis-Driven Simulation Studies. The requirements analysis presented in Chapter 4 has the goal of deriving requirements for scientific hypotheses in simulation and identifying methodological shortcomings in their integration in simulation studies. Based on these requirements, Chapter 5 proposes an integrated procedure model for the conducting of Hypothesis-Driven Simulation Studies. Moreover, to assist the verification of hypotheses by means of simulation studies, this chapter introduces logical components that are required for the execution of the process and outlines an abstract architecture for an assistance system. To this end, a detailed specification of all logical components as well as the interconnections between these components are presented in Chapter 6.

Finally, in the third part, the proposed approach is applied to and evaluated in a practical simulation scenario, which is focused on in Chapter 7. For this purpose, a supply chain simulation model is introduced and a respective scenario is defined. In Chapter 8, conclusions are drawn and an outlook on future work is given.

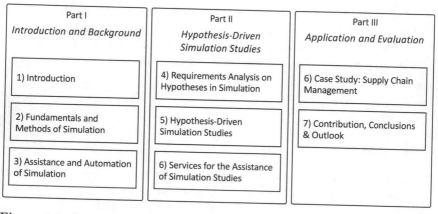

Figure 1.1: Structure of this thesis.

2 Foundations and Methods of Simulation

The increasing feasibility and popularity of applying simulation for planing, analyzing, and optimizing complex systems is a result of computational advances, e.g., web-based cloud computing and GPU computing (Nance and Sargent, 2002). In this regard, simulation has been established as a third pillar of science between induction and deduction (Axelrod, 1997). It is used amongst various disciplines and no longer limited to natural or information sciences such as information systems research (Hudert et al., 2010). Also in humanities, especially in social sciences, simulation has become a standard means for analyzing population dynamics (Gilbert and Troitzsch, 2005). To illustrate the underlying epistemological process of gaining knowledge by means of simulation, (Turnitsa and Tolk, 2008) applied Ogden's semiotic triangle (cf. Figure 2.1). Accordingly, the model can be seen as the conceptualization of the natural (real world) system which is represented by a simulation. Still, like other scientific methods, the starting point of simulation is existing knowledge and the goal is to generate new knowledge (Tolk et al., 2013b).

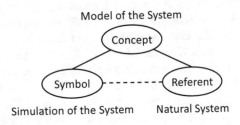

Figure 2.1: Semiotic triangle applied to simulation (Turnitsa and Tolk, 2008)

Advancing knowledge by means of simulation is possible but challenging. In particular it requires compliance with the principle of *reproducibility*, which is a major requirement of all scientific methods and approaches. Asendorpf et al. (2013, p. 1) emphasized that "replication is more than hitting the

© Springer Fachmedien Wiesbaden GmbH, part of Springer Nature 2019
F. Lorig, *Hypothesis-Driven Simulation Studies*,

lottery twice". The *National Institute of Standards and Technology* defined reproducibility as the

> *"closeness of the agreement between the results of measurements of the same measurand carried out under changed conditions of measurement".*

(Taylor and Kuyatt, 1994, p. 14, VIM 3.7)

In the narrowest sense and transferred to simulation, the replication of simulation studies and of respective results implies that if two persons execute the same simulation experiment or conduct the same simulation study, the observed model behavior must be equal. In a wider sense, one might neglect the necessity of equal results for each run and assess reproducibility by the similarity of the final results only. In non-deterministic environments such as simulation models, where the behavior of probabilistic components is observed, it is challenging or even impossible to meet these requirements (Freire et al., 2012). Dalle (2012) identified different challenges for reproducibility such as the human factor or technical issues. Therefore, he proposed four levels of reproducibility which are more suitable with respect to the demands of stochastic simulation models that consist of probabilistic components. Besides the requirement of a detailed specification of both the scenario and the instrumentation that was used for executing simulation experiments, he also suggests a more loose specification of reproducibility in terms of *similarity*.

In the MANET community, which focuses on the simulation of Mobile Ad Hoc Networks, Kurkowski et al. (2005) surveyed the 2000 to 2005 proceedings of the MobiHoc symposium on Mobile Ad Hoc Networking and Computing. Even though 75.5% of the 151 surveyed papers used simulation, the authors discovered that only 15% of the presented approaches are repeatable. Among the main issues for limited repeatability the authors identified missing information regarding the simulator that was used for the execution of experiments, missing information on the number of replications, and shortcomings in the application of statistical techniques.

Reproducibility of simulation is especially challenging due to different competences that are required for the application of simulation. To allow for the reproduction of simulation results, the competences and contributions of all involved experts must be documented as well. Timm and Lorig (2015) discussed three perspectives of tasks as well as three groups of experts which are involved in the conducting of simulation studies. Strategic, tactical, and operational tasks must be mastered by experts from computer science, information systems research, and the respective application domain the modeled system originates from. Considering the required competences and responsibilities, it becomes apparent that multiple experts are required to conduct a sound simulation study. Yet, all involved actors have different know-how relating to the system that is modeled but also on simulation methods and techniques. Furthermore, differences in experience as well as the capability of abstraction must be assumed and the reproducibility of results becomes more challenging as more experimenter bias must be expected (Bley et al., 2000).

The application of simulation in accordance with the above mentioned requirements is a subject of the *Modeling & Simulation* discipline. As the name implies, this process can be separated into two distinct tasks. First, a *model* needs to be built that adequately represents the system which is analyzed by means of simulation. Following this, as a second step, *simulation* is used to execute the model and to observe the behavior of the modeled system under specific circumstances.

In the literature, the required terms and concepts are not ambiguously defined. This is challenging with respect to the goal of this thesis. To reduce experimenter bias and methodological uncertainties when answering research questions in simulation studies, the underlying concepts must be defined properly. Thus, in this chapter, the foundations of simulation and especially of Modeling & Simulation are introduced. This includes relevant aspects of simulation and how they are interconnected, i.e., the real-world system which is simulated, the model, and the experiments, as well as an overview of how simulation is used in information systems research. Furthermore, challenges in simulation are illustrated and implications for intelligent assistance are derived.

2.1 History of Simulation

When speaking of the origins of simulation, *Buffon's Needle Problem* (1777) is often mentioned as the first documented problem whose solution was approximated by means of simulation (Goldsman et al., 2010). In this mathematical problem, the probability is searched that a needle of a specific length (l) which is tossed on the floor intersects parallel lines of equal distance (d) that are painted on the floor (cf. Figure 2.2). From today's perspective, one possible solution for estimating the searched probability can be classified as *Monte Carlo experiments*: The repeated process of tossing needles on the floor and calculating the percentage share of needles that lie across

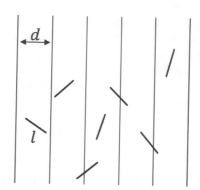

Figure 2.2: Buffon's needle problem (Aigner and Ziegler, 2014).

a line for approximating the respective probability. However, besides the mathematical approach he pursued, it is doubtful that Buffon was aware of the fact that this problem can be solved by means of simulation.

In the history of modern simulation, first attempts reach back more than 70 years. Goldsman et al. (2010) refer to the era from 1945 to the 1970s as the *formative period* of simulation where today's understanding of simulation was shaped. In the 1940s, the invention of ENIAC enabled scientists to automatically execute mathematical computations for solving numerical problems (Bednarek and Ulam, 1990). Initially, the "general purpose electronic computing machine" (Goldstine and Goldstine, 1946, p. 97) was developed for calculating fire tables during World War II. One of the earliest examples of modern computer simulation is the development of the hydrogen bomb. A group of scientists around Ulam used ENIAC to simulate neuron diffusion. Applying Monte Carlo methods they investigated how different materials interfere with the travel of neurons (Goldstine and Goldstine, 1946; Bednarek and Ulam, 1990).

Since then, the availability of computers increased, the hardware for executing simulation experiments was enhanced, and the application areas expanded. As a result, during the 1950s an 1960s, simulation gained popularity which resulted in the development of methods for the application of simulation. Goldsman et al. (2010) refer to *The Art of Simulation* as the first method-based textbook on simulation, which was published by Keith D. Tocher in 1963. In the following years, the first frameworks, e.g., GPSS (Gordon, 1981), and languages, e.g., *SIMSCRIPT* (Kiviat et al., 1968), for the specification and execution of simulation experiments were developed.

From a scientific perspective, the development of simulation can be reconstructed by means of the archive of one of the most established and influential conferences on computer simulation: the *Winter Simulation Conference*. Initiated in 1967 as the *Conference on Applications of Simulation Using the General Purpose Simulation System*, the scope of the conference was extended in the following year. From 1968, the conference was no longer limited to GPSS but called for contributions independent from language and framework. As the Winter Simulation Conference has taken place annually from 1968 on until today (except for 1972), it presents itself as "the premier forum on simulation practice and theory" (Wilson et al., 1996, p. 6). Considering the conference's history, it can be assumed that the archive of the conference provides an overview of relevant work conducted in context of simulation. Lately, almost 500 contributions were presented and published annually as part of the conference. This includes papers, posters, and keynotes from over 20 different tracks such as *Modeling Methodology*, *Manufacturing Application*, and *Social and Behavioral Simulation*.

In the following decades, simulation developed in various directions and the history of simulation must be pursued for each of the resulting topics or subdisciplines. With respect to the goal of this thesis, the history of simulation methodology and especially the execution of simulation studies is the most relevant. To this end, and due to the large number of openly accessible contributions from multiple decades, it seems reasonable to analyze the archive of the Winter Simulation Conference to reconstruct trends and advances in the methodology of simulation. The results of this survey that are presented in this thesis were also published by Timm and Lorig (2015). A first brief evaluation of the contributions revealed that the greater part of articles focus on the development of simulation models for practical applications rather than acquiring or introducing guidelines for performing sound and successful simulation studies. Generating reliable and reproducible results appears not to be of central relevance.

Considering the development of the conference over time as well as the range of subjects that are covered by the contributions, a trend can be identified. In the late 1960s and early 1970s, when simulation was still in its early stages of development, contributions on how to improve the technique of simulation can be occasionally found. The issues considered by the authors were related to the estimation of reliability in simulation experiments (Fishman, 1968), the use of experimental design techniques in simulation (Frank, 1968), or the necessity of a methodology for simulation (Mihram, 1973). Thereafter, up to the mid and late 70s, methodological and process-oriented aspects of simulation were neglected. The tracks of the conference mostly focused on the creation of simulation models for solving social, technical, medical or economical issues. Examples include health service (Kennedy, 1973), financial markets (Frankfurter and Horwitz, 1971), or even aerospace engineering (Flanagan et al., 1973). Towards the end of the 70s, a reorientation of the conference can be observed. Henceforth, papers and tracks regarding methodology of simulation were no longer uncommon but became an inherent part of the conference.

Nance and Sargent (2002) discuss a variety technical factors that drove and still drive the evolution of simulation. They distinguish between *external* factors, which originate from computing technology and shape the evolution of simulation, and *internal* factors, which are attributed to the community of simulation researchers and practitioners. Besides the evolution of computer hardware and the advances in computer software, Nance and Sargent identified a number of driving technologies which can be neither classified as hardware nor software. Examples are developments in *human-computer interaction* though which a decoupling of simulation developers and users was achieved. Due to interactive simulation models, detailed knowledge of the model was no longer required to work with the model. Through this, models became accessible for users that are not the developers of the respective model. As internal factors, Nance and Sargent identified assistance functionalities such as stand-alone pseudo random number generators or event list management tools. The reuse of such functionalities facilitates the development and execution of simulation models. Accordingly, methodologies for analyzing simulation results are still proposed and improved. This includes output analysis, experimental designs, optimization approaches, or variance-reduction techniques which allow for tactical planning of simulation studies. Finally, the development of their own *"theory of simulation"* (Highland, 1977, p. 4) promoted the development and application of simulation (Zeigler et al., 2000).

Nowadays, simulation is applied in various disciplines and has become an essential means in scientific research (Banks, 2014). By observing and adjusting simulation models, hypotheses concerning the behavior of artificial systems can be evaluated and the impacts of modifying real systems can be estimated ex ante.

However, findings made by analyzing artificial systems are often used for drawing conclusions in regard to the real world. Especially in the context of investment decisions, simulation is frequently used for planning alternative approaches. Common areas of application are, for example, factory planning including material-flow simulation (Kuhn, 2006) or traffic simulation when building new road networks or redesigning traffic junctions (Lattner et al.,

2011c). Therefore, it is obvious that general conditions and guidelines are required to assure a certain level of quality. Reliable results can only be generated if preparation and execution of simulation experiments are conducted under well-defined or even standardized conditions. Only in this case can results be used as a profound basis for decision-making or as starting point for further research. Simulation has become established as its own discipline and respective methods and techniques became an inherent part of the spectrum of research methods of various disciplines. As simulation is rooted in many of those disciplines' methods, it became unimaginable to carry out research without the use of simulation.

2.2 Fundamentals of Simulation

As previously mentioned, the discipline that emerged from the increasing application of simulation in many scientific disciplines is referred to as *Modeling & Simulation* (Zeigler et al., 2000). This name emphasizes the importance of two distinct yet closely linked tasks that have to be performed when applying simulation: The building of a model and the execution of simulation experiments. Sokolowski and Banks (2009) characterize Modeling & Simulation as a discipline with its own body of knowledge, theories, and research methodology.

The key element of each simulation is the model that is used for the execution of experiments. Simulation models can be defined as "approximations of the real world" (Sokolowski and Banks, 2009, p. 3). In this regard, simulation is a technique that allows for the repeated observation of the behavior of such models. The observed behavior is then analyzed for drawing conclusions with respect to the real world system based on which the model was built. Accordingly, the aim of simulation and also of Modeling & Simulation is to artificially generate the behavior of a system to allow for its analysis. In the following, relevant terms from Modeling & Simulation are introduced and the relationships between the respective concepts are described. This chapter especially focuses on three major entities: the system whose behavior is to be analyzed, the model which contains the relevant mechanisms and entities of the system, and the simulator which is used to execute the model and to generate the observable behavior (cf. Figure 2.3). In this regard, especially the *modeling relation* between the system and the model as well as the *simulation relation* between the model and the simulator are outlined in this chapter.

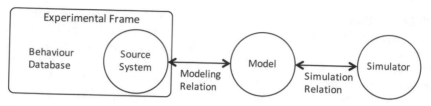

Figure 2.3: Basic Modeling & Simulation entities and their relationships (Zeigler et al., 2000).

Usually, the desire or need to apply simulation is motivated by the demand to analyze a specific object or phenomena. When scientifically investigating phenomena, this object of interest is often referred to as a *system*. In systems theory, a system is defined as "a number of elements in interaction" (*interrelated parts*) with given spatial and temporal boundaries which is located in an environment (von Bertalanffy, 1968, p. 83). They consist of states that describe the system's condition at certain points in time and which transform inputs from the system's environment into outputs that are returned to the environment. To evaluate hypotheses which aim at explaining a certain phenomena of a system, i.e., the relationship between inputs and outputs, *experiments* are conducted (Wilson, 1990). When performing an experiment, the system itself is varied or observed under changed conditions with the goal of studying the effect the modification or the new conditions have on the system and its behavior (Gooding, 1990). In the classical sense, experiments are directly conducted with the system under investigation. However, experimentation with the original system is not always feasible or reasonable due to various reasons. These include but are not limited to economic reasons, i.e., experiments with the real system are too expensive, as well as pragmatic reasons, e.g., the system might not be accessible due to safety or spatial restrictions, the system's state or existence does not allow for experimentation, or the system would be modified and the system's state would be negatively affected by the experiments. In all of the described cases, the conducting of experiments based on an artificial copy of the system seems to be promising for bypassing the mentioned issues. With regard to the application of simulation, this section presents foundations of simulation models and experiments.

2.2.1 Simulation Model

The simplified representation of a system (*source system*) in which only purposefully selected aspects are considered is referred to as a *model*. In some disciplines, e.g., engineering or physics, models are built as a physical copy of a system and thus provide a visual representation for the examination of the system (*physical model*) (cf. Figure 2.4 a). An example of a physical model is a replica of a car which is placed in a wind tunnel to analyze its aerodynamics. The aspect of the real system which is relevant for investigating its aerodynamics is the outer shape of the car. Accordingly, the model is reduced to this aspect and inner components such as the interior or motor compartment are not part of the physical model.

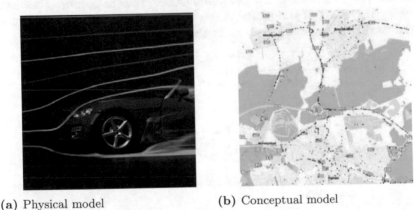

(a) Physical model　　　　　(b) Conceptual model

Figure 2.4: Examples of two different types of models: a) Flow simulation of a car (Bulmahn, 2009) and b) MAINSIM traffic simulation (Dallmeyer, 2013).

In contrast, the representation of a system or some aspects of a system by means of conceptualization is called the *conceptual model* (cf. Figure 2.4 b). A conceptual model of a system often consists of assumptions regarding the interactions of the system's components to explain its behavior in a logical or mathematical way by applying commonly accepted principles. Yet, the real world existence of the model's source system is not mandatory as virtual or fictional systems can be modeled, too. Either way, the source system of a model is often referred to as *real-world system*. This relates to the fact that this system is the one on which conclusions are drawn. The goal of this thesis is the assistance and partial automation of simulation studies.

Accordingly, only conceptual models are considered and the terms "model", "simulation model", and "conceptual model" are used as synonyms.

Especially when developing a conceptual model of a system, it is important to ensure that the real-world system and the model are similar. From a systems theory perspective, the similarity between systems can be defined on different levels. Zeigler et al. (2000) discriminates between five levels of morphism. While level 0 only demands that inputs, outputs, and the time bases of the systems correspond to each other, simulation requires the systems to be *homomorphic*. This implies that the structure of the real-world system is preserved during the modeling process, i.e., that both systems go though the same state sequence and that the states of both systems are identical (cf. Figure 2.5). The *homomorphism* concept requires that each state or transition of the modeled system must correspond to a state or transition of the real-world system but not vice versa.

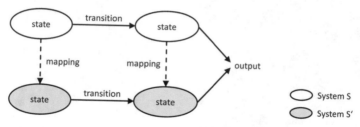

Figure 2.5: The homomorphism concept preserves state transitions (Zeigler et al., 2000).

To introduce relevant aspects of simulation models, the remainder of this section is structured as follows. First, a distinction is presented of inputs and outputs of models which are required to control and observe the behavior of a model. Then, a discrimination is provided between different types of models and discrete-event simulation is introduced in particular. Finally, this subsection presents approaches for the verification and validation of simulation models to ensure the correctness of the model as well as its suitability for investigating the respective real-world system.

Inputs and Outputs of Simulation Models

A model can be described in two ways: by its *structure* or by its *behavior*. The structure represents the inner architecture of a model and consists of possible states and rules how and when states are transformed into other states. A system's structure may consist of multiple subsystems and individual systems can be coupled to a larger system (Zeigler et al., 2000). This perspective corresponds to the definition of systems in systems theory (von Bertalanffy, 1968). In contrast to the inner structure, the behavior of a system characterizes the relationship between the system's inputs and outputs, i.e., sets of external input data that influence the system and corresponding sets of output data that can be used to measure the behavior of the model (cf. Figure 2.6). During the experiment-driven research process, most hypotheses assume or propose a certain behavior of a model under given inputs, which are then verified by conducting corresponding experiments.

In this thesis, a black box approach is pursued where the inner structure of the model is not of relevance or even unknown. The focus on the functional capabilities of a system is a common approach in information systems research and stands in contrast to a formal perspective with a focus on the efficient and effective application of information systems (Hevner et al., 2004; Österle et al., 2011). In this regard, a model is only defined by its *input-output behavior* whose analysis is the goal of a simulation study. In this regard, the model can be seen as a function $f: X \mapsto Y$, which maps explicit symbolic inputs X to corresponding outputs Y. The model itself can be considered as a subsymbolic system where the behavior is implicitly modeled and which does not allow insights into the generation of the behavior. This is contrary to white box approaches and models, where the states of the model as well as the transition mechanisms between states are explicitly specified. The input-output behavior of a model is defined by a set of inputs

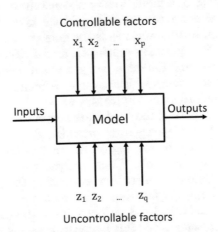

Figure 2.6: Black box view of a modeled system (Montgomery, 2013).

(*exogenous variables*) and corresponding outputs (*endogenous variables*) (Birta and Arbez, 2013). It is assumed that the outputs of a model change in accordance with the inputs and the relationships of the model.

Yilmaz (2015) presented three distinctions of exogenous model inputs: *qualitative vs. quantitative, discrete vs. continuous*, and *controllable vs. uncontrollable inputs*. Quantitative inputs, such as the number of workers in a factory, are characterized by numerical values. In contrast to this, qualitative inputs, as the queuing discipline of job processing, are nominally scaled and do not provide a hierarchy of values. Still, nominal values can be used to encode different levels, e.g., $1 \rightarrow$ FIFO and $2 \rightarrow$ LIFO (Sanchez and Wan, 2012). As qualitative inputs do not provide an ordered range of values, a differentiation between discrete and continuous inputs can only be applied for quantitative inputs. The main difference between discrete and continuous inputs is the data type of the variable. While discrete inputs can only take a countable number of values (e.g. Integer or a specific set of floating-point values), continuous inputs may take any real-number value and are only limited by specific upper and lower bounds (Sanchez and Wan, 2012). Accordingly, for instance, the quantitative input that defines the number of workers in a factory is discrete. In contrast to this, examples of continuous inputs are weight, size, or volume of a product. Depending on whether or not the inputs can be influenced, a distinction between *controllable* and *uncontrollable* inputs can be made (cf. Figure 2.7). In this regard, Winsberg (2010) refers to *parameters* when speaking of uncontrollable inputs of a model that are constant over time. In contrast to this, *input variables* are controllable and take values that vary over time. An example of a controllable variable is the number of machines or the used queuing disciplines in a job shop simulation model. Uncontrollable variables are of statistical origin and the values are generated randomly. Consequently, they take probabilistic values which can not be manipulated, e.g., the inter arrival time between orders or service times.

The observable outputs of the model are computed during the execution of the simulation. Just like exogenous variables, these endogenous variables can also be distinguished depending on whether the output is constant or influenced by chance (random). When analyzing a modeled system, it is often necessary to define measures for evaluating the performance of the model. These *measures of effectiveness* are usually not part of the model's outputs and need to be calculated on the basis of the model's *response* and respective *output variables*. For this purpose, it seems to be reasonable to define one or many layers of *intermediate variables* (*auxiliary variables*) as the precursor of target variables.

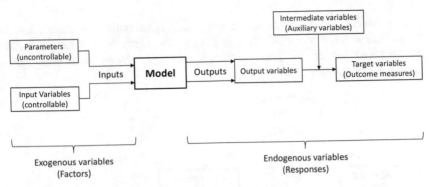

Figure 2.7: Classification of inputs and outputs of a simulation model.

Types of Simulation Models

In case the formalized model is not too sophisticated, mathematical methods can often be used for deducing a precise analytic solution of the model's input-output-behavior. When analytical solutions cannot be derived within a reasonable period of time or not at all for complexity reasons, e.g., due to the scope of the models, *simulation* provides an alternative approach for analyzing these models. In contrast to mathematical methods, simulation executes the model with specific input values or a range of values to practically observe how the model's outputs are affected by the inputs.

Table 2.1: A taxonomy of experiments (Vallverdú, 2014).

Experiments	Material	Nature	*In vivo*
		Laboratory	*In vitro*
	Non-material	Computational	*In silico*
			In virtuo
		Throught	*In mente*
	Hybrid	Computational-material	*In mixtura*

As most of the experiments with formalized models are conducted *in silico* (cf. Table 2.1), this type of simulation is referred to as *computer simulation*. This stands in contrast to *in vitro* experiments with physical models, e.g., crash tests with cars or aerodynamic flow simulations of planes. Accordingly, simulation is dependent on the mathematical modeling of systems for conducting experiments when analytical solutions are not feasible or reasonable (cf. Figure 2.8). In this thesis, the terms "computer simulation" and "simulation" are used as synonyms and imply the *in silico* execution of models and experiments.

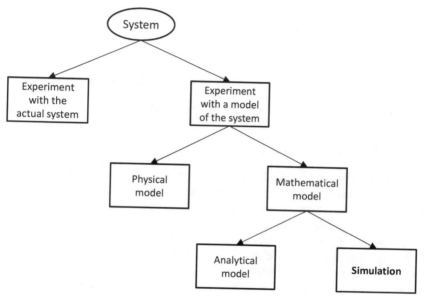

Figure 2.8: Ways to study a system (Law, 2014).

According to Law (2014) and Harrell et al. (2012), mathematical models used in simulation (*simulation models*) can be distinguished by three dimensions: *dynamics, randomness,* and *progress of time.*

Dynamics: Simulation models mostly represent systems, in which time plays an important role as the system changes over time. This type of simulation models is referred to as *dynamic simulation models.* The area of application includes but is not limited to manufacturing and logistics as these systems operate over time. In contrast, when a model represents the state of a system at a specific point in time or when time is not existent in the system, a simulation model is said to be *static.* Static models are used for Monte Carlo experiments where random samples are drawn for statistically solving problems. In finance, for instance, Monte Carlo simulation is used for determining the estimated distribution of outcomes when analyzing portfolios (Raychaudhuri, 2008).

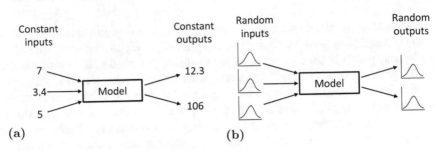

Figure 2.9: Examples of (a) deterministic and (b) stochastic models (Harrell et al., 2012).

Randomness: When the inputs of a simulation model are not influenced by randomness, the model is *deterministic* (cf. Figure 2.9). Consequently, a given initial state of a model determines all possible future states of the model as no random or unforeseen events might occur. The outputs of the model are predetermined likewise and will remain constant regardless of the number of iterations. Thus, deterministic models need to be executed only once to obtain exact results. An example of a deterministic simulation model is a set of differential equations describing dynamics in manufacturing, e.g., average flow of products (Armbruster et al., 2006; van den Berg et al., 2008). In contrast, if one or more inputs are probabilistic, the simulation model is referred to as a *stochastic model*. The outputs of the model depend on probabilistic inputs, which results in the observation of random outputs from an (unknown) probability distribution. In this case, each execution of the model only allows for one observation of the system's behavior. In consequence, stochastic simulation models must be executed multiple times to estimate the parameters of the distribution of output values and to derive statistical performance indicators, e.g., average values. In manufacturing, systems with varying process times and resulting uncertain throughput times are modeled stochastically.

Progress of time: Depending on how the states of a system are formalized, models can be either *discrete* or *continuous*. The state of continuous models changes steadily over time, which is why sets of differential equations can be used here as well. Examples are models of moving objects, e.g., vehicles or planes, as well as the consumption of a substance or material over time, e.g., fuel in vehicles or certain operating materials in manufacturing. Here, the behavior of the model can be observed at arbitrary points of time.

In most cases, the continuous modeling of systems is not feasible. Computers, which are used for executing the model, work in discrete units and real data, which is used to calibrate or evaluate the model, is also available for discrete points of time. To cope with these circumstances, discrete models can be used to represent the system by using a reduced number of states that change at discrete points in time. Usually, changes of states are caused or triggered by events occurring in the system. They cause an instantaneous change of the state, e.g., incoming orders, failure of machines, or the completion of a manufacturing process. Discrete models benefit from a reduced complexity as periods of time without relevant actions do not need to be simulated in detail, computing capacities can be saved, and transitions between states are simplified. In fact, this results in a further abstraction of the source system. Yet, for most applications of simulation this is still sufficient.

Discrete-Event Simulation

In this thesis, the focus lies on models that are discrete, dynamic, and stochastic. Such models are subject to *discrete-event simulation*, where states of the model change at specific points in time (Nance, 1993). Often, a distinction is made between this type of simulation and *continuous* or *Monte Carlo* simulation. Examples of discrete event simulation are queuing models as they can be found in customer service, e.g., call centers, inquiry desks, or restaurants, but also inventory management, e.g., in manufacturing or warehousing. The *discrete-event* characteristic of such simulation models relates to how the system evolves over time. In contrast to continuous simulations, the states of the model change instantaneously at specific points in time upon the occurrence of specific *events*. An example of an event is the arrival of a customer in the waiting queue of an information desk or the receipt of an order in a production line. The benefit of discrete-event simulation is that time intervals between the occurrence of two events do not need to be simulated as it is assumed that no relevant action takes place. Thus, the computation of such models is more efficient as such periods of time can be skipped (cf. Figure 2.10). Likewise, when multiple events occur in a short time interval which could not be differentiated in time-equidistant simulation, discrete event simulation allows for the consideration of each individual event. Yet, scheduling of events as well as obtaining dynamic behaviors is challenging as specific assumptions might apply (Özgün and Barlas, 2009).

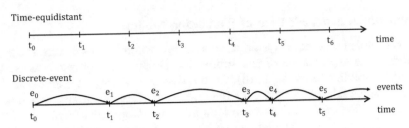

Figure 2.10: Time steps in time-equidistant and event-driven simulations (Law, 2014).

Law (2014) illustrates the benefits of discrete-event simulation using an example of a service facility. To estimate the expected average delay in a queue of customers arriving at an information desk at an airport by means of a discrete-event model, only three variables are required: the status of the server, the number of waiting customers, and the point of time each customer arrived at the desk. Depending on the status of the server, an arriving customer is served immediately or needs to wait in the queue. When a customer leaves from the desk after being served, the server becomes idle in case the queue is empty or serves the next customer from the queue. Accordingly, two types of events can occur: the arrival of new customers and the departure of customers after they were served. The average delay is then determined as the average delta between the time of arrival and the time of departure of each customer. In case the server is idle and no customer is waiting in the queue, the time until the next customer arrives can be skipped and does not need to be simulated. Likewise, when a new customer is served, the time until the departure of the customer can be skipped, too, except when new customers enter the queue.

In contrast to continuous simulations, the behavior of the system can only be derived for specific points of time. Accordingly, no conclusions can be drawn about the dynamics of the system between the occurrence of two events. In case all events that are relevant for thoroughly answering the underlying question are modeled, this might be an advantage. Time slices in which no event occurs do not need to be simulated, which saves computation time and leads to a more efficient execution of the model. Discrete event simulation also allows for the simulation of events that take place in parallel, as they are sequentialized by the event list but still take place at the same time slice of the model. Finally, discrete event simulation allows for the parallel and distributed simulation of models (Fujimoto, 1990).

Verification and Validation of Simulation Models

Regardless of whether a system is designed as a continuous or discrete-event model, the significance of the simulation study strongly depends on the model's validity (Sargent, 2013). To increase the validity of a model and to ensure the quality of a model for the execution of sound experiments, means of *verification and validation* must be applied. Petty (2009) defined related terms with respect to modeling and simulation from a quality management perspective: *Verification* describes a testing approach in which an object's consistency with individual specifications or regulations is measured and assessed. Transferred to Modeling & Simulation, verification refers to the assessment of whether the executable implementation of a model corresponds to the specification of the model. An analyze is made of whether the conceptual model is correctly implemented by the program code. In other words, verification analyzes whether the model was built *right* (Balci, 1998, p. 336).

In contrast to this, *validation* takes an external perspective in quality management and evaluates whether a product corresponds to the customers' requirements. In Modeling & Simulation, this refers to the behavior of the model. If the correspondence of the model's behavior with the behavior of the real-world system is satisfying, a model is considered *valid*. However, a famous quote that is often attributed to physicist Murray Gell-Mann states that "the only valid model of a complex system is the system itself" (Beautement and Broenner, 2011, p. 38). This aims at the issue that models can never be able to adequately represent every aspect and mechanism of the real world as they might even be unknown. For that reason, Sargent (2013) redefines the requirements for a model to be valid such that the criterion of accuracy is weakened. Instead of absolute accuracy, Sargent demands an accuracy which lies in an acceptable range and that is sufficient for the purpose of the simulation. In this thesis, models to which common techniques and methods of validation were applied are referred to as *validated models*. This corresponds to Sargent's definition of validity and implies at the same time that the model's behavior does not fully correspond to the real-world system's behavior, yet, the level of inaccuracy is acceptable. Accordingly, validations analyzes whether the *right* model was built (Balci, 1998, p. 336).

Figure 2.11 illustrates how verification and validation fit into the process of simulation studies (Petty, 2009). Verification establishes a relationship between the requirements that define which aspects of the real-world system must be part of both the conceptual model and the executable model. It must be assessed, whether all requirements are met by the conceptual

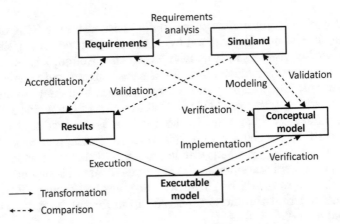

Figure 2.11: Comparisons in verification, validation, and accreditation (Petty, 2009).

model. Furthermore, verification also takes place between the conceptual model and the executable model. The goal of verification is to ensure that all aspects of the conceptual model are sufficiently implemented in the *executable model* that was developed using a programing language or simulation framework. In contrast to this, validation can be located between the *simuland* (experimenter), the real-world system of interest, and the conceptual model but also between the simuland and the behavior or results generated by the executable model. Between the simuland and the conceptual model, validation evaluates whether the aspects of the simulation were modeled adequately and to their full extent. Additionally, observations of the simuland are compared to the results of the simulation. Validation assures that the behavior of the artificial system corresponds to the behavior of the real-world system with sufficient accuracy. Finally, Petty (2009) introduces *accreditation* as a third process that takes place between requirements and results. Unlike verification and validation, accreditation is a decision process with the goal of deciding whether or not a model is suited for a specific purpose.

A process that is closely related to validations is *calibration*. Instead of comparing the model's behavior to the real system, the aim of calibration is to find a parametrization that results in a specific desired output behavior of the model (Banks, 2014). Calibration is an iterative process in which the values of the model's inputs are adjusted with respect to minimizing the deviation between the outputs of the models and the outputs observed from the real-world system under corresponding circumstances (Kleijnen, 1995). This can, for instance, be achieved by means of optimization algorithms such as *simulated annealing* (Bates, 1994; Kasaie and Kelton, 2015).

Building proper simulation models is a challenging and time-consuming task (Sargent, 2013). It requires a large amount of domain expertise and knowledge of respective mechanisms that are part of the artificial representation of the real-world system. In this thesis, it is assumed that approaches were successfully applied for the verification, validation, and accreditation of the model. Accordingly, when referring to a model that is provided by a user for conducing a simulation study, it is assumed that this model's reliability and validity were tested by means of adequate techniques. Furthermore, it is presumed that the model's accreditation for the intended study was confirmed as well.

2.2.2 Simulation Experiment

After building a simulation model and assuring its quality, the next step towards answering research questions is the execution of *simulation experiments*. The aim of simulation experiments is to identify and understand changes in the observable behavior of a model that are caused by the variation of the values of the model's inputs. With respect to the goal of this thesis, the identification and design as well as the execution and analysis of those experiments are crucial for answering the hypothesis. Especially when investigating models with a large number of inputs and admissible values per input, not all possible input value combinations can be investigated by experiment. Instead, a limited number of experiments with parametrizations that provide evidence for answering the hypothesis *(relevant experiments)* must be executed. For instance, if it can be proven that a specific input does not influence the behavior of a model, it might not be necessary to execute experiments for each possible value of this input. Respective experiments can then be considered *irrelevant* for answering the hypothesis.

For this reason, the concept which is presented in Chapter 5 and specified in Chapter 6 addresses these steps thoroughly. It discusses how experiments can be assisted and automated with respect to systematically answering research questions. To avoid redundancies and with respect to the structure of this thesis, only concepts and terminology which are of superior relevance for understanding the presented approach are introduced in this chapter. The aim of this subsection is to impart a basic understanding of what scientific simulation experiments are, why the proper design of experiments is an important and challenging task, and how this task can be supported by means of theoretical frameworks. To outline the fundamentals of simulation experiments, it is structured as follows. After providing a definition of simulation experiments, the influence randomness has on the design and execution of simulation experiments is illustrated. Finally, theoretical frameworks are presented that provide assistance for the design of simulation experiments.

Scientific Simulation Experiments

For the generation of credible simulation results, it is not sufficient to just observe the behavior of a model under any circumstances upon execution. To provide reliable answers to model-related research questions, it is necessary to understand how different circumstances systematically affect the behavior of the model. It is essential to investigate and analyze a model's *cause-and-effect relationships* in terms of how variations of the model's inputs influence the model's outputs (Montgomery, 2013). Furthermore, it is also desirable to identify which inputs influence a specific output. This is the goal of *simulation experiments*. In Modeling & Simulation, a simulation experiment can be defined as

> *"a test or series of runs in which purposeful changes are made to the input variables of a process or system so that we may observe and identify the reasons for changes that may be observed in the output response".*

> (Montgomery, 2013, p. 1)

In each of the runs that Montgomery refers to, the model's behavior is observed under different circumstances. Technically, those circumstances are defined by the model's inputs and more particularly by the values of the model's inputs. To execute the model, specific values must be assigned to each input of the model. A tuple that contains an individual value for each input of the model is referred to as the *parametrization* of the model. Accordingly, each simulation run that is performed as part of an experiment is defined by an individual parametrization of the model.

Randomness in Simulation Experiments

If the model consists of random inputs (cf. Section 2.2.1), the design and execution of simulation experiments is more difficult compared to deterministic models that are not comprised of stochastic behavior. This is because the statistical certainty of the generated results must be assessed and considered.

To include probabilistic values in simulation models, *stochastic probability distributions* are used. They consist of mathematical functions that provide information on how likely the observation of specific outputs of an experiment is. When rolling a 6-sided dice, the sample space of possible outcomes is $S = \{1, 2, 3, 4, 5, 6\}$ where each observation is equally likely, namely $1/6 \approx$ 16.67%. Accordingly, the corresponding probability distribution of rolling a fair dice is uniformly distributed (cf. Figure 2.12).

A differentiation can be made between *continuous* and *discrete* probability distributions (cf. Figure 2.13). The probability distributions of rolling a dice or tossing a coin consist of a countable number of discrete events that can be observed. Each observation can be assigned to one specific and predefined value of the respective discrete random variable. In contrast to this, a continuous probability distribution defines the probability of a continuous random variable taking a specific value. Such distributions consist of an infinite and uncountable number of possible values. Accordingly, the likelihood to observe one specific value is zero and only the probability to observe a value from a range of values is determined by the distribution. Continuous probability distributions can be utilized to describe outcomes of processes where times are measures, e.g., the processing time of orders in a manufacturing environment. However, considering the accuracy of the measuring tool, continuous distributions might be discretized due to a lack of granularity. For instance, the precision of stop watches that are used for measuring waiting or processing times is often limited to a hundredth or thousandth of a second. Thus, measured times are discretized accordingly. This corresponds to the distinction between discrete and continuous inputs of a model as presented in Section 2.2.1.

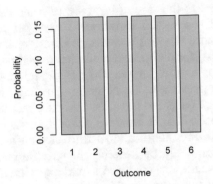

Figure 2.12: Probability mass function of a 6-sided fair dice.

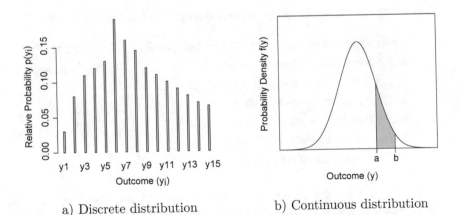

a) Discrete distribution   b) Continuous distribution

Figure 2.13: Discrete and continuous probability distribution (Montgomery, 2013).

Theoretical Frameworks for Designing Experiments

To consolidate all aspects that are of importance when designing simulation experiments, several theoretical frameworks were proposed that provide assistance and structure relevant processes. Montgomery (2013) proposed seven guidelines (steps) for designing simulation experiments (cf. Table 2.2). These guidelines shape a procedure for the design and analysis of simulation experiments with respect to an exact understanding of the study's goal, the extent and form of collected data, as well as a qualitative understanding regarding the analysis of these data. The first step of Montgomery's guidelines proposes both a **recognition and statement of the study's underlying problem**. Only by keeping the specific reason for executing experiments in mind can a targeted and sound experimentation be ensured. This proceeding is not exclusive for simulation experiments but can also be discovered in procedure models for simulation studies as a part of which experiments are executed (cf. Section 2.3.3). When discussing reasons for simulation experiments, Montgomery distinguished between *factor screening, optimization, confirmation, discovery*, and *robustness*. This emphasizes, that the process of executing experiments must be varied in accordance with the specific reason.

Table 2.2: Guidelines for designing an experiment (Montgomery, 2013).

1. Recognition of and statement of the problem   (Pre-planning)
2. Selection of the response variable   (Pre-planning)
3. Choice of factors, levels, and ranges
4. Choice of experimental design
5. Performing the experiment
6. Statistical analysis of the data
7. Conclusions and recommendations

As a next step, the **selection of the response variables** is proposed to adequately measure the performance or behavior of the model during experimentation. In this regard, the conducting of multiple simulation iterations is suggested to reduce the measurement error that might occur in dynamical models. The first and second step of the proposed guidelines can be summarized as *pre-experimental planning*. They are conducted in advance of the experimentation and serve as a methodological frame for the following steps.

In the third step, the **choice of factors, levels, and ranges** takes place. In *Design of Experiment* terminology, (*design*) *factors* are inputs that can be varied during an experiment. Montgomery (2013) discriminated between *potential design factors*, those that are varied by the experimenter during the experiment, and *nuisance factors*, which are not of particular interest for the current experiment. Still, nuisance factors might affect the performance of the model and thus need to be taken into account during experimentation. After the experimenter has defined which *design factors* will be varied, the second task is to determine which values (*levels*) or ranges of values will be simulated for each factor. At this point, a trade-off between the coverage of the parameter space and the computational complexity needs to be made. For the selection of relevant design factors, detailed process knowledge is required. Approaches exist for the systematic identification of important factors, e.g., factor screening. However, such approaches are difficult to apply and several preconditions need to be met (Kleijnen et al., 2005).

The fourth step of Montgomery's experiment guidelines intends the **choice of an experimental design**. Besides the required number of replications, the order in which the simulation runs are executed as well as potential reductions of the parameter space can be provided by experimental designs. A more detailed presentation and discussion of approaches for designing simulation experiments is provided in Section 6.3.

After an experimental design was chosen, **performing the experiment** is the fifth of the seven presented guidelines. Montgomery emphasizes the importance of executing the experiments in exact accordance with the experiment plan, which was defined in the previous steps. He furthermore points out that errors in the execution of experiments may drastically reduce or even entirely undermine the validity of the results. As a major source of error in the execution of simulation experiments, Montgomery identifies the person performing the experiments. While he suggests the involvement of a second person with the task of checking experiment settings, it seems that the assistance and automation of respective tasks, as proposed in this thesis, is more efficient with respect to reducing experimenter bias (Tolk, 2017a).

The **statistical analysis of the data** is the sixth step of experimentation. To ensure the objectiveness of the output data analysis and to facilitate the respective process, it is recommended to apply statistical methods. Those methods are able to assess the reliability and validity of the results by means of confidence levels and error estimations. However, they cannot prove that a factor indeed has a specific effect (Montgomery, 2013). Thus, a combination of statistical methods and domain knowledge is required to enable a sound and reasonable interpretation of the experiment's results.

Finally, as a last guideline, **conclusions and recommendations** must be made. This includes drawing *practical conclusions* from the results that were analyzed in the previous step. According to Montgomery, this last step can also include the execution of *follow-up runs* to confirm or disconfirm findings. Experimentation can be understood as an iterative process, where the results of one experiment lead to new problems and result in new experiments.

To summarize, simulation experiments have dynamic and individual properties, which need to be applied thoroughly and carefully. In this regard, Teran-Somohano et al. (2014) speak of a *life cycle of experiments*, taking account of a systematic design of experiments presented by Lorscheid et al. (2012) (cf. Table 2.3). With the goal of contributing to a more standardized simulation research process, Lorscheid et al. opened the "black box of simulations" to develop an approach for the systematic analysis of simulation models. Teran-Somohano et al. picked up on their approach, revised and specified the steps with respect to the computational assistance of experiments, and referred to it as the *experiment life-cycle*.

The experiment life-cycle consists of three phases and eight stages, which mostly correspond to the guidelines of experimentation proposed by Montgomery (2013). Teran-Somohano et al. argue that many tools and frameworks exist for managing the conducting of simulation experiments. However, they criticize that these tools do not take the entire life-cycle of simulation experiments into account. To counteract this shortcoming, experiments are modified as part of the extended process and with respect to experimental objectives.

The development of experiment process models such as guidelines for executing simulation experiments can, among other reasons, be attributed to a lack of (sound) experiments (Himmelspach, 2007). However, this is not a new topic. Already 20 years ago, Tichy (1998) discussed a lack of experimentation for testing theories and emphasized the importance of experimentation for computer science.

2.3 Application of Simulation

Combining the perspectives on modeling and experimentation, the focus of this section lies on the application of simulation, which is introduced in a twofold way. First, practical aspects of the application of simulation are presented. This includes the introduction of areas in which it is applied as well as software support for the execution of models and the conducting

Table 2.3: Phases and stages of the experiment life-cycle (Teran-Somohano et al., 2014) based on Lorscheid et al. (2012).

Phase	Stage	Output
I: Exp. preparation	1. Experiment objective formulation	List of experimental objectives
	2. Variable classification	Variable classification table
II: Exp. execution	3. Definition of response variables and factors	Response list, Factor table (including levels and values)
	4. Design selection	Experiment design matrix
	5. Estimation of experimental error variance	Number of required replications for statistical reliability
	6. Experiment execution	Final effect matrix
	7. Analysis of effects	ANOVA table, Effect strength and direction table, Factor and interaction significance table
III: Analysis of experiment	8. Outcome analysis with respect to experiment objective	Updated response and factor list

of experiments. In this regard, different domain-specific and multi-domain procedure models are presented. Second, theoretical aspects of applying simulation are focused including a discussion on advantages and disadvantages of simulation. To conduct methodologically sound simulation studies using the presented simulation software, this section introduces procedure models that structure the application of simulation studies.

2.3.1 Areas of Application

Simulation has been established as a third pillar of science and its application is no longer limited to computer science and information systems research. Banks (1998) summarized a wide range of potential areas of application. An obvious area of application is *manufacturing*, where simulation is used to analyze production planning models and machine shop operations (Mönch et al., 2003). This is especially promising with regard to the *"Digital Factory"*, a strategic goal of many enterprises in the production industry (Wenzel et al., 2005). The Digital Factory benefits from simulation as production processes can be planned, optimized, and changed as they take place. This also enables a more dynamic handling of unpredictable events such as failures in the manufacturing process. In this case, simulation can support the decision-making by investigating potential alternative manufacturing scenarios in no time.

Also in *logistics* and *supply chain management*, simulation has become a standard technique (Thiers and McGinnis, 2011). Many specialized software frameworks, e.g., Arena (Rockwell Automation) or Plant Simulation (Siemens AG), were developed to analyze logistics networks and resource distribution (Pawlewski and Borucki, 2011). Specific scenarios are allocation or scheduling of resources as required in warehousing and distribution of goods. Kleijnen (2005b) presented four types of simulation that are applied in logistics and supply chain simulation: *Discrete-event dynamic system simulation, spreadsheet simulation, system dynamics*, and *business games*. *Discrete-event dynamic system simulation* is closely related to discrete-event simulation, which represents individual events and incorporates uncertainties. By this means, complex supply chains can be simulated where random variables, e.g., production times or delays, need to be considered. In the broader sense and according to Banks (2014), the simulation of pedestrian flows is part of logistics simulation as well. This includes the flow of customers in a company's building, e.g., passengers in an airport terminal, but also of people in general, e.g., the evacuation of sport fans from a soccer stadium in case of fire or other emergencies. To this end, as well as for the simulation of logistics supply networks, agent-based simulation is often applied, which imposes scalability challenges (Timm and Pawlaszczyk, 2005).

Traffic and transportation simulations are comprised of road traffic, shipping, and aviation. On land, the planning and optimization of (long distance) road traffic and transportation networks (Taniguchi and Shimamoto, 2004) as well as the evaluation of strategies for traffic light circuits and traffic guidance alternatives (Dallmeyer et al., 2015) can be supported by simulation. In addition to these areas of application, Davidsson et al. (2005) provide a comprehensive overview of further applications of simulation in transport logistics. On water, simulation is applied to optimize port traffic (Cortés et al., 2007) or in container terminal management (Henesey, 2006) including connections to the hinterland (Iannone, 2012). In the air, the areas of application range from the training of pilots in flight simulations to the airflow simulations for the design of aircrafts and spacecrafts (Lee, 2005). However, in aviation, discrete-event simulations are rarely used.

In terms of *business processes* management, simulation can be applied to reduce costs or to improve efficiency. Accordingly, it can be applied as a method in business process reengineering (Greasley, 2003). Like in logistics, numerous simulation frameworks exist that facilitate modeling and simulation of processes in or between companies. For this purpose, process models that were described by means of traditional business modeling paradigms, e.g., BPMN (Wagner et al., 2009) or PetriNets (Jansen-Vullers and Netjes, 2006), can be executed and analyzed (van der Aalst et al., 2010). Potential applications of business process simulation are diverse and extend from call center staffing (Atlason et al., 2008) to patient treatment processes in hospitals (Djanatliev and Meier, 2016).

Also in *social sciences*, simulation has been established for modeling artificial populations with the aim of investigating human behavior. The emerging sub-discipline is referred to as *computational social science* (Conte and Paolucci, 2014) where modern computer-assisted approaches are applied to analyze social phenomena. A prominent example is the research field of *agent-based social simulation* where methods from social sciences, computer simulation, and agent-based computing are combined (Davidsson, 2002). Related methods are well suited to analyze social phenomena on a micro scale by representing individuals or groups of individuals as software agents (Gilbert and Troitzsch, 2005). In this regard, the potentials of combining sociology and artificial intelligence were also studied in the research field of *socionics* (Malsch and Schulz-Schaeffer, 2007). Yet, the application of simulation in social sciences is not limited to the analysis of human behavior. Simulation is also applied for estimating and understanding socio-demographic development, e.g., unemployment (Münnich and Rässler, 2005) or care-demand (Berndt et al., 2017).

Finally, for the sake of completeness, *military* applications of simulation must be mentioned. Military simulation includes domestic and international scenarios of defense and disaster management as well as combat missions and reconnaissance. Relevant fields include logistics and operational planning where supply networks (Hussain et al., 2015) or emergency strategies (Brachner, 2015) are evaluated. Furthermore, simulation is used to gain tactical advantages by optimizing the location of decoys (Mattila et al., 2014) or naval mines (Floore and Gilman, 2011). But also human performance can be analyzed and optimized by means of simulation. An example is the detection of and adaption to team behavior by autonomous mobile robots (Wimpey et al., 2015). Finally, to prevent and mitigate the effects of cyber attacks, modeling and simulation of different attack scenarios and counter-measures seems suitable (Cayirci and Ghergherehchi, 2011). Another common application of simulation in a military context is the development of serious games. Through this, both training and education of military staff can be improved, e.g., the importance and effects of international humanitarian law and ethics can be taught in role plays (Veziridis et al., 2017). At the same time, this application of simulation also emphasizes and justifies the importance of a code of *ethics* for the application of simulation (Tolk, 2017b).

2.3.2 Appropriateness and Advantages of Simulation

As stated in this chapter, simulation is an established technique for analyzing real-world systems by means of artificial models. Based on validated models, experiments are executed to systematically investigate the model's behavior and to derive conclusions regarding the behavior of the real-world system. Even though simulation is applied in various disciplines and for multiple purposes, simulation is no silver bullet and the opportunities provided by simulation must be considered carefully before its application. Thus, this subsection discusses circumstances under which the application of simulation is appropriate as well as benefits and pitfalls of simulation.

Section 2.3.1 introduced various areas in which simulation is applied. This gives only a first impression regarding the extensive field of application of simulation. The question of whether or not simulation can be applied in a specific situation or under specific circumstances cannot be answered by only considering the respective domain. To assess if the application of simulation is appropriate, e.g., for solving a problem or analyzing a system, the underlying purpose must be considered as well.

According to Banks (2014), traditional purposes where simulation is appropriate include but are not limited to *studying complex systems* or systems within systems as well as to *treat internal interactions of complex systems*. Moreover, *observing how changes of the inputs affect the outputs of a system* is a major task where simulation can be applied just like *analyzing effects of environmental changes* by investigating how the model's behavior changes in accordance with changes of the environment. By these means, dependencies and mechanisms within the model as well as between the model's variables can be identified. Finally, simulation is appropriate to *evaluate new designs or policies before implementation*,

In contrast, several circumstances exist where the application of simulation is not appropriate. Banks and Gibson (1997) refer to "ten rules for evaluating when simulation is not appropriate" (cf. Table 2.4). While some of the provided rules focus on the solvability of the underlying problem, others target quantitative factors such as costs or time.

Table 2.4: Ten rules for evaluating when simulation is not appropriate (Banks and Gibson, 1997).

1) The problem can be solved using "common sense analysis".

2) The problem can be solved analytically.

3) It's easier to perform direct experiments on the real system.

4) The cost of the simulation exceeds possible savings.

5) There aren't proper resources available for the project.

6) There isn't enough time for the model results to be useful.

7) There is no data - not even estimates.

8) The model can't be verified or validated.

9) Project expectations can't be met.

10) If system behavior is too complex, or can't be defined.

The primary rule for not applying simulation is the question whether it is necessary and efficient to use simulation. If the application of simulation takes too long compared to alternative analytical solutions, it is not recommendable to use simulation even though it might be useful. As an example, Banks and Gibson (1997) mention steady-state queuing models and probabilistic inventory models where probabilities in the system can be determined more efficiently by means of (closed form) equations. Furthermore, under some circumstances it might be easier to perform real-world experiments if the respective system as well as the obtained results will not be modified, harmed, or affected in any other negative way.

From an economic perspective, the appropriateness of applying simulation can be assessed monetarily. If the cost savings that can be achieved based on the simulation's results do not cover the expenses of the required simulation study, the application of simulation is not appropriate. Likewise, if there is not sufficient time to conduct a simulation study, e.g., due to long-winded model building or as the available time window is too narrow, it is also not appropriate to use simulation. Finally, if the model cannot be verified and validated or if no data is available for the execution of sound simulation experiments, it is not reasonable to simulate.

After evaluating whether the application of simulation is appropriate based on the individual circumstances, the consideration of further advantages and disadvantages of simulation is necessary. In addition to enabling the analysis of possible futures of a system, Banks (2000) discussed 21 aspects for and against the use of simulation. With respect to the goal of this thesis, the most relevant aspects are the *exploration of possibilities*, the *identification of constraints, difficulties in interpreting results*, and the *inappropriate use of simulation*.

Shannon (1998) also discussed advantages and disadvantages of the application of simulation. To emphasize the advantages of simulation, Shannon compares simulation to other approaches for analyzing systems such as analytical and mathematical models. Besides the improved *comprehensibility* of simulation, which is an advantage if the underlying concepts need to be explained to customers or managers, he points out the increased *credibility* of simulation models. Also for the *identification of bottlenecks*, e.g., in processes where the flow of information or products is analyzed, simulation is an adequate means. With respect to the goal of this thesis, the aspect of *hypothesis testing* for the investigation of phenomena is a major advantage of simulation. However, Shannon also discusses disadvantages of simulation such as *extensive training, dependence on the quality of input data*, and the fact that simulation models are not solved but *run*. Thus, they do not per se provide an optimal solution.

In summary, numerous advantages and disadvantages of simulation exist. Before applying simulation, one needs to thoroughly trade off these aspects against each other to assess whether or not simulation is an appropriate technique in a specific context. This thesis assumes that the appropriateness of the application of simulation was confirmed in advance of the planning of the simulation study. The proposed approach neither questions the suitability of simulation nor proposes alternative approaches for solving a problem. To ensure the generation of valid results, the feasibility of alternative approaches must be investigated by the experimenter.

2.3.3 Procedure Models for Simulation Studies

In the previous two sections, two key components of simulation studies were introduced: simulation models and simulation experiments. For each of the two components, individual research areas were established such as *agent-based modeling* (Bonabeau, 2002) and *design of experiments* (Kleijnen, 1998). Yet, to conduct successful and sound simulation studies, a thorough and systematic coordination between both components is required. When applying simulation in terms of studies, such coordination of the simulation process can be achieved and ensured by means of *procedure models*.

Procedure models are applied for process modeling and consist of a number of ordered steps with the intention to facilitate the achievement of a process goal. At first glance, this definition of procedure models seems to correspond to the definition of simulation experiments. Montgomery (2013) defines experiments as a series of tests in which the *input-output relationship* of a model is investigated. However, in this thesis, a differentiation between simulation studies and experiments is made such that experiments do not necessarily need to follow a systematic approach. While arbitrary parametrizations can be tested during an experiment, the process of a study as a first step requires the formulation of a research question. All remaining steps of the study are then aligned to contribute to systematically answering this question. In this regard, experiments can be seen as an essential part of simulation studies, yet, they can also be executed in isolation and apart from a study.

A large amount of procedure models was proposed during the last decades (Timm and Lorig, 2015). In the discrete event simulation community, the procedure model proposed by Law (2014) has been established as a *de facto standard* (cf. Figure 2.14). Hence, as a representative for other procedure models, Law's perspective on simulation studies is introduced.

Law's procedure model consists of ten linked sequential steps. As a first step of each simulation study, Law advises thoroughly **formulating the problem of the study**. This includes the definition of the overall objectives of the study in terms of questions that will be answered during the study. It also implies the definition of requirements for the model which will be developed during the study, based on objectives that are defined by the decision-maker. The boundaries of the modeled system are defined at this stage, too. Furthermore, performance measures for the assessment of the model's efficiency or for the comparison of different parametrizations of the model are defined at this stage of the simulation study.

The second step proposed by Law covers both the **collection of data and definition of a model**. Real-world system data that needs to be collected during this step in the study is required for the specification of the parameters of the developed model. Yet, not only the determination of relevant parameters but also the identification of respective ranges of admissible values as well as *input data analysis* for identifying and fitting respective probability distributions are part of this step. The result of the second step is a detailed documentation of assumptions that must be met

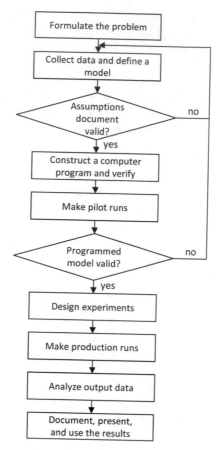

Figure 2.14: Procedure model for simulation studies (Law, 2014).

regarding the model as well as a specific data basis which is often referred to as the *conceptual model*.

In the next step, an evaluation is made whether the **assumptions document is valid**. Law suggests that this task, the *conceptual-model validation*, can be achieved by means of a structured walk-through of the respective documents. In case the validity of the assumptions document cannot be confirmed in this step, the document has to be updated before proceeding with the fourth step of the study. This means that, depending on the identified shortcomings, it might be necessary to repeat step 2 or even to start over with the entire procedure. Multiple iterations of the improvement process might also be required.

After the successful validation of the assumptions document, the next step's goal is the **construction and verification a computer program**. The development of an executable model includes the specification of the model using adequate means such as class or sequence diagrams as well as the implementation of the model. To implement the model, either profession simulation software, e.g., NetLogo, AnyLogic, or Repast Symphony (Kravari and Bassiliades, 2015), or proprietary implementations written in programming languages such as Java or C++ can be used. The verification of the implemented model can be evaluated using dynamic testing approaches such as *unit testing* but also by means of static techniques like *model checking* or *software metrics* (Chockler et al., 2006; Sawyer and Brann, 2009). At this point of the study, the model can be used to **make pilot runs**. The data acquired during these pilot runs can then be used for the validations in the following step of the study.

The sixth step analyzes whether the pilot runs provided sufficient evidence that the **programmed model was valid**. Law discriminates between *results validation* and *face validity* when referring to the correctness of simulation models. Results validation can be achieved by comparing the model's observed behavior to the behavior of the real-world system. Face validity, in contrast, can also be achieved without respective data from a real-world system. Instead, the reasonableness of the observed behavior is evaluated and assessed by experts. In case the model's behavior is compliant with the experts' expectations, the model has face validity. At this step, an identified lack of validity results in the reiteration of the previous steps and the revision of the model assumptions as well.

After the model's validity is confirmed, the model building part of the simulation study is successfully completed and the process of the study continues with the experimentation part. The seventh step of simulation studies according to Law, and the first step of the experimentation, focuses on the **design of experiments**. The goal of this step is to specify under which conditions each parametrization of interest is executed. This includes but is not limited to the definition of individual warm-up periods, run length, and number of replications per simulation run. Especially when simulating stochastic models that require many replications for each parametrization, a large number of individual executions of the model might be necessary. To avoid the combinatorial explosion of simulation runs and iterations, *factorial designs*, e.g., 2^k *fractional design* or *Latin hypercube sampling*, should be applied at this step (Kleijnen et al., 2005). Based on the runs that were defined in the previous step, the next step of a simulation study is to **make production runs**. For this purpose, the simulation software that was chosen in step 4 is used to execute the model.

During the execution of the model which was performed in step 8, output data is generated for each iteration of each parametrization. With respect to answering the research question or the problem that was stated as the first step of the study, the second last step of a simulation study deals with **output data analysis**. Maria (1997) identified two major tasks during output data analysis. First, descriptive statistics need to be applied to calculate numerical estimates of the model's performance with respect to the performance measure defined in step 1. This includes the calculation of the arithmetic mean or confidence intervals. Second, these data shall be used to test hypotheses about the performance of the model. For this purpose, Law suggests comparing the outputs of alternative parametrizations of the model in a relative sense. Yet, the application of a statistical hypothesis testing approach is also reasonable and applied frequently (Hofmann, 2016).

Finally, to complete the simulation study, it is necessary to **document, present, and use the study's results**. This is of particular importance with respect to the reproducibility of the study's results. For this purpose, the assumptions that were made during the study, the executable model, the outputs generated by the model, and the results must be thoroughly documented. Additionally, Law emphasizes that the presentation of the study's results is important, too, when completing a simulation study.

In this section, a brief overview of the steps of simulation studies was given with respect to their definition in procedure models. In the further course of this thesis, a more detailed discussion of individual differences between the procedure model presented here and other existing procedure models is provided (cf. Section 4.2.1). Furthermore, each of the steps that are related to the execution of experiments will be analyzed with respect to the verification of research hypotheses. For this purpose, more detailed specifications of those steps will be presented in Chapter 6.

3 Assistance and Automation of Simulation

In the previous chapter, simulation was introduced as an approach where computer models of real-world systems are applied to facilitate analyzing, planning, and optimizing of these system. This thesis aims at integrating research hypotheses into the process of simulation studies, to assist the identification, design, execution, and evaluation of important experiments to prove or disprove such hypotheses. Especially in models with a large number of inputs, the resulting degrees of freedom require an extensive number of similar experiments. The repetitiveness of this task might lead to carelessness by the experimenter, which is a thread to the quality of the results. Moreover, the large number of design decisions that must be made during a study might unwillingly lead to experimenter bias.

To overcome this, this thesis claims that an assistance or even automation of the entire process of simulation studies and its respective steps is required. With respect to this goal, this chapter provides a *state-of-the-art* overview of existing approaches for assisting and automating simulation. Based on the results of the literature survey, potentials and opportunities but also gaps and shortcomings of existing approaches are identified. Accordingly, existing approaches can be extended and combined so that they contribute to the overall goal of Hypothesis-Driven Simulation Studies.

To examine the current state of the art in the design, assistance, and automation of simulation studies, two major areas need to be covered: theoretical and practical approaches. As a first step, formalisms such as description languages and other theoretical frameworks are considered. Such approaches provide assistance as they structure and define both the process of simulation as well as individual tasks, steps, and entities. This includes interchange formats and specification languages, methodology and quality guidelines, as well as systematizations of the simulation process. In a second step, practical implementations such as software toolkits and frameworks for the automation of simulation are surveyed. The aim of this investigation is to examine their capabilities for assisting the life-cycle of simulation studies defined by procedure models.

© Springer Fachmedien Wiesbaden GmbH, part of Springer Nature 2019
F. Lorig, *Hypothesis-Driven Simulation Studies,*

The survey that is conducted to identify related contributions is inspired by the literature *snowballing* approach (Wohlin, 2014), which enables systematic literature studies. The snowballing procedure consists of three major iterative steps, which are executed until no new relevant papers are found. For this purpose, reference lists of relevant contributions as well as publications that reference these contributions are analyzed to identify further papers, articles, and books that are of importance with respect to the initial question or problem. The relevance of a contribution is assessed stepwise by its title, abstract, and the full text. This process is repeated until no additional references are found during the analysis of the gathered reference lists. Hence, snowballing allows for more reproducible and systematic literature studies.

To search for relevant publications, *Google Scholar*[2] was used, an academic search engine that indexed nearly 100 million documents (Khabsa and Giles, 2014). In a second step, results found when using Google Scholar were complemented by searching the quality-assured *DBLP*[3] database, which lists more than 4 million computer science publications. Combining these two search engines enables a comprehensive overview over a wide range of scientific publications which is complemented by relevant contributions from major conferences and journals in computer science.

The following sections present the relevant publications. As a differentiation can be made between theoretical and practical contributions, this section has a two-fold structure. First, it presents theoretical approaches for the assistance of simulation including interchange formats and specification languages as well as guidelines for and systematizations of the application of simulation. Then, practical approaches are introduced that refer to toolkits and software frameworks for the automation of simulation experiments or studies.

3.1 Description Languages and Theoretical Frameworks

This first section surveys theoretical approaches for the assistance of simulation. Interchange formats and specification languages are developed to facilitate the communication of simulation concepts, e.g., description and configuration of experiment, models, or performance indicators. An overview of relevant domain-specific languages is provided in Section 3.1.1. After-

---

[2] https://scholar.google.de/ [Retrieved Jul. 2019]
[3] https://dblp.uni-trier.de/ [Retrieved Jul. 2019]

wards, Section 3.1.2 introduces guidelines for both the methodology as well as the quality of simulations. Such guidelines provide theoretical frames that guide the application of simulation. Finally, Section 3.1.3 presents systematizations of the procedure of simulation studies. In addition to guidelines, such approaches align relevant aspects of simulation and establish a methodological connection between them. Such theoretical frameworks address and assess the epistemological contribution of simulation.

3.1.1 Interchange Formats and Specification Languages

To allow for the specification of simulation models and experiments, numerous XML-based model interchange formats and specification languages have been developed (Smith et al., 2010). This subsection presents different approaches for specifying simulation-related artifacts and entities. Each approach is briefly introduced, if available, the application domain is specified, and a discussion is provided on both advantages and disadvantages of the introduced approaches.

Schützel et al. (2014) discriminate between four different types of modeling and simulation support languages: *workflow languages, domain-specific languages, languages to instrument data collection,* and *languages to support validation and analysis.* The authors identified a paradigm shift in Modeling & Simulation towards a more structured process of simulation studies in terms of scientific workflows. Multiple workflow languages were proposed to specify simulation processes as scientific workflows. An example is BPMN, a language that aims at the specification of business processes, which can also be automatically transformed into simulation models (Schepers et al., 2014). In contrast to this, domain-specific languages are not multi-purpose approaches and the vocabulary is defined with respect to one particular domain. As they are implemented using general-purpose programming languages, e.g., *Scala* (Ewald and Uhrmacher, 2014), or frameworks for the development of programming languages, e.g., *Xtext* (Doud and Yilmaz, 2017), they can be extended assuming the user has sufficient knowledge of the respective language or framework. To limit the volume of collected data by means of a targeted data extraction, it is reasonable to apply data collection languages. According to Schützel et al. (2014), the specification of such languages requires three design decisions: target addressing ("Which entities contain relevant information?"), collection of metadata ("How are groups of values formed and aggregated?"), and frequency of data collection ("During which phase will data be collected?"). Finally, languages that support validation and analysis of simulation models and experiments provide techniques that enable, e.g., automated model checking. An extensive overview of domain-specific languages is provided by van Deursen et al. (2000), although not all of the presented languages were developed with respect to the application in the context of simulation. Additionally, Bruce (1997) presents principles for assessing the quality of domain-specific languages.

In computer network research, the *ns-3* simulator enables the specification and execution of discrete event simulation experiments (Riley and Henderson, 2010). To keep the entry barrier for working with ns-3 low, Riley and Pekley (2011) proposed *ns3xml*, an XML experiment description language for ns-3. By this means, the user is no longer required to have programming skills in C++ but can design and specify simulation experiments as XML files. The syntax of ns3xml is simple but even though it is specified in XML, the developers do not provide an XML schema. Instead, the ns3xml program ensures the consistency of the generated document as it enforces required sub-elements of each element.

The *SAFE* framework (Simulation Automation Framework for Experiments) provides assistance for the use of the *ns-3* simulator by automating workflows for the design and execution of experiments. As an extension of the SAFE framework, Hallagan (2011) developed two XML-based languages: *NEDL* (ns-3 Experiment Description Language) and *NSTL* (ns-3 Script Templating Language). The goal of these languages is to describe network simulation experiments and models. While NEDL can be used for specifying experiments, NSTL provides a set of tools that enable the exchange of information between NEDL and the underlying simulator.

Another extension to the SAFE framework is *SLED* (SAFE Language for Experiment Description), a domain-specific language for the description and configuration of simulation experiments in SAFE (Schützel et al., 2014). SLED was developed after NEDL and NSTL and in contrast to these languages, the goals of SLED are improved readability as well as the automated generation of experiments. For this purpose, SLED is not based on XML but makes use of the JSON format instead. It was the developers' intention to fully replace NEDL.

A need for sharing and reusing models and respective experiments was also identified in computational biology and biochemistry. To meet the communities' demand for a more detailed description of how simulation were executed, Köhn and Le Novère (2008) proposed the simulation experiment description markup language *SED-ML*. SED-ML corresponds to the requirements of MIASE, guidelines that define minimum information about a simulation experiment, and is compliant with XML-based models (Waltemath et al., 2011).

Another domain-specific language for the specification of experiments that originated in tge domain of computer networks is *OF-NEDL* (OpenFlow Networking Experiment Description Language) (Liang et al., 2012). OF-NEDL is a language for describing networking experiments in *OpenFlow*, which is a communications protocol for Ethernet network switches (McKeown et al., 2008). OpenFlow enables the user of the switch to modify a switch's flow-table with the aim of evaluating experimental routing settings. The interventions required for the execution of such experiments affect internal functionalities of the switch. Thus, the manufacturer of the switch would need to reveal functionalities to allow for these experiments. To keep the company's secrets, manufacturers might refuse to do so. OpenFlow is a compromise that does not require the vendor to reveal the internal workings of the switch while researchers are able to execute experiments. It provides a physical separation of the network forwarding and control function.

An OF-NEDL specification of experiments is written in XML and consists of five components: *information, topology, deployment, control,* and *output.* Topology, deployment, and control contain network simulation specific data. In contrast, information and output contain more generalizable data. The information component consists of the experiment's metadata such as the person that defined the experiment as well as parameters that define the start and end time of the experiment. The output component consist of data that is required to evaluate the performance of the network experiment.

The *PMIF* approach of Smith and Llado (2004) makes use of software performance engineering techniques for the development of a performance model interchange format. The goal of the proposed interchange format is to close the gap between software performance engineering tools and different performance modeling tools. Through this, the quantitative assessment of a system's performance is facilitated. This corresponds to the definition of performance indicators as it is known in simulation studies.

In the following years, a more general concept for the specification of simulation experiments was proposed by Smith et al. (2007). In terms of queuing network models, the *Experiment Schema Extension* (Ex-SE) can be used to define a set of simulation runs as well as the desired outputs. According to the authors, Ex-SE is capable of specifying simulation iterations, alternations, assignments of variable values, and other features of simulation experiments. It allows for the definition of parameter values and ranges that are executed in an automated way, model executions that depend on the result of previous executions, the use of outputs values as inputs of subsequent runs, and the specification of individual output metrics. Some aspects of Ex-SE were transfered into individual specification languages such as *Output*

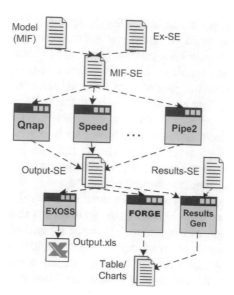

Figure 3.1: Ex-SE model interoperability framework (Llodrà et al., 2011).

Schema Extension (Output-SE) and *Result Schema Extension* (Result-SE) (Smith et al., 2011). Thus, the idea behind both schema extensions is closely related to Ex-SE (cf. Figure 3.1). While Output-SE specifies the XML format of simulation experiment output metrics, Result-SE provides information to automatically transform those output metrics into processable results.

Ex-SE is based on *PMIF*, which facilitates the exchange of model-related information between different simulation tools (Smith et al., 2010). In PMIF, queuing network models are defined by a set of nodes and arcs that connect those nodes as well as workloads that represent transactions between nodes. The respective experiment extension (*PMIF-Ex*) consists of variable declarations, solution specifications and output specifications (Smith et al., 2011). The declaration of variables includes the assignment of values to input parameters of the model as well as the automated iteration over these values. Solutions are specified so that stop conditions and alternations are applied in case given tests are passed or failed. Finally, outputs are specified by means of metrics such as throughput or utilization. The specifications of PMIF-Ex and Ex-SE are mostly equal, yet, PMIF-Ex considers additionally structural analysis for outputs. Besides, the experiment schema extension is not a closed system but can be extended or adapted according to more specific requirements. Melia et al. (2008) enhanced Ex-SE such that it satisfies the requirements of Petri nets analysis, e.g., constraints on tokens, invariant analysis, or reachability analysis.

As one of the last steps of a simulation study, the outputs generated by the model must be analyzed to derive conclusions. In practice, measures that are required for investigating the model's performance are often not part of the output variables. Accordingly, techniques are required to close the gap between the outputs of the model and the performance measures that are required for analyzing the results of the study. A first step towards the evaluation of simulation experiments is to convert data into more comprehensible tables. To assist this step, Llodrà et al. (2011) proposed *FORGE*, a "friendly output to results generator engine". FORGE works hand in hand with Results-SE as it generates a Result-SE file based on the model's PMIF outputs (cf. Figure 3.1). This file is then processed to generate more readable tables which facilitate manual analysis of simulation results. Additionally, the authors developed *EXOSS* (EXperiment, Output to SpeadSheet). In contrast to FORGE, EXOSS only aggregates XML outputs from different simulation experiments and presents them in one single xls spreadsheet.

A general purpose approach for specifying, analyzing, and designing complex systems is *OMG SysML* (OMG Systems Modeling Language). In contrast to other approaches presented in this section, SysML is a graphical modeling language and based on the well-known modeling language *UML 2* (Booch et al., 2005). Its area of application is not limited to simulation, yet simulation-specific applications exist. Peak et al. (2007) presented an approach for using SysML in *simulation-based design*. Furthermore, Huang et al. (2007) illustrated how SysML can be applied for developing object-oriented models of systems that include the structure and behavior of people, material, and other resources. The authors emphasize that using SysML in Modeling & Simulation enables the development of formal system models that can be directly linked to formal simulation languages. By this means, such models can be automatically parsed into executable models.

Besides the presented general-purpose languages, *domain-specific languages* were proposed to solve problems in a specific application domain or a specific type of problems. *SESSL* is a domain-specific language that is implemented in *Scala* and that is applied for specifying simulation experiments (Ewald and Uhrmacher, 2014). Scala is a functional and object-oriented programming language which can be executed on a Java virtual machine as the source code is compiled to Java bytecode. The compatibility to Java improves the simplicity of SESSL. It is easy to use with many simulation frameworks and only rudimentary programming skills are required to read

```
1   import sessl._
2   import sessl.james._
3
4   execute {
5     new Experiment with Observation {
6       model = "file-sr:/./SimpleModel.sr"
7       scan("r1" <~ (0.5, 1, 1.5))
8       replications = 10
9       stopCondition = AfterWallClockTime(seconds=1) and AfterSimTime(10e4)
10      observe("A")
11      observeAt(range(100, 50, 9000))
12      withRunResult {
13        result => println(result ~ "A")
14      }
15    }
16  }
```

Figure 3.2: Specification of an experiment using SESSL (Ewald and Uhrmacher, 2014).

and modify SESSL code (cf. Figure 3.2). SESSL can be used for experimental design, performance analysis, result reporting, and simulation-based optimization on models from various disciplines and independent from the underlying simulation framework. It is closely related to the JAMES II framework, however, other frameworks can be used as well. SESSL supports different types of simulation experiments such as observations, parallel executions, or reports. Especially the observation of simulation outputs is relevant with respect to answering research hypotheses. To specify a simulation experiment, a reference to the model file itself as well as a list of parameters and respective value ranges to be scanned during the simulation is required. Furthermore, replications, stop conditions, and the observed performance indicator can be specified.

One of the latest approaches discussed in this thesis is the domain-specific language *XPerimenter* (Yilmaz et al., 2017). According to the authors, the declarative XPerimenter language is dedicated to the specification of simulation experiments. It is independent of the host programming environment and allows for a high level of abstraction. The target environment entities that are generated by the translator of XPerimenter are those utilized by scientific workflow management system. In this regard, the authors mention Kepler as the reference system that is used for replicating experiments and for managing experiment variants even though the approach itself is platform-neutral. The interface between XPerimenter and scientific workflow management systems is specified such that the fragments of the simulation experiment are mapped to the features of the respective workflow system. To facilitate experiment management, a distinction between *"true users"*, those that are not programmers, and *"power users"* that are capable of writing and interpreting code, is made. The flexibility of power users is increased as they can properly use the syntax of the domain-specific language. In contrast to this, true users require more high-level tools that rely on variability models. Such models describe variants of the experiment and thereby simplify the use of the proposed language.

The efforts at developing a standard specification language for communicating models and experiments are not only related to computer science. In biology, the specification language *SBML* became a de-facto standard for the description of simulation models (Hucka et al., 2003). In mid-2018, 290 SBML-compatible software packages were listed by the developers of the language and the initial publication in which SMBL was presented was cited more than 2,900 times according to Google Scholar. The main goal of the *Systems Biology Markup Language* is the representation and exchange of biochemical reaction network models with respect to increased interoperability. Examples of such networks of biochemical phenomena are infectious diseases or metabolic networks.

Another markup language that must be mentioned when referring to SBML is *CellML* as these languages are closely related (Smith et al., 2014). While SBML aims at the exchange of information about models by means of language elements, CellML describes models in a more numerical way using variables, mathematical expressions, and metadata. However, it is possible to translate SMBL to CellML and vice versa (Smith et al., 2014).

In the domain of discrete event simulation, to which this thesis contributes, one of the most important and generally applicable specification formalisms is *DEVS*. The *Discrete Event System Specification* was introduced by Zeigler in 1976 and targets the issue that many simulation models are "prisoners of their simulation language implementations or algorithmic code expressions" (Zeigler et al., 2000, p. 6). To this end, DEVS utilizes concepts of systems theory and modeling and provides a formalisms for describing model behavior. A DEVS specification consists of input and output values as well as specific states and transitions between these states. This facilitates the determination of the model's output based on a given state or a set of inputs. Nowadays, multiple (partially domain-specific) extensions of Classic DEVS exist (cf. Figure 3.3). This includes *P-DEVS* (Parallel Discrete Event System Specification), *RT-DEVS* (Realtime Discrete Event System Specification), and *FD-DEVS* (Finite & Deterministic Discrete Event System Specification) (Wainer et al., 2011).

In conclusions, numerous domain-specific and multi-domain specification languages exist. Most languages focus on the specification of simulation

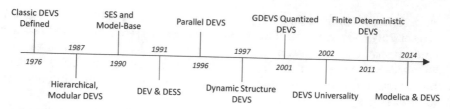

Figure 3.3: Some highlights in DEVS development (Zeigler, 2016).

experiments while others can also be used for the formal description of simulation models. With respect to the goal of this thesis, a de facto standard language for specifying simulation experiments cannot be identified. An overview of the surveyed languages is provided in Tables 3.1, 3.2, and 3.3.

Table 3.1: Interchange formats and specification languages for simulation (part 1/3).

Reference	Name	Purpose	Format	Domain	Focus	Extension
(Altintas et al., 2004)	MoML	Actor hierarchies in models	XML	Workflows	Model	
(Ewald and Uhrmacher, 2014)	SESSL	Specification of experiments	Scala	Multi-domain	Exp.	Related to JAMES II framework
(Hallagan, 2011)	NEDL	Description of ns-3 experiments	XML	Ad hoc networks	Exp.	
(Hallagan, 2011)	NSTL	Exchange of information between NEDL and ns-3	XML	Ad hoc networks	Exp.	
(Hucka et al., 2003)	SBML	Description of biological models	XML	Biology	Model	Can be translated into CellML
(Liang et al., 2012)	OF-NEDL	Specification of networking experiments	XML	Ethernet networks	Exp.	
(Llodrà et al., 2011)	FORGE	From output to performance measure	XML	Multi-domain		Works together with Result-SE
(Llodrà et al., 2011)	FORGE	From output to spreadsheet	XML	Multi-domain		

Table 3.2: Interchange formats and specification languages for simulation (part 2/3).

Reference	Name	Purpose	Format	Domain	Focus	Extension
(Melia et al., 2008)	PN-Ex	Ex-SE for petri nets	XML	Petri nets	Exp.	Extension of Ex-SE
(Oinn et al., 2004)	Scufl	Simple conceptual unified flow language				
(Peak et al., 2007)	SysML	Specification of complex systems	UML 2	Multi-domain	Model	
(Perrone et al., 2012)	SLED	Configuration of experiments in SAFE	JSON	Ad hoc networks	Exp.	Replacement of NEDL
(Riley and Pekley, 2011)	ns3xml	Design of ns-3 experiments	XML	Ad hoc networks	Exp.	
(Smith et al., 2007)	Ex-SE	Definition of simulation runs	XML	Multi-domain	Exp.	Based on PMIF
(Smith et al., 2010)	PMIF	Exchanging models among tools	Lisp-style notation	Performance models	Model	
(Smith et al., 2011)	Output-SE	Definition of simulation outputs	XML	Multi-domain	Model	

Table 3.3: Interchange formats and specification languages for simulation (part 3/3).

Reference	Name	Purpose	Format	Domain	Focus	Extension
(Smith et al., 2011)	Result-SE	Tranformation of outputs	XML	Multi-domain	Model	Works together with FORGE
(Smith et al., 2011)	PMIF-Ex	Experiment specification	XML	Queuing networks	Exp.	Mostly equal to Ex-SE
(Smith et al., 2014)	CellML	Technical specification of biological models	XML	Biology	Model	Can be translated into SBML
(Waltemath et al., 2011)	SED-ML	Sharing and reusing experiments		Bio- chemistry	Model and exp.	Corresponds to MIASE
(Yilmaz et al., 2017)	Xperimenter DSL	Specification of experiments		Workflows	Exp.	Related to Kepler
(Zeigler et al., 2000)	DEVS	Description of model behavior	Own formalism	Discrete event systems	Exp.	Multiple extensions exist

3.1.2 Guidelines

In addition to specification languages, methodological guidelines are another approach to provide a theoretical framework and to assist simulation studies. In this context, guidelines can be understood as non-mandatory information or recommendations regarding how to conduct specific tasks in simulation or entire simulation studies. This is reminiscent of procedure models for the conducting of simulation studies which were presented and discussed in Section 2.3.3. In contrast to procedure models, guidelines are of a more general character and do not necessarily describe the step-wise process of an entire study. As some procedure models are formulated as recommendations, they can also be considered as guidelines for simulation. However, the guidelines discussed in this subsection go beyond procedure models and mostly consist of best-practices collected by experienced researchers in the field of simulation.

As in many disciplines, a lack of reusability of simulation models and experiments was identified in the field of biology. It was attributed to an insufficient availability and description of models. Instead of proposing a standard description format, LeNovère et al. (2005) proposed minimum quality standards for describing biochemical simulation models. These quality standards are formulated as a set of rules which define procedures for the annotation of models. Models that correspond to these rules can be systematically parsed by simulation frameworks without the need for human translation. The *Minimum Information Requested in the Annotation of Biochemical Models* (MIRIAM) consists of six rules that must be met by a model in order to correspond to the defined standard. Instead of predetermining a particular specification language, MIRIAM only requires the use of a public, machine-readable format that is supported by specific software applications such as Mathematica or MATLAB. The authors mention *SBML* and *CellML* as examples and require that the models fully comply with the standard that is defined by the selected language. Furthermore, a *reference description* must be provided such that the user is aware of the process the models reproduce and the models' structure must correspond to the biological process that is referred to in the reference description. Finally, the model must be equipped with a parametrization such that it can be instantiated and executed without further ado. In this regard, the results defined in the reference description must be reproduced by the simulation. This includes both qualitative reproduction, e.g., oscillation or chaos, and quantitative reproduction, e.g., values of variables or relationships between variables.

The MIRIAM requirements for simulation models are extended by the *MIASE* guidelines which define "Minimum Information About a Simulation Experiment" (Waltemath et al., 2011). By this means, the reproducibility of simulation experiments can be facilitated and improved. MIASE does not define a specific language in which the information must be provided. Instead, it can be used with any description formalism for simulation experiments, e.g., experiment specification languages (cf. Section 3.1.1). The MIASE guidelines can be divided with respect to three subjects: *information about the models*, *information about the simulation steps*, and *information about the output* (cf. Table 3.4). As this thesis pursues a black box approach and only focuses on the experimentation part of simulation studies, information about the model itself is not discussed. For the reproduction of simulation steps, the authors define four requirements for a sufficient description. Besides a detailed description of the algorithm and the model that was used for the simulation, all information required for the implementation of the simulation steps as well as the order of these steps must be stated. The authors emphasize that reproduction of experiments extends the repetition of experiments and that the provision of algorithms used by closed-source computer programs is necessary. Finally, for the reproduction of the results of stochastic models, a detailed description is required of how to execute the models such that the results can be reproduced. This includes all post-processing steps of output analysis.

Table 3.4: MIASE rules for the description of simulation experiments (Waltemath et al., 2011).

1. All models used in the experiment must be identified, accessible, and fully described.
2. A precise description of the simulation steps and other procedures used by the experiment must be provided.
3. All information necessary to obtain the desired numerical results must be provided.

In its early days, SED-ML was named *MIASE-ML*, which emphasizes that the intended use of this markup language was the realization of the respective guidelines. Furthermore, the MIASE guidelines were developed in accordance with the MIRIAM requirements. Both MIASE and MIRIAM are projects related to the *MIBBI* initiative for "Minimum Information for Biological and Biomedical Investigations" (Taylor et al., 2008). MIBBI

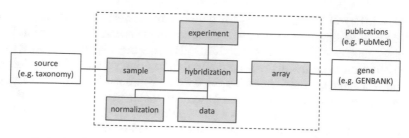

Figure 3.4: A schematic representation of six components of a microarray experiment according to the MIAME guidelines (Brazma et al., 2001).

comprises various efforts and recommendations to ensure that research data can be verified, analyzed, and interpreted by the respective community.

Analogous to MIASE, the *MIAME* guidelines define a standard for "Minimum Information About a Microarray Experiment" (Brazma et al., 2001). Microarray analysis refers to techniques that are applied in life sciences for analyzing data generated from DNA-related experiments after genome sequencing. As the amount of data is very large, a need for standardization was identified to compare gene expression data. This affects both databases of microarray laboratories as well as publication data. The authors identified six components that are essential for representing a microarry experiment: *experimental design, array design, samples, hybridizations, measurements,* and *normalization controls* (cf. Figure 3.4). Even though most components are domain-specific, the gap MIAME closes between empirical data, central repositories, and publications is also applicable for other disciplines. The samples that are described by means of MIAME and that are used for experiments consist of biological material as well as a corresponding taxonomic definition of respective organisms. Based on these samples, the goal of the proposed approach is to provide a systematic array design considering how the samples were used in specific experiments. This takes place with respect to the publication of these experiments in public repositories or gene databases where they can be accessed by other researchers. Furthermore, an experimental design must be provided for each experiment that is published, i.e., the contact information regarding the author as well as detailed information on the experiment itself, e.g., experiment type, variables, parameters, or research questions.

In addition to the presented domain-specific guidelines, more general multi-domain guidelines also exist. The "guidelines for designing simulation experiments" by Sanchez (2007) cannot be broken down into a list of recommendations or instructions. Instead, they introduce basic concepts of experimental design and emphasizes their importance for simulation. Accordingly, Sanchez discusses pitfalls to be avoided during experimentation and presents helpful use cases. A common pitfall in simulation experiments is the application of poor designs, e.g., the *one-factor-at-a-time* method. When analyzing the importance of a model's inputs by varying one factor at a time, one can easily forget to analyze whether correlations exist between different inputs. Accordingly, effects of the model are ignored and wrong decisions might be made. Similar guidance was also provided by Kleijnen et al. (2005), who published a user's guide to designing simulation experiments. In their work, the authors present a toolkit of designs whose target group are users of simulation with limited knowledge about designing experiments.

In his *guidelines for designing successful experiments*, Casler (2015) emphasized that experimental designs are more than just general-purpose instructions. Instead, he describes experimental designs as "creative series of decisions that are meant to solve one or more problems" (Casler, 2015, p. 692). To solve these problems in a methodologically sound way, he defines four basic pillars of experimental design that require proper consideration: *replication, randomization, blocking*, and *size of experimental units*. Identifying the optimal size of experimental units, i.e., the smallest units which are observed in experiments, as well as blocking or grouping of experimental units are challenges that are of particular relevance for life sciences. In contrast, replication and randomization are also of cross-domain relevance. The guidelines aim at reducing the probability of failure and thus increase the reproducibility of simulation experiments.

An example of more mandatory guidelines is the *DSEEP* standard for distributed simulation engineering and execution (Lutz, 2011). *DSEEP* was proposed by the IEEE and is a high-level process framework that provides recommended practices. It consists of seven steps that guide the user when developing and executing simulation environments. The steps cover the entire process, from the definition of the objective of the simulation environment to the analysis and evaluation of the results. For each step, different activities are stated that should be executed by the user. Even though the processual structure of DSEEP also fortifies a classification as systematization (cf. Section 3.1.3), it was classified as a guideline due to the mandatory recommendations. An example of a well-known framework that was developed according to the IEEE DSEEP standard is *HLAcloud* (cf. Subsec 3.2.2).

Similar mandatory guidelines that specify the application of simulation in logistical, material flow, and production system are published by the VDI (*Verein Deutscher Ingenieure*; English: *Association of German Engineers*). VDI is the association of German engineers and has the goal of promoting technological advances as well as representing the interests of both individual engineers and companies that work in the field of engineering. The association has issued more than 2,000 guidelines on the state of the art in engineering. Multiple guidelines discuss the utilization of simulation in various areas of application. However, only guideline 3633 provides a comprehensive overview and defines the simulation process from an engineering perspective (VDI, 2016). Even though the guidelines are published by a German association, they are provided both in German and English to avoid language and application barriers. In 13 different sheets, VDI guideline 3633 specifies all aspects of simulation that are relevant for the simulation of logistics systems. This includes but is not limited to organizational tasks such as the definition of functional specification documents and differentiation criteria for the choice of adequate simulation tools. Furthermore, more technical aspects of simulation are also considered, e.g., experiment planning, optimization, verification, and validation. Finally, as engineers embody practitioners of simulation, cost aspects as well as the integration of simulation into operational processes are also addressed.

The proposition of guidelines that assist the conducting of simulation is not a new phenomenon. Almost 30 years ago, Balci (1990) presented guidelines for successful simulation studies as a life-cycle model (cf. Figure 3.5) which practitioners can follow to increase their chances of conducting successful simulation studies. The life-cycle model consists of 10 phases (rectangular boxes), 10 processes (dashed arrows), and 13 stages of credibility assessment (solid arrows). Even though Figure 3.5 depicts a sequential process, the author emphasizes that the life-cycle is meant to be iterative and that reverse transitions are intended. The process of the life-cycle consists of 10 phases, which reminds of standard procedure models for simulation studies (cf. Section 2.3.3). In contrast to existing procedure models, Balci focuses on the transitions between the phases. He discriminates between processes that relate the steps to each other and credibility assessment stages that provide an overall evaluation scheme to ensure the credibility of the simulation results. With respect to the model building part of simulation studies, the life-cycle model provides detailed guidance and systematization. However, the design, execution, and evaluation of simulation experiments is only considered by two processes. This does not correspond to the extensive requirements of this thesis.

Even though Balci refers to the life-cycle model as guidelines, it does not fully correspond to this thesis's definition of guidelines. The primary goal of the presented approach is not to formulate recommendations for the conducting of simulation studies. Instead, what is provided by Balci can also be considered as a detailed systematization of the entire process of simulation studies.

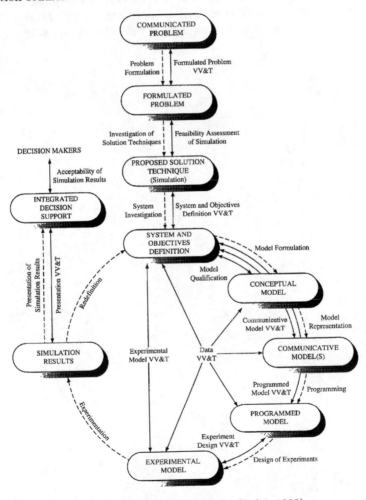

Figure 3.5: The life-cycle of a simulation study (Balci, 1990).

The guidelines presented in this subsection assist the conducting of simulation studies as they provide a theoretical framework (cf. Table 3.5). They facilitate the execution of simulation studies as they consist of best practices or recommendations for performing specific tasks. However, not all guidelines are non-mandatory collections of recommendations for action by other researchers. Standards can also be considered as guidelines even though they have a more prescriptive character. They enforce a specific procedure and require the user to comply with these standards.

Table 3.5: Guidelines for the application of simulation.

Reference	Name	Purpose	Domain	Type	Relatedness
(Balci, 1990)	-	Life-cycle model of simulation studies	Multi-domain	Life-cycle model	
(Brazma et al., 2001)	MIAME	Minimum information about microarray experiments	DNA and genome sequencing	Components	
(Casler, 2015)	-	Reproducibility of design of experiments	Multi-domain	Pillars	
(Kleijnen et al., 2005)	-	User guide to design of experiments	Multi-domain	Theoretical toolkit	
(LeNovère et al., 2005)	MIRIAM	Minimum quality standards for biochemical models	Biochemirsty	Rules	SMBL and CellML must be MIRIAM compliant
(Lutz, 2011)	IEEE DSEEP	Distributed simulation engineering	Multi-domain	Recommended practices	
(Sanchez, 2007)	-	Design of simulation experiments	Multi-domain	Concepts	
(Taylor et al., 2008)	MIBBI	Minimum information for biological/medical investigation	Biochemistry	Recommendations	MIASE and MIRIAM are related to MIBBI
(VDI, 2016)	VDI 3633	Definition of simulation process	Engineering and Logistics	Process	
(Waltemath et al., 2011)	MIASE	Minimum information about experiments	Biochemistry	Requirements	Formally represented by SED-ML

3.1.3 Systematizations

In this thesis, a distinction is made between guidelines and standardizations (*systematizations*). Like guidelines, systematizations provide a theoretical framework for simulation studies. While guidelines often embody optional or mandatory recommendations for actions, systematizations structure the simulation process so that relationships and hierarchical dependencies between the steps are emphasized and specified. This subsection presents different systematizations. This includes workflow specifications, method comparisons, and life-cycle considerations of simulation processes.

To assist or even automate recurring processes in research, data centric science (eScience) makes use of scientific workflows (Taylor, 2011). The conducting of methodologically sound simulation studies, which is the subject of this thesis, is a process which is well-suited for the specification as scientific workflow. The potential for the assistance and management of simulation experiments was also recognized by other scientists from the simulation domain. Thus, custom workflow systems for simulation were developed and multi-purpose workflow systems were customized and applied to simulation-specific tasks. A major shortcoming of general-purpose scientific workflow systems is that domain-specific concepts are not considered, e.g., statistical approaches for input and output data analysis or expertise for the design of experiments (Teran-Somohano et al., 2014).

Kepler is an open-source system for capturing, designing, and executing research activities as scientific workflows (Altintas et al., 2004). Kepler extends *Ptolemy II*, another open-source software framework that supports the design and simulation of actor-oriented models (Hylands et al., 2003). Scientific workflows are similar to workflows as they occur in business processes, e.g., job shops in manufacturing or the application of service-oriented architectures. Yet, scientific workflows also consider aspects that are not necessarily part of business workflows. Altintas et al. (2004) emphasized two major differences: First, scientific workflows operate on complex heterogeneous databases and produce large amounts of data, which need to be stored and maintained for reutilization in future workflows. Second, in contrast to control-oriented business workflows, scientific workflows are more dataflow-oriented and thus are more closely related to signal-processing tasks. Kepler's features include prototyping as well as distributed execution of scientific workflows but also the connection of databases and other execution environments like Python or R. Yilmaz et al. (2017) demonstrate how Kepler can be utilized for the specification of simulation experiments.

The problem solving environment *SCIRun* allows for the specification of modeling and simulation processes as scientific workflows (Johnson et al., 2000). It supports the execution of large-scale simulations as well as the visualization of the generated data and is closely related to Kepler. However, SCIRun supports only a single dataflow execution model while Kepler allows for the parallel execution of multiple dataflow models (Altintas et al., 2004). In practice, SCIRun is used for technical and biomedical simulations and visualizations such as electrocardiography (Coll-Font et al., 2014) as well as for transcranial direct current stimulation of the human head (Dannhauer et al., 2012).

Another scientific workflow environment which comes from the domain of bioinformatics is *Taverna* (Oinn et al., 2004). In contrast to SCIRun and Kepler, Taverna models each step of the workflow as an individual web service. For the specification of workflows, Taverna makes use of the *Scufl* (simple conceptual unified flow) language. In Scufl, workflows consist of three major entities: *processors* (transformations), *data links* (flow of data), and *coordination constraints* (links and controls processors). Furthermore, each step of a workflow is modeled as an individual atomic task. By this means, Taverna allows for the integration of services from all over the bioinformatics community into one scientific workflow.

Systematizations of simulation processes do not necessarily need to consist of workflows. Lorscheid et al. (2012) pursue an alternative approach towards increasing the understanding and transparency of simulation studies. By "opening the black box of simulations", the authors' goal is to facilitate the systematic design of simulation experiments and to contribute to the establishment of more standardized research processes. For this purpose, they present a systematic procedure for the assistance and guidance of simulation practitioners (cf. Figure 3.6). The presented approach particularly focuses on the experimental analysis of models as well as on the communication and reusability of results.

Yet, the authors are not alone in their endeavor. According to Lorscheid et al. (2012), other authors pursue similar efforts to define more standardized research processes and for further establishing computer simulation as a scientific method. For instance, Grimm et al. (2006) proposed *ODD*, a protocol for the specification of agent-based models. The *ODD sequence* covers seven elements: *purpose*, *state variables*, *process overview*, *design concepts*, *initialization*, *input*, and *submodels*. They can be divided into three aspects of modeling: *overview*, *design concepts*, and *details* (cf. Table 3.6).

The authors describe the logic behind ODD as follows: First, the *overview* aspect provides general information as well as the context of the model. This

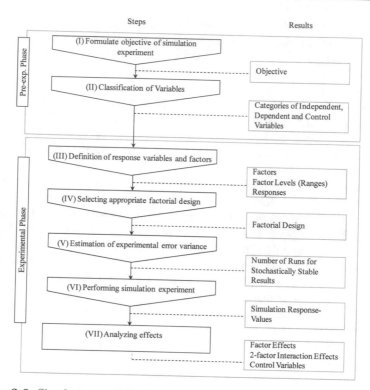

Figure 3.6: Simulation model analysis process (Lorscheid et al., 2012).

Table 3.6: Elements of the ODD protocol (Grimm et al., 2006).

Aspect	Element
	Purpose
Overview	State variables and scales
	Process overview and scheduling
Design concepts	Design concepts
	Initialization
Details	Input
	Submodels

includes the purpose of the model (why the model was built), information on state variables (entities that are described by the model as well as hierarchical dependencies between the entities), and a process overview (a conceptual specification of the processes that are modeled). Second, *design concepts* are stated in terms of more strategic considerations of the model's structure. Concepts that should be considered in here include sensing, interactions, and resulting emergent effects. Finally, technical *details* are provided so that the execution of the model is facilitated. This aspect specifies the initialization of the models in terms of initial values of the state variables, the dynamics of the model that are determined by the model's inputs and how they change over time, as well as potential submodels that are integrated into the considered model. When specifying the design of the model, the authors refer to "the mathematical skeleton of the model" (Grimm et al., 2006, p. 119) which consists of rules and equations that define the model. This facilitates the replication of agent-based models.

Richiardi et al. (2006) proposed a common protocol for agent-based social simulations. To develop this common protocol, the authors identified methodological pitfalls that might occur in agent-based simulations or that are made in scientific contributions that present agent-based simulations. These pitfalls include the link with the literature (i.e., the number of pages granted in scientific papers and journals is not sufficient to present the model's structure in sufficient detail) and the structure of the model (i.e., the main features of the model are not clearly stated in scientific publications which makes them difficult to understand). Besides, analyzing the model's behavior as well as the replicability of the model's results are subject to methodological pitfalls. Both tasks are more challenging in agent-based simulation as respective models do not consist of a compact set of differential equations, which can be solved by means of algebraic techniques. Furthermore, diverse programming languages and representation formalisms are used during the model building process. To address these pitfalls, the authors propose a three-staged process with respect to the definition of a common methodological protocol in agent-based social simulation. The steps consist of the creation of working groups to develop a questionnaire, which will then be sent to authors that submit their work to journals or conferences. Next, the authors are asked to fill in the questionnaire and the results are used for the definition of standards for each type of simulation model. Finally, reviewers can be provided with checklists that correspond to these standards to evaluate future submissions.

In addition to systematizations that can only be applied to specific types of simulations, domain-specific systematizations exist as well. To facilitate

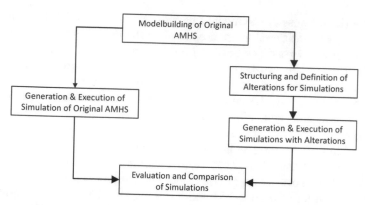

Figure 3.7: Workflow for the automation of simulation experiments with models of automated material handling systems (Wagner et al., 2013).

simulation and analysis of potential automated material handling system alterations in semiconductor manufacturing, Wagner et al. (2013) proposed a systematic approach for the automated planning, execution, and evaluation of simulation experiments. To this end, the authors specify a five-step workflow starting with the construction of a suitable model (cf. Figure 3.7). Afterwards, the process continues twofold: On the one side, alterations of the model's parametrization are systematically defined and applied and respective simulations are automatically generated and executed to observe and evaluate the model's behavior. On the other side, the real-world system with respect to which the model was built is observed under the same conditions to receive reference data. Finally, the simulations' output data are analyzed with regard to the reference data collected from the real-world system.

From a more general-purpose perspective, efforts were made to unify processes in Modeling & Simulation to improve the reuse of practices across disciplines. The *MS-SDF* (M&S System Development Framework) proposed by Tolk et al. (2013a) pursues this goal by unifying systems engineering processes and modeling and simulation processes. By this means, a systems engineering approach for capturing requirements, conceptual modeling, as well as verification and validation are adapted and transferred according to the requirements of modeling and simulation. For this purpose, assumptions made by the decision makers are aligned with theoretical concepts to derive suitable approaches for their implementation.

The *goal-hypothesis-experiment framework* by Yilmaz et al. (2016) specifies connections between goals, hypotheses, and experiments in simulation studies. The authors pursue a model-driven science approach from which an iterative discovery process emerges. The framework's underlying architecture supports the classification of the three mentioned components with respect to the discovery process. To specify goals of simulation experiments on a conceptual level, the consideration of multiple dimensions is required. This includes the *object of study* as well as the *purpose, focus, viewpoint*, and *context* of the experiment. The specification of hypotheses takes place on an operational level. On this level, the authors discriminate between three types of hypotheses: *phenomenological, mechanistic*, and *control hypotheses*. Finally, on a tactical level, experiments are specified. The aim of experiments is to answer the hypotheses stated on the previous level. Thus, the outcomes of the experiments are fed back into the system with respect to the revision of goals, hypotheses, and experiments. The presented framework implements experiment life-cycle management concept by Teran-Somohano et al. (2015).

Peng (2017) proposed TAECS (Tool for Adaptation, Execution and Checking of Simulation experiments), which links simulation experiments that were conducted for validation purposes with respective models. By this means, the reuse of experiments is enabled in case the models they were annotated with are reused, e.g., for building new models. The comparison of the results of the experiments then allows for the evaluation of whether the original model's behavior is still shown by the new model or to assess how the model behavior changed due to reuse. The specification of the experiments is implemented using SESSL.

The *AssistSim* approach targets the systematization and assistance of simulation experiments in manufacturing and logistics (Lattner et al., 2011a). The presented methodology addresses two aspects of simulation studies, the design of experiments and the execution of experiments. While the design is assisted via the thorough identification and capturing of relevant information about the object of investigation, the parameter space is systematically investigated and measurements are stored in a central experiment database. The resulting process is specified by means of an extensive procedure model, that systematizes and aligns relevant tasks and decisions.

With regard to systematizations for the assistance and automation of simulation, state of the art approaches that only target the experimentation part of simulation studies need to be mentioned as well. Relevant contributions especially include the proposition of a life-cycle management framework for reproducible simulation experiments (Lorscheid et al., 2012). Yet, as these works are of great relevance for the specification of Hypothesis-

Driven Simulation Studies, they were discussed in detail in the foundations chapter (cf. Section 2.2.2). To extend their approach and to increase the practical applicability of the proposed methodological framework, Teran-Somohano et al. (2015) also developed a web-application. In this regard, they propose a more application-oriented systematization of the experiment life-cycle approach. The authors pursue a model-driven engineering approach and define a framework for the interchange of design of experimentation strategies between platform-specific and platform-independent domains. For this, experiment feature models as well as design of experiment ontologies are developed and presented. The resulting distributed system consists of multiple interconnected services and can be considered as a software framework for the automation of simulation experiments. Other related software-technical approaches for the automation of simulation are discussed in the following section of this chapter.

Finally, systematizations that focus on specific application areas are often provided as workflows. The amount of experiment workflows is too large to be presented here. To enable the central management, sharing, and reusing of workflows, research repositories are reasonable. *myExperiment* is an example of a repository for bioinformatics workflows where computer experiments and data analyses can be specified as a series of composed activities (Goble et al., 2010). Users can choose between three approaches to search the repository. This includes topic tags, a full-text keyword search, or the workflow's affiliation to specific groups or users. As of beginning of 2018, myExperiment consisted of more than 3800 workflows.

This section provides a systematic and comprehensive overview of theoretical frameworks for the assistance and automation of simulation (cf. Tables 3.7 and 3.8). This includes formal description and specification languages by means of which aspects of simulation can be unambiguously described and published, e.g., in public simulation repositories or as part of scientific publications. Moreover, guidelines that provide mandatory or non-mandatory recommendations on how to conduct specific simulation-related tasks are presented and discussed. Finally, an overview of systematizations that structure the simulation process or specific sub-processes is provided. Such systematizations emphasize how entities that are involved in this process interact with each other and define hierarchical dependencies between these components. Often, scientific workflows are used to specify such processes. In summary, it can be concluded that many valuable approaches exist which serve as a theoretical frame for the assistance and automation of simulation. However, aspects of systematic hypothesis testing as well as specific recommendations for actions are rarely provided.

Table 3.7: Approaches for the systematization of simulation (part 1/2).

Reference	Name	Purpose	Domain	Focus
(Altintas et al., 2004)	Kepler	Capturing research activities as scientific workflow		Workflow
(Grimm et al., 2006)	ODD	Specification of agent-based models	ABM	Protocol / Sequence
(Johnson et al., 2000)	SCIRun	Execution of large-scale simulations	Biomedical	Workflow
(Lattner et al., 2011a)	Assist-Sim	Systematization of experiments in logistics	Manufacturing and Logistics	Systematic procedure
(Lorscheid et al., 2012)	-	Assistance of simulation practitioners		Systematic procedure
(Oinn et al., 2004)	Taverna	Integration of services in workflows	Bioinformatics	Workflow
(Peng, 2017)	TAECS	Reuse of experiments		Systematization of M&S process
(Richiardi et al., 2006)	-	Identification of methodological pitfalls	ABSS	Pitfalls

Table 3.8: Approaches for the systematization of simulation (part 2/2).

Reference	Name	Purpose	Domain	Focus
(Teran-Somohano et al., 2015).	-	Life-cycle management of experiments		Life-cycle
(Tolk et al., 2013a)	MS-SDF	Unification of systems engineering and M&S processes		Unified process
(Wagner et al., 2013)	-	Automated planning, execution, and evaluation of experiments		Workflow
(Yilmaz et al., 2016)	GHE	Connections between goals, hypotheses, and experiments		Theoretical framework

3.2 Toolkits and Software Frameworks

To complement the view on theoretical approaches for the assistance of simulation that was presented in the previous section, this section's goal is to present and compare practical approaches and implementations of assistance functionalities. In particular this includes software toolkits and frameworks for the assistance and automation of simulation. A major distinctive feature of such framework is the range of application. While some frameworks were only developed with respect to the assistance of simulation in specific domains or disciplines, others provide more general-purpose assistance. Thus this section is structured as follows: First, in Section 3.2.1, domain-specific toolkits and frameworks are introduced. Subsequently, in Section 3.2.2, general-purpose toolkits and frameworks are presented.

Most of the approaches, frameworks, and software toolkits that are presented and discussed in this section pursue *model-driven engineering* approaches. Unlike other software development methodologies, where the model is used for documentation purposes, the model takes a key role in model-driven engineering (da Silva, 2015). Respective approaches provide sophisticated methods for the formulation and construction of models. These models then serve as a basis for the automated creation of software systems.

In this regard, a paradigm shift can be identified (Schmidt, 2006). Conventional software development methodologies often pursue a *"construct-by-correction"* approach. Here, an incomplete software artifact is developed at first and completed according to a specific development process, e.g., test-driven development. In contrast to this, model-driven engineering pursues a *"correct-by-construction"* approach. Its goal is the development of complete and fully functional software artifacts based on conceptual models of specific systems or mechanisms. By the use of standardized models and domain-specific design guidelines or patterns, this improves reusability of and compatibility between the resulting systems.

Besides the frameworks presented in this section, there are a large number of further frameworks and toolkits. This includes commercial software such as AnyLogic, Arena, Enterprise Dynamics, Plant Simulation, or Simio. However, open source frameworks exists as well, e.g., MASON, NetLogo, Repast Symphony, or SeSAm. Even though assistance or even automation functionalities are provided by most of these frameworks, their primary goal is to facilitate the building and execution of models. Hence, such Modeling & Simulation frameworks are not presented in this section and the focus lies on software whose main contribution is the automation of simulation.

3.2.1 Domain-Specific Toolkits and Frameworks

The assistance and automation of simulation is challenging as it consists of multiple sophisticated and interdependent steps that need to be executed in a methodologically sound way. As simulation is applied across various domains and purposes, it also seems reasonable to develop software toolkits or frameworks for specific domains or purposes. This subsection presents toolkits and frameworks which are only applicable to specific areas.

For the simulation of computer networks, the *ns-3* network simulator is a commonly used framework (Riley and Henderson, 2010). After *ns-1* and *ns-2*, which are no longer maintained, it is the third and most recent software product in this family of simulators. It is a discrete-event simulator with a focus on realism, reuse, and ease of debugging of the developed models. The implementation of a simulation experiment workflow in ns-3 can be divided into four distinct steps. First, the user is required to implement the network topology, i.e., nodes, channels between nodes, and network protocols. Then, the data demand of the network is implemented. In computer networks, data is generated by network applications that either send data to the network or receive data from the network. As a third step, the model is executed according to the event list and until the event list contains no more entires. Finally, the trace files generated by ns-3 are analyzed. To simplify the operation of ns-3, specification languages like ns3xml, NEDL, and NSTL were developed (cf. Section 3.1.1).

SWAN is another framework from the domain of network simulation (Liu et al., 2001). It is a high-performance framework which can be utilized for large-scale simulations of wireless ad hoc networks. SWAN was developed with respect to achievements in signal processing and microelectronics, which allow for the construction of large-scale sensor networks. As such networks easily consist of several thousand nodes, simulation is challenging. The SWAN framework emerged from the combination of two existing softwares: the *Dartmouth Scalable Simulation Framework* (DaSSF) and *WiroKit*, a software developed by *BBN Technologies*. The DaSSF framework facilitates the development of discrete-event simulation models of Internet protocols as well as large and complex networks (Cowie et al., 1999). It serves as "structural glue" (Liu et al., 2001, p. 10) for the integration of models. WiroKit is a router for wireless ad hoc networks, which uses the same interface definitions in both the code that is used for the simulation and the one that is used in the real-world mobile radio units. By this means, configurations that were analyzed by means of simulation can easily be distributed to the corresponding devices in reality. However, the assistance

SWAN provides mainly focuses on the aggregation of different types of sub-models, i.e., terrain models, dispersion models, operating system models, and wireless sensor models.

The web-based interface developed by Kenna (2008) is part of the SWAN project. It extends SWAN and its primary goal is to enhance the believability of simulation studies by replicating the behavior of real-world mobile ad hoc networks via computer simulation. It supports the parallel and distributed execution of experiments, stores the respective results in a central database, and facilitates the analysis of gathered data.

To overcome SWAN's shortcomings in assisting systematic experimentation with network models, *SAFE* (Simulation Automation Framework for Experiments) was developed (Perrone et al., 2012). According to the authors, the development of SWAN was only a proof-of-concept, which is why the project was discontinued. Instead, the authors made use of the experiences they collected during SWAN's development and from then on focused on the extension of the ns-3 simulator (cf. Section 3.1.1). In this regard, SAFE aims at providing assistance to novice users that are inexperienced in the design and conducting of simulation studies using the ns-3 simulator. The assistance consist of an automation of the workflow that starts with the initialization of the model's parameters, includes the launching of relevant experiments, and ends with the visualization of the generated results.

The Java-based *VSEit* (Versatile Simulation Environment for the internet) simulation environment focuses on the application of simulation in social sciences, especially for analyzing interdependencies between social, economic, and natural processes (Brassel, 2001). It provides a visual interface that facilitates the specification, control, and recording of simulation experiments.

For the automation of MATLAB simulations, Dominka et al. (2008) developed a tool that replaces the operator during simulation and optimization runs. The presented *simulation-automation-system* automatically compares the actual state of the simulation results to a defined target state and operates the simulation accordingly. The assistance provided by this tool is rather static as specific objective functions are selected and applied automatically.

The approach proposed in this thesis is not limited to specific domains or areas of application. Accordingly, domain-specific toolkits and software frameworks are only briefly introduced in this chapter. The number of existing frameworks is considerably higher than the selection presented here. However, with respect to the goal of this thesis, the most relevant frameworks were introduced in this section (cf. Table 3.9). This provides an overview of how frameworks are used in different domains and disciplines to assist and automate the conducting of simulation studies.

Table 3.9: Domain-specific frameworks for the automation of simulation studies.

Reference	Name	Purpose	Languages	Domain	Relatedness
(Brassel, 2001)	VSEit	Simulation environment	JAVA	Social sciences	
(Dominka et al., 2008)	Simulation-automation-system	Automated optimization	MATLAB	Engineering	
(Kenna, 2008)	-	Web-based interface for experiments		Ad hoc networks	Web interface for SWAN
(Liu et al., 2001)	SWAN	Large-scale simulations	C++	Ad hoc networks	Combination of DaSSF and WiroKit
(Perrone et al., 2012)	SAFE	Automation of experiments		Ad hoc networks	Replaces SWAN
(Riley and Henderson, 2010)	ns-3	Network simulator	ns3xml, NEDL, NSTL	Ad hoc networks	

3.2.2 Multi-Purpose Toolkits and Frameworks

Based on a SysML system specification, the *HLAcloud* framework proposed by Bocciarelli et al. (2013) enables the automated implementation of a distributed simulation model. It makes use of general HLA-based model transformations for the automated generation, deployment, and execution of the model. The framework is capable of generating Java code from SysML models and thus facilitates the development of distributed simulation models. A similar approach was presented by Schonherr and Rose (2009) where simulation models are generated based on SysML specifications as well. However, they do not utilize cloud computer infrastructure for the automated implementation of model code.

The idea of a simulation framework that makes use of plug-ins for the dynamic loading and integration and exchange of simulation components and services is not new. TORNADO, a framework that is mostly used in the water quality domain, dynamically integrates numerical solvers that are required for solving non-linear ordinary differential equations (Claeys et al., 2006). This is required for the evaluation and optimization of simulation models during modeling and virtual experimentation. By this means, the maintainability of the framework as well as the computational efficiency increase while the diversity of programming languages decreases.

In some situations, it is not reasonable to systematically derive necessary experiment configurations from the hypothesis a simulation study tries to answer. Instead, it is more suitable to execute a large number of simulation runs with different parametrizations to generate a vast amount of data to investigate a phenomenon. This approach to analyzing the landscape of a simulation model is referred to as *data farming*. To facilitate large-scale data farming, Król et al. (2013) introduced *SCALARM*.

The assistance provided by Çakırlar et al. (2015) also focuses on the validation of simulation models. *RatKit*, a repeatable automated testing toolkit for agent-based modeling and simulation, facilitates verification and validation of agent-based simulation models as well as the automated execution of tests. For this purpose, test scenarios are defined in which the investigated model is executed under different circumstances. Instead of developing RatKit from scratch, the authors made use of the generic testing framework developed by Gürcan et al. (2013) and extended it.

Teran-Somohano et al. (2015) presented a model-driven engineering approach for managing the design, execution, and analysis of simulation experiments. By this means, the management of the entire life-cycle of simulation experiments is facilitated (Teran-Somohano et al., 2014). The authors in-

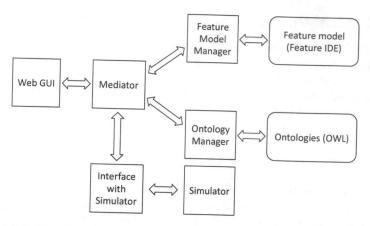

Figure 3.8: Prototype of an assistance system for the design of experiments (Teran-Somohano et al., 2015).

troduce a web-based experiment design wizard, which addresses simulation practitioners that are capable of model building but lack training regarding the conducting of experiments. For this purpose, an experiment ontology as well as a feature model are utilized to capture and manage experimentation knowledge. The ontology covers basic terms from design of experiment and the relationship between these terms, for instance, sampling methods or design matrices. In addition, the feature model specifies components that are not equal between multiple experiments such as the number of input factors and respective factor levels. Finally, a prototypical implementation of the developed experiment management system is presented (cf. Figure 3.8).

Griffin et al. (2002) developed and introduced SOS, a set of "Scripts for Organizing 'Speriments". With the aim of supporting the execution of a large number of simulation experiments, SOS provides functionalities for the automated variation of input parameter values as well as for the management of the resulting output data generated by the model. Additionally, output data can be plotted to enable visual analyzes of the generated output landscape. SOS was developed using Perl and MySQL which makes it difficult for users that are unfamiliar with the respective languages and programs. Furthermore, basic expertise with bash commands is required as it is intended to control the scripts via the command line interface. According to the developers, a web interface does not exist and they do not intend to develop such an interface.

The *FASE* approach provides a framework for the formal automated analysis of simulation experiments as well as for hypothesis testing (Doud and Yilmaz, 2017). In contrast to the goal of this thesis, FASE focuses on mechanistic hypotheses, which make assertions on the inner structure of simulation models. The framework is platform independent, includes a domain-specific language for the specification of hypotheses, and makes use of automated model checking to evaluate hypotheses. FASE is closely related to the Goal-Hypothesis-Experiment framework by Yilmaz et al. (2016), which defines and provides its scope. While the Goal-Hypothesis-Experiment framework provides a domain-specific language for the specification of experiments, FASE extends these efforts by the analysis of the results of such experiments. The only input of the FASE system is a specification of a simulation experiments using the domain-specific language of the Goal-Hypothesis-Experiment framework. The specification is then transformed into two separate tasks. On the one side, the hypothesis is converted into linear temporal logic. For this purpose, the hypothesis is syntactically analyzed and corresponding temporal properties are identified. Furthermore, a distinction is made whether the hypothesis refers to an event or a logic statement. On the other side, experiments are prepared and executed by the system. This includes the identification of relevant variables for the data recording as well as the generation of batch files for the execution of individual simulation runs. The output data generated during all simulation runs is then used to build a Markov Chain in accordance with the underlying hypothesis. At this point, a PRISM model is generated, which allows for formal model checking. Additionally, an omega automata is constructed by the PRISM system based on the linear temporal logic for assessing the probability of acceptance and for evaluating the initial hypothesis. As a conclusion, the authors emphasize that the speed of scientific discovery can be increased by means of automation.

Finally, the workgroup of Adelinde M. Uhrmacher from University of Rostock proposed a variety of frameworks, toolkits, and assistance systems with the aim of facilitating the methodologically sound and technically rigorous conduction of computer simulation. These software systems are complemented by the SESSL language, which was presented in the previous section (cf. Section 3.1.1).

Systematically guiding simulation experiments is the primary goal of the *GUISE* (GUIding Simulation Experiments) tool developed by Leye and Uhrmacher (2012). By integrating multiple experimentation methods, different goals of experimentation such as optimization or validation can be flexibly pursued. In GUISE, simulation experiments are divided into six tasks that provide an explicit structure: *specification of the experiment, selection of model parameters, execution of simulations, data collection, analysis of collected data,* and *evaluation of the results.* In this regard, GUISE facilitates the identification and combination of suitable methods and thus assists each of these steps. For this purpose, it utilizes the plug-ins of the JAMES II framework which it is based on.

A more technical assistance framework that focuses on the selection of well-suited simulation algorithms for a specific task was proposed by Ewald (2012). Often, simulation systems provide a large number of different problem solving algorithms. In this case, the user is often overwhelmed by the task of selecting one of these algorithms, as criteria for the assessment of each algorithms' appropriateness are unclear. The approach presented by the author is implemented as an extension of the JAMES II system. This also allows for the automatic configuration of simulation systems as adequate algorithms can be identified and selected independently.

Most of the presented approaches from the University of Rostock extend the multi-domain modeling and simulation framework *JAMES II* or serve as plug-ins (Himmelspach, 2007). JAMES II assists both major components of simulation studies, the creation of simulation models as well as the flexible, scalable, and parallel execution of simulation experiments. It allows for switching the simulation engine at runtime as model and simulator are entirely separated. To retain the flexibility of the simulation framework, JAMES II implements a *"plug 'n simulate"* concept (Himmelspach and Uhrmacher, 2007), which enables the integration and reuse of external algorithms. JAMES II is not limited to specific modeling paradigms or languages, however, the authors focus on variants of DEVS such as PDEVS or PdynDEVS.

Even though the assistance provided by JAMES II is comprehensive, the detailed documentation of the study's process was not supported by the framework. To improve the credibility of scientific results that were generated by means of simulation, a thorough documentation of applied methods and techniques is inevitable. Especially when considering the large number of plug-ins that might be integrated into the process of simulation studies using JAMES II, the need for rigorous documentation arises. As plug-ins are dynamically integrated during runtime of the framework, the identification of selected and utilized plug-ins is challenging or even impossible once the simulation study is finished. At the same time, the combination of different perspectives on simulation studies in one framework makes the system more transparent which simplifies the generation of respective documentations. Still, the task of collecting relevant information is extensive and time-consuming. The *WorMS* (WORkflows for Modeling and Simulation) workflow system developed by Rybacki (2016) addresses this issue of automatically documenting the execution of predefined workflows in JAMES II. By this means, gathering relevant information regarding the creating, verification, and validation of the model but also of the execution of simulation experiments is facilitated.

Besides the presentation of JAMES II, in his work Himmelspach (2007) provides an extensive comparison of 23 related simulation frameworks. Criteria that were applied for presenting the frameworks include the utilized simulation formalism (discrete, continuous, or hybrid), the execution of the model (distributed or sequential), the user interface (editor, debugger, visualization, and analysis). Furthermore, information is provided regarding utilizable types of models (Java, XML, etc.) and whether model building, experimentation, or both aspects are supported by the frameworks. Considering the goal that is pursued in this thesis, the presented survey provides only technical details regarding functionalities provided by each framework. Information on the experimentation assistance is limited to the general support of experiments. Specific aspects of experimentation such as design, execution, and analysis are not discussed in detail. Similar surveys on platforms that assist the development of simulation models as well as the execution of experiments are also provided by Railsback et al. (2006), Tobias and Hofmann (2004), Kravari and Bassiliades (2015), and Nikolai and Madey (2009).

Compared to the domain-specific frameworks, the number of frameworks that are not limited to a specific discipline is higher in this literature review. Most of the presented frameworks focus on the automation of isolated steps of simulation studies, e.g., distribution, execution, or documentation (cf. Tables 3.10 and 3.11). In this regard, they provide a valuable contribution to the automation of simulation. However, it must be noted that an assistance or automation of the entire life-cycle of a study is not provided by these frameworks and that hypotheses are mostly not considered. FASE stands out, because it automates testing of mechanistic hypotheses by means of temporal logic. Yet, this approach is not applicable for the verification of phenomenological hypotheses on the behavior of a model.

Table 3.10: Multi-purpose frameworks for the automation of simulation studies (part 1/2).

Reference	Name	Purpose	Original Domain	Type of Automation	Relatedness
(Bocciarelli et al., 2013)	HLAcloud	Automated implementation of models	Distribution simulation	Generation, deployment, execution	System specification in SysML
(Çakırlar et al., 2015)	RatKit	Verification, validation, and testing	Agent-based Modeling and Simulation	Repeatable execution of tests	Based on (Gürcan et al., 2013)
(Claeys et al., 2006)	TORNA-DO	Dynamical integration of numerical solvers	Water quality	Loading, integration, and exchange of components	-
(Doud and Yilmaz, 2017)	FASE	Automated mechanistic hypothesis testing	Software engineering	Model checking and verification	Utilizes PRISM
(Ewald, 2012)	Automatic Algorithm Selection	Setup of simulation experiments	Modeling & Simulation	Simulation algorithm selection	Part of JAMES II

Table 3.11: Multi-purpose frameworks for the automation of simulation studies (part 2/2).

Reference	Name	Purpose	Original Domain	Type of Automation	Relatedness
(Griffin et al., 2002)	SOS	Organization and execution of large number of experiments	Network simulation	Generation and execution of simulation runs	Developed for SSFNet
(Himmelspach and Uhrmacher, 2009)	JAMES II	Plugin-based M&S framework	Modeling & Simulation	Integration and reuse of services	Multiple plug-ins
(Król et al., 2013)	SCALARM	Automated execution of simulation runs	Computer science	Systematic execution of runs for data farming	-
(Leye and Uhrmacher, 2012)	GUISE	Systematic guidance of experiments	Modeling & Simulation	Flexible pursue of different experimentation goals	Based on JAMES II
(Rybacki, 2016)	WorMS	Automated documentation	Modeling & Simulation	Automated execution and documentation of workflows	Based on and JAMES II
(Teran-Somohano et al., 2015)	Model-driven engineering framework	Facilitates well-designed experiments	Computer science and systems engineering	Design and execution of experiments	Life-cycle management framework

3.3 Methodological Shortcomings and Research Gap

The goal of this thesis is to enable and assist the design, execution, and evaluation of Hypothesis-Driven Simulation Studies. As shown in this chapter, there are a variety of valuable specification languages, formalisms, theoretical frameworks for the description as well as functionalities and frameworks for the assistance and automation of simulation. Most of these approaches focus on individual aspect or specific steps of simulation studies (e.g., verification and validation of models, data preparation and processing, or execution of predefined experiments) or are limited to particular domains (e.g., biology, logistics, or engineering). Others cover the multiple steps of the process of simulation studies or can be applied across different domains. Frameworks exist which combine and interrelate individual assistance functionalities to integrated workflows with the aim of providing more a extensive assistance of the entire life-cycle of simulation studies.

With respect to the required assistance for both formal specification and systematic revision of hypotheses in simulation studies that is pursued in this thesis, deficits of existing assistance systems can be identified. This chapter presented a variety of systematizations for the assistance and automation of computer simulation. Besides general-purpose systematizations, many of the presented approaches are either intended for specific types of simulation or only applicable to specific domains. Most of the discussed systematizations consist of a high-level perspective on simulation and fail to provide specific instructions regarding their application. Furthermore, the verification of research hypothesis is not considered by most of these systematizations. They instead focus on the automated variation of parameter configurations. However, the identification of relevant parameterizations of the model is not considered. Moreover, most of the presented approaches only address individual aspects related to hypothesis testing and systematic experimentation in simulation studies. As a consequence, the experimenter still has to make important design decisions regarding the selection and integration of suitable components. This might result in experimenter bias that negatively influences both reproducibility and credibility of the study's results.

In simulation, like in other disciplines, the formation and verification of hypotheses plays an important role in the process of knowledge acquisition and decision support. Yet, approaches for systematically integrating research hypotheses into simulation studies rarely exist. As shown in this chapter, automating both formulation and testing of scientific hypotheses by means of simulation is not a new idea. In other scientific disciplines, e.g., biochemistry or wireless networking, such approaches are well established. Accordingly, a research gap can be identified such that scientific hypotheses in simulation studies need to be formally described for their integration into the simulation process. This allows for the systematic design, execution, and evaluation of relevant simulation experiments, for providing evidence for or against the stated research hypotheses, and for accomplishing the goal of the study.

Part II

Hypothesis-Driven Simulation Studies

4 Requirements Analysis on Hypotheses in Simulation

The research gap identified in the previous section reflects an insufficient representation and consideration of research hypotheses in the process of simulation studies. This stands in contrast with the vision of this thesis of enabling and facilitating the methodologically sound and reproducible verification of research hypotheses on the behavior of simulation models. To overcome this gap, existing procedure models, which define the methodology of simulation studies, must be extended so that the entire life-cycle of a study is covered, from the formulation of hypotheses to their reliable and replicable answering. For this purpose, the process must be advanced to allow for the dynamic integration of hypotheses as well as for the adaptation of the individual steps of the process. To achieve this, this thesis proposes an innovative methodology for the conducting and intelligent assistance of Hypothesis-Driven Simulation Studies.

In contrast to existing procedure models, this thesis aims at the formal specification of the research hypothesis as part of the simulation study. To this end, an integrated procedure model is proposed so that the hypothesis becomes the key element of the study and accordingly is able to guide the process of the study. This allows for the systematic design, execution, and evaluation of relevant simulation experiments based on a specific hypothesis. Furthermore, the aggregation of the experiments' results with respect to proving or disproving the hypotheses is facilitated. The presented process serves as a methodological framework for planning and conducting Hypothesis-Driven Simulation Studies. Nevertheless, it is not limited to the theoretical integration of hypotheses into simulation studies but also allows for their automated conduction.

As a first step towards conceptualizing and enabling Hypothesis-Driven Simulation Studies, this chapter performs a requirement analysis to determine the specifications of the developed approach. With respect to the integration of hypotheses into the process of simulation studies, the theoretical concept of scientific hypotheses is investigated first. This includes the analysis of the structure of scientific hypotheses with regard to their formulation and

© Springer Fachmedien Wiesbaden GmbH, part of Springer Nature 2019
F. Lorig, *Hypothesis-Driven Simulation Studies*,

formalization for the use in an intelligent assistance system. This theoretical perspective on research hypotheses is aligned with the requirements that arise from the epistemology of simulation and to derive requirements on scientific hypotheses in simulation. Moreover, this chapter analyzes how the identified theoretical requirements are met in practice. This requires the thorough investigation of the methodological integration of hypotheses in the process of simulation studies as well as the identification of methodological shortcomings. Together, the defined requirements as well as the identified shortcomings serve as a basis for the development of an integrated procedure model for the conduction and assistance of Hypothesis-Driven Simulation Studies.

4.1 Scientific Hypotheses

To improve the targeted integration of hypotheses into simulation studies, a first necessary step is the definition of requirements regarding to what extent and for which purposes hypotheses shall be integrated. In the approach presented here, hypotheses contribute to the production and validation of knowledge in simulation studies. Thus, the aim of this section is to identify and derive epistemological requirements for the conceptualization and integration of hypotheses in simulation.

Before systematically integrating hypotheses into the process of simulation studies, this section provides a discussion as well as a definition of the term *hypothesis* in the context of simulation. First, the scientific process of developing and verifying hypotheses is analyzed in different disciplines and over time. Perspectives from logical-analytical, empirical, and philosophical domains are presented. Based on this, the theoretical structure of hypotheses as well as different reasoning techniques for drawing conclusions from hypotheses are introduced and distinguished. Secondly, these approaches are compared to the epistemological demands of simulation. To this end, the epistemic contribution simulation results can make is defined by the purpose or context of the application of simulation. Thus, a respective discussion of the epistemological opportunities and limits of verifying scientific hypotheses in computer simulation is presented in this section. The identified requirements are then summarized and general requirements on scientific hypotheses in simulation are defined.

4.1.1 Formalization of Scientific Hypotheses

This first step towards the systematic integration of scientific hypotheses into the process of simulation studies analyzes the history of as well as the scientific discourse on hypotheses. It derives common characteristics of hypotheses and provides a definition of hypotheses as it is used in this thesis. To conceptualize scientific hypotheses in terms of simulation studies, a discussion of respective approaches and techniques for their formulating and testing is provided. The presented techniques are then aligned with the theoretical concept of hypotheses to derive implications for Hypothesis-Driven Simulation Studies.

The term *hypothesis* was already used by ancient philosophers. However, it differed from today's use and originally did not involve an approach in science (Storey and Allan, 2014). In the late modern period, one of the first debates that involved hypotheses as part of a scientific method was held between John Stuart Mill and William Whewell. The reason for this debate was a disagreement on how the validity of suppositions can be methodically proven by different techniques of experimental inquiry (Achinstein, 1990).

In the 19th century, Mill defined hypotheses in a scientific context as follows:

> "An hypothesis is any supposition which we make (either without actual evidence, or on evidence avowedly insufficient) in order to endeavour to deduce from it conclusions in accordance with facts which are known to be real; under the idea that if the conclusions to which the hypothesis leads are known truths, the hypothesis itself either must be, or at least is likely to be, true."

(Mill, 1872, Book III, Chapter XIV, §4)

The driving idea of Mill's *inductive* approach for the verification of hypothesis is to make generalizations from observed facts. This bottom-up-approach is based on an argumentation such that the presence of the hypothesized cause implies the presence of the hypothesized effect. Vice versa, the absence of the hypothesized cause implies the absence of the hypothesized effect. According to the observation that mortality can sooner or later be observed for any human, a generalization can be inferred that any newborn human is mortal, too. Based on individual observations of a phenomenon (mortality), common patterns and circumstances that are capable of explaining the phenomenon are searched for (being human). Based on such similarities between the observed objects, hypotheses are formulated

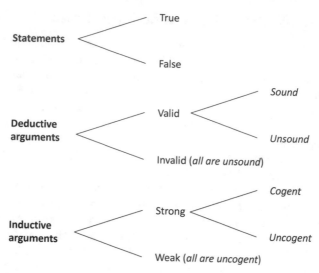

Figure 4.1: Terminology of deductive and inductive arguments (Hurley, 2012).

regarding the cause of the observation and general theories are derived ("All humans are mortal."). As the conclusion is only based on a certain number of observations, the correctness of the inferred theory remains uncertain. Consequently, it is still possible that the theory is false as one contradictory observation is sufficient to disprove it (Mill, 1882).

Instead of classifying such hypothesis as valid or invalid, inductive conclusions need to be assessed by their strength based on the number of confirming observations (cf. Figure 4.1). If the suppositions of the hypothesis provide probable support for the conclusion, the hypothesis is *strong* on a structural level. Furthermore, if the hypothesis is strong and there is empirical evidence for all suppositions to be true, one should believe in the conclusion. Such a hypothesis is referred to be *cogent*. However, according to Giere (1997), a strong and cogent inductive hypothesis or theory can never be proven with certainty, no matter how many affirming observations are made.

In contrast to inductive reasoning, Whewell argued in favor of *Deduction*, which pursues an argumentative top-down approach (Whewell, 1847). Here, the hypothesis is not defined based on observations. Instead, a theory serves as a basis for the definition of one or many hypotheses. Unlike the inductive approach, empirical observations are made after the statement of the hypothesis, e.g., by means of experiments that prove or disprove the hypotheses. The structural precondition of a deductive hypothesis is validity.

For valid hypotheses, it is impossible that true suppositions result in a false conclusion. Based on deductive validity, soundness is defined such that the suppositions are in fact true. Thus, the conclusion is logically certain (Hurley, 2012).

> *"Deduction justifies by calculation*
> *what Induction had happily guessed."*
>
> (Whewell, 1847, Vol. 2, pp. 92-93)

For the justification of hypotheses, Whewell demands the underlying theories to pass a number of tests before they can be confirmed as truth. The tests evaluate *prediction, consilience,* and *coherence* of the theory. Firstly, the theory must be capable of correctly predicting phenomena. As theories consist of universal principles and rules, respective hypotheses that are derived from true theories must be able to foretell phenomena. Secondly, consilient theories must be able to explain phenomena that are different from those that have been thought of when formulating the hypotheses. Finally, a theory is coherent if the hypotheses are able to predict and explain new classes of phenomena without adding new suppositions to the theory itself. Thus, the coherence should increase over time when the theory develops (Zack, 2010).

Besides test criteria for confirming theories and hypotheses, Whewell also proposed a method for performing these tests. His *hypothetico-deductive model* consists of three components: *hypotheses, deduction,* and *conclusions* (Grove and Menton, 2015). Based on a theory, hypotheses are defined such that the predicted observations contradict the theory. This is done in a way that all potential influencing factors are considered which can be used for explaining the theory. In case the hypothesized observation, which contradicts the theory, can indeed be made, the theory is disconfirmed and the respective factor must be ignored when improving the theory. Otherwise, if the observation does not follow the contradictory phenomenon, the hypothesis must be rejected, the factor is of importance, and the theory remains valid. In summary, the *hypothetico-deductive model* makes the assumption that hypotheses aim at explaining observations. However, experiments and further observations are required to verify such hypotheses. This stands in contrast to the inductive approach which pursues a vice versa approach (cf. Figure 4.2).

The modern understanding of hypotheses in science is particularly attributed to the thoughts of philosopher John Dewey and mathematician Karl

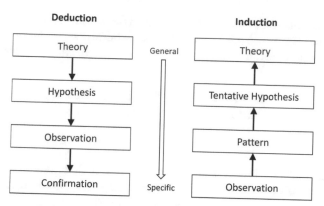

Figure 4.2: Deductive versus inductive reasoning (Repko et al., 2017).

Pearson (Manicas, 2011). Around the turn of the 20th century, both scientists presented methodical approaches for scientific investigations (Dewey, 1910a; Pearson, 1900). Even though Pearson focused on science and Dewey addressed inquiry in general, both approaches are similar and promote a data-based *scientific method*. Dewey was especially critical of the notion of science being the body of acquired knowledge. In his opinion, a shift from the imparting of knowledge, concepts, and theories to an improved understanding of methods for scientific inquiry was necessary to advance science. The focus of the proposed methodical approach to science lies on improving and establishing empirical reasoning as scientific *"habit of mind"* (Dewey, 1910b, p. 143).

The scientific method proposed by Dewey consists of multiple steps (Dewey, 1910a). Based on a perceived and defined problem, one or many possible solutions are suggested. The quality of the solutions is then evaluated through experiments, which are not necessarily physical. Thus, by means of contradiction, possible solutions are discarded until only one solution remains. Pearson proposed a similar, yet more data-driven, process where scientific laws are discovered from empirical observations (Pearson, 1900). From today's perspective, both Dewey's suggestion of possible solutions and Pearson's creative discovery of laws from measured data whose final acceptance requires critical assessment match previous definitions of hypotheses. Dewey's scientific method in particular can be classified as an advanced *hypothetico-deductive method* following Whewell's definition.

The scientific method has evolved since its first proposition and domain-specific adaptations have been made. However, its main characteristics have

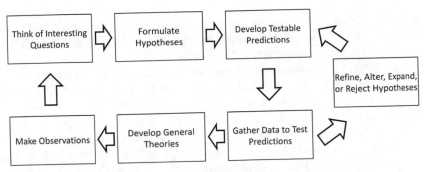

Figure 4.3: Formulation and testing of hypotheses as part of the scientific method (Haig, 1995).

not changed. The formulation and testing of hypotheses as well as systematic observations and experiments for proving or disproving these hypotheses are still essential elements. This results in an iterative and universal process for developing general theories, which consists of multiple steps (cf. Figure 4.3) (Haig, 1995). The first step of the process is the formulation of a research question proceeding from observations or thoughts that were made. At this point, the answer to the question is still uncertain. Based on the research question, possible factors as well as explanations for the phenomenon are identified and research hypotheses are formulated. Assuming the correctness of each hypothesis, testable predictions are developed whose occurrence is expected in case the hypothesis is correct. In a following step, data is acquired from literature or as part of an experiment to evaluate whether or not the predicted phenomenon indeed occurs. The empirical or experimental contradiction of a hypothesis requires a reformulation of the hypothesis until the assumed predictions can be confirmed. Finally, general theories are developed based on the confirmed hypothesis. In the scientific method, the definition of research hypotheses still meets Mill's definition of a hypothesis. The suggested explanation provided in a hypothesis is neither proven or disproved. It might be the result of an educated guess.

The process shown in Figure 4.3 corresponds to Whewell's hypothetico-deductive model where testable predictions are developed based on the research hypotheses and data is used to accept or reject these hypotheses. Even though both methods provide valuable and well-established approaches for working with hypotheses in science it is challenging to assist or automate these methods by means of information systems (Uhrmacher, 2012). For automatically processing hypotheses, both a machine-readable formalization of hypotheses and an algorithmic representation of the respective methods are required. Yet, neither of these requirements are provided in the hypothetico-deductive model or in the scientific method.

Nowadays, hypothesis-related reasoning methods, as presented in this chapter, belong to the scientific discipline of *logic*. Logic is the scientific discipline that aims at developing methods and techniques for evaluating arguments (Hurley, 2012). This includes formalisms for the specification of facts and circumstances as well as automatable reasoning approaches. Even though the term hypothesis is used differently in formal logic, the described characteristics of research hypotheses correspond with the definition of *arguments*.

Inductive and deductive reasoning, as discussed by Mill and Whewell, are the two most common approaches for revising theories in logic. In both approaches, theories are formulated as arguments. Thus, in the following, the logical concept of arguments is introduced well as other logical concepts that are closely related to arguments, i.e., *nonarguments* and *conditional statements* (Hurley, 2012).

Both *deductive* and *inductive arguments* consist of one or many *premises* that are linked to one *conclusion*. In deductive arguments, the premises provide evidence that implies or supports the conclusion and the conclusion is claimed to necessarily follow from the premises. Consequently, if all premises are true, the conclusion must as well be true. Inductive arguments are less certain with respect to the inferential claim. The premises claim to support the conclusion as well, but only with limited certainty. Even though the premises are true, one can only infer that the conclusion is also *likely* to be true. This is because of the fact that opposing observations might falsify the argument and corresponds to Popper's concept of *falsifiability* (Popper, 2002). The following example emphasizes the inferential link between the premises and the conclusion.

Premise 1: The payment of the employees was increased by 15%
Premise 2: and the number of vacation days was increased by 5,
Conclusion: thus, the manufacturing rejection rate decreased by 9%.

In logic, premises and conclusion of arguments are statements that are either true or false. To this end, groups of statements can be logically connected. Yet, a group of statements is not per se an argument, Depending on the link of the logical statements, they can also be classified as *nonarguments*. An example of a nonargument is an *explanation* where the statements are differentiated into *explanandum* and *explanans*. In contrast to arguments, explanations do not provide evidence for new theories but describe established knowledge or facts instead. Unlike the conclusion of an argument, the explanandum is the statement which describes a phenomenon that is generally accepted. Accordingly, the explanans is a single statement or a group of multiple statements that aims at explaining the explanandum.

> *Explanans:* *Because the supplier was not able to deliver in time,*
> *Explanandum: the production of the goods was delayed.*

A more elementary form of a nonargument is a *conditional statement*. The structure of a conditional statement can be separated into the *antecedent* followed by the *consequent* part or vice versa. Even though the structure is similar to arguments, conditional statements differ from arguments in a way that arguments require the premises to provide evidence and thus to be true. Furthermore, the conclusion of an argument must be implied by the premises. In a conditional statement, both the antecedent and the consequent may either be true or false. The assertion of a conditional statement is that in case the antecedent is true, the consequent must be true as well. For a true antecedent and a false consequent, the conditional statement is false. If the antecedent is false, the conditional statement is always true, regardless of whether the consequent is true or false. The fact that anything follows from contradiction is referred to as the principle of explosion (*ex falso quodlibet*) (Bertossi et al., 2005).

> *Antecedent:* *If the number of machines is doubled,*
> *Consequent: the number of manufactured goods will increase by 50%.*

Concluding, arguments, explanations, and conditional statements consist of groups of statements (cf. Figure 4.4). However, the order but also requirements regarding the relation between statements and the truth values of statements are defined differently. While arguments are based on true premises with the purpose of proving a statement, the explanans in explanations only claims to explain a statement, which consists of accepted facts. Also, arguments are based on the foundation of the claimed link (the premises) while explanations are based on the result of the claimed link (the explanandum). Conditional statements are similar to arguments. Yet, the statements that are part of conditional statements must neither express

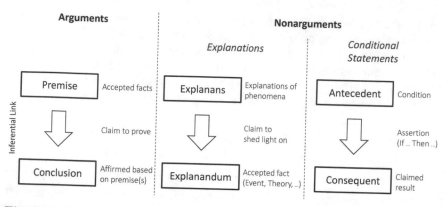

Figure 4.4: Inferential structure of arguments, explanations, and conditional statements (Hurley, 2012).

evidence nor imply something. Still, a conditional statements might be part of an argument as premise or conclusion.

At first, Mill's definition of hypotheses seems to correspond to the definition of a conditional statement. Mill defined hypotheses as a supposition whereby facts which are known to be true are used to deduce a conclusion. In conditional statements, the consequent is a logical consequence of the antecedent as well. However, the expression of a causal connection between the antecedent and the consequent is not necessary for a conditional statement. In Mill's definition of hypotheses, the ability to deduce the conclusions from the facts is essential. This is more similar to logical arguments where the conclusion must be implied by the arguments as well. Furthermore, sound (deductive) arguments require all premises to be true and the argument to be valid such that it is impossible for the conclusion to be false. Thus, it can be concluded that the logic concept of arguments seems to mostly correspond to the definition of scientific hypotheses. To evaluate whether respective testing approaches can be applied in a simulation context as well, it has to be investigated whether further parallels exist between the two approaches. Thus, the next subsection analyzes if the steps of the scientific method correspond to the approach pursued when utilizing computer simulation in research.

4.1.2 Epistemological Demands of Simulation

To assist the integration and verification of scientific hypotheses in simulation studies, this section adapts the previously presented techniques to the epistemological demands of simulation. For this purpose, the presence and importance of hypotheses in simulation is analyzed as well as their contribution to the epistemic process. The contribution primarily depends on the expressiveness and scope of simulation results, which is determined by the simulation's purpose of application. To this end, this section provides a differentiation and discussion of different purposes of simulation and derives implications on the epistemological contribution of simulation. This includes but is not limited to simulation's ability to verify research hypotheses.

Axelrod (1997, p. 4) postulates that simulation has established as a "third way of doing science" between theory and experiment, a view, which is also shared by other researchers (Dodig-Crnkovic, 2002). Considering real-world experiments, e.g., in empirical research, statistics provides suitable methods for the evaluation of observed results. In this regard, in particular the concept of *statistical hypotheses* is applied where an assertion is made regarding the parameter or parameters of an unknown distribution of a random variable (Hanneman et al., 2013). Similarly, the aim of simulation is to gain knowledge by means of virtual experiments (Tolk, 2015). Thus, the questions arises how the quality of the knowledge that is obtained by simulation can be evaluated and how their trustworthiness can be ensured. These questions are related to the epistemology of simulation.

This thesis aims at the integration of formally specified hypotheses into the process of simulation studies in accordance with the approaches presented in Section 4.1.1. To this end, an analysis is required of the implications hypotheses have for the epistemology of simulation. Simulation is applied in many different ways and for many different purposes. To understand the epistemological challenges in simulation, which arise from such diverse applications, different scientific uses of simulation are compared and differentiated first. Based on this, specific epistemological demands on the application of hypotheses in simulation are derived with regard to the sound acquisition and validation of knowledge.

Perspectives on the Epistemology of Simulation

As simulation is a scientific method, the epistemology of simulation was examined by researchers and practitioners from various domains. The domains range from computer science to philosophy of science but also include practical aspects. In the following, different perspectives are introduced, differences and similarities between the presented perspectives are identified, and the epistemic contribution is classified that can be provided by simulation. As the perspective of each author must be taken into account when analyzing different purposes of simulation, their respective professional background is illustrated in Figure 4.5. Additionally, Table 4.1 provides an aggregated overview of the different purposes of simulation that are presented by the authors.

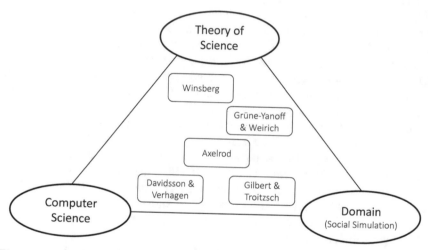

Figure 4.5: Professional background of the surveyed authors.

Grüne-Yanoff and Weirich (2010) take a philosophical perspective on the epistemology of simulation, which is inspired by social sciences. They discriminate between four different scientific usages of computer simulation: *proof, prediction, explanation*, and *policy formulation*.

To discuss the suitability of simulations to prove theories and assumptions, the authors quote the computer-assisted proof for *Kelper's sphere packing problem*, which was initially presented by Thomas Hales around the turn of the millennium (Hales, 2005). As no formal analytical proof was available at that time, Hales developed a computer program to solve a minimization problem for proving the theory. The computational results he presented were too extensive and the reviewers were not able to confirm the presented proof with absolute certainty. Still, the results were published by the *Annals of Mathematics* journal and Hales was awarded the *Fulkerson Prize* for outstanding papers (American Mathematical Society, 2010). Grüne-

Yanoff and Weirich describe the shortcomings of computer-assisted proof as *epistemic opacity*. Even though proof can be provided, hardware problems and software bugs might unknowingly bias the results. Simulations and other computations can be used for theorem proving. Yet, the verification of every detail of the results is challenging and partially not possible at all.

Moreover, the authors claim that simulation is often used for predicting that a certain event will occur at any point. However, the prediction of an event is not necessarily associated with the explanation of the event. Even though the simulation of an airplane's flow behavior in a wind tunnel might be used for predicting the plane's flight characteristics, it cannot be used to explain them physically and through laws of nature.

In contrast to this, simulations cannot predict phenomena whose principles and mechanisms that are not part of the conceptual model. As the observed behavior results from these mechanisms it can be assumed that explanations can be provided, too. Some simulations are based on natural laws but discrete-event simulations of production, logistics, or customer queuing models do not primarily depend on natural laws. Instead, mechanisms and algorithms as well as their respective probabilities are statistically estimated from empirical data or expert knowledge. Grüne-Yanoff and Weirich conclude that the predictive power of simulations depends on the modeled mechanisms and that the validity of these mechanisms is limited due to its empirical origin. Thus, they discriminate between *structural* and *predictive validity*. In structurally valid models, the mechanisms of the real system are used to produce the behavior of the model. Predictive validity only describes the simulation's capability to match a set of data. Thus, they conclude that some simulations indeed predict phenomena but fail to explain them.

Despite this, the authors state that scientific papers still claim the presented simulation is capable of explaining phenomena. Thus, they differentiate the explanatory power of simulations into three categories: *full explanations*, *partial explanations*, and *possible explanations*. *Full explanations* are provided by simulations that explain the reason as well as the characteristics of a certain phenomenon that occurred. This relates to the mechanisms that produced the phenomenon or the history of causalities that lead to it are provided. Yet, Grüne-Yanoff also argues that full explanations are challenging as the used model most likely lacks validity. In contrast to full explanations, *partial explanations* do not consider all factors for the explanation of a phenomenon. Due to complexity, most models abstract the real system and disregard factors that are not relevant for the simulation's purpose. Nonetheless, these simulations can still be applied to explain some of the factors that are responsible for the occurrence of a phenomenon.

Finally, some simulation models cannot be adequately validated, e.g., because the real system does not exist or because it cannot be accessed. Thus, such simulations can neither provide full nor partial explanations. In this case, simulations can still provide *possible explanations* or *candidate explanations* (Epstein, 2006). *Possible* or *potential explanations* are not actual explanations but do support the development of them. Thus, Grüne-Yanoff (2009, p. 43) described the epistemic contribution of a simulation as "an instance of the simulated system's functional capacities". Rather than expecting causal explanations, possible functional settings are provided and may be used to explain the observed phenomenon.

The fourth purpose of simulation presented by Grüne-Yanoff and Weirich is *policy formulation*. Simulation is applied to support the formulation of policies, for instance in terms of computational economics. In agent-based computational economics, intelligent software agents are used to analyze economic processes by modeling them as system of interacting agents (Tesfatsion, 2003). Yet, policy formulation by means of agent-based simulation is not limited to computational economics. Agent-based social simulation has been established for modeling and analyzing complex social phenomena in many areas including sociology (Gilbert and Troitzsch, 2005), management (Hare and Deadman, 2004), and psychology (Smith and Conrey, 2007).

The authors argue, that the kind of policy decisions which can be made strongly depends on the validity of the simulation. As agent-based simulations do not usually allow for correct predictions, cost-benefit-analyses and utility maximizations are not possible. Instead, they provide a set of possible scenarios based on the modeled mechanisms and allow for exploring the plausibility of these scenarios with respect to the real system. Policies can then either be formulated to minimize the worst-case outcome of the model or to perform better than other policies regarding a set of scenarios and a defined goal of the new policy. The term *scenario*, as it is used by the authors, refers to the general circumstances under which a simulation is executed. It is not to be mistaken with the term *scenario* as it is used in this thesis and which is introduced and defined in Section 5.1.

In contrast to Grüne-Yanoff and Weirich, the view of **Axelrod** (1997) is more practical. He presents a differentiation of seven purposes of simulation. Besides *prediction* and *proof*, Axelrod names *performance, training, entertainment, education,* and *discovery* as further purposes. These additional purposes shed a more practical light on simulation. They include but are not limited to the conducting of simulation for the performance of specific tasks and decision making, e.g., speech recognition and medical diagnosis.

The purpose of training, e.g., by simulating an environment, work tool, or object to be investigated, is closely related to the purposes of entertainment and education. Flight simulation, for example, can either be used to educate pilots or as computer game for leisure-time activities. Educational simulation are often referred to as *serious games*, as they are similar to computer games, yet, entertainment is not their only purpose. They also enable the user to experiment with the system to playfully experience how mechanisms work and what impacts changes or interventions have on a system's behavior, e.g., to illustrate transformation processes of socio-ecological systems (Lorig et al., 2016) or to teach Distributed Artificial Intelligence (Timm et al., 2008).

Finally, Axelrod states the discovery of new relationships and principles as another purpose of simulation and describes it, together with prediction and proof, as the major value of simulation. He identifies these three purposes as the main purposes of simulation with respect to its scientific application. Discovery is closely related to the purpose of explanation which has been discussed previously.

The purpose of *discovery*, as described by Axelrod, is part of what Grüne-Yanoff and Weirich outline as the purpose of *policy formulation*. Axelrod describes simulative discovery as the process of discovering and understanding the effects the modeled mechanisms have on the system's behavior. According to Grüne-Yanoff and Weirich, an important part of policy formulation is *exploratory modeling*. Simulation experiments are executed to observe the behavior of the system and to explore the effects of the modeled mechanisms. Summarizing, the discovery of the effects or mechanisms can be used for evaluating the impact different policies have on the behavior of a system.

Davidsson and Verhagen (2013) described potential purposes for simulation from a computer science perspective. With regard to other work published by the authors it seems that this view on purposes of simulation is also motivated by the practical application of simulation in social sciences (Davidsson, 2002). The authors discriminate between purposes of simulation where the user is *observing* the simulation and purposes where the user actively *participates* in the simulation. The observation of a simulation takes place for analyzing the system. Mentioned examples of use are *management, design*, or *engineering* of a system as well as evaluation, verification, and understanding of a system. In this regard, Davidsson and Verhagen refer to the use of simulation as a tool when introducing advantages for the support of design decisions when developing a system. Furthermore, they also emphasize the methodical application of simulation for evaluating, comparing, and verifying theories, models, or hypotheses. In contrast to this, the user's participation in the simulation might be reasonable with respect to *education, training,* or *entertainment.* These purposes were as well identified by Axelrod.

The perspective of Davidsson and Verhagen is closely related to the perspective of **Gilbert and Troitzsch** (2005). In addition to Davidsson and Verhagen, Gilbert and Troitzsch provide a social science view on the utilization of simulation as research technique. They discriminate between seven uses of simulation: *understanding, prediction, substitute for human capabilities, training, entertainment, discovery,* and *formalization.* The purpose of understanding is defined in accordance with Davidsson and Verhagen and the purpose of prediction corresponds to the definitions provided by Grüne-Yanoff and Weirich as well as Axelrod. The use of simulation as a tool for the substitution of human capabilities has not been mentioned before. However, in correspondence with the purpose of management which was proposed by Davidsson and Verhagen as Gilbert and Troitzsch name expert systems as an example for such a substitute. Training and entertainment are as well uses of simulation which were mentioned by other authors. Finally, discovery and formalization is emphasized as a major reason for social science's interest in simulation. The authors describe the discovery of consequences of theories which is facilitated by modeling parts of a real system. Yet, the purpose of discovery was also identified by Axelrod.

Winsberg (2010), whose research mainly focuses on epistemological considerations of simulation from a philosophy of science perspective, describes three main purposes of application (cf. Figure 4.6). For one thing, it can be used for *heuristic* reasons. In this case, a distinction is made according to the purpose of the simulation. It can either be used for communicating knowledge (e.g., visualizing (natural) processes by simulation for improving the understanding of the process) or for representing information (e.g., to communicate features of a system or structure to others by making them explorable using simulation). Summarizing, and referring to Axelrod's purposes of education and training, this view on simulation makes the user experience the results and thus imparts knowledge. Furthermore, depending on the availability of input data, simulation can as well be used for *understanding* and *prediction* purposes. In case data is not available, simulation can create artificial copies of real-world systems for further consideration. In doing so, the expected behavior of a system can be evaluated under certain conditions and data can be collected. In case data exists which describes the system's behavior, simulation can be used for understanding the mechanisms leading to this behavior and how certain events occur. This corresponds to the purpose of explanation as defined by Grüne-Yanoff and Weirich (2010).

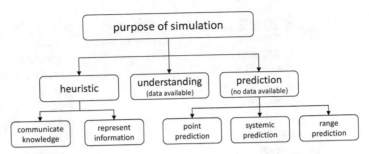

Figure 4.6: Purposes of simulation according to Winsberg (2015).

They focus on simulation as a scientific technique and how research can be conducted and supported by means of simulation. Axelrod, in contrast, presented a more comprehensive and more practical perspective on purposes of simulation. Davidsson and Verhagen complement a computer science perspective and combine both a theoretical and practical perspective. The view of Gilbert and Troitzsch is more practical as they utilize simulation as research technique in social sciences. Finally, Winsberg provides a meta perspective seizing aspects from all other perspectives. Table 4.1 summarizes all purposes of simulation that were presented by the authors.

Classification of the Use of Simulation

On closer inspection, similarities can be identified between the discussed purposes of simulation. Based on the presented definitions, the purposes of education and training as well as the heuristic purposes presented by Winsberg, i.e., communication of knowledge and representation of information, seem to target the same circumstance. All three uses of simulation provide information to the user or with the aim of educating the user by extending his or her knowledge or skills. This purpose is closely related to entertainment where educational simulations are utilized as well. However, as the transfer of knowledge or skills is not of primary interest, the purpose of entertainment is considered separately. Another major use of simulation is the imitation and substitution of human capabilities. This includes tasks, which can be executed by humans, yet the use of simulation is more efficient, economic, or faster. Examples are the performance of certain tasks, e.g., speech recognition, decision support for the management of systems, and proof. Considering the three previously presented purposes it can be observed that they imply a practical use of simulation.

Author(s)	Purpose	Author(s)	Purpose
(Axelrod, 1997)	discovery education entertainment performance prediction proof training	(Gilbert and Troitzsch, 2011)	discovery entertainment formalization prediction substitute of human capabilities training understanding
(Davidsson and Verhagen, 2013)	design education engineering entertainment management training	(Grüne-Yanoff and Weirich, 2010)	explanation policy formulation prediction proof
		(Winsberg, 2010)	heuristic prediction understanding

Table 4.1: Overview of purposes of simulation by authors in alphabetical order.

The remaining purposes can also be divided into three groups. In the first group, uses of simulation can be summarized, which analyze consequences of theories or mechanisms. This includes discovery, formalization, and policy formulation. The aim is to model specific aspects of a system to discover the consequences or phenomena that occur when certain theories, policies, or mechanisms apply. The second group includes purposes where simulation provides explanations for a specific behavior of the modeled system and improves the understanding of the considered system. Finally, in the third group, purposes can be summarized, which evaluate systems. This use of simulation is common in case the real-world evaluation is too uneconomic and difficult or even impossible. Yet, this stands in contrast to the question of the appropriateness of the application of simulation, which can be questioned here (cf. Section 2.3.2). It includes the design and engineering of complex systems as well as the evaluation and verification of theories, models, systems, and corresponding hypotheses. Furthermore, in this regard one must refer to the prediction of phenomena and possible futures which result from a set of inputs and modeled mechanisms. In contrast to the three practical purposes of simulation which were presented prior to this, the latter uses of

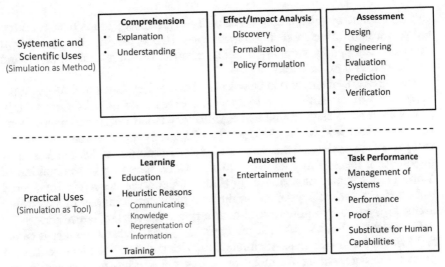

Figure 4.7: Classification of systematic and practical use of simulation.

simulation imply a more scientific and systematic application of simulation.

The presented purposes are derived from the presented contributions (cf. Figure 4.7) and lead to an even greater variety of aspects and goals of simulation. Regarding the heterogeneous areas of application discussed here it is obvious that no methodological silver bullet exists for the conducting of all simulation studies. Depending on the purpose, individual procedure models must be applied. Hence, a suitable differentiation of simulation purposes is required.

Considering the presented purposes, a twofold usage of computer simulation can be observed. In literature, the terms *tool* and *method* are used when differentiating the application of simulation. However, it appears that these terms are often used without questioning their actual meaning or even as synonyms. Still, they seem to be appropriate for a fundamental differentiation of the fields of application (Timm and Lorig, 2015).

On the one side, there are purposes for simulation that imply an instrumentalized use of simulation, which can be compared to the use of a *tool*. In the context of simulation, Fishwick described a tool as "handy and useful" (Fishwick, 1997, p. 59). This description corresponds to the statements of other authors, classifying simulation as a research tool. Schmidt (1984), for example, described the use of simulation for evaluating whether components of a system accomplish their purposes during systems analysis. He justified this statement by outlining the similarity of necessary steps being conducted to those of other modeling approaches. Hence, he described particular functions fulfilled by simulation in the context of operations research and thus declared it to be a tool.

The purposes of simulation that were presented by Gogg and Mott (1993) imply a use of simulation as a tool as well. From their point of view, simulation is an "analytical tool that can significantly facilitate the problem-solving process" (Gogg and Mott, 1993, p. 9). When creating a representation of a real process or system, simulation can help to determine which input is most qualified for generating a desired output. Corresponding to the opinion of Maria (1997) it may be summed up that simulation is frequently considered to be a useful technology for the evaluation of the performance of a, possibly artificial, system by applying and comparing different configurations.

Compared to the tool-like use of simulation, a procedural manner is essential for the methodical use of simulation. Contrary to the aforementioned practical understanding of simulation, a method emphasizes systematic and adaptive properties of a technology. Especially when seen from an epistemological perspective, a method describes the entire process. Analogous to the scientific method, the method of simulation starts with a hypothesis and aims at generating causal explanations for a hypothesized phenomena (Carter and Little, 2007).

According to Tolk (2015), simulation is able to support the process of theory building and testing which makes it a useful method. A variety of disciplines, which are traditionally not familiar with the use of software systems, took note of these opportunities and adopted simulation as an essential part of their research process. Sociologists, for instance, create artificial societies using simulation. Based on these virtual worlds, experiments, which cannot be performed in real-world environments, can be carried out. Thus, the possibility of detailed observation can be provided and new insights can be gained.

Gilbert refers to the new set of opportunities becoming available to research disciplines by the use of simulation as *simulation-based research* (Gilbert and Troitzsch, 2005). Social scientists, for example, are enabled to set up hypotheses or research questions concerning theoretical scenarios and complement the model by using assumptions or empirical observations. However, the demand of simulation approaches initiated or requested by other research disciplines, e.g., social sciences, is not unilateral. It has been perceived by computer science as well. Davidsson (2002) took up the social scientists' demand of a computer science view on social simulation and positioned it as a research method between the two disciplines. The mentioned examples represent the *methodical* use of simulation, as they describe a procedure for approaching a particular goal.

Seen individually, both of the presented ways of using simulation are scientifically justified and provide practical benefits (cf. Figure 4.7). However, they are not equally well-suited for being assisted by the approach proposed by this thesis. The focus of the approach presented here lies on the use of simulation as research technique for answering questions regarding the behavior of a simulation model in accordance with the scientific method. Thus, this thesis only considers purposes of simulation that are related to the systematic and scientific use of simulation as research method.

Utilizing simulation as a tool for evaluating the performance of a system or for visualizing system behavior is an important area of application. However, this purpose of simulation does not always correspond to the scientific method and cannot be generally represented by a comprehensive research process. When using simulation as a tool, the experimentation itself is in focus. The process is mostly reduced to the execution of the model and the observation of results. In contrast to this, a methodical approach of simulation implies a systematic and adaptive procedure where the experimentation is embedded into the epistemological process. This results in a more extensive and dynamic procedure as multiple scientific requirements need to be met to ensure the soundness of both the process and the generated results.

Still, the two major purposes of simulation that have been differentiated can be transferred into each other. The methodical use of simulation can be limited and reduced to the experimentation. As a result of this, the expressiveness of the simulation's results decreases as the interpretive framework is removed. One can still measure or observe the behavior of the model during experiments. However, due to a lack of systematics, the results of the experiment may not be used as a basis for generalizations or for deriving insights. Otherwise, in case the user who applies simulation as a tool can formulate an appropriate model-related research question, a methodical approach can be pursued. This results in additional effort compared to the initial way of application. The process becomes more comprehensive at the expense of the simple and straightforward conducting of simulation experiments. Yet, these opportunities and the associated consequences might not be in the users' interest.

4.1.3 Requirements on Scientific Hypotheses in Simulation

As shown in Section 4.1.1, the concept of hypotheses is not exclusive to simulation. It is used in many scientific disciplines and is an inherent part of the scientific method. For the formulation and testing of scientific hypotheses, different approaches have been proposed. Yet, these approaches are of general nature and cannot be applied to simulation without adaptations. Thus, initially, a conceptualization of research hypotheses in simulation is required. The aim of this conceptualization is to enable the integration of such hypotheses into a methodology for simulation studies. Both the intelligent and hypothesis-based design as well as the systematic conducting of simulation experiments shall be facilitated by this means. Consequently, the first requirement reads as follows:

Requirement 1: *Research hypotheses in simulation must be specified such that they can be integrated into a methodology for assisting the systematic design and automated conduction of experiments.*

To achieve this requirement, two preconditions need to be achieved first, which build on one another. In Section 4.1.1 it has been concluded that the concept of arguments, as it is used in logic, seems to mostly correspond to the definition of scientific hypotheses. When transferring hypotheses to concepts from logic, reasoning and testing approaches that are applied for proving or disproving these hypotheses need to be adapted as well. The approach developed in this thesis aims at the systematic verification of research hypotheses by means of experiments. Thus, the structure (*syntax*) of simulation-related hypotheses must be defined such that it becomes machine-readable and that reasoning and testing approaches can be systematically applied. This results in the following subrequirement, which specifies and substantiates requirement 1:

Requirement 1.1: *The structure of hypotheses in simulation must be defined by means of relevant components to allow for the systematic application of reasoning or testing approaches.*

After defining the structure of hypotheses as they are used in the methodical application of simulation, the next step is the development of a formalisms that can be used for specifying hypotheses. Current approaches describe hypotheses using natural language. On the one hand, this is beneficial as the hypothesis can be read and understood by anyone. On the other hand, this results in two difficulties. Firstly, natural language is often not sufficiently specific to avoid misinterpretations and misunderstandings. Secondly, the computer-aided processing of natural language is challenging. Even though the characters can be easily interpreted on a syntactical level, the semantical interpretation of natural language and the assessment of a statement's intention also involves the risk of misinterpretations. To avoid this, formal specifications are used to describe properties or systems and to generate machine-readable statements. Still, the interpretation of such specifications is challenging in terms of controlling simulation studies. The resulting subrequirement 1.2 is related to the definition of *semantics* of formally specified hypotheses:

Requirement 1.2: *Taking account of the superior structure of hypotheses, a formalism must be developed which allows for the specification, interpretation, and systematic integration of hypotheses in simulation studies.*

Besides the logical structure of hypotheses, the epistemological classification of hypotheses in simulation as well as the scientific contribution they provide must be considered by the developed approach. From a methodical perspective, the content of hypotheses is neither predetermined nor limited. Any conceivable claim can be formulated as a scientific hypothesis. Yet, for facilitating the systematic formulation and testing of hypothesis, it has been concluded that arguments in logic correspond to the concept of scientific hypotheses. According to Section 4.1.1, the truth content of the comprised statements is crucial for logical arguments. Additionally, the epistemology of simulation further limits the claims that can be verified by means of simulation experiments. This results in the second main requirement:

Requirement 2: *The explanatory power of hypotheses in simulation must be analyzed to define and adequately consider epistemological opportunities and limitations of Hypothesis-Driven Simulation Studies.*

As discussed in Section 4.1.2, the explanatory power of hypotheses is predefined and restricted by the purpose of simulation. Considering all potential applications of simulation, a distinction between the use of simulation as tool and method was made. The focus of this thesis lies on the scientific use of simulation as a research method. To ensure that the developed approach adequately meets the demands of a research technique, the first specification of this second requirement is:

Requirement 2.1: *The methodical use of simulation as research technique shall be assisted and facilitated by the developed approach.*

The purpose of prediction is an area of application which is often described in simulation literature. When building a model, one might be interested in how the model's behavior changes under certain parametrizations or and how likely it is for a phenomenon or event to occur. The prediction of the behavior of a modeled system, which is based on a specific set of input parameter values, may not be mistaken by the explanation of the system's behavior. Even though a phenomenon may be predicted in case the structure of the original system is modeled correctly and sufficiently detailed, the simulation does not necessarily provide an explanation for the behavior. In simulation, where all mechanisms need to be explicitly modeled, these two purposes are intercoupled. Virtual models cannot predict phenomena whose mechanisms are not explicitly modeled. Still, structural validity of the model must be assumed such that the model correctly reproduces the behavior of the modeled system. This results in the following requirement:

Requirement 2.2: *The developed approach must be capable of integrating hypotheses that predict the behavior of structurally valid models.*

The following third subrequirement is closely related to the second one, as prediction and explanation are inseparable in simulation. Still, it is argued that full and also partial explanations, which causally explain why and how a phenomenon occured, can mostly not be provided by simulation. This results from a lack of validity and from simplifications, which are part of the model building process. Instead, simulation provides possible functional explanations as the functional capacities of the simulated system are discovered during simulation experiments. Consequently, when simulation is expected to systematically provide explanations, the developed approach must allow for the identification and determination of potential functional explanations. The corresponding requirement can be formulated as follows:

Requirement 2.3: *The approach must be capable of providing and verifying potential functional explanations that explain the behavior of the model.*

Considering requirements 2.2 and 2.3 as well as the fact that a black box approach is pursued in this thesis, it is challenging to predict and functionally explain the behavior of a model without a structural analysis of the model itself. Still, the approach can explore the outer behavior of the model under different parametrizations and use this information to verify research hypotheses. By this means, a variety of plausible behaviors of the model is simulated and can be used for predictions and for providing functional explanations. The challenge is to identify and restrict the relevant parameter space and to systematically test a large set of possible scenarios to adequately analyze the model's behavior. Consequently, the fourth requirement is:

Requirement 2.4: *Hypotheses must be systematically tested over a sufficiently large set of possible parametrizations to evaluate the performance of the model.*

The requirements on the logical structure and the epistemological classification of hypotheses in simulation are defined with respect to the integration of a hypothesis into the process of simulation studies. To enable the systematic design and conduction of simulation experiments and to identify relevant experiments, hypotheses must be integrated into and aligned with other existing methods. In simulation, a variety of valuable and sophisticated methods, services, and techniques exists. Yet, the identification of appropriate and reasonable methods for the verification of specific hypotheses as well as the targeted and dynamical logical linking of these methods is challenging. This results in the third main requirement for the approach which is developed in this thesis:

Requirement 3: *Suitable methods must be identified and logically linked to allow for the systematic design and conducting of relevant simulation experiments based on a given formalized research hypothesis.*

To guide the identification and linking process, the first necessary step is the development of a procedure model. By providing a methodology, both the epistemological and the structural perspective of hypotheses in simulation can be combined in a joint framework. On the one hand, a methodology defines an operational framework and thus guides the user's actions and decisions during the research process. On the other hand, the contribution of a methodology facilitates a more standardized, replicable, and reproducible application of simulation with respect to the verification of hypotheses. Therefore, the first subrequirement with respect to the targeted integration of methods is:

Requirement 3.1: *To allow for a systematic experimentation, an integrated and adaptive procedure model for Hypothesis-Driven Simulation Studies must be designed.*

In addition to this, enabling and facilitating the practical application of the developed methodology is part of this thesis. Methodologies provide a valuable guide for the operation of processes. However, transferring the approaches and procedures of a theoretical framework into practice is challenging. Methodologies only define a scope of action which does not prevent variations in the practical application. For this purpose, the development of an assistance system is reasonable. Such systems provide aid to the experimenter as they keep track of the procedure, which is defined by the methodology. Furthermore, when the sequence of process steps is defined by case-specific decisions, an assistance system can support the experimenter to plan a suitable and methodologically sound progress for the study in accordance. This is, to reduce experimenter bias and results in the seconds subrequirement:

Requirement 3.2: *An assistance system must be designed and developed that facilitates the conducting of Hypothesis-Driven Simulation Studies.*

This subsection aimed at defining general requirements on scientific hypotheses in simulation. For this purpose, the logical and scientific requirements for formulating and testing research hypotheses (cf. Section 4.1.1) were compared as well as the epistemological demands from simulation as scientific method (cf. Section 4.1.2). To bridge the identified gap, requirements were defined on the logical structure and the epistemological classification of hypotheses in simulation. Furthermore, this subsection presented general requirements for integrating hypotheses into the methodological process of simulation and for aligning existing methods with hypotheses. The next step, after defining theoretical requirements, is the analysis of practical approaches to simulation. It is analyzed if and to what extent they meet the defined requirements. In case a gap can also be identified here, approaches must be developed that close this gap and meet the requirements.

4.2 Hypotheses in Simulation Studies

This section analyzes whether the previously defined requirements are sufficiently met by practical implementations of simulation. The practical scientific application of simulation as a scientific method takes place in simulation studies. Accordingly, this section provides a perspective on how hypotheses practically contribute to the epistemological process in simulation studies and whether the defined requirements are met.

This section provides two perspectives on simulation studies: a *processual* perspective and a *structural* perspective. The process of simulation studies is defined by procedure models. Thus, methodological procedure models for simulation studies are introduced and it is evaluated how the theoretical concept of hypotheses is considered by these procedure models. Additionally to providing a logical segmentation of the study's process, procedure models also structurally organize simulation studies. While the processual structure of a simulation study represents the sequence in which the individual steps take place, the logical components of the study hierarchically represent the artifacts of the simulation study. They define hierarchical dependencies between the structural components of simulation studies as well as transitions to convert these components into one another. Thus, the structure of simulation studies is also addressed by this section. From both perspectives, it is analyzed how hypotheses are integrated into simulation studies as well as the effect hypotheses have on the both the structural and processual elements of the simulation study.

After discussing the structural decomposition of simulation studies, the aggregation of the outputs that are generated by the individual components of simulation studies has to be conceptualized as well. Here, two aspects must be considered. On the one hand, the outputs of the simulation steps and iterations need to be summarized and statistical measures of central tendency must be applied for averaging the responses. On the other hand, it has to be ensured that the aggregated results are interpreted within their context. To this end, this section discusses requirements for the aggregation of simulation outputs. Finally, considering the requirements defined in Section 4.1, methodological shortcomings are identified in the integration of hypotheses in simulation studies. They serve as a basis for the design of a process of Hypothesis-Driven Simulation Studies in Section 5.

4.2.1 Methodological Integration of Research Hypotheses

After terminologically defining and epistemologically classifying hypotheses in terms of simulation, the role is analyzed that hypotheses play in simulation studies. For this purpose, this subsection presents the results of a literature survey on procedure models for the conduction of simulation studies. In addition to this thesis, the results of this survey were separately published by Timm and Lorig (2015). Based on these models, it is assessed what impact hypotheses have on the process of simulation studies.

Procedure models are developed and used to ensure reliable results in simulation studies. Describing the simulation process by means of procedure models improves and accounts for quality assurance (Kettinger et al., 1997). To evaluate the community's state of discussion regarding process organization in simulation, this section presents the results of a literature survey of the archive of the *Winter Simulation Conference* (WSC) for articles proposing or discussing procedure models in simulation. Since 1968, WSC has taken place annually (except for 1972) and presents itself as "the premier forum on simulation practice and theory" (Wilson et al., 1996, p. 6) which, considering the conference's history, indicates an overview of relevant work conducted in context of simulation. The online archive of the WSC contains more than 8500 contributions[4], is publicly available, and due to the long existence of the conference it seems appropriate to be used for reflecting the community's state of discussion and its evolution. Based on this, a preselection of the most relevant articles was performed by evaluating both titles and abstracts of all on-topic contributions as well as their references. These articles were then analyzed in detail and classified with respect to the creation of an overview on relevant steps and their order in simulation studies.

As a result of the previous advances in simulation research, the first procedure models considering the entire simulation process were presented as part of WSC in the early 1980s. However, even though simulation is used by diverse scientific disciplines, a review of the relevant contributions reveals a number of apparently universal procedure models (cf. Table 4.2).

Considering the most cited publications in the context of simulation processes, Law and its former coauthor Kelton are mentioned frequently. As long ago as in 1982, the two researchers identified and published essential steps in simulation studies. In ten steps they describe the **procedure of a simulation study**. Each step is explained briefly and in a comprehensible way and most of the elements of a simulation study mentioned by Law appear in later models as well, even though interpretation and order might vary. The authors reference Shannon (1975) and Gordon (1978) as influences on their work. Yet, Gordon is not considered any further within this section as his work focuses on techniques for system simulation and ignores the modeling aspect.

Even though Shannon did not propose a procedure model to WSC until 1998, he suggested stages of simulation studies that "may be distinguished" (Shannon, 1975, p. 23) already back in 1975. Shannon's as well as Law's procedure models mainly differ in two aspects. On the one hand, Shannon makes a distinction between system data, describing the boundaries and behaviors of a system, and input data, for executing the model. On the other hand, the experimental design is double-checked in Shannon's model. After a preliminary **experimental design** is defined, the final design is specified after the verification and validation process, before the experiments are conducted (Shannon, 1998).

---

[4] According to Alexopoulos et al. (2017), Barton et al. (2017), and Sargent et al. (2017), more than 8500 papers, Titan talks, case studies, and vendor presentations were presented at the Winter Simulation Conference between 1982 and 2017.

The remaining models are not presented in detail as they mainly refer to the works of Shannon and Law. Instead, only remarkable extensions, comments or unique features are emphasized that are relevant for this thesis. The entire outline of each model is shown in Table 4.2.

Table 4.2: Comparison of different simulation procedure models: Steps numbered consecutively in chronological order. Additional letters imply the combined execution of the steps.

	Balci (1990)	Banks (2014)	Carson (2004)	Centeno (1996)	Friedman (1996)	Law (2014)	Maria (1997)	Montgomery (2013)	Musselman (1994)	Pegden et al. (1995)	Pritsker and O'Reilly (1999)	Sadowski (1992)	Schmidt (1984)	Shannon (1975)
Define the problem	1	1	1_a	1	1_a	1_a	1	1_a	1_a	1_a	1_a	1	1	1_a
Define objectives	2_a	2	1_b	$2/4$	1_b	1_b		1_b	1_b	1_b	1_b	2	2	1_b
Plan the study			1_c			1_c		1_c	1_c	2		3		2
Collect real system data	2_b	5	$3/4$	3	2_a	2_a	2_a	2	2	3	3_b	4_a	3	3
Create conceptual model	3_a	4	2		3_a	2_b	3		3	4	2	4_b	$4/6$	4
Validate conceptual model					3_b	3						5	5	
Collect input data	3_b				2_b		2_b			4	6		7	6
Select response variables					2_c				3					
Translate model in simulation language	4	6	$3/4$	5	4_a	4_a	4_a		5	7	3_a	6	8	7
V&V of model	*	$7/8$	5_{ab}	6_{ab}	4_{bc}	$4_b/6$	$4_b/5$			6_{ab}	8_{ab}	4_{ab}	$9/10$	8_{ab}
Experimental design	5	9	6_a		5_a	7	7	4			$5/9$	3_c		$5/9$
Conducting of experiments	6_a	10	6_b	7_a	6	$5/8_a$	8	5	10_a	10	5	7	11_a	10_a
Number of runs		12			5_b	8_b			10_b					10_b
(Statistical) analysis of output data	6_b	11	7	7_b	7	9	9	6	7	11	6	8	11_b	11
Documentation	8	13	8	8		10	6		8	12	7	9		12
(Re)Validation	7							7					12	

For visualizing procedure models, most authors have chosen sequence diagrams. By this means, they illustrate the modular structure of the models and underline the interdependency between the individual steps. These requirements, which are closely related to software projects, indicate that simulation studies have to be planned properly as well, in order to support a successful progress. While Law and Shannon recommend this step, the other surveyed approaches do not mention it.

Another central component of most procedure models analyzed during the survey is the aspect of **verification and validation** (Sargent, 2013). To validate a program or model, the verification needs to be completed successfully. In case of simulation, verification and validation is applied to the conceptual model and the simulation model as well as to the results. However, all authors, except for Montgomery and Sadowski, recommend verification and validation of the simulation model, whereas validating the conceptual model is not even suggested by half of them. Balci even complements verification and validation with testing techniques and proposes applying them during the entire study. Finally, the validation of the results and, as the circumstances require, a revalidation of the model are only proposed by Montgomery and Schmidt.

When executing simulation experiments, the steps proposed by the procedure models differ the most. Some authors limit their requirements to the execution of the simulation experiments. Other authors, in contrast, emphasize the importance of defining variables for the **surveillance of the model** during experimentation. Furthermore, estimating a sufficient number of simulation runs is another underestimated challenge when performing studies. These general conditions are taken into account by less than half of the procedure models.

In summary, it can be concluded that most of the procedure models presented here consist of three major components: The planning of the simulation study including the collection of relevant data describing the system to be modeled, the definition and development of a simulation model and environment (tool or framework), and the conducting of the actual simulation experiments. Considering, that individual experts are required for the realization of these components, a main challenge in simulation studies is to integrate and synchronize the collaboration in a suitable way.

The simulation domain proposed various procedure models for the conduction of simulation studies. The profession of the authors varies from theorists to practitioners and they have different professional backgrounds as they come from different domains. Regardless of the authors' perspectives, all procedure models share the definition of the problem to be solved as first necessary step of a simulation study. In most procedure models, this step is immediately followed by a the formulation of objectives and the planning of the study. Besides a planning phase, all surveyed procedure models for simulation studies have two more phases in common: the definition and development of the simulation model and the conduction of the experiments. However, differences can be observed in the level of detail in both the number of steps of each phase as well as the specific guidance that is provided for each step.

Some of the presented procedure models provide very detailed descriptions or specification of important steps in simulation studies and how can be transfered into practice. Yet, with respect to the goal of this thesis, the initial definition of the study's problem is not sufficiently integrated and referenced in the following steps. Even though the overall problem is occasionally mentioned in later steps, specific instructions or approaches for individually addressing the problem's epistemological demands and for verifying underlying research hypotheses can rarely be identified.

Taking into account the requirements that were defined in Section 4.1 leads to the identification of two major shortcomings: First, the problem of the study and consequently also the resulting hypothesis of the study are not sufficiently specified for the application of respective concepts from logic. All presented procedure models require the definition of a problem the study addresses. Yet, with respect to the reproducibility of they study, they do not provide approaches or techniques for specifying and communicating the identified problem. When published, the problem is stated in natural language which is not sufficient for the scientifically sound reproduction of the study's results. Second, the purpose of the simulation study is not adequately represented by the procedure models. In Section 4.1.2, it was concluded that the purpose of simulation studies strongly influences and predetermines the epistemological contribution of the study's results. Both the opportunities and limitations of different purposes were introduced and a methodical differentiation of the purposes has been presented. The surveyed procedure models are neither purpose-specific nor is the methodology adjusted depending on the purpose of the study. Only general purpose procedure models are proposed which obviously cannot take specific epistemological demands into account. As a consequence, existing procedure models must be extended such that they can dynamically adapt to different purposes of simulation.

4.2.2 Structural Components of Simulation Studies

In addition to the process of simulation studies, structural components of simulation studies can be derived from these procedure models as well. The process of simulation studies consists of multiple steps, some of which take place in an iterative and parallel manner. During these steps, different structural components of simulation studies are created, modified, and transferred into one another. In this subsection, these different components are identified, specified, and their hierarchical dependencies are outlined. Based on this, each components' contribution to the verification of research hypotheses is examined.

Simulation studies are conducted to achieve a better understanding of how a system works and behaves under different conditions by conducting experiments with a model of the system. In the classical sense, simulation studies consist of two parts, the conception and implementation of the simulation model (*modeling*) as well as the design, execution, and evaluation of simulation experiments based on the model (*experimentation*) (Shannon, 1998). The modeling part requires a high domain-specific expertise for the development of a valid model which appropriately represents the real-world system (cf. Figure 4.8) (Huang et al., 2011). As a result of this, models are highly individual, it is difficult to compare or assess a model's quality, and the assistance of the modeling part of a simulation study is challenging.

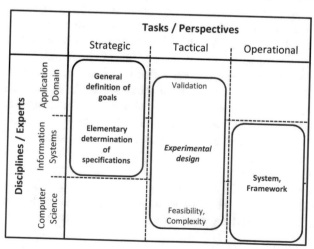

Figure 4.8: Disciplines involved in simulation study and their task fields.

To successfully conduct simulation studies, the modeling part is not always of primary interest. A model of the studied system may already exist and can be reused. Furthermore, depending on the aim of the study, the use of an existing model might be necessary, e.g., if the study aims at reproducing results of previous research or when hypotheses of earlier studies are revised and need to be tested again. Nevertheless, even though the individual assessment of the model's appropriateness may vary, the credibility and replicability of a simulation study also depends on the design, execution, and evaluation of the experiments. No matter how high the model's quality is, if the process that is applied to test the assumption and hypotheses of the model does not follow scientific standards, the results lack expressiveness and soundness (Tolk, 2017a). In contrast, when studying a poor model with a sound experimentation process, the derived results are expressive with respect to the model. Yet, the appropriateness of the underlying model must be questioned and thus the modeling part of simulation studies is neglected in the approach presented here. Instead, the focus lies on the well-documented, replicable, and assisted conduct of the experimentation part of simulation studies.

The experimentation aims at investigating the system's behavior (*input-output relationship*) with the objective of providing evidence for or against the simulation studies' leading question or assumption, i.e., the goal of the study (Montgomery, 2013). Thus, the inner structure of the model is of less relevance, i.e., states and mechanisms of the model. Besides, it cannot be assumed that the inner structure of models is published or accessible. Consequently, when developing a universal process for systematically answering research questions based on a simulation model, it is reasonable to pursue a black box approach where the experimentation only relies on the observable behavior of a model. Hence, this thesis defines the term *simulation study* as the targeted and systematic process of experimenting with a black box model and the goal of investigating a question or an assumption regarding the model's behavior.

Simulation studies implement a hierarchical structure, where experiments need to be derived from the study's goal on the one hand and consist of complex processes and respective sub-processes on the other side. Thus, a terminological distinction of both the components that are relevant in simulation studies and the interdependencies between the components needs to be made to allow for the systematic assistance of simulation studies. The suggested distinction is presented in Figure 4.9.

Regardless of the separation between modeling and experimentation, Winsberg (2010) defines *simulation studies* as inferential processes that investig-

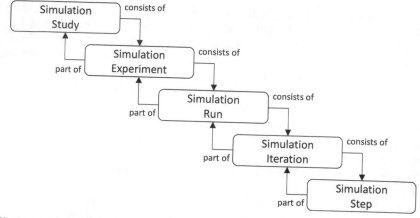

Figure 4.9: Structural components of a simulation study.

ates complex phenomena by means of computational techniques. In contrast to this, Law (2003, p. 66) provided a more practical definition of simulation studies. He describes it as "a sophisticated systems-analysis activity" and underlines that knowledge of simulation methodology, probability theory, statistics, and project management are required. In practice, most users who perform simulation studies do not have these skills as their training is often limited to the application of a specific simulation framework. At the same time Law (2003) emphasizes that programming the model is only a minor task in simulation studies, which demands 25% to 50% of the overall time.

With regard to the survey of procedure models for simulation studies (cf. Section 4.2.1) it must be emphasized that simulation studies cover more than just the implementation and execution of a model. They consist of a large number of steps or stages with the aim of investigating properties of a real system (Shannon, 1975). Simulation studies enable the investigation "of the dynamics of a system, how it changes over time and how subsystems and components interact" (Carson, 2004, p. 11). As pointed out, the key element of a simulation study is its goal. It specifies the objective and purpose of the study and thus drives the entire experimentation process.

To achieve the objective of a simulation study, i.e., addressing specific research questions (Shannon, 1998), corresponding performance measures are specified and *simulation experiments* are conducted. The aim is to analyze and compare the influence different parametrizations of the model have on the values of the performance measures (Law and McComas, 1991). Each experiment describes a "series of tests" where changes are made to the inputs of the model to observe changes of the outputs (Maria, 1997, p. 9). They are conducted with regard to the investigation of which inputs are responsible for the observed behavior of the model (Montgomery, 2013). A simulation study consists of at least one simulation experiment per question that is stated about the system.

For each experiment, an appropriate design must be defined. The main goal of experimental design is to provide an estimation of how different levels of the model's factors affect the outputs of the model (Kelton and Barton, 2003). According to Maria (1997), relevant aspects or questions that must be considered during the design of experiments include type, quantity, and form of data, which are required to accomplish the study's goal. Generally speaking, this includes the selection of a performance measure as well as a small set of input factors which influence the performance measure and respective factor levels. In case the number of possible factor-level-combinations is too large to be simulated, Maria recommends the use of fractional factorial designs to reduce the number of simulated configurations. Finally, if the simulation model is not designated to terminate or in case specific parametrizations or software faults result in infinitive loops of simulation, termination conditions must be defined for each experiment (Barton, 2013).

As defined by Montgomery (2013, p. 1), experiments are "series of runs", where each experimental run represents an individual test of the model with a specific parametrization. For each simulation experiment, one or many *simulation runs* are designed in which the system's response to a specific set of inputs is observed (Maria, 1997). Usually, each factor-level-combination which was defined during the design of experiment defines one parametrization of the model and thus an individual simulation run.

In contrast to deterministic simulation models that do not contain random variables, simulation runs that execute stochastic models with probabilistic inputs require multiple *simulation iterations* (*replications*). This is to allow for a statistical assessment of the distribution of the results and to achieve reliable results (Hoad et al., 2007). Centeno (1996) pointed out the risk of confusion and illustrated the difference between simulation runs and iterations as follows. When executing simulation models, a run is defined by a specific parametrization and starts when the experimenter clicks on the start button of the simulation framework or sends the respective command line instruction. It ends when the framework simulated the last event or time step. When the model is executed, multiple iterations can be simulated in sequence. The simulation iteration is defined to take place between the start of the simulation watch and its end, i.e., from the first to the last tick. Consequently, the outputs of the iterations differ, while the summarized outputs from each run are the same. However, this only applies if a run is initiated multiple with equal random number streams. In summary, each iteration of a stochastic simulation run is initiated with the same inputs but a different stream of random numbers, which results in different output values (Carson, 2004).

Finally, depending on how progress is calculated in the simulation model, each simulation iteration consists of multiple *simulations steps (tick)*. Each step represents progress of the simulation clock and the computation of a new state of the model. Especially for the consideration of warm-up periods or for defining the time-based termination of simulation iterations, the application of simulation steps is reasonable (Sanchez, 2007).

The presented differentiation of structural components in simulation studies illustrates, how each component is logically linked to the goal of the study and to the hypothesis whose verification the study pursues.Out of the five presented structural components, the hypothesis is closest related to the simulation study itself. It defines the goal of the simulation study and thus provides direct and fundamental implications for the execution of the study. Simulation experiments are directly derived from the study. Each experiment consists of a series of tests, in which different parametrizations are applied to analyze the model and their effect on the behavior of the model (Maria, 1997). Thus, the aim of simulation experiments is to define a landscape of relevant parametrizations or to cover all parametrizations that are of interest. Because of the black box approach which is pursued in this thesis, potential functional explanations for the model's behavior must be defined as different parametrizations of the model. Thus, experiments define and test a variety of potential functional explanations for a certain hypothesized behavior. Simulation runs, which are dependent on experiments, define individual scenarios with specific parametrizations of the model. With respect to the hypothesis, each run then provides a prediction of one possible future of the model.

As this thesis focuses on probabilistic models, repeating a simulation run must not necessarily lead to the same outputs, even though the parametrization of the model remains unchanged. To take probabilistic model behavior into consideration, the observed behavior must be evaluated stochastically. In this regard, each iteration of a simulation run contributes to minimizing the statistical uncertainty of the results. Accordingly, the necessary number of iterations must be estimated individually and the required level of certainty must be defined as part of the research hypothesis. Finally, the use and specification of simulation steps is not mandatory. They can be beneficial for modeling specific circumstances and thus for answering particular research questions. If applied, the concept of step-wise simulations allows for answering more detailed research questions. As each step provides time-discrete outputs of the model, the temporal progress of the model can be observed, time series can be derived, and more specific information regarding the behavior of the model is obtained. Based on this, more specific potential functional explanations are provided, which enables the researcher to formulate more detailed research questions.

4.2.3 Aggregation and Interpretation of Results

Each of the presented structural entities either produces genuine outputs themselves or they process outputs from other, hierarchically subordinate, entities and pass them along the hierarchical structure of the study. With respect to the systematic verification of hypotheses, these outputs must be reaggregated. This subsection presents pitfalls that might occur during the aggregation of outputs and systematizes the aggregation process to cope with these pitfalls.

The presented process combines two aspects, the numerical summarization and averaging of the generated output values as well as the contextual interpretation of the aggregated results. In a simulation study, the fragmentation of the study's hypothesis into individual simulation experiments, runs, and iterations in only one half of the overall task. After performing simulation runs and their respective iterations, the responses of each iteration must be collected and aggregated in a suitable and sound way to allow for drawing conclusions and to confirm or disconfirm the assumptions of the study (see Figure 4.10). The outputs of the simulation model are gathered in every simulation iteration or, if supported by the model, in each simulation step. After a successful simulation iteration, the model returns the current values of all output variables. These values allow for the analysis of the response of the model.

In contrast to this, each simulation step provides a snapshot of the system's behavior at a specific point in time. These time-discrete pieces of data, the stepwise responses of the model, can be assembled. This results in a time series of response for the respective simulation iteration. In this case, either the model's outputs at a specific point in time, e.g., the last step of the simulation, or the arithmetic mean of the outputs over a period of time can be defined as the response of the respective simulation iteration. When averaging output values, both the consideration of the values of all steps or the reset of the statistical measures of central tendency after a defined warm-up period are feasible (Chung, 2004). In addition, each step's outputs can be seen as an individual sample and analyzed accordingly.

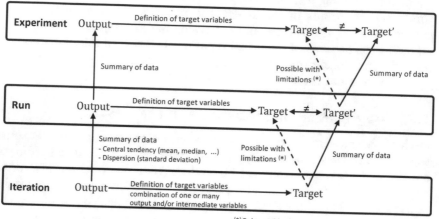

Figure 4.10: Aggregating output variables to target variables and performance measures in simulation studies.

To overcome the expressiveness gap between the outputs of the model and the performance measures that are part of the study's underlying hypothesis, target variables are formally specified based on the model's output variables. First, the iterations' responses are defined and extracted from the time series of output data in step-based simulation models or directly by observing the output values in unspecified simulation models. Next, the values of the specified target variables need to be calculated based on the model's output and aggregated for each simulation run to obtain each run's results. Here, the order in which these two steps are applied is of particular relevance as they are not interchangeable without the risk of generating biased and incorrect results. This is because the summarization of output or target variables and the calculation of target variables are not necessarily commutative (Lorig et al., 2017a). The issue is formally defined, discussed, and a solution to overcome this issue by means of an assistance system is presented in Section 6.1.3. At this point, for the definition of the integrated procedure model, it is important to take the existence of this pitfall into account. Otherwise, methodological uncertainties may lead to epistemological weaknesses in terms of the interpretation of the results. Ultimately, this impacts the testing of the statistical hypothesis and consequently also the verification of the initial research hypothesis as the sampled data basis is biased.

The consequences of disregarding this issue can be illustrated by the following example. It assumes an ABSS study, where the transactions on a marketplace are simulated as interactions between customers and companies. From a company's perspective, relevant performance indicators might be the *customer lifetime value* (CLV) as well as the *economic order quantity* (EOQ). Neither of the two indicators is provided as output of the model and thus has to be defined as a new variable. As the marketplace is a probabilistic model, several iterations of the simulation model are executed for each parametrization and the gathered outputs need to be summarized to gain every run's results. The CLV must be calculated for each iteration, as it relates to the decisions and actions a specific customer has performed in each execution of the simulation model. It represents the profit that has been generated by a customer during its relationship with the company (Berger and Nasr, 1998) and can be simplified as follows:

$$CLV = (\text{Revenue per customer and year}$$
$$\times \text{ Customer relationship in years})$$
$$- \text{ Promotion costs per customer and year}.$$

In this example, the CLV is equal to the price of all products the customer has bought during the simulation. Assuming that the simulation's output includes information on all purchases that have been made by the customers, the required target variable needs to add up the price of the purchases per customer. The CLV per customer and iteration can then be calculated and the average CLV can be determined over all iterations. However, one could also first summarize the purchase data from each iteration and calculate the CLV based on the aggregated dataset. In this specific case, the results would not differ as addition and averaging are commutative operations.

Considering the EOQ, this is not possible. The EOQ results from a trade off between the order costs, i.e., fixed setup cost and cumulated unit costs, and both interest and depreciation on stored goods (Harris, 1990). It can be determined by dividing the double sum of the annual demand and the fixed costs per order by the annual storage cost per good:

$$EOQ = \sqrt{\frac{2 \times \text{Annual demand} \times \text{Fixed order cost}}{\text{Annual storage cost per unit}}}.$$

Assuming that all required values are provided as outputs of the model, each iteration's outputs must be calculated before averaging each iteration's EOQ to achieve the result of the simulation run. Averaging annual demand, fixed costs per order, and the annual storage cost per good before calculating the EOQ would cause mathematically incorrect results. The concatenation of division and averaging is not commutative and thus needs to be differentiated with respect to the study's hypothesis. The same differentiation applies for the aggregation of results from different simulation runs for drawing conclusions from a simulation experiment. To avoid this pitfall, and for receiving sound results, the process of aggregating performance measures needs to be planned thoroughly.

In conclusion, the following challenge can be summarized for the consideration in Hypothesis-Driven Simulation Studies. The behavior of the simulation model is observed on the lowest structural layer. Here, outputs are generated which must be summarized and aggregated to allow for a targeted interpretation with respect to the initial hypothesis. During this process, methodological uncertainties may lead to epistemological weaknesses in terms of the interpretation of the results.

4.2.4 Methodological Shortcomings

With respect to the epistemological requirements that were defined in Section 4.1, this section discusses and analyses the integration of scientific hypotheses in simulation studies. To this end, three relevant perspectives were identified. First, the methodological integration of hypotheses in simulation studies in terms of procedure models was investigated. Second, in addition to the processual perspective, a structural perspective was chosen and the components of simulation studies as well as their hierarchical dependencies were presented with respect to the integration of hypotheses. Finally, the aggregation and interpretation of the model's outputs that were generated during the study was addressed to allow for sound hypothesis testing. Based on these perspectives, gaps were identified between the defined theoretical requirements and the perceived practical implementation and integration of hypotheses in simulation studies. These gaps are consolidated in this subsection and addressed during the development of an integrated procedure model for the design, conduction, and evaluation of Hypothesis-Driven Simulation Studies.

Different purposes for the application of simulation that were presented in Section 4.1.2 were revisited in Section 4.2.1. Depending on the purpose of the study, the epistemological contribution simulation can make is influenced and predetermined. The presented investigation and comparison of different procedure models for simulation studies revealed that they are neither designed for purpose-specific modifications nor enable methodological adjustments of the process. All models that were part of the survey focused on general-purpose simulation studies and did not take specific epistemological demands into account. As a result of this, the purpose of the simulation study cannot be adequately considered. Furthermore, the hypothesis is not sufficiently specified by the investigated procedure models so that the immediate application of hypothesis-testing concepts from logic is not possible.

Subsequently, Section 4.2.2 differentiated structural components of simulation studies and defined the hierarchical relationships between the components. In the presented distinction, the simulation study itself was introduced as superior component from which experiments, runs, iterations, and optional steps are derived. The study results from the scenario and thus represents the research hypothesis. The degree to which experiments, runs, and iterations can take the research hypothesis into account is predetermined by existing logical connections. Consequently, hypothesis-specific adaptations of the process must be planned and implemented in a top-down approach. The proper and targeted definition of the study as well as the systematic derivation of dependent components is challenging. To facilitate different purposes of simulation, e.g., the provision of functional explanations, the structural components of the study must be derived accordingly. Yet, the logical and contextual dependencies and transitions between the structural components of the study are not sufficiently conceptualized.

Finally, Section 4.2.3 investigated the aggregation and interpretation of the outputs that were generated by the structural components introduced in Section 4.2.2. Identified shortcomings do not address the aggregation of basic output values but the application and integration of more advanced performance indicators. Examples presented in this regard are key performance indicators which are domain-specifically defined and utilized for measuring the performance of a system. Underlying formulas may contain various mathematical operators, which interrelate the values of different input or output variables of the model. Pitfalls occur as it cannot be assumed that these operations are commutative. The correct order of the operations must be derived from the hypothesis to avoid methodological uncertainties and misinterpretations.

4.3 Conclusions

This chapter presented and discussed the results of a requirement analysis. To this end, it defined requirements for scientific hypotheses in simulation and presented an investigation of the status quo of the practical integration of hypotheses in simulation studies. A gap can be identified such that the stated requirements are not adequately met in practice. To close this gap, existing procedure models for simulation studies must be extended to allow for the integration and verification of scientific hypotheses.

With respect to the vision of this thesis, a need for research arises, which can be summarized in terms of three major challenges: First, there is a need to tighten the methodological alignment of the study's process on the investigated research hypothesis. Instead of only recommending the definition of a problem as a first step of a study, it is necessary to formally specify testable hypotheses. Each subsequent step of the study must then be planned and executed with respect to answering this hypothesis. For this purpose, an integrated procedure model is required that focuses on answering scientific hypotheses by means of simulation.

Second, the logical link between the structural components of the study must be conceptualized. This link allows for the integration of external methods or techniques into the process of the study such that existing approaches can be reused as part of the integrated procedure model. Moreover, the specification of the logical link between all involved components enables the intelligent assistance of the process by means of a software. This is essential to relieve the experimenter from repetitive tasks and to avoid experimenter bias.

Finally, the targeted and consistent aggregation and interpretation of the generated outputs must be enabled over all structural layers of the study and with regard to the verification the initial hypothesis. Each iteration and run of a simulation experiments generated individual outputs that must be gathered, analyzed, and interpreted to provide evidence for or against the validity of the investigated hypothesis. In this regard, the process of aggregating these outputs strongly depends on the hypothesis and must take the underlying assumption into account.

5 Hypothesis-Driven Simulation Studies

As part of the requirement analysis, challenges were defined for the formalization of hypotheses. Yet, it seems that these requirements are insufficiently met in practice. With respect to the replicable and reproducible verification of hypotheses in simulation studies, shortcomings of existing procedure models for simulation studies were identified. To overcome these limitations, this section proposes an integrated procedure model for the conducting of Hypothesis-Driven Simulation Studies. In contrast to conventional procedure models, the one developed and presented in this thesis focuses on the methodological integration of research hypotheses in the process of simulation studies. For this purpose, the procedure of the study must be aligned with the research hypothesis and the steps of the study need to be adjusted and combined accordingly.

This chapter addresses the logical connection of existing assistance functionalities with respect to facilitating and automating the conducting of Hypothesis-Driven Simulation Studies. It provides an overview of all involved entities (i.e., tasks, functionalities, and services) that contribute to the process of a simulation study. Furthermore, this chapter provides a specification of all connections between the interfaces and outline the way each component contributes to achieving the goal of a simulation study.

Finally, the development of an assistance system seems reasonable considering the large number of entities that are involved in the practical conducting of Hypothesis-Driven Simulation Studies. Thus, the last section of this chapter proposes an abstract architecture for an assistance system and illustrates how simulation users and experts operate with this system. This allows for the automation of large parts of the simulation study and relieves the experimenter of repetitive tasks. Examples of such tasks are the systematic variation of model parameters or the execution of respective simulation runs.

© Springer Fachmedien Wiesbaden GmbH, part of Springer Nature 2019
F. Lorig, *Hypothesis-Driven Simulation Studies*,

5.1 Integrated Procedure Model

In this subsection, different perspectives on hypotheses in simulation studies are joined into an integrated procedure model for the assistance of Hypothesis-Driven Simulation Studies. For this purpose, classical procedure models for simulation studies are extended and refined to overcome the described shortcomings of existing approaches and to meet the identified requirements for systematically integrating research hypotheses in simulation studies.

The requirements for formulating and testing scientific hypotheses serve as a basis for the proposed procedure model. Based on this, conventional procedure models for simulation studies are adapted such that the entire process of the study is aligned with the formulated hypothesis. By this means, structural components of the study can be systematically derived, modified, and connected with respect to the study's goal. Additionally, not only the decomposition of the study's components but also the aggregation of the outputs generated by these components is systematized.

The presented process aims at closing the gap between the structure and procedure of simulation studies on the one side and the epistemological requirements for systematically answering research questions by means of simulation on the other side (cf. Figure 5.1). This section introduces the integrated procedure model stepwise. Both the process steps as well as the transitions between the steps are presented in detail. Moreover, the process's potential for assisting the design and conducting of Hypothesis-Driven Simulation Studies is illustrated. For this purpose, this section introduces and applies an example from the domain of industrial manufacturing process simulation.

The structure of this section follows Figure 5.1. First, the scenario is introduced, which provides the context of the simulation study (top of the figure; Section 5.1.1) Based on this scenario, the study's hypothesis is specified (Section 5.1.2). To illustrate how both scenario and hypothesis are interconnected to the process of the study, this section introduces and applies an exemplary case from logistics. Next, and referring to the presented example, all relevant steps for the design of experiments, runs, iterations, and steps are presented (left side of the figure; Section 5.1.3). Subsequently, the outputs generated during these steps are aggregated in reversed order which allows for answering the stated hypothesis (right side of the figure; Section 5.1.4). This section considers each step of the study, assuming the provision of an implemented, executable, and verified simulation model.

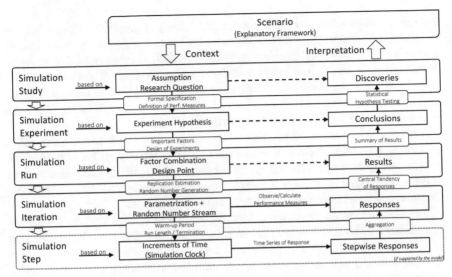

Figure 5.1: Process model for the conducting of Hypothesis-Driven Simulation Studies.

5.1.1 Introduction of the Study's Scenario

According to most simulation procedure models, e.g., Law (2014), Banks (1998), or Shannon (1998), the necessary first step of a simulation study is the proper definition of the goal (cf. Section 4.2.1). This is essential, as the study's goal specifies the objective and implies the purpose of the study. It drives and influences the entire experimentation process as relevant experiments need to be derived from the goal to achieve it (Conway and McClain, 2003). The boundaries for defining reasonable goals are determined by the model under study, as it mainly provides the study's context. In the literature, this context is often referred to as the *scenario* of the study. To adapt this terminology in this thesis, the term *scenario* is discussed and defined in tis section. Furthermore, to illustrate how the scenario of the study affects each step of the proposed procedure model, an exemplary case from logistics is introduced and used through this chapter.

Scenarios in Simulation Studies

In information technology, the term *scenario* is defined in various ways. Ahmed and Sundaram (2009) discussed different perspectives on and definition of scenarios from an information systems perspective. The definition they provide describes scenarios as "a complex combination of data, model, and solver" (Ahmed and Sundaram, 2009, p. 1030). In this regard, a scenario is defined as a *model* that is instantiated by a certain set of *data* and that is tied to *solvers*. In their definition, a *solver* is described as an algorithmic software component, which applies behaviors to the *model*. The aim is to separate the behavior of the model from its structure.

Transferred to simulation, the solver can be compared to the simulation software, which executes the model and thereby generates its behavior. In most cases, this is a specific and possibly commercial simulation framework or toolkit, e.g., AnyLogic, Repast Symphony, or Enterprise Dynamics. However, proprietary and individual solutions may also be used.

In practice, most simulation models are inseparably tied to a specific simulation software. Hence, the exchange of this software often results in additional effort as specific interfaces must be reimplemented or even newly development. Approaches exist where simulation models are defined using particular meta description languages, e.g., Modelica (Fritzson and Engelson, 1998). This improves the cross-platform flexibility as such models can be imported into and utilized by multiple of simulation frameworks. However, the number of frameworks is still limited and the extension of the scope of supported frameworks requires the development of additional wrapper or importer classes. Furthermore, cross-compatibilities exist between certain frameworks, e.g., between Repast Symphony and NetLogo, where the ReLogo language allows for the execution of simpler NetLogo models using the more powerful Repast Symphony engine (Ozik et al., 2013). In summary, the simulation software used for implementing and executing simulation models corresponds to the definition of a solver given by Ahmed and Sundaram (2009).

In accordance with the presented definition of a scenario, in this thesis the scenario of the simulation is defined as the combination of simulation *data*, *model*, and *software*. Ahmed and Sundaram (2009) defined data as the representation of facts that describe value and data type of discrete information. Accordingly, in the black box approach which is pursued here, data is provided and integrated via the inputs of the model (cf. Section 2.2.1) and the scenario of the simulation study consists of a set of data. It can be one specific full parametrization of the model, which strongly predetermines the behavior of the model. Yet, partial parametrizations that leave out variables or the definition of admissible values or ranges of values for the input variables of the model are also possible data sets. The simulation model together with an explicit parametrization and an appropriate framework

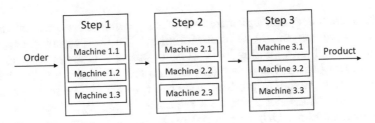

Figure 5.2: Setup of the exemplary case.

form an executable system. Thus, the scenario can be used to generate the behavior of the simulation model and to analyze possible futures of the modeled system.

Here, the epistemological importance and impact of scenarios in simulation studies becomes apparent. On the one hand, the scenario of a study limits the extent to which questions can be answered by the simulation. The more restrictive the scenario has been designed, i.e., due to a specific parametrization of the model, the less explanatory power the simulation has as the dynamics are restricted as well. Accordingly, the amount of possible hypotheses is also restricted as variations of parameter values are not longer intended. On the other hand, the scenario provides a context for the interpretation of the results. Without a scenario, the results of a simulation are only plain values whose sound and context-related interpretation is challenging. The simulation's scenario defines and provides the semantics that are required for the interpretation. Both the direction of each variable's effect and the range of admissible values for the relative classification of a specific value are defined.

Exemplary Case: Production Line Logistics

To illustrate how the scenario influences each step of a simulation study, this chapter introduces an example from the practical application of simulation. In manufacturing, simulation is applied to analyze, plan, and optimize production processes in factories. This example case assumes a factory that operates an assembly line for the production of a simple unspecified product, e.g., chairs or tables. The assembly of the product consists of multiple consecutive steps and each step is executed by a specific type of machines (cf. Figure 5.2). For reasons of parallelization and redundancy, groups of equal machines of each type exist and incomings orders are distributed among the machines within a group.

The assessment and optimization of the performance of a production line is a common aim of a simulation study. In the presented setup, the performance of a production line can be evaluated via the number of orders that are finished during a day shift or in a specific time slot. In this case, the maximum number of products that can theoretically be manufactured in the considered time slot serves as a reference for the highest performance of the production line. Other potential performance measures are the average utilization of the machines or the rate of products that are rejected due to manufacturing defects.

This example emphasizes that it is essential to take the scenario and particularly the underlying data of the model into account when evaluating simulations. Assuming that 20 orders arrive on a simulated day, the average number of products per order is 4, and the standard deviation of the number of products per order is negligibly small. The simulation's result is the successful manufacturing of 10 orders. In another model, 20 orders arrive on one day as well. In contrast to the first simulation, the average number of products per order is only 2, the standard deviation is likewise small, and the result of the simulation is the completion of 18 orders. By only comparing the number of completed orders, one could conclude that the second model results in a higher performance of the system as almost the double amount of orders was completed, e.g., due to improved queuing disciplines. Yet, the scenarios of the two simulations differ and consequently the results of the simulation cannot be directly compared. Interpreting the results in the context of each simulation's scenario reveals the potential bias. Relating the number of completed orders to the average number of products per order indicates that the first model manufactured 40 products while the second model was only able to manufacture 36 products. With due regard to the data of the model, the performance of the first models seems to be higher. However, further experiments are required to finally and reliably assess and compare the performance of the two models.

To utilize the presented exemplary case for the conduction of a Hypothesis-Driven Simulation Study, a research questions must be stated first. In the domain of manufacturing simulation, a variety of research questions can be thought of. Lattner et al. (2011a, p. 122) presented the following manufacturing-related investigation question in their work: "Is the current storage still sufficient in case of a change in volume and content of the orders?". They point out, that verbal statements like the one presented are often stated as research questions in simulation studies. At the same time, they also emphasize that experiments cannot directly be derived from such verbal statements.

For illustrating the methodology of the proposed procedure model, a more comprehensible research question is required to demonstrate the hypothesis-driven process of a simulation study. In contrast to the storage-related research question that consists of an ambiguous and hardly testable assertion, there is a need to formulate a more specific and quantifiable goal of the simulation study. In the initial situation, a fully implemented simulation model of a production line in a factory is available, which can be run by means of a corresponding simulation framework. As part of a manufacturing simulation, a possible question that drives the simulation study could read as follows:

Will the manufacturing cycle efficiency increase by more than 50% if the number of machines increases from 3 to 5?

To evaluate and compare business processes, quantitative criteria (*key performance indicators*) are defined in economics (Parmenter, 2015). These performance indicators enable and facilitate the assessment of the success of a specific process. Success can be defined narrowly, e.g., as rejection rates in a manufacturing process, but also as the achievement of superior process goals, e.g, the satisfaction of customers. The *manufacturing cycle efficiency* (MCE) is a performance indicator, which is used to assess the relative amount of wasteful or uneconomic time in a production process (Mowen, 2013). This is important, as the goal of process management is to increase the efficiency of business processes by decreasing or even eliminating uneconomic times. The equation that defines the MCE calculates the ratio between the value-added time and the manufacturing cycle time (throughput time) of a process. Accordingly, it can take values between 0 and 1 (0 - 100%). An MCE of 0.25 implies that 75% of the production time is spend on activities where no value is added to the products, e.g, waiting, moving, or queuing. The ideal or most desirable MCE is 1, implying the elimination of all non-value-added time in a process.

$$MCE = \frac{\text{Processing Time}}{\text{Manufacturing Cycle Time}(MCT)}$$

$$MCT = \text{Processing Time} + \text{Move Time} +$$
$$\text{Inspection Time} + \text{Waiting Time}$$

In the following sections, the presented example case is used to illustrate how the stated question can be systematically answered as part of a simulation study. To this end, the behavior of the model is measured via the MCE performance indicator.

5.1.2 Specification of Hypotheses

After emphasizing the importance of the scenario of a simulation study and introducing an exemplary case, the process model for Hypothesis-Driven Simulation Studies is presented in three consecutive steps. This includes the specification of hypotheses, the design and structural decomposition of relevant experiments, as well as the aggregation and analysis of the generated outputs. As a first step, one or more testable hypotheses need to be specified for each research question that is stated as a goal of a simulation study. In accordance with the types of experiment hypotheses that were defined by Yilmaz et al. (2016) (cf. Section 3.1.3), only *phenomenological hypotheses* are considered by the proposed approach. Such hypotheses make assertions about the behavior (*input-output-relationship*) of a model, i.e., which form the outputs take in the case of specific input values.

When evaluating and verifying phenomenological hypotheses according to the requirements defined in Section 4.1.1, it is most challenging to check whether or not the observations from the experiments do indeed contradict the hypothesis. When applying probabilistic models in simulation, a single observation rarely allows drawing sound conclusions about the modeled system. It is unclear, how the observation can be classified compared to the amount of possible observations defined by the model's basic population. This challenge is closely related to hypothesis testing in statistics (Montgomery, 2013). Hence, this section introduces and applies an approach for the specification of hypotheses on the behavior of simulation models which is inspired by statistical hypotheses.

Specification of Statistical Hypotheses

In contrast to computer science and theory of science, statistical hypotheses are not expressed as a statement, which consists of a number of premises and one inferentially linked conclusion. Instead, in statistics, pairs of hypotheses are constructed in which the outcome of a probabilistic experiment is supposed. The pair of hypotheses is mutually exclusive, meaning that each possible outcome of the experiment is covered by either of the two hypotheses. Here, the hypothesis that formulates the default statement, i.e., that the observed outcome of the experiment is a result of chance, is referred to as *null hypothesis*, while the hypothesis claiming the existence of causality is the *alternative hypothesis*. The distribution of the system's population is unknown and the observations from the experiments are considered as a random sample drawn from this population. The aim of the statistical hypothesis test is then to assess how likely or unlikely the made observations is compared to the result expected from pure chance or in relation to other possible outputs. The threshold defining the boundary between chance and causality (*significance level*) is defined in advance and domain-specific standards apply.

The assumptions as well as the approach of statistical hypothesis testing correspond to the requirements of hypothesis testing as identified in Section 4.1. In computer science, the outcome which is generated by a model during experimentation can also be viewed as a sample drawn from an unknown probability distribution. Accordingly, the question of whether or not the observed outcome is representative for the population or whether the observed improvement was a result of chance arises as well. The approach's limitation on phenomenological hypotheses furthermore implies that the conclusion of the initial research hypothesis makes a statement on the behavior of the model. This can be measured via the output variables of the model or respective performance indicators derived from or based on these variables. The average value of such an output variable or performance indicator can analogously be used as a test statistic in statistical hypothesis testing. Thus, in this thesis, statistical hypotheses testing approaches are applied to evaluate and verify phenomenological hypotheses in simulation studies.

To make preparations for the application of hypothesis tests, some requirements must be met. Mainly, a null hypothesis as well as a corresponding alternative hypothesis have to be formulated and a data sample needs to be drawn respectively. As the aim of this approach is to test the initial research hypothesis of the simulation study by means of statistical hypothesis tests, both null and alternative hypothesis need to be derived from the goal of the study. Accordingly, the alternative hypothesis describes the assumption that the model's behavior will change under the defined conditions while the null hypothesis assumes that any changes made to the parametrization of the model or the model itself will not have any effect on the model's behavior, i.e., the model's response. For defining a set of corresponding hypotheses, measures need to be defined first, which provide information that can be used for assessing the response of the model. To verify phenomenological hypotheses it has been argued that output variables or performance indicators seem to be suitable measures.

Specification of Hypotheses on the Performance of Simulation Models

Performance indicators are goal-specific and usually not part of the outputs of a simulation model. Instead, output variables need to be mathematically combined to new variables (*target variables*), which can then be used for assessing the performance of the model. Referring to the manufacturing example introduced in this chapter, all output variables that represent non-value-added times, i.e., *waiting time, inspection time*, and *move time*, must be summed up and added to the *processing time*. The result is the length of time that has passed from the start of a product's production until its completion. In logistics, this timespan is referred to as *manufacturing cycle time* (MCT) and it is reasonable to label the resulting variable accordingly. As such variables are created artificially with respect to assessing the performance of the model, but are not directly used as performance measures, they are termed *intermediate variables* (Barton, 2013). As a next step, the output value of the *process time* is divided by the intermediate variable MCT to receive the target variable MCE, which was defined as a performance indicator.

In the example provided here, the formulated question consists of a relative statement regarding the behavior of the model, i.e., a 50% increase of the MCE in case the number of machines is increased by two. For applying statistical hypotheses tests, a test statistic has to be defined that summarizes the dataset. As the study's goal consists of the assessment of the MCE indicator, the central tendency (e.g., the arithmetic mean) of the MCE's distribution is a suitable test statistic. Consequently, a possible pair of statistical experiment hypotheses can read as follows:

H_0: If the number of machines increases from 3 to 5,
    the mean MCE will **not** increase by more than 50%.
H_1: If the number of machines increases from 3 to 5,
    the mean MCE will increase by more than 50%.

To enable a systematical assistance of this process, the goal of the study in terms of the resulting research hypothesis, the respective pair of experiment hypotheses, and the process for deriving these hypotheses from the study's goal need to be formally specified. This allows for the systematic parametrization and evaluation of simulation studies and thus also for the automated evaluation of the constructed hypotheses. For the formal specification of hypotheses and with respect to their automated evaluation, three relevant components are identified.

Formally specified and statistically testable hypotheses on the behavior of models in simulation studies must consist of three parts: the *parametrization of the model*, *information on the statistical hypothesis*, and additional *test constraints*. This allows for both the automated parametrization and evaluation of simulation studies as necessary experiments are systematically derived from the hypothesis, resulting simulation runs are executed, and outputs are analyzed with suitable hypothesis tests. In addition to this thesis, the presented approach for the formal specification and automated verification of hypotheses in simulation studies was published by Lorig et al. (2017a).

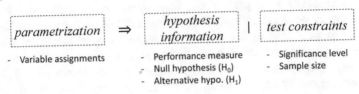

Figure 5.3: Structure of a experiment hypothesis in simulation studies.

Figure 5.3 illustrates the structure of a formally specified experiment hypothesis. The three parts of the hypothesis are linked in a way that the parametrization of the model implies the hypothesis information and additional test constraints apply globally. In the parametrization part, specific values or ranges of values are assigned to the independent variables of the model. This approach presumes the closed world assumption and thus demands either the explicit declaration of the input values or the use of predefined standard values. Based on the parametrization of the model, detailed information on both null and alternative hypothesis is provided in the *hypothesis information* part of the expression. In particular the expected behavior of the model is defined here. Besides the definition of both a set of output or target variables that serve as performance measures and a respective statistical measure, which is used for determining the central tendency of the performance measures, e.g., arithmetic mean, both null and corresponding alternative hypothesis are formulated based on values or value ranges of performance measures. Finally, superior *test constraints*, e.g., significance level and sample size, must be stated. As the proper definition of test constraints is challenging, assistance is provided for this step of the simulation study as well. Approaches for assisting the definition of test constraints are formally presented and integrated in the next chapter. Leaving out the test constraints at first, the following expression illustrates how a formally specified hypothesis could be stated in the context of the manufacturing example.

$$ParSet1(machines(5)) \land ParSet2(machines(3)) \land \#$$
$$\Rightarrow \mu_1(MCE) \land \mu_2(MCE) \land$$
$$(H_0(\mu_1 - \mu_2 \leq 50\%) \lor H_1((\mu_1 - \mu_2 > 50\%))$$

The parametrization part of the formalized hypothesis consists of two distinct parameter sets, *ParSet1* and *ParSet2*. The increase of the mean MCE, as it is stated in the pair of statistical experiment hypotheses, is not stated as absolute value but relative to the increase of the number of machines. Consequently, two samples need to be drawn with individual parametrizations of the model to enable the comparison of the mean MCE before and after increasing the number of machines. The samples only differ in the value of the factor *machines* and further specific factor values are not stated in the experiment hypotheses. Thus, the ceteris paribus symbol *(#)* is added to the parametrization part implying the use of standard values for all remaining inputs.

As two sampled need to be compared in this example, the hypothesis information part of the formally specified hypothesis must relate both samples to each other. First, the feature must be defined to enable the execution of statistical hypothesis tests. In this case, the arithmetic mean of the MCE measured for each of the two parameter sets is defined as feature of the test (μ_1 and μ_2). Then, null and alternative hypothesis (H_0 and H_1) are formulated such that the difference between the two mean values is calculated and a threshold is defined ($\mu_1 - \mu_2$). According to the experiment hypotheses, the threshold is 50%. While the null hypothesis assumes that the difference is less or equal to 50% (no effect) and the alternative hypothesis assumes that the difference is greater than 50% (causality).

To enable the automated testing of experiment hypotheses, a gap needs to be closed between the outputs that are provided by the model and the data that are required to verify whether or not the hypothesis holds. Different approaches have been proposed for the formal specification of dependent variables such as performance measures, e.g., the use of *MathML* (Teran-Somohano et al., 2015). These approaches as well as their advantages and shortcomings were discussed in Chapter 3.

5.1.3 Design and Structural Decomposition of Experiments

As a next step, simulation experiments need to be conducted to generate outputs and to test whether or not the experiment hypotheses hold (left side of Figure 5.1). According to the definition of simulation experiments that is provided in Section 4.2.2, conducting experiments includes the systematic variation of the model's inputs for observing changes of the outputs. *Design of Experiment* is challenging, as decisions need to be made regarding which input variables (factors) are altered and which values are both relevant and feasible with respect to computational complexity and coverage of the parameter space (Kleijnen et al., 2005). Furthermore, as the required test statistic needs to be defined in advance, a suitable hypothesis test needs to be selected at this stage (Montgomery, 2013). This also influences the design of the experiments, as the experimentation process must be aligned with the hypothesis tests' requirements to be able to observe and gather the values of the test statistic during the experimentation process. For each resulting relevant parametrization, individual simulation runs must be executed to obtain comprehensive and sound results.

In the example presented here, the simulation study consists of a single simulation experiment with a corresponding set of experiment hypotheses. Based on this pair of hypotheses, a two-sample test is required for testing whether or not the null hypothesis holds. In the presented example, a *two-sample t-test* for normal populations and independent observations is suitable for testing the hypotheses (Lehmann and Romano, 2005). Consequently, individual yet comparable samples need to be drawn by means of simulation for each of the parameter sets, i.e., 3 and 5 machines. This results in two major groups of simulation runs, those with a parametrization of 3 machines and those who require that the number of machines is set to 5 as part of the parametrization. For executing simulation runs, specific values need to be assigned to all input variable, also the ones whose factor levels are not part of the experiment hypothesis' parametrization. This is challenging, as relevant factor levels of the remaining input variables depend on the performance measure of the study. Furthermore, for important factors, the execution of multiple simulation runs with different factor levels is reasonable to fully assess the response surface of the model's performance measure. Thus, important factors need to be identified among the input variables as the variation of all factor's levels is impracticable due to the combinatorial explosion of the number of simulation runs. This limitation especially applies for extensive and complex models with a large number of input factors.

The identification of relevant factors is challenging. As the importance of each factor is relative and depends on the considered performance indicator, it is hardly possible to determine such dependencies *ex ante* and without detailed knowledge of the model's mechanisms. Thus, the determination of important factors must be performed individually for each performance measure. When identifying important factors, two results can be expected. Either a small number of factors has a major impact on the observed outputs or a great number of factors is of importance for the observed behavior. The second case contradicts the idea of limiting the parameter space in favor of the computational complexity of the simulation study. In case a large number of factors is identified as having a strong influence on the outputs of the model, the conclusiveness of such a model must be questioned as well. If the effect cannot be attributed to a small number of factors, there is a reason to doubt the simplicity and thus also the testability of the model and accordingly of the results that were generated by it. In this case, the model's suitability for the epistemologically sound verification of phenomenological research hypotheses is inherently limited. This scientific issue has also been discussed in the domain of simulation. According to the *parsimony principle* (*Occam's razor*), the identification of a minor set of factors that has a major impact on the performance measure is advisable (Kleijnen, 2015).

For this specific purpose, different *factor screening* approaches have been proposed and improved during the last years (Morris, 2006), e.g., Morris method (Morris, 1991) or sequential bifurcation (Bettonvil and Kleijnen, 1996). Compared to the Morris method, the advantage of sequential bifurcation is that it requires a smaller number of simulation runs (Shi et al., 2016). All variations and extensions of sequential bifurcation, e.g., CSB, or CSB-X, provide promising and reliable approaches for identifying important factors of a simulation model. They extend the initial approach and take dependencies between input factors into account as well. Yet, each approach requires an individual set of conditions to be met by the model, e.g., whether correlations between factors are allowed. Thus, and because of the advanced mathematical understanding, which is required for applying sequential bifurcation, it is desirable to assist the selection and application of factor screening approaches in simulation studies. Technically, sequential bifurcation pursues a *divide and conquer* approach for identifying each factors effect on the simulation output by systematically altering the input factor levels (Bettonvil and Kleijnen, 1996). The results of this approach can be visualized as tree where each layer is the result of splitting a group of factors in two smaller groups (cf. Figure 5.4).

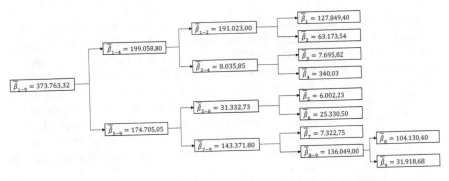

Figure 5.4: Search tree of the sequential bifurcation factor screening.

After identifying a set of factors that is of importance with respect to the study's performance measures, the systematic variation of suitable factor levels in terms of individual simulation runs must be planned. To decrease both the number of required simulation runs as well as the computational efforts, different factorial designs were proposed in the *design of experiments* field, e.g., 2^k *factorial designs* or *latin hypercube designs*. They systematically limit the amount of factor levels to be tested by defining a subset of levels for each factor, which is applied to parametrize the model for the simulation (Sanchez, 2007). In the example presented in this chapter it seems promising to apply sequential bifurcation for identifying important factors. Furthermore, the 2^k *factorial design* seems well suited as both techniques use two levels for each factor, i.e., a low and a high value. Each possible combination of the identified factor levels results in a specific configurations of the model (*design point*) and consequently defines an individual simulation run.

Finally, when performing the designed simulation runs, the impact stochastic inputs have on the variation of the simulation outputs needs to be taken into account. By replicating simulation runs, i.e., executing a model multiple times with the exact same parametrization, a larger sample is drawn. Accordingly, statistical measures of dispersion can be applied, the variance can be quantified, and statements can be made about the underlying population. To determine or estimate the number of replications that is required to allow for a sufficient estimate of the performance measure's mean, different approaches exist. According to Hoad et al. (2007), these include the *rule of thumb*, different *graphical methods*, and the utilization of *confidence interval with specified precision*. Neither the rule of thumb, where the number of required iterations is estimated based on experiences from previous studies and without considering specific features of the model, nor graphical methods, where the sufficiency of the number of iterations is determined by expert estimations based on the smoothness of the plotted mean value, seem to be sufficiently reliable and reproducible for the assistance of simulation studies. Thus, to assist and automate the simulation process, an approach that is based on confidence intervals seems most applicable. It depends least on the individual expertise of an analyst, makes use of statistical inference, and thus can be algorithmically described based on a given significance level (Lattner et al., 2011b).

Each simulation iteration that is derived from the same simulation run shares the same parametrization but differs in the random number stream. The variation of the random number stream is important to take into account all possible random events that can take place in a probabilistic model when drawing a sample for hypothesis testing (L'Ecuyer, 1990). *Seed* values are used to initialize a pseudorandom number generator at different positions of the random number stream. For drawing representative samples, the seed value of each simulation iteration must be determined randomly. Yet, the seed values must still be recorded as they are required for the replication of simulation iterations. When executing a simulation model with both equal parametrization and equal random number stream, an exact replication of the results is assumed. However, reproducibility of simulation is challenging due to different aspects, e.g., human factors and technical issues as software bugs or interferences with the operating system (Dalle, 2012).

For some types of models, simulation iterations can be divided into individual simulation steps. An example are discrete-event simulations, where the states of the model change at discrete points in time and a simulation clock keeps track of the model's current time. In contrast to real-world time progress, simulation time skips periods where no events occur and instantly jumps forward to the point of time the next event takes place (Fujimoto, 2000). Each simulated point in time is an individual step of the simulation. By this means, the implementation of time constraints that are part of the study's hypothesis is facilitated. This includes temporal termination conditions or *warm-up* periods where approaches exist for the automated estimation of the length (Hoad et al., 2010b). Furthermore, the simulation analyst as well as the assistance system can keep track of the response variables' progress over time.

5.1.4 Aggregation and Analysis of Outputs

After the simulation study has been fragmented into its structural components with due regard to the study's hypothesis, simulation runs and their respective iterations are performed. For each iteration, the values of all output variables must be collected and aggregated in a suitable and sound way (right side of Figure 5.1). This is to allow for drawing conclusions and to confirm or disconfirm the assumptions of the study (cf. Figure 4.10). Pitfalls which have to be considered when aggregating outputs in simulation studies were presented and discussed in Section 4.2.3. They address possible methodological uncertainties that may result in misinterpretations of the simulation model's behavior when summarizing and averaging observations inappropriately.

Model outputs are generated on the lowest structural layer of a simulation study. Depending on the type of model used during the study, the simulation's progress is either segmented and observable as time-discrete steps or occurs as one single coherent step from the experimenter's perspective. In case the model allows for a stepwise execution, the current value of all output variables might be observed after each step. This results in a time series of output values, which represent the model's response in the form of discrete steps. To obtain the aggregated response of the model, these step-wise responses can either be averaged, with or without taking into account the values generated during a specific warm-up period, or the last value is chosen as it represents the final result of the simulation (Rossetti, 2016). When performing simulation studies with models that do not implement a step-wise progress of time or do not allow for observing output values respectively, the model's response is defined by the simulation iteration's output values.

Subsequently, each iteration's responses must be aggregated with respect to the assessment of the superior simulation run. The result of each simulation run depends on and follows from the responses that were observed or determined in the respective simulation iterations. As the simulation run is the structural layer of a simulation study on which the specific parametrization of the model is defined, the result of a simulation run provides information on how this parametrization affects the model's behavior. When utilizing probabilistic models for the verification of hypotheses, output values cannot be assessed individually as the stochastic variations of the values do not allow for drawing conclusions on the underlying distribution function. Instead, they need to be assessed under consideration of multiple output values generated by the model or the underlying distribution of possible values. Thus, it is not sufficient if the result of simulation runs only consist of a summarized value. Instead, statistical measures of central tendency e.g., arithmetic mean or median, must be applied together with suitable measures for quantifying the dispersion of the summarized data, e.g., standard deviation or interquartile range (Lehmann and Romano, 2005). By this means, the result of a simulation run can be contextualized as the variation of the underlying iterations is specified.

In the further process, the calculated results of the simulation runs are used for verifying the experiment hypothesis that has initially been stated. After aggregating both the responses of all performed simulation iterations and the results of each run, statistical hypothesis tests are applied to the data of each experiment to draw respective conclusions. The aim is to statistically test the pair of hypotheses that was defined at the beginning of the study based on the study's goal and to prove or disprove the respective hypotheses. The selection of an appropriate test has taken place at an earlier stage of the process as the experiments have to be designed accordingly to ensure all samples that are required for performing the hypothesis test are correctly drawn. After rejecting the null or alternative hypothesis based on the results of the hypothesis test, the initial assumption or research question of the study can be assessed or answered and the simulation study is completed. However, the discoveries from the study will only gain significance when interpreted with respect to the study's explanatory framework, i.e., the scenario of the study. The interpretation of the results takes place outside of the scope of the procedure model and is performed by the user of the system (cf. Section 4.2.3).

5.1.5 Implications for the Assistance of Simulation Studies

To take into account the stated requirements and the three presented steps for the verification of hypotheses, this section presented an integrated procedure model for the conducting of Hypothesis-Driven Simulation Studies (cf. Figure 5.1). The aim of this procedure model is to provide a frame for addressing the shortcomings that were identified in Section 4.2 to accomplish the requirements from Section 4.1. In this regard, requirement 2 is addressed in particular by the proposed process. The epistemological challenges that arise from Hypothesis-Driven Simulation Studies are addressed by a systematic frame. Likewise, the methodical use of simulation as research technique is facilitated as the process defines and guides the conduction of studies. Epistemological demands are met in different ways. Potential functional explanations for the model's behavior can be tested if formulated as parametrizations of the model, derived as set of important factors, or provided as part of the experiments' conclusions. Additionally, the process intends and promotes the systematical investigation of the model under different scenarios. Due to the full integration of all relevant structural components, different parametrizations that result from one or many scenarios can be systematically applied to the model and the respective results can be analyzed accordingly.

Furthermore, shortcomings that were identified in Section 4.2 can be overcome with the aid of the presented procedure model. The procedure model implements a multi-layer architecture. Beginning with the simulation study itself and its guiding research question, a top-down-approach is pursued to derive and specify all hierarchically subordinated structural components of the study, i.e., experiments, runs, and iterations. Different purposes of simulation can thus be represented by this approach as the required components can be derived accordingly. Also the pitfalls that might occur during the aggregation of the model's responses can be weakened or eliminated by utilizing the process. Methodological uncertainties that promote these pitfalls can be controlled through the presented approach. Finally, the defined scenario serves as an explanatory framework of the entire study and the research hypothesis is formulated based on the scenario. Thus, methodological shortcomings can be addressed such that suitable steps existing procedure models for simulation can be individually identified, adjusted, and combined with respect to specific hypothesis. This ensures that hypothesis testing in simulation studies is performed in a targeted and reproducible manner.

The presented procedure model defines an extensive process. It consist of multiple layers that are bidirectionally linked, transitions between the layers are defined by a plurality of methods, and in each step the respective actions must be be planned and executed with regard to the study's research hypothesis. Numerous model- and hypothesis-related questions have to be answered during the process and decisions that might have epistemological consequences have to be made. In Section 4.1, it was argued that experimenters, which meet important design decisions in simulation studies, might unwillingly bias the results (Uhrmacher et al., 2016). To address this issue, the development and provision of an assistance system seems reasonable (Lattner, 2013).

5.2 Logical Connection of Services

This section lays the foundations for the implementation of an assistance system. The goal of this assistance system is to dynamically link, adjust, and apply existing approaches and services to facilitate the conducting of Hypothesis-Driven Simulation Studies. It covers all aspects of the proposed procedure model, starting from the design and execution of relevant experiments to the analysis of the generated outputs. Through this, the task of the experimenter is limited to the specification of a research hypotheses in accordance with the study's scenario and the interpretation of the generated results. To achieve this, this section identifies relevant logical components that are involved in the process of the study based on the process model. Moreover, it outlines how each component contributes to the conducting of Hypothesis-Driven Simulation Studies.

Figure 5.5 illustrates the identified logical components as well as their interactions. The figure consists of two major parts: the left side it shows the steps of the simulation study as it is conducted by the researcher who is using the assistance system. The right side, in contrast, illustrates the flow of information into, within, and out of the assistance system. Each rectangle represents a logical entity within the process. On the side of the researcher, each rectangle is a step of the simulation study, as defined by common procedure models (cf. Subsec 4.2.1). In the assistance system, each rectangle describes an individual service that is required for the systematic design, execution, and conduction of the study's experiments. The arrows between the rectangles represent the unidirectional flow of information or data. The arrowheads indicate the direction of the information flow and the shape of the arrows, e.g., solid or dashed, expresses whether transitions are explicit or implicit. A transition is implicit if the respective part of the process is accomplished by other steps, which finally lead to the same result. Considering the illustrated process of the researcher, the experimentation part of the study is marked as implicit. This emphasizes the aim of this thesis, where the user provides only a research question and an executable model, the assistance system identifies, executes, and analyzes necessary experiments, and the results are returned to the user of the system.

To outline how the components contribute to the implementation of the proposed integrated procedure model, the process of Hypothesis-Driven Simulation Studies is revisited, which was presented in Section 5.1. In contrast to the processual perspective that was chosen in the preceding section, the focus lies on the technical interactions of the referred components. Still, an example applied here as well to improve the understanding of the emerging system's functionality. The following description of a simulation study's process emphasizes the contribution of each component as well as the links between the components and the information which is exchanged between the components. Each step of the study is considered, starting from the provisioning of the simulation model, the experimental design as well as the conduction of the experiments through to the evaluation and interpretation of the results.

To adequately illustrate the use and procedure of the assistance system, a more detailed and advanced example is required. Thus, to outline the entire process, a more comprehensive model and respectively also a more sophisticated research question are introduced. Furthermore, this subsection is not limited to the functional introduction of the assistance system itself. It also presents how the assistance system can be integrated into the user's research process. For this purpose, the presented use case covers the entire process of conducting a scientific simulation study, as it was introduced in Section 4.2.2.

Simulation studies consist of an initial model building step. For this example, it is assumed that the collection of data and the structural definition of a modeled system as well as the implementation, verification, and validation of a computer program are complete. Thus, in the initial situation of this example, the experimenter provides a simulation model, which was implemented using a common simulation framework.

For consistency reasons, the model used as an example in this section describes a manufacturing process as well. It models a production line where products are manufactured on different machines or groups of machines, which are connected. Machines are controlled by employees and a lack of employees results in delays or even the idleness of the machines. In each stage of production, the products are stored in machine-specific storages and are processed according to global queuing disciplines. To quantify how the measured cycle time changes depending on the number of employees that are part of the manufacturing process, it is assumed the experimenter wants to conduct a simulation study.

In summary, a possible **goal of the study** can be formulated as follows:

The study aims to show that an increasing number of employees will result in an increase of the MCE.

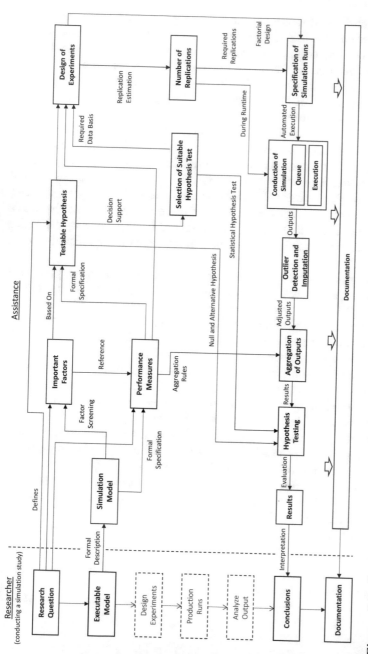

Figure 5.5: Components of the assistance system and interactions between these components.

For enabling the systematic and computer-aided design and conducting of simulation experiments with respect to accomplish the study's goal, a **formal specification of the simulation model as well as its input and output variables** is required. This includes the formal description of inputs and outputs, i.e., label, admissible values, and data type, as well as the initialization of the model by means of the used simulation framework. Furthermore, minimum and recommended system requirements for the execution of the model must be part of this specification as well, e.g., operating system, number of processor cores, memory, or external libraries. Usually, detailed instructions on how to initialize and execute the model are part of the documentation or the manual, yet, such documents lack machine-readability. Information regarding the operation of the simulation model needs to be systematically accessed by the developer of the model or a user that is at least aware of how to parametrize, adjust, and execute the model. In this thesis, the provided simulation model is treated as a black box. Thus, it is not possible to apply deductive approaches for automatically deriving information about inputs and outputs from the inner structure of the model, e.g., static model testing techniques like structural analysis (Balci, 1998).

To construct a machine-readable specification of the simulation model's attributes, the assistance system has to systematically question the user with respect to the model. Here, the focus lies on the detailed description of the model's input and output variables. This includes but is not limited to the data type of the variable as well as minimum, maximum, and standard values. Furthermore, this includes technical details as the variables' labels, which are used in the model and additional command line parameters which are required to execute the model. As the model's internal labels for variables are often shortened and difficult to read, the definition of self-explanatory labels as well as a short description of each variable's purpose are reasonable. A standardized language for the specification of a model's inputs and outputs can facilitate this step as necessary information can be provided along with the model by the developer. After this step, the assistance system can make use of the formal specification of the simulation model for providing a model-specific guidance of the user through the process of the simulation study and for automating or semi-automating the execution of each process step.

In this thesis, simulation studies are applied to answer research hypotheses. Thus, as a first step after formally specifying the model, the **research hypothesis** needs to be defined based on the study's goal and must be **formally specified** as well. Statistically, a hypothesis consists of an assumption about the probability distribution of a variable under specific conditions. Transferred to simulation, a hypothesis is an assumption on the distribution of an output or target variable under a specific set of input variables. Considering the presented example, a possible hypothesis which corresponds to the goal of the study reads as follows:

> If the input variable representing the *number of employees* is increased by 10 units and the input variable representing the *order queuing discipline* is set to *FIFO*, the assumption is that the value of the performance indicator MCE increases by at least 20%.

Performance indicators or target variables are not initially part of the simulation model. They are calculated or derived from output variables and serve as individual performance measures for evaluating the behavior of a simulation model. Consequently, after formally specifying the input and output variables of the simulation model, the **specification of the performance measures** that are used for formulating the hypothesis is an important step. In this step, the experimenter must be provided with a list of the model's output variables and needs to logically and mathematically define or construct the required performance measures. Intuitively, when formulating hypotheses, it can be assumed that the input variables (*Explanans*) must be defined prior to the specification of the assumption about the output variables (*Explanandum*). This is not reasonable in simulation studies. The Explanandum has to logically result from the Explanans by means of deduction to make a reliable statement. Hence, with respect to the formulation of a testable and sound research hypothesis, it is necessary to assess whether or not it is feasible to draw conclusions from specific input variables about the chosen performance measure.

Certainly when dealing with complex models that provide a large number of input variables, the process of testing which input variables influence which output variables or performance measures is challenging and cannot be executed for all possible combinations of inputs and outputs (Kleijnen, 2015). Instead, it seems more promising to first define a performance measure of interest and to use approaches for identifying *important factors* of this specific performance measure afterwards.

The **identification of important factors** is conducted based on the performance measure that was defined or selected in the previous step. By executing a set of simulation runs where the values of the input variables are systematically changed, it can be determined which input variables influence the selected performance measure (Kleijnen, 2005a). For this purpose, metamodels are used as an approximation of the input-output-behavior of simulation models. As a full coverage of all possible values of input variables is too extensive, factorial designs are used here to reduce the computational effort (Sanchez and Lucas, 2002). If available, information regarding factor levels that are expected to result in low and high outputs may be provided by the user and applied here.

After both the performance measure of interest and the respective important input variables were identified, the **formal specification of the research hypothesis** can be conducted. This is required, as design as well as conducting and evaluating the simulation experiments is assisted with respect to answering the hypothesis. Thus, a formal representation of the hypothesis is required for planning and adjusting the process of the simulation study. To specify the experiment hypothesis, the experimenter must be provided with an overview of all input, output, and target variables that were defined up to this point. For the specification of the parametrization part of the hypothesis, each of the model's input variables may be assigned a specific value. However, the use of important factors is recommended here and input variables that were not shown to be important regarding the selected performance measure should be avoided. This reduces the complexity of the study as only parametrizations that are likely of relevance are evaluated. The expressiveness and efficiency of the simulation study can be increased by the assisted construction of the hypothesis as the design and conduction of promising runs is facilitated.

To test the specified experiment hypothesis, a **suitable statistical hypothesis test** must be identified. Even though data for the test was not generated yet, the selection of a hypothesis test is important at this point of the process. There exists a large number of different hypothesis tests which can be differentiated by various criteria, e.g., parametric or non-parametric tests, dependency of the samples, and one- or two-sided tests (Freedman et al., 2007). As each test requires specific preconditions for its application, the assistance system must pursue and ensure the fulfillment of these requirements. In particular the extent and number of required samples affect the specification of simulation experiments. Therefore, the selection of an appropriate hypothesis test takes place before the design of experiments.

After the hypothesis was formally specified and a suitable test was selected, the experiments of the simulation study must be designed. The **experimental design** defines the combinations of values that are simulated for each input variable. This is challenging, as extensive hypotheses with a large number of factors might result in an combinatorial explosion of possible parametrizations. In addition to *full factorial designs*, where all possible combinations of values for each input variable are simulated, there are experimental designs that try to minimize the complexity. Such *fractional factorial designs* derive a subset of parametrizations from all possible parametrizations following a specific pattern (Sanchez and Wan, 2012). As part of the assistance system, experimental designs have to ensure that all factors that influence a specific performance measure are considered and that a set of factor values is chosen to cover the relevant parts of the parameter space.

The experimenter is encouraged to specify the hypothesis by using factors that were identified as important with respect to the defined performance measure. However, he or she might refuse to do so, which does not decrease the quality of the hypothesis but affects the further procedure. In case input variables that were classified as important are not included in the hypothesis, they still need to be considered by the experimental design. This is to ensure that all relevant simulation runs are conducted that are required to answer the hypothesis by taking into account the effect these factors have on the model's behavior. When lacking alternative approaches, low and high values of each input variable that were specified during the model description phase can be applied. Yet, more sophisticated factorial designs are also possible (Kleijnen, 2005a).

When performing experiments with probabilistic models, the **number of necessary replications** needs to be determined for each run that was defined during the *design of experiment* step. Due to the randomness of the model's behavior, formulas for calculating a statistically sufficient number of replications in advance do not exist. Instead, different techniques were proposed to estimate the number of replications based on the observed behavior. Besides expert estimations, which are not viable in an semi-automated assistance system, statistical approaches that make use of confidence intervals were proposed. The estimated replication count defines how many simulation iterations are required for each simulation run. Most approaches that can be utilized for a replication estimation require the sample to be normally distributed, which must be tested first.

As a next step, all specified simulation runs and their respective iterations need to be processed to executable and queueable simulation tasks that contain all necessary information for the *execution of the simulation model*. The **specification of simulation iterations as individual tasks** enables the parallel but also unsupervised and time-independent execution. For one thing, a **central simulation (task) queue** can be used for storing tasks and sorting them based on established queuing disciplines or other priority rules. For another thing, simulation tasks can be distributed to different servers where the actual simulation is conducted. This enables an efficient utilization of available hardware as task generation and conduction are decoupled. By this means, a dynamic distribution to suitable hardware is facilitated and parallelization of simulation runs and iterations is enabled. For example at night or on the weekend, when servers and other IT hardware are less or not at all occupied and have free capacities, simulation tasks can be taken from the central queue which allows for an even utilization of available hardware.

Even though the queuing of simulation tasks takes place centrally, the **conducting of simulation** is performed in a decentralized manner. For this reason, each simulation task contains all necessary information for the execution of the respective run or iteration. This includes the file, archive, or link to the executable simulation model as well as a specification of the model itself in terms of its input and output variables including performance measures. Additionally, the parametrization of the simulation run and necessary technical details are provided, e.g., commands for stating the simulation, if required the paths of input files, and break conditions in case the simulation does not terminate.

Available hardware for executing simulation runs usually varies in the provided computing capacity, e.g., number of processor cores or available memory, but also simulation models impose different requirements, e.g., minimal number of CPUs for parallelization or minimal amount of RAM. Still, neither a full utilization of all CPU cores that are provided by the hardware, e.g., due to the application of single-thread simulation frameworks like MASON, nor the demand of a large amount of memory can be observed for many simulation runs (Lorig et al., 2015). Consequently, a need-based assignment of hardware and simulation tasks seems reasonable to achieve an adequate utilization of the available servers.

Finally, after all necessary simulation runs and iterations for answering the initially stated hypothesis have been conducted, the outputs of all runs need to be collected, centrally aggregated, and evaluated. The evaluation of the results is performed by means of the statistical hypothesis test, which has been selected in advance. For this purpose, **data cleansing** needs to be performed to exclude sets of inaccurate, inplausible, or missing output data (*outliers*) from the statistical analysis. However, excluded samples must be documented properly to allow for the reproduction of the results. Afterwards, the selected **hypothesis test** is applied to the cleansed data set and the user of the assistance system is provided the hypothesis testing results, i.e., whether or not the experiment hypothesis needs to be rejected

based on the outcome of the hypothesis test. Additionally to this, a detailed
documentation of all steps and decisions as well as applied approaches and
techniques within the process of the simulation study is generated and
provided.

5.3 Abstract Architecture of an Assistance System

To implement and facilitate the logical connection of services, this section
proposes an abstract architecture for a software system that assists and
partially automates the conducting of Hypothesis-Driven Simulation Studies.
For the application of the presented procedure model, a variety of different
services and methods must be adapted, executed, and coordinated. To
relieve the simulation user of these tasks and to facilitate conducting a study,
the development of an assistance systems seems reasonable. In this regard,
the introduced procedure models provides the methodological frame of the
assistance system and the outlined logical components represent the entities
that must be coordinated by the system.

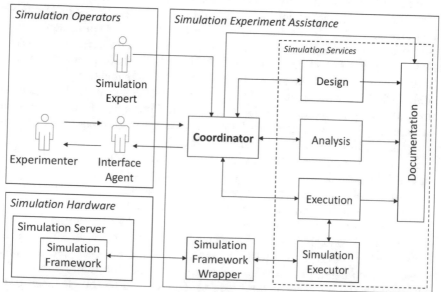

Figure 5.6: Abstract architecture of the simulation experiment assistance.

The abstract architecture of the assistance system consists of three major components: *simulation operators*, *simulation hardware*, and the *simulation experiment assistance*. Each of these components consists of multiple entities such as services, methods, or actors which can be human or virtual entities. This section outlines the tasks and responsibilities of each of the three components and illustrate how they control each other. Moreover, it presents the entities that are dedicated to each component and outlines their interactions with other entities within the same components or between different components. To this end, this thesis focuses on the specification of the *simulation experiment assistance* to support the procedure of the study. Thus, the design of both the interface agent of the operator as well as the technical utilization of simulation hardware are presented and discussed on a conceptual level.

The *simulation experiment assistance* is the key feature of the assistance system and of this thesis. It combines and controls all simulation services that were introduced in this chapter. This includes services for the *design*, *execution*, and *analysis* of simulation experiments that are required to conduct Hypothesis-Driven Simulation Studies. In the proposed architecture (cf. Figure 5.6), these three components represent all services and methods that are related to the respective step of the study. For instance, the *design* component comprises services that are required for factor screening or the application of experimental designs.

Besides this, a *documentation* service and a *simulation executor* service are proposed in the architecture as part of the simulation services. The *documentation* service receives data from the design, execution, and analysis services. This allows for the reproduction of each step and decision that was made during the assistance of the study. Moreover, intermediate data and final results of the simulation are stored and can be used for further analysis. The simulation executor provides an interface for the connection of external simulation hardware. As the execution of simulation runs often requires technically sophisticated hardware, specific requirements are made regarding the number of CPU cores or the RAM capacity. To efficiently utilize this server hardware and to execute the simulation model, *simulation frameworks* are used. These frameworks serve as an execution layer between the server and the model.

As a high number of different simulation frameworks exists, the execution of the model must be planned with due regard to specific features or restrictions of the used framework. This contrasts with the concept of a general simulation experiment assistance. Thus, it is necessary to decouple the simulation experiment assistance from specific hardware and software requirements of the model or the framework. Instead of accessing and operating the simulation framework directly from the simulation executor, the proposed architecture suggests the use of a *simulation framework wrapper*. The wrapper is a framework-specific service that converts instructions and data from the simulation executor into commands and formats that can be processed by the framework. Hence, an individual wrapper service must be developed for each framework that shall be supported by the assistance system.

Finally, to manage all services that contribute to the study, the simulation experiment assistance requires a central *coordinator*. Instead of fully connecting all services of the simulation experiment assistance, this section proposes the implementation of a central unit that is in charge of the management of the study. Each service is connected to the coordinator, receives tasks from it, and returns the results back to it. This design decision allows the knowledge base of the experiment assistance to be maintained by the coordinator. It includes information on the procedure of the simulation study such as the order of the steps as well as guidelines or instructions for the adaptation, execution, and assessment of data generated during the steps.

The coordinator is also the only service of the simulation experiment assistance that provides an interface for the simulation operators. Accordingly, simulation tasks that are submitted to the system are taken by the coordinator. It is feasible to design the coordinator as intended by the *mediator design pattern* (cf. Figure 5.7), which intends the encapsulation of interactions between other objects, in this case, of the simulation services (Gamma, 1995). In this regard, the coordinator takes the role of the *mediator* which coordinates the communication between multiple *colleague* objects, e.g., the services for the design, execution, and analysis of the experiments. For this purpose, each colleague object is aware of its mediator and communication which usually directly occurs between colleague objects takes place with the mediator instead. The mediator then routes requests of the colleague objects between them. By applying the mediator design pattern, the colleague classes are decoupled, the interactions are simplified, and the control of the system is centralized. A similar approach is used in the architecture of the simulation experiment management system presented by Teran-Somohano et al. (2015).

A differentiation can be made between two types of operators that interact with the coordinator of the experiment assistance. To maintain the knowledge base of the coordinator, detailed information on the procedure of the study must be provided by a *simulation expert*. In this thesis, the proposed procedure model contains this process knowledge as it determines the order

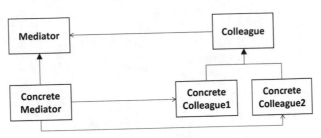

Figure 5.7: Structure of the mediator design pattern (Gamma, 1995).

of the study's steps. Moreover, the knowledge base must also include information on the logical connections of the services as well as of the interfaces of each service. The proposed architecture is inspired by *expert systems* from Artificial Intelligence. Thus, reasoning algorithms can be applied to the knowledge base to determine a specific sequence of actions to verify a hypothesis by means of simulation experiments.

A study is initiated by a *simulation user* (experimenter) who might be inexperienced in conducting simulation studies or who might want to reduce its effort. Thus, the provision of a user-centered assistance seems reasonable here. The required assistance corresponds to the *interface agent* concept introduced by Maes (1994). Here, specific tasks are delegated to a virtual representative (*agent*) which then solves these tasks independently. Initially, the agent is provided with a minimum of background knowledge on conducting simulation studies. It then autonomously acquires further knowledge that is required to solve specific tasks.

Four sources are available for the acquisition of additional knowledge and for the learning of further competences (cf. Figure 5.8): First, interface agents can directly learn from the user of the system and *imitate* its behavior when controlling the application or system. Especially when observing the user's actions over a longer period of time, recurring behavior pattern can be identified and adapted by the agent. Second, the user can provide the agent with *feedback* on its actions and inform the agent to omit certain actions. This feedback can also be given indirectly in case the user does not follow the suggestions of the agent. Third, the agent can learn new behavior from *examples* given by the user. In these examples, the user might suggest suitable actions for certain situations. Finally, if multiple interface agents exist, one agent can *ask* other agents for assistance.

In summary, for the conceptualization of the *simulation experiment assistance*, a decentralized architecture seems suitable such that functionalities are

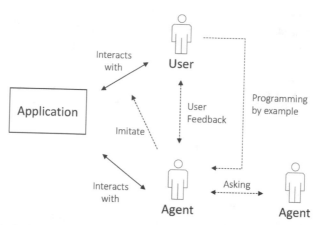

Figure 5.8: Different ways of learning by an interface agent (Maes, 1994).

provided by independent services. The use of decentralized services enables the development of a highly dynamic system. First, the same functionality can be provided by one or more different services ensuring a permanent supply of the service, e.g., in case of system failures or increased demand. For implementing a specific service, different approaches might exist, e.g., the estimation of the number of replications can be based on confidence intervals or be performed graphically. Even though both approaches lead to suitable results, users of the assistance system might have different preferences regarding which implementation of the service should be used. Likewise, specific disciplines or research areas might require the use of certain services for the verification of knowledge.

The implementation of these functionalities as individual services has further benefits. On the one hand, the services do not have to be centrally provided. Instead, anyone may contribute to such an assistance system by developing webservices according to predefined requirements, e.g., interfaces, datatypes, or namespaces. This also allows the provider to host the service itself and keep the algorithms closed source. On the other hand, it improves the flexibility and adaptability of the assistance system. The process of simulation studies is model-driven, highly individual, and not standardized. Thus, the selection and order of services to perform a simulation study varies and flexible approaches are required. Web services are not statically connected but can be dynamically combined and recombined to an extensive process. To achieve this, the interface of each type of web service needs to be defined, i.e., what type and quantity of data is expected and returned by the web service, such that an exchange of data between the services is enabled and the development of new compatible services is facilitated.

5.4 Conclusions

The goal of this chapter was the presentation of an integrated procedure model for the conducting of Hypothesis-Driven Simulation Studies. The model addresses shortcomings in current procedure models for simulation study and allows for the systematic integration and verification of hypotheses by means of simulation experiments. Based on the scenario of the study, which provides the context of the study, a testable hypothesis is formalized on the behavior of a model. In the course of the study, relevant simulation experiments, runs, and iterations are derived with respect to the stated hypothesis and to provide evidence for or against its validity. The responses of the iterations, runs, and experiments are then aggregated so that statistical hypotheses tests can be applied. By this means, the experimenter is guided through the process of the study and the initial hypothesis can be confirmed or refuted in a replicable and reproducible way.

Useful approaches and methods exist that implement most functionalities that are presented and aligned in the procedure model. Yet, the main challenge is to identify, adapt, and combine functionalities that are required to conduct Hypothesis-Driven Simulation Studies. To this end, this chapter not only identifies relevant logical components but also logically links them in terms of the procedure model. The result is a sequence of steps that can be practically executed to answer hypothesis by means of simulation experiments.

To answer a hypothesis, it might be necessary to execute a large number of experiments to cover the relevant parameter space. Moreover, with respect to the statistical reliability of the generated results, the execution of a sufficient number of replications must be ensured. For the operator, this results in monotonous and repetitive tasks that need to be carried out with adequate care. To support the work of an operator, this chapter finally presented an abstract architecture for the development of an assistance system. To this end, the proposed procedure model and the logical connection of the required components provide a theoretical frame for the automation of the process of conducting Hypothesis-Driven Simulation Studies.

With respect to the implementation of such an assistance system, the logical connection of the services is not sufficient. Instead of considering each service as a black box, the mechanics of the services must be specified.

This also includes the specification of information that is required by each service and information that is provided by each service. Based on these specifications, it can be assessed whether existing services are applicable for the assistance of the study's process. Furthermore, the specification enables the identification of shortcomings of existing functionalities so that they can be adapted or extended.

6 Services for the Assistance of Simulation Studies

This thesis presents a methodology for the conducting of Hypothesis-Driven Simulation Studies. Unlike existing procedure models for simulation studies, the presented process fully integrates the study's goal as a specific research hypothesis on the behavior of the model. By this means, all important steps of the study are aligned with the research question, in order to answer it in a sound and reproducible way. When conducting studies in accordance with the procedure model, the experimenter is still in charge of the process management which might unwillingly result in experimenter bias. To avoid this and to assist the application of the procedure model as well as conducting simulation studies, the development of an assistance system is reasonable. Yilmaz et al. (2014, p. 2798) emphasize that

> "the provision of such automated tools will help to improve the state of the art in practice in replicability of models and reproducibility of simulation experiments".

With the aim of facilitating the conducting of Hypothesis-Driven Simulation Studies, an abstract architecture for the implementation of an assistance system was proposed in the previous chapter. The architecture requires the combination of different methods and techniques to provide a comprehensive assistance of the entire process of the study. To facilitate the selection of appropriate components, this chapter formally specifies all logical entities that are required for assisting the scientific process of knowledge generation in simulation studies (cf. Figure 5.5). To this end, this chapter specifies the interfaces of these components, i.e., mandatory inputs and returned outputs. Moreover, it defines the task that is expected from each entity and how this task contributes to the overall goal of the assistance.

Aligned in accordance with the abstract architecture, these components form a distributed system that serves as a platform for the systematic verification of phenomenological hypotheses. Rather than developing a new simulation system or framework, the presented specification and combination of simulation services forms an assistance, which operates in accordance with

© Springer Fachmedien Wiesbaden GmbH, part of Springer Nature 2019
F. Lorig, *Hypothesis-Driven Simulation Studies,*

a simulation system instead of replacing it. In this regard, the assistance consists of the logical combination of methods and techniques. This is challenging, as a large number of potential approaches exist that must be selected and joined up depending on the hypothesis to be tested.

The selection of services that is introduced in this chapter is based on the requirements of the proposed procedure model. Most services can be assigned to a specific step of the study, i.e., the design, execution, or analysis of experiments. These services are not directly accessed or operated by the user of the assistance. In contrast to this, the simulation model as well as the research hypothesis are components of the assistance that are provided and defined by the experimenter. As other services rely on the model and the hypothesis, these two components are specified first. The remaining services are then introduced and formally specified according to the steps of simulation studies which are assisted by the respective services. They are introduced ordered by their utilization in the three major steps of simulation studies that are assisted by the proposed system: design of experiments, conduction of experiments, and analysis of experiments. Finally, conclusions for the implementation of the resulting assistance system are discussed in the last section of this chapter.

6.1 Simulation Model

To assist Hypothesis-Driven Simulation Studies, the simulation model must be executed as specified by the process proposed in Section 5.1. Thus, the assistance system must, among other things, systematically identify important factors, apply different parametrizations, run simulations, and aggregate as well as interpret results for assessing the model's behavior under certain conditions. To minimize experimenter bias in this process, both control of and decision-making within the process are the primary responsibility of the assistance introduced in this chapter. For this purpose, the assistance must be capable of perceiving and operating the simulation model. The specification of a simulation model that is presented here includes the inputs and outputs of the model, the execution function for generating the model's behavior, and metadata that describe the model.

Simulation models are computer-based representations of theoretical models of real-world systems (Vincent, 1998). According to Maria (1997), a simulation model consist of four components: *system entities*, *input variables*, *performance measures*, as well as *functional relationships*. This thesis pursues a black box approach where the inner states and mechanisms of the model are not accessible or considered. Thus, the model is only defined by its input-output-behavior instead of its inner states (cf. Figure 6.1). For the human user of the simulation model, relevant information on the model itself as well as on its operation are part of the respective documentation. Such documents are written in natural language and usually do not follow a general standard. Thus, it is not feasible to automatically interpret model documentations for identifying the model's interfaces or controls and a formal specification is required.

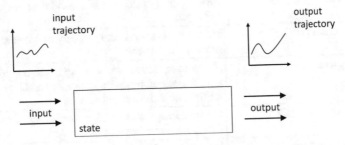

Figure 6.1: Black box representation of a simulation model (Zeigler et al., 2000).

In this section, all components are presented that are required for the black box specification of a simulation model. Besides metadata that describe the model, this section specifies inputs and outputs as essential components of a simulation model.

6.1.1 Model Metadata

To allow for the replicable conduction of simulation experiments and for the reproduction of results, it is not sufficient to store detailed information on the experimentation process, e.g., parametrizations and results. A detailed description of the utilized model needs to be documented as well. In this subsection, such information is referred to as *metadata* of the model. As simulation is used in various disciplines, it is challenging to define a general standard for model and experiment metadata. In the following, different definitions and perspectives on model metadata are presented and discussed to specify required metadata for the assistance.

Meléndez-Colom (2001) discussed the challenge of a model metadata standard from an ecology perspective. She examined both computer and ecological models and identified seven common metadata elements: *identifi-*

ers, *responsible parties, descriptors, access or availability, metadata source, variable description*, and *literature* (cf. Table 6.1).

Table 6.1: Common metadata elements of simulation models (Meléndez-Colom, 2001).

Common category of element definition	Specific corresponding element definitions
Identifiers	Model long name or ID, model short name or acronym
Responsible parties	Model creator or author, metadata creator, contact person, institution
Descriptors	Keywords, temporal coverage, geographic coverage, cross reference to other datasets or models, additional information source
Access or availability	Constraints, availability, ordering procedures, costs, software requirements
Metadata source	Metadata related information
Variable description	Name, acronym, definition, max and min values, range, units, data type
Literature	Title, year, journal or publisher, pages, volume, issue, editor, ISBN, ISSN, URL

Typical identifiers for simulation models are the model's name or any other ID code. As models are advanced and extended over time, multiple versions of the same model might exist with the same name. Hence, the version number seems to be suitable metadata, too, assuming that the combination of model name or ID and version number serves as an unique identifier. By this means, other researchers are able to relate to the specific model which was used during the simulation study.

The development of simulation models is an extensive process and the documentation of the model creation might be incomplete, incomprehensible, or non-existent. Thus, when utilizing models of other researchers, contact information of the responsible developer are valuable. This includes the name and affiliation of the contact person, postal or e-mail address, and even a phone number. As many models are developed in an academic context, keeping such information up to date is challenging due to changes of the employer, PhD students leaving academia, or retirement (Himmelspach, 2007).

To facilitate the usage of a model, a description of the model should be provided by the developer. Similar to scientific publications, feasible means are an abstract and a list of keywords. This allows for a first classification of the model's subject or purpose. Additionally, it is reasonable to provide the scope of the model, related models or datasets, and further information.

Another major issue is the permanent availability of the model, which is related to the challenge of up-to-date contact information. Often, models are provided as download via the website of the researcher's institution. In this case, the model's availability cannot be guaranteed when the researcher leaves the institution. For this reason, repositories for collection and long-term archiving of simulation models are founded and developed, e.g., *OpenABM*[5] (Janssen et al., 2008) or *AnyLogic Cloud*[6]. Other information that is related to access and availability of the model is more technical. This includes software and hardware requirements, restrictions of the operating system, and specific expertise which is required for controlling and executing the model.

Remaining information, the source of the metadata, the description of the model's variables, and respective literature, are not discussed in this subsection. The metadata source includes technical information regarding name, version, and date of the metadata. However, this information is not relevant during this phase of the approaches specification. In contrast, the description of the model's variables is highly relevant and thus is subject to the following two subsections. Finally, the literature might well be part of the description of the models which was already presented.

The presented common metadata elements are the result of a domain-specific analysis of requirements. In accordance with the model repositories that were introduced for long-term archiving models, frameworks and repositories also require the user to provide metadata. In the following, three environments are introduced: a simulation framework (*Simulink*[7]; Angermann et al., 2007), a framework that also provides an own repository for models (*NetLogo*; Tisue and Wilensky, 2004), and a framework-independent online repository for agent-based simulation models (*OpenABM*[8]; Janssen et al., 2008).

---

[5] https://www.comses.net/codebases/ [Retrieved Jul. 2019]
[6] https://cloud.anylogic.com/ [Retrieved Jul. 2019]
[7] https://mathworks.com/products/simulink.html [Retrieved Jul. 2019]
[8] As of mid-2018, the *OpenABM* repository has become part of the *CoMSES Net Computational Model Library*. As a result of this, the repository is no longer limited to agent-based models and consists of different computational models of social and ecological systems.

Simulink is closely related to MATLAB and enables the simulation of dynamic systems, which are modeled as block diagrams. For each simulation, Simulink provides the user with a metadata object that consists of five properties: *model, execution,* and *timing information* as well as two user-defined fields for *single string* or *arrays* of data. While the latter two properties are empty by default, the simulation framework collects relevant model, execution, and timing information during the simulation. Model information consists of general information such as the model's name, version, and path. It also includes information on the used simulation framework, operating system, and Simulink version as well as simulation specific information such as the start and stop time of the simulation. Execution information can be used for debugging simulation runs. It contains information on the reason why the simulation stopped and provides detailed insights into diagnostics. Finally, times which were measures during the simulation, e.g., initialization, execution, and termination time, as well as the wall clock time are stored as timing information. Considering the metadata described by Meléndez-Colom (2001), only the collected model information corresponds to what was described as *model metadata.*

In *NetLogo*, the concept of metadata is more prosaic. According to the official documentation of NetLogo, the *info* section of the model shall provide an introduction to the model. However, there are no mandatory fields which have to be specified by the developer. In Version 6.0, newly created models provide nine headings and the developer is recommended to provide sufficient information for each section. Yet, the developer might change the headings or even delete them without replacement. The default headings address general model information such as what the models is trying to show or explain, how the model works, how it can be used, what the user should notice or try when conducting experiments, how the model can be extended, and specific NetLogo features that are utilized by the model. Furthermore, the developer is asked to refer to related models and provide credits and necessary references. Due to the lack of structured information, searching the associated *ModelingCommons* repository[9] for models is difficult and only possible by the model's name, optional tags, or free text search.

The *OpenABM* repository provides more structured and detailed information on each model. Besides name, affiliation, and contact information on the developer, the repository provides a description of the model's purpose and keywords as well as publications associated with the model. Furthermore, technical information is provided, e.g., platform (framework), programming

---

[9] `http://modelingcommons.org/` [Retrieved Jul. 2019]

language, operating system, and instructions how to run the model. Finally, all required model files (code, docs, and other files) are provided as well as all available versions of the model. In contrast to the NetLogo repository, metadata of OpenABM models is more detailed and structured. Furthermore, it corresponds to the common metadata elements presented by Meléndez-Colom (2001).

Other approaches like the *model description language* (MDL) have the goal of sharing knowledge by facilitating and unifying the understanding of models (Smith et al., 2017). The structure of MDL consists of multiple objects which define *model, parameters, data,* and *task properties* (cf. Figure 6.2). For particular tasks, which includes simulation studies, the *MOG object* (Modeling Objects Group) is used to specify all objects required for this task. In terms of the model's meta-information, only the MOG object is of relevance. The other objects are used to describe specific information which are relevant during experimentation. Similar to NetLogo, only a brief set of information is provided by the MOG object which includes the model's name and the problem statement. In summary, even dedicated model description languages do not provide comprehensive meta information on the model itself and focus on the description of experiments instead.

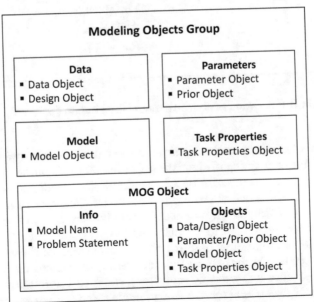

Figure 6.2: Objects of the Model Description Language (Smith et al., 2017).

$$
\begin{aligned}
ModelMetadata \quad &= \quad \{ \quad Identifier, \\
&\qquad\quad Responsibility, \\
&\qquad\quad Description, \\
&\qquad\quad Requirements, \\
&\qquad\quad Files \quad \}
\end{aligned}
$$

$$
\begin{aligned}
Identifier \quad &= \quad \{ \quad \text{Model Name,} \\
&\qquad\quad \text{ID (URI),} \\
&\qquad\quad \text{Date of Creation,} \\
&\qquad\quad \text{Version,} \\
&\qquad\quad \text{Citation,} \\
&\qquad\quad \text{Initial Model (URI)} \quad \}
\end{aligned}
$$

$$
\begin{aligned}
Responsibility \quad &= \quad \{ \quad \text{Full Name,} \\
&\qquad\quad \text{Mail Address,} \\
&\qquad\quad \text{Postal Address,} \\
&\qquad\quad \text{Affiliation,} \\
&\qquad\quad \text{Phone} \quad \}
\end{aligned}
$$

Figure 6.3: Specification of simulation model metadata (part 1/2).

The aim of the proposed assistance is to enable and improve the reliable and replicable conducting of simulation studies. For this purpose, a thorough and consistent meta description of the simulation model is essential. On the one hand, the name of the model is not sufficient for the unambiguous identification of simulation models. A combination of name, version, and platform of the model together with detailed information on the developer of the model is required to describe which model was used for a particular simulation study. On the other hand, for storing and managing the results of simulation studies in a suitable repository, detailed information is required for comfortably searching for simulation models and studies and for enabling reutilization and reproduction.

$$
\begin{aligned}
Description \quad &= \quad \{ \quad \text{Abstract,} \\
&\qquad \text{Keywords,} \\
&\qquad \text{Related Work,} \\
&\qquad \text{Related Models,} \\
&\qquad \text{Instructions} \quad \} \\
\\
Requirements \quad &= \quad \{ \quad \text{Framework,} \\
&\qquad \text{Operating System,} \\
&\qquad \text{Programming Language,} \\
&\qquad \text{Software Requirements,} \\
&\qquad \text{Hardware Requirements,} \\
&\qquad \text{Expertise} \quad \} \\
\\
Files \quad &= \quad \{ \quad \text{Model Files,} \\
&\qquad \text{Data Files,} \\
&\qquad \text{Documentation Files,} \\
&\qquad \text{Additional Files} \quad \}
\end{aligned}
$$

Figure 6.4: Specification of simulation model metadata (part 2/2).

Definition 6.1 (Model Metadata) *Model metadata provides basic information for the identification and description of a simulation model. This includes a unique* Identifier *of the model, information on the developer of the model (*Responsibility*), a* Description *of the model, as well as* Requirements *and* Files *for the execution of the model.*

Based on the presented perspectives on model metadata, the specification proposed in this thesis consists of five objects: *Identifier, Responsibility, Description, Requirements,* and *Files* (cf. Figures 6.3 and 6.4 as well as Definition 6.1). The *identifier* provides all information required for the ambiguous identification of a simulation model. Furthermore, in case a model is the result of an advancement of another model, a reference to this model should be provided. The *responsibility* object contains detailed information on the person who is or was in charge of the model's development and who accordingly can answer questions regarding the model. The *description* of the model consists of a brief abstract on the model's purpose and respective keywords but also refers to related work or related models. Additionally, instructions on how to utilize and execute the model are given. For the execution of the model, *requirements* apply and specific expertise might be assumed. If used, the framework the model was developed in, for instance, NetLogo or Repast Symphony, but also requirements with respect to the operating system, programming language and other software and hardware requirements are summarized here. Finally, *files* that are required for the execution of the model must be provided. Besides the model files itself, input data files but also the developers documentation files are part of this.

6.1.2 Input Variables and Parameters

Two major components that define a model are its *inputs* and *outputs*. They are essential for generating and analyzing the model's behavior. The inputs influence the behavior of the model as they affect the states as well as the transition of states within the model. In the approach presented in this thesis, these dynamics are not directly observable as the model is a black box and its inner operations and processes cannot be viewed during runtime. Still, outputs allow for detailed insights and enable the observation of the model's behavior retrospectively, i.e., after the execution of the model or of a single simulation step. This subsection specifies the inputs of a model (cf. Figure 6.6) while the following subsection defines the outputs.

Inputs of a simulation model represent exogenous factors that independently affect the model's behavior (Banks, 2014). As they are not influenced by or dependent on other factors, they need to be defined and their values need to be set before the execution of the model. Inputs can be divided into *input variables* and *parameters* (cf. Figure 6.5).

Input variables represent changing inputs of the model whose values depend on probability distributions. Their purpose is to represent external factors that physically or logically affect the model, e.g., the arrival of orders in a factory. Parameters, in contrast, are constant values that influence the system's behavior, e.g., the number of machines in a factory (cf. Section 2.2.1).

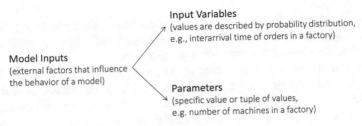

Figure 6.5: Differentiation of model inputs into *input variables* and *parameters*.

Definition 6.2 (Inputs and Domain of Inputs) *Let X be the set of model inputs. For all inputs $x_i \in X$ with $i = 1, ..., n$ and $n \in \mathbb{N}$, there is a domain $\mathbb{D}_i$ that defines the range of admissible values.*

Regardless of whether an input $x_i \in X$ with $i = 1, ..., n$ and $n \in \mathbb{N}$ is an input variable or a parameter, each x_i is defined by both a type and range of values (*domain*; $\mathbb{D}_i$) it can take. Both properties are determined by the model (cf. Definition 6.2). An example of the type of an input are whole numbers ($\mathbb{Z}$ or *integer*). The domain of an input might be defined as an interval (e.g., $[1, 100]$), where 1 is the smallest and 100 the largest admissible value. In this case, the corresponding formal specification of the domain reads as follows:

$$\mathbb{D}_i = \{z \in \mathbb{Z} \mid 1 \leq z \leq 100\}.$$

The values of simulation inputs can either be constant or stochastic. Inputs with constant values (*input parameters*) are used to represent basic features of the real-world system in the model. Examples of parameters are steady quantities of objects, e.g., the number of machines in a production system, or constant periods of time, e.g., the maintenance interval of a machine that is defined by the manufacturer. Suitable values of parameters can either be observed in the real-world system or result from calibration processes. In special cases, a parameter's range of admissible values may contain only one value, which helps avoiding calibration difficulties. An example is the weight of an industrial feedstock, if the weight of an manufactured product is required as an output of the simulation. Assuming that pure iron is used during the production process, the only reasonable admissible value of the density parameter is 7.874 g/cm^3 (Bauccio, 1993). Such parameters are referred to as *constants* or *constant parameters*.

In simulation models, the values of parameters are not necessarily limited to single constant values (cf. Definition 6.3). Time series or any other collection of constant inputs can as well be a parameter of a simulation model. For example, an order list that defines the arrival times of orders in the production process. In this case, the parameter's values are represented by an ordered n-tuple (ordered list) of $1 \le n < \infty$ elements. However, for some input parameters the representation as a tuple or list is not reasonable with respect to the conducting of sound simulation studies. Even though the use of specific order lists and arrival times seems promising, the estimation and use of probability distributions is recommended here (Kleijnen, 2001).

Definition 6.3 (Input Parameter) *An input $x_i \in X$ with $i = 1, ..., n$ and $n \in \mathbb{N}$ is called* parameter, *if x_i equals one specific value or a specific tuple (*time series*) of values $x_i = \{x_{i1}, ..., x_{in}\}$ of its domain $\mathbb{D}_i$.*

Regardless of the constant values parameters have, they might cause stochastic behavior of the simulation model. Depending on the structure of the model, the parameter of a stochastic probability function can be defined by an input of the simulation model, e.g., the λ-parameter of a *Poisson distribution* that is used to model a randomized arrival process in queuing simulation (Law, 2014). In contrast to input parameters of simulation models, the quantity of parameters of probability distributions can not directly be derived from the real system but needs to be estimated based on empirical observations.

In contrast to parameters, some inputs of simulation models are not constant and cannot be controlled. For example the daily number of orders that arrive at a manufacturing facility or the size of each order are uncertain and might vary. As variation and uncertainty of inputs affect the behavior of the system, they need to be considered as part of the inputs of the system's model. *Input variables*, as a second type of inputs, represent random inputs whose values cannot be determined with certainty but by means of probabilities (cf. Definition 6.4). To describe and specify the randomness of input variables, stochastic processes are used (Nelson, 2010).

Definition 6.4 (Input Variable) *An input $x_i \in X$ with $i = 1, ..., n$ and $i \in \mathbb{N}$ is called* input variable, *if*

$$x_i = \varphi(w_i) \text{ with } \varphi : [0, 1] \to \mathbb{D}_i, \quad w_i \in [0, 1].$$

Here, φ is the inverse cumulative distribution function *(quantile function) of a specific probability distribution.*

For stochastic input variables, the range of admissible values is implicitly given by the probability distribution. In this regard, w_i is a random variate drawn from a continuous *uniform distribution* on the interval $[0, 1]$. Based on w_i, the *inverse cumulative distribution function* of any desired probability distribution function can be used to generate respective random variates. For a specific probability $w_i \in [0, 1]$, the *inverse cumulative distribution function (quantile function)* defines the value of the random variable such that the probability is less or equal to this probability (Gilchrist, 2000).

An example of a probability distribution is the *Bernoulli distribution*. A Bernoulli distributed variable can take exactly two values with probabilities p $(0 < p < 1, p \in \mathbb{R})$ and $q = 1 - p$. Bernoulli distributions can for example be used to describe the outcome of a fair coin toss with $p = q = 0.5$. In this case, the outcomes 0 and 1 would represent *head* and *tail*.

$$\varphi(w_i) = \begin{cases} 0, & w_i < 0.5, \\ 1, & w_i \geq 0.5. \end{cases}$$

A differentiation between admissible values and reasonable values of an input parameter needs to be made. The range of admissible values of an input parameter which defines the number of machines in a manufacturing simulation are all natural numbers including zero ($\mathbb{N}_0$). Negative values are excluded by definition as a negative number of machines cannot exist. In contrast, defining the number of machines as zero is not reasonable, as no production can take place even though this value is admissible. While the estimation of reasonable values of a simulation model's input parameters is part of the user's responsibility, the restriction of admissible values is part of the model building process (Biller and Gunes, 2010). Thus, an assistance must ensure the parametrization's compliance with the range of admissible values during the conduction of simulation experiments.

Besides input variables and parameters, Montgomery (2013) distinguished exogenous variables of simulation models between *potential design factors* and *nuisance factors*. While potential design factors are the inputs which the experimenter intends to vary during the study, nuisance factors are not of primary interest even though the effect they have on the model's behavior might be large. Potential design factors can be differentiated according to their relevance for the current experiment into *design factors*, *held-constant factors*, and *allowed-to-vary factors*. Design factors are those factors which were chosen to be varied during the experiments, i.e., the model is executed with different levels of each design factor during each simulation run. Accordingly, factors which are not of interest for the current experiment and whose values are not varied, for instance because it is challenging to vary those factors, are referred to as held-constant factors. Finally, allowed-to-vary factors are represented by probability distributions to cover possible values by means of randomization. Analogously, nuisance factors can be discriminated into *controllable*, *uncontrollable*, and *noise factors* (Sanchez, 2007). While controllable factors can be set by the experimenter, uncontrollable factors are part of the experiment's environment, e.g., humidity or gravity. Noise factors are uncontrollable as well, however, they are controllable in simulation experiments. An example of a noise factor is "weather".

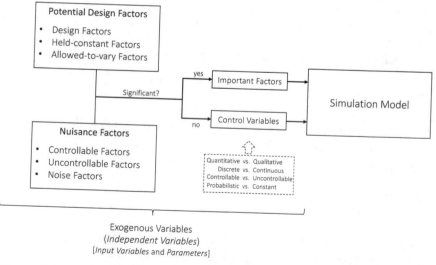

Figure 6.6: Inputs of a simulation model.

The determination of a factor's importance is challenging. It depends on the performance indicator, which has been selected for measuring the behavior of the model. As it is part of the design of experiments, respective approaches are presented and formally specified in Section 6.3.1.

Based on the definition and differentiation of simulation model inputs, characteristics of inputs can be derived. Depending on whether the value of an input describes a specific value or a distribution of probable values, a distinction between quantitative and qualitative inputs can be made. Furthermore, the controllability as well as the constancy of the inputs' values can be differentiated. In conclusion, simulation models consist of different types of inputs, which can be differentiated and specified as illustrated in Figure 6.6.

The decision whether an input is classified as potential design factor or nuisance factor is another potential source of experimenter bias. Even though nuisance factors are not of primary interest, they might still have a major impact on the model's behavior and thus must be considered when designing experiments. Likewise, the experimenter might define potential design factors that do not influence the behavior of the model and thus do not need to be varied during the experimentation. By assessing the significance of the inputs, the presented assistance is capable of reassigning the model's inputs. Accordingly, two new sets of inputs arise: *important factors* that must be varied as they affect the behavior of the model and *control variables* that are held constant. It is the goal of the experimentation to investigate how important factors influence the behavior of the model and whether the hypothesized behavior can be observed.

6.1.3 Output Variables and Performance Measures

Analogously to inputs of simulation models, *outputs* of simulation models can be differentiated into more specific types of variables. In contrast to the independent inputs of a model, its outputs are dependent (*endogenous*) variables. They are generated by the model and enable the experimenter to observe the behavior of the model. Often, the observable variables that are provided by the model differ from the demands for measuring the performance of the model, which are defined by the simulation study. Already in an early step of the study, case-specific measures or indicators are defined. They are later used to assess the performance of the model. Based on these measures, it is defined whether or not the goal of the study is fulfilled or accomplished. Thus, a gap needs to be closed between the observable outputs that are provided by the model and the measures that are required to allow for the

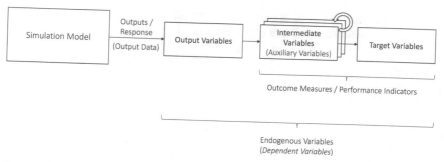

Figure 6.7: Outputs of a simulation model.

achievement of the study's goal. This subsection differentiates and specifies outputs that are provided by the model as well as different types of variables and measures that need to be derived from the model's outputs with respect to the study's goals (cf. Figure 6.7).

According to Law (2015), the output of a DES simulation model is the output of a stochastic process resulting from the randomness of inputs or components of the model. The output of the model, also referred to as the output data of the model, consist of one or many output variables. Each output variable describes the observable behavior of one of the system's components, e.g., the total amount of breakdowns a machine has had during a shift, or provides information on the performance of the system, e.g., the processing time of each manufactured product. Law emphasizes that neither the independence of these variables nor the fact that these variables are identically distributed can be assumed. As a result of this, classical statistics are not applicable or only applicable with limitations for the analysis of simulation outputs. Even though this issue results from the characteristics of the model's outputs, it must be taken into account during the analysis of the results. Thus, approach for handling these specific features are introduced, specified, and applied in Section 6.5.3.

To enable the targeted conducting of simulation studies, specific performance indicators are defined as part of the study's problem statement. Zeigler et al. (2000) emphasized these indicators' characteristics to measure how effective systems are in accomplishing specific goals. He described how different parametrizations of the model can be evaluated making use of such *outcome measures*. Even though Maria (1997) referred to *performance measures* instead, the definitions correspond mostly. She defined performance measures as "quantitative criteria on the basis of which different system configurations will be compared and ranked"(Maria, 1997, p. 8). In accordance with most definitions, Zeigler pointed out that outcome measures are computed based on output variables that are provided by the model. Accordingly, output variables itself are not considered as performance measures of simulation models even though their values might be used to assess the performance of a model. Law and McComas (1998, p. 88) affirmed this view and discriminated between "basic simulation output data" and "performance measures computed from them".

In contrast to the definition of simulation models presented in Section 6.1, performance measures are not necessarily an inherent part of simulation models. Even though performance measures may be represented by output variables, they are not limited to them. A performance measure might for instance be an arithmetic combination of output variables. An example from the manufacturing domain for a potential performance measure is the rejection rate of a manufactured product. The rejection rate is defined by the quotient of the output variables that represent the number of accepted and rejected products. However, any other mathematical combination, modification, or extension of the output variables' values, e.g., the normalization of logistical key performance indicators for comparing the performance of different scenarios, are also potential performance measures in simulation studies. The specification of performance measures based on a provided simulation model includes the combination and modification of the model's output variables in a way that new variables are created. As these new variables often serve as target functions to the simulation, they are also referred to as *target variables*.

The decision regarding which performance measures are required for assessing the model's behavior in a simulation study strongly depends on the identified goal and cannot be met ex ante, during the development of the model. Instead, the definition and implementation of performance measures must be conducted as part of the simulation study. To guide users though the process of defining target variables and performance measures of a simulation model, the definition of intermediate steps seems reasonable to facilitate the process. One approach is to divide the definition of a complex *target variable* into the definition of many simple *intermediate variables* (Dekker, 1984). Such intermediate variables are also referred to as *auxiliary variables* (Biles et al., 2007) and are directly computable from the model's output variables or from other auxiliary variables. They may be used as performance indicators even though, by definition, this is not their main purpose (Bossel, 2014).

Definition 6.5 (Inventory range in days)

$$Inventory\ range\ in\ days = \frac{Average\ inventory}{Average\ demand\ per\ day}$$

$$Average\ inventory = \frac{Inventory\ current\ period\ +\ Inventory\ prior\ period}{2}$$

The assisted combination of existing intermediate variable to target variables is more reasonable than the definition target variables from scratch considering the susceptibility to error. For example, when simulating logistical processes, the use of storekeeping parameters as performance indicators is suitable, e.g., the *inventory range* in days (cf. Definition 6.5). The inventory range is defined as the consumption time in days of the average inventory assuming a steady demand of goods. Thus, the intermediate variable *average inventory* should be calculated first, which is defined as the mean of the current and the last period's inventory.

To provide a service that is capable of assisting the definition of performance measures of a simulation model by means of intermediate and target variables, the service requires model-specific information in advance. This includes the formal description of the model as well as of its output variables (Y) that were defined in Section 6.1. Each output variable $y_j \in Y$ ($j = 1, ..., m$ and $j \in \mathbb{N}$) can be linked to an intermediate variable $y^I \in Y^I$ by the function $\bar{g} \colon Y \to Y^I$. Intermediate variables may also consist of other intermediate variables, i.e, $\bar{g}$ can also be provided elements of its co-domain as input. However, as all elements of Y^I can also be expressed by elements of Y, the domain of $\bar{g}$ does not need to be extended. The same applies for target variables and the corresponding function $\hat{g} \colon Y^I \to Y^T$. It links elements from Y^I or elements from Y^T to elements in Y^T (cf. Definitions 6.6 and 6.7).

Definition 6.6 (Output and Target Variables) *With respect to the analysis of the behavior of a simulation model, the outputs of a model can be divided into:*

- *a set of* output variables $Y = \{y_1, ..., y_m\}$, $f(X) = Y$, $m \in \mathbb{N}$ *and*

- *a set of* target variables Y^T *as a result of the combination of output variables with* $g(Y) = Y^T$.

Y^T *is a o-dimensional space with*

$$g := \begin{pmatrix} g_1(Y) \\ \vdots \\ g_o(Y) \end{pmatrix}.$$

Each function $g_1, ..., g_o$ is a combination of admissible operators (cf. Figure 6.9). To facilitate the process of defining target variables, the use of intermediate variables *is reasonable (cf. Definition 6.7).*

Definition 6.7 (Intermediate Variables) *An* intermediate variable $Y^I = \{Y_1^I, ..., Y_P^I\}$, $p \in \mathbb{N}$ *is any variable that is defined as an interim stage between output and target variables.*

Consequently, the composition $g(Y) = (\hat{g} \circ \bar{g})(Y) = \hat{g}(\bar{g}(Y))$ applies where

$$\bar{g} \colon Y \to Y^I \text{ and } \hat{g} \colon Y^I \to Y^T.$$

Both intermediate and target variables may not only consist of one but of multiple output variables or respective mappings of output variables (cf. Figure 6.8). The linkage of variables can be defined by arithmetical operations, e.g., elementary arithmetic operations such as addition, subtraction, multiplication or division but also more advanced operations are possible as for instance modulo or the least common multiple. Furthermore, numeric values can be applied to output, intermediate, and target variables by means of arithmetical operations. This is reasonable, if for example a multiple or fraction of a specific variable if required for the definition of a performance measure, e.g., the taxation of a price by a certain factor.

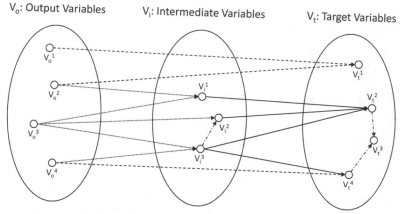

Figure 6.8: Relationship between output, intermediate, and target variables.

To enable the definition of performance measures for a simulation models as part of the assistance, the set of output variables (Y) that was specified for the model must be extended by the experimenter. The respective service must allow for the definition of one or many output variables as performance measures. Alternatively, it must allow for the definition of new intermediate and target variables based on the given output variables, which will be used as performance measures. The decision of which variables are supposed to serve as performance measures is highly individual and depends on the hypothesis the experimenter wants to test. Thus, the implementation of a guided user dialogue seems reasonable. During this process, the concept of intermediate variables can be used to facilitate the user-driven definition of new variables that are required for conducting the study. However, algorithmic solutions for defining a set of performance measures based on model criteria, e.g., standardized performance indicators based on the domain of the model, can further facilitate the process. The result is a set of performance measures (P), which are defined by a set of mapping rules based on the model's output variables. Additionally, the intermediate (Y^I) and target (Y^T) variables that are defined during the process are also part of the process's result and extend the formal specification of the simulation experiment.

> **Definition 6.8 (Performance Measures)** Performance measures
> $P := Y \cup Y^T$, $P \neq \emptyset$ *are one or many output (Y) and target variables*
> *(Y^T) that are used for the investigation of the model's behavior with*
> *respect to answering the research hypothesis.*

This section focuses on the formal specification of performance measures
for simulation models (cf. Definition 6.8). To utilize such performance
measures for the assistance of Hypothesis-Driven Simulation Studies, this
approach as well as the requirements and dependencies that were defined
must be made applicable. For this purpose, the use of a language seems
suitable. Grammar 6.1 and 6.2 formally specifies respective dependencies
and constraints for linking of output, intermediate, and target variables as
a language. The syntax of the language is defined using the *Backus-Naur*
form. The structure of the language is defined by rules that specify how
valid expressions are build. Moreover, performance measures can be formally
specified, using and combining operators and variables according to the
defined rules and in accordance with Figure 6.24. Here, only the basic
mathematical operators addition, subtraction, multiplication, division, and
modulo are presented. This selection can be expanded by any other operator
that combines numeric or symbolic inputs or outputs of simulation models.
In the grammar presented here, an *input* can be both *input variable* or
parameter (cf. Section 6.1.2).

As with previous steps in the process of a simulation study that is pursued
in this thesis, a black box specification of the simulation model under
investigation was presented. Besides metadata, the specification consist of a
set of input and output variables that can be used for assessing behavioral
aspects of the model. The formal description of the service in Section 6.1.3
determines that a set of specified output variables is passed to the service.
Consequently, the service is capable of utilizing information regarding *type*,
name, *description*, and *identifier* of each output variable of the model for
the process of defining performance measures.

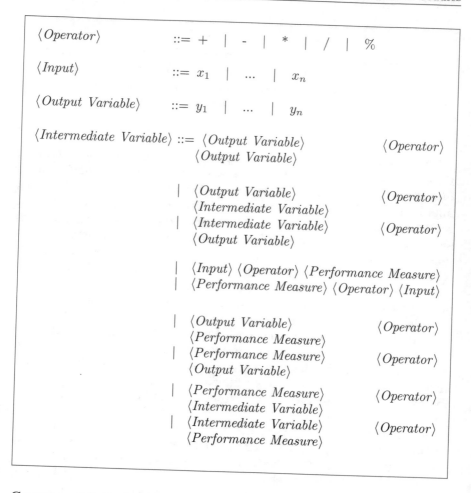

Grammar 6.1: Backus-Naur form of the specification of performance measures (part 1/2).

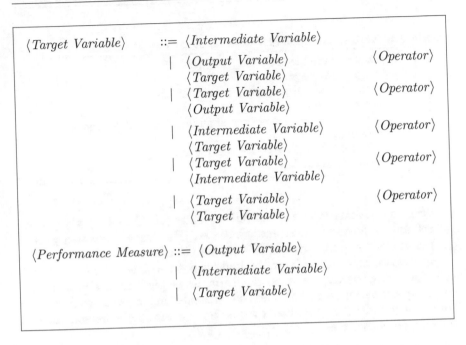

Grammar 6.2: Backus-Naur form of the specification of performance measures (part 2/2).

The methodology for simulation studies that is presented in this thesis aims at proving or disproving a research hypothesis on the distribution or value of a performance measure of a simulation model. The hypothesis, which is formally specified at a later stage of the simulation study, is provided by the user of the assistance system and represents the user's individual assumption on how the models behaves. Thus, it can be assumed that the user is aware of both the performance measures that are required for testing a specific hypothesis and the way output variables can be suitably combined to define required target variables. Because of this, the definition of performance measures by means of a guided user dialog seems reasonable and a fully automated approach for defining performance measures is not pursued, e.g., based on standardized performance indicators. Yet, experienced users might provide the required specification of the performance measure along with the model.

Code 6.1: XML specification of simulation model output variables.

```
<outputVariable uid="var_out_736537">
<type>int</type>
<label>Average processing time</label>
<description>
The average processing time of all manifactured products.
</description>
<identifier>avgProcTime</identifier>
</outputVariable>
```

Based on information on all output variables (cf. Code 6.1), the process of defining performance measures is initiated. The user is presented with all of the model's output variables (Y). In case that all required performance measures are represented by individual output variables, the process ends after selecting the respective output variables as performance measures. If output variables need to be combined to create target variables first, a set of operators (O) is required that define how variables can be combined to intermediate variables Y^I (cf. Definition 6.9).

Definition 6.9 (Intermediate and Target Variables) *To combine output variables to intermediate and target variables, operators O are required. Each operator $o_l \in O$ is defined by a set of functions $o_l = \{\alpha_{l1}, ..., \alpha_{ln}\}$ where each function α defines a possible linkage of the variables with $l = 1, ..., n$ and $l \in \mathbb{N}$.*

Each operator (o_l) is defined by a set of functions $\{\alpha_{l1}, ..., \alpha_{ln}\}$, where the domains of each function α_{lk} with $k = 1, ..., n$ and $n \in \mathbb{N}$ describe permissible variable types of the arguments, e.g., only numerical variables as *Integer* ($\mathbb{N}$) and *Double* ($\mathbb{R}$) (see Figure 6.9). For numerical variables, a possible definition of the "+" operator is the addition of two arguments (addends) as it is defined for real numbers. Each addend can either be the value of a variable of the model or a real number. When the addends are of type *Integer*, the result of the addition operation ($\mathbb{N} \oplus \mathbb{N} \rightarrow \mathbb{N}$) is a new numerical variable that is of type *Integer*, too. Like all operators, the "+" operator can be individually defined for multiple variable types. Besides the addition of real numbers, it can for example also be defined as the concatenation of

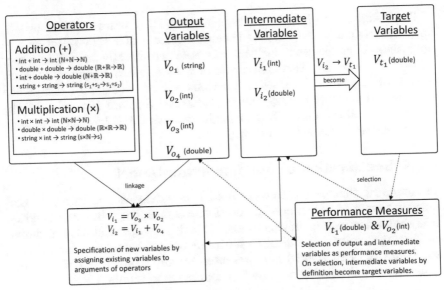

Figure 6.9: Specification of performance measures based on operators and output variables.

characters for two or more textual variables, e.g., *String* ($\mathbb{S}$), or the addition of *Time* and *Date* values ($\mathbb{D}$). In this case, the resulting variable is of a textual respectively temporal variable type. For each operator o_l and each number of arguments, the permissible variable types of each argument, the type of the resulting variable, and the specific operation are to be defined separately as an individual function $\alpha_{lk} \in o_l$. For instance, for the addition operator $o_l = +$, possible functions α_l are: $\alpha_{l1}: \mathbb{N} \oplus \mathbb{N} \to \mathbb{N}$, $\alpha_{l2}: \mathbb{R} \oplus \mathbb{R} \to \mathbb{R}$, $\alpha_{l3}: \mathbb{N} \oplus \mathbb{R} \to \mathbb{R}$, and $\alpha_{l4}: \mathbb{S} \oplus \mathbb{S} \to \mathbb{S}$ with $\mathbb{N} \equiv Integer$, $\mathbb{R} \equiv Double$ and $\mathbb{S} \equiv String$. To this end, each variable Y^I that has been newly defined may serve as argument of an operator for the specification of further variables.

At first, all created variables are considered as intermediate variables. They are neither genuine output variables nor were they selected as performance measures or defined as target variables, yet. This step is a necessary interim stage for the specification of the actual performance measures. In a second step, the performance measures are selected from the sets of output and intermediate variables. Through the selection of an intermediate variable as performance measure, this variable becomes a target variable by definition, while output variables remain output variables.

The resulting set of performance measures (P) consists of elements of Y and former elements of Y^I that became elements of Y^T by selection and definition. Each element of P that was selected directly from Y is a new variable Y^I, a combination of elements of Y by means of operators O. Each operator o_l is defined by a set of functions α_{lk}, where each α_{lk} defines the types and the quantity of arguments (variables) that are demanded by the operator as well as the specification of the operation, i.e., how the operator's arguments are combined to new variables.

6.1.4 Specification of the Simulation Model

In summary, the specifications of model metadata as well as inputs and outputs presented in the previous sections result in the following definition of a simulation model. In this thesis, a black box representation is chosen so that the model is reduced to its input-output-behavior. Accordingly, the behavior of the model is represented by an *execution function* which generates the observable outputs based on a set of inputs.

Definition 6.10 (Simulation Model) *A simulation model M is defined by a four-tuple $M := (X, Y, f, \mathbb{M})$ with*

- *X is the set of* Inputs, *i.e., $X = \{x_1, ..., x_n\}$ with $n \in \mathbb{N}$ and $X \neq \emptyset$,*

- *Y is the set of* Outputs, *i.e., $Y = \{y_1, ..., y_m\}$ with $m \in \mathbb{N}$ and $Y \neq \emptyset$,*

- *the* execution function $f \colon X \to Y$,

- *and a set $\mathbb{M}$ of metadata.*

A simulation model (M) can be specified by the following four components: its *inputs* (X), its *outputs* (Y), a function (f) for *executing* the model and for conducting simulation experiments, and the model's *metadata* $(\mathbb{M})$ (cf. Definition 6.10). f executes the model with a tuple of inputs $X = (x_1, ..., x_n)$, the parametrization of the model, and returns the observed behavior of the model as outputs $Y = (y_1, ..., y_m)$. In this regard, n is the number of inputs and m is the number of outputs where both n and m are by definition greater or equal one. It is assumed, that the model either comprises the simulation framework or can be linked to a simulation framework by defined interfaces, e.g., based on wrapper classes. Relevant information for the execution of the model is part of the model metadata ($\mathbb{IM}$). Either way, it is ensured that the conducting of experiments is possible such that the corresponding outputs Y can be determined for a specific set of inputs $X : X \to Y$.

6.2 Research Hypothesis

After specifying the simulation model as well as the model's input and output variables, the research hypothesis that shall be answered as goal of the simulation study is another relevant component of the assistance. It is the most challenging input, as it has to be provided by the user and is usually formulated in natural language. For the systematic and (semi-)automated conduction of simulation studies, the research hypothesis must be specified formally to allow for answering it precisely, reproducibly, and in an automated way. For this purpose, this section analyzes the structure of research hypotheses and specifies essential components of formalized hypotheses.

6.2.1 Formal Specification of Hypotheses

To specify research hypotheses in simulation studies, this thesis presents the *FITS* language. Parts of this section such as the concept of *FITS* and an approach for the automation of simulation experiments based on formalizes hypotheses were separately published by Lorig et al. (2017a). Approaches for testing the hypothesis that complement *FITS* are not part of this section and are addressed in the analysis section of this chapter instead (cf. Section 6.5.3).

As a first step towards the formal specification of research hypotheses that make assumptions on the behavior of a simulation model, the concept of research hypotheses is revisited (cf. Section 4.1.1). In accordance with the theory of science view presented in Section 4, the term hypothesis refers to an operationalized proposition that assumes relations between two or more variables in information systems research (Recker, 2013). This can be a speculative guess or a scientifically grounded assumption. In this definition, the variables describe the object of investigation. To allow for testing such hypotheses, the application of approaches and techniques from statistics seems suitable. In simulation, it is common to use statistical hypothesis tests for analyzing outputs of simulation studies (Banks, 2014). However, the statistical definition of hypothesis is more technical and specific. In statistics, a hypothesis is an assumption about the partially known probability distribution of one or more random variables, which is examined in a test (Tietjen, 1986). To formally specify research hypotheses in a way that they are compatible with these requirements, relevant attributes and components of hypotheses must be identified first. After that, it is necessary to consider and define the interdependencies between the hypothesis and the simulation model.

The aim of the specification presented in this subsection is the description of a hypothesis such that it is testable by means of parametric hypothesis tests. The t-test, as an example of a parametric hypothesis test, is used to determine if the mean values of two datasets differ. Depending on whether a one-sample or two-sample test is used, one empirical and one synthetic and idealized dataset or two empirically sampled datasets are required. Either way, the research hypothesis specified in this subsection must provide information on the circumstances (*model parametrization*) under which the sample is drawn. Furthermore, an assumption regarding the mean values of the datasets must be formulated. With respect to the application of hypothesis tests, the formulation of both a null hypothesis and a corresponding alternative hypothesis is reasonable. Finally, additional information such as the required significance level or the number of replications of the model must be specified.

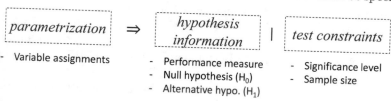

Figure 6.10: Structure of a hypothesis in *FITS*.

For this purpose, a *FITS* expression of an experiment hypothesis consists of three parts: *parametrization*. *hypothesis information*, and *test constraints* (cf. Figure 6.10). The *parametrization* part contains information on the values of the inputs under which the stated assumption is supposed to apply. In addition, the *test constraints* part defines the model's performance measure and states the values of the performance measure for which the hypothesis applies. Finally, *FITS* expressions specify *test constraints* for the application of statistical hypotheses tests.

Definition 6.11 (Parametrization Part of a Hypothesis) *The parametrization of a hypothesis assigns a specific value or series of values from its domain $\mathbb{D}_i$ to each input parameter $x_i \in X$ with $i = 1, ..., n$ and $n \in \mathbb{N}$ of a model.*

The first part, the *parametrization*, includes the assignment of specific values to the model's inputs X (cf. Definition 6.11). Depending on the number of model inputs, this part of the hypothesis can be extensive. Thus, in a *FITS* expression it is possible to shorten the assignment by using the number sign ("#"). Here, the symbol has the meaning "ceteris paribus" (*all else being equal*). Accordingly, initial standard values are assigned to the remaining variables whose values were not explicitly defined. Alternatively, an assignment of values which was used in previous studies or any other predefined assignment could be used.

After this *parametrization* part of the hypothesis, a separator and the *hypothesis information* part follow, which define properties of the hypothesis (cf. Definition 6.12). For the first separator of a *FITS* expression, an arrow is used in accordance with describing implications in logic. This reminds of the formal structure of a conditional clause which a scientific hypothesis is (implicitly) based on (cf. Section 4.1.1). *Hypothesis information* includes information on the considered feature (performance measure) as well as an assumption regarding a specific value or the relationship between the mean values. For example, in an model where the average processing time (PT) of a product ($\mu(PT)$) is measured, it can assumed that the average processing time is less or equal to 120 minutes (H_0: $\mu(PT) \leq 120$). A potential corresponding alternative hypothesis is the assumption that the production takes longer than 120 minutes (i.e., H_1: $\mu(PT) > 120$).

Hypothesis information consists of aggregated values of the performance measures ($\tilde{P}$) as well as a mutual exclusive pair of statistical hypotheses (H_0 and H_1). As performance measures of a simulation model are either output or target variables, the aggregated values of the respective variables ($\tilde{Y}_t$ and $\tilde{Y}_t^T$) must be gathered over all executed simulation experiments w. A more detailed specification of the aggregation process is provided in Definition 6.35.

Definition 6.12 (Information Part of a Hypothesis) *Hypothesis information I consists of a triple $I := (\tilde{P}, H_0, H_1)$ such that*

– $\tilde{P}$ *are the aggregated values of the performance measures (P) with*

$$\tilde{P} := \tilde{Y} \cup \tilde{Y}^T, \qquad \tilde{Y} = \bigcup_{t=1}^{w} \tilde{Y}_t, \text{ and} \qquad \tilde{Y}^T = \bigcup_{t=1}^{w} \tilde{Y}_t^T \text{ where}$$

   - $\tilde{Y}_t$ *is the set of aggregated output variables from experiment t,*
   - $\tilde{Y}_t^T$ *is the set of aggregated target variables from experiment t,*
   - w *is the total number of executed experiments, and*

– *two mutually exclusive statements on the actual value of the performance measure, a null hypothesis H_0 and a corresponding alternative hypothesis H_1.*

Between the *hypothesis information* part and the final *test constraints* part, another separator is inserted. To avoid misinterpretations and as the *test constraints* part refers to the hypothesis in general, the vertical bar symbol ("|") is used, which also serves as delimiter in other contexts. In the *test constraints* part, the experimenter defines overall conditions for testing the hypothesis such as significance level α and sample size n for the subsequent execution of a significance test (cf. Definition 6.13). Depending on the type of hypothesis, additional information might be required, which can be stated in the *test constraints* part of the hypothesis as well.

Definition 6.13 (Test Constraints Part of a Hypothesis) *Test constraints C are defined as tuple $C := (\lambda, n)$ with significance level λ and sample size n.*

Within all three introduced parts, the conjunction symbol "$\wedge$" is used to concatenate multiple subexpressions. The disjunction symbol "$\vee$" is used to separate the null hypothesis from the alternative hypothesis.

$\langle Statement \rangle$	$::=$	$\langle Parametrization \rangle$ '$\Rightarrow$' $\langle Hypothesis\ Inf. \rangle$ '$|$' $\langle Test\ Constraints \rangle$
$\langle Parametrization \rangle$	$::=$	$\langle Value\ Assignments \rangle$
$\langle Value\ Assignments \rangle$	$::=$	$\langle Value\ Assignment \rangle$ $|$ $\langle Value\ Assignment \rangle$ '$\wedge$' $\langle Value\ Assignments \rangle$
$\langle Value\ Assignment \rangle$	$::=$	$\langle Input\ Variable \rangle$ '(' $\langle Instance \rangle$ ',' $\langle Value \rangle$ ')' $|$ $\langle Input\ Variable \rangle$ '(' $\langle Class \rangle$ ',' $\langle Value \rangle$ ')' $|$ #
$\langle Hypothesis\ Inf. \rangle$	$::=$	$\langle Features \rangle$ '$\wedge$ $((H_0(\mu$' $\langle Relation \rangle$ $\langle Value \rangle$ ')) $\vee$ $(H_1(\mu$' $\langle Relation \rangle$ $\langle Value \rangle$ '))))'
$\langle Features \rangle$	$::=$	$\langle Feature \rangle$ $|$ $\langle Feature \rangle$ '$\wedge$' $\langle Features \rangle$
$\langle Feature \rangle$	$::=$	'μ(' $\langle Performance\ Indicator \rangle$ ')'
$\langle Relation \rangle$	$::=$	'$<$' $|$ '$\leq$' $|$ '$>$' $|$ '$\geq$' $|$ '$=$' $|$ '$\neq$' $|$ ...
$\langle Test\ Constraints \rangle$	$::=$	'α(' $\langle Value \rangle$ ') $\wedge$ n(' $\langle Value \rangle$ ')'

Grammar 6.3: Backus-Naur form of the *FITS* language for expressing hypotheses.

The use of a language such as *FITS* seems reasonable for the specification of hypotheses in simulation studies. A trade-off between the expressive power and the efficiency of the reasoning needs to be made. Natural language in writing (e.g., English or German) is capable of expressing a desired content in great detail. However, computer-aided processing of natural language is challenging and error-prone. In order to formulate hypotheses on the behavior of an investigated model, a formal language seems more suitable. This can be used by researchers independent of their subjects. The language is used to specify a parametrization of the simulation model and to determine which significance level is required. Thus, the acronym *FITS* was chosen as name of the language which stands for "**F**ormulating, **I**ntegrating and **T**esting of Hypotheses in Computer **S**imulation". The language can be used without a simulation system to formulate hypotheses and to share them with other researchers. Grammar 6.3 defines how valid *FITS* expressions can be constructed by means of the Backus-Naur form.

Using *FITS*, a possible specification of a hypothesis from the manufacturing domain might look as follows:

$$machines(8) \; \wedge \; workers(3) \; \wedge \; queuingDiscipline(SPT) \; \wedge \; \#$$
$$\Rightarrow \mu(ProcessingTime) \wedge (H_0(\mu \leq 240) \vee H_1((\mu > 240)) \wedge \alpha(5) \wedge n(100)$$

The stated example specifies a hypothesis about a simulation model of a production line. In this model, the number of machines and workers can be varied as well as the queuing discipline used for processing incoming orders. A possible translation of the example in natural language could read as follows:

> *If the production line consists of 8* machines *and 3* workers *control these machines and the* queuing discipline *"shortest processing time" is applied for processing orders ceteris paribus, then the observed processing time per order will be lower than 240 minutes on average and this assumption will be tested with a significance level of 5% and a sample size of 100 simulation runs.*

The character "μ" denotes the expected value of a random output variable of the model. In this sample, this is the operation time which is also the feature of investigation. The subexpressions of the null hypothesis H_0 and the alternative hypothesis H_1 consist of a statement about that feature which will be evaluated by means of hypotheses testing approaches. In summary, in this thesis research hypotheses on the behavior of simulation models are defined as specified in Definition 6.14.

Definition 6.14 (Research Hypothesis) *In simulation studies, a research hypothesis H is defined as tuple* $H := (X, I, C)$ *with*

- X *the parametrization of the model (cf. Definition 6.10),*

- *hypothesis information* $I := (\tilde{P}, H_0, H_1)$, *and*

- *test constraints* $C := (\lambda, n)$.

6.2.2 Documentation of the Solution Process

To confirm or refute a given hypothesis in a replicable and reproducible way, it is essential to thoroughly document all steps that were executed to receive a solution. The goal of this step is to preserve the explanatory potential of the conducted study and evidence for or against the validity of the hypothesis. Documented information includes all decisions that were made during the process of the study as well as interim and final results. The documentation is not a single step of a simulation study but accompanies the entire process, starting with the formulation of the research hypothesis, the design, execution, and analysis of experiments, through to the interpretation of the results. This subsection presents criteria and best practices for the documentation of simulation studies. Furthermore, it specifies information and data that need to be documented to allow for the reproduction of the study's results.

Approaches for the documentation of simulation studies exist for both models and experiments. To allow for the documentation of simulation models, taxonomies for the classification of simulation models (Highland, 1979) or minimum information for the annotation of models (LeNovère et al., 2005) were proposed. But also for the documentation of simulation experiments, approaches exist that propose a minimum set of required information (Waltemath et al., 2011) or that define an *experimental frame* (Zeigler et al., 2000).

The definition varies of what extent of information is sufficient to be considered as *documentation*. Some authors argue that a written report or presentation of the simulation which describes how to run the model might already serve as documentation (Rossetti, 2016). In this regard,

Chung (2004) discussed ten written report guidelines that should be considered when writing a final report. The guidelines include the *problem statement, project planning, system definition, input data collection and analysis, model formulation, model translation, verification, validation, experimentation and analysis,* and *recommendations and conclusions.* However, the author does not provide detailed information regarding what aspects must be considered for each guideline. With respect to the goal of this thesis, the *experimentation and analysis* guideline seems to be most suitable. Rossetti (2016) presented questions that might be answered to fulfill this guideline. This includes the description of a typical simulation run, the determination of both run length and number of replications, a detailed description of the experimental plan, and a discussion of the results.

To ensure the correctness, completeness, consistency, and unambiguity of all documentations that were created during a simulation study, Balci (1998) proposed *documentation checking* as an informal verification and validation technique. This is especially important if the logic of the model or the conducted experiments are modified. In this case, the documentation must be updated, however, this step is often forgotten or ignored. Uhrmacher et al. (2016) also addressed the incompleteness of documentation which results in a lack of reproducibility. The authors emphasized that existing approaches for the facilitation of simulation documentation require major effort. Yet, they attribute shortcomings in the reproducibility of simulation results not only to an insufficient description of the model. In addition, they outline how a lack of documentation might hide other mistakes in the execution of simulation experiments, e.g., a too small number of replications. To overcome such issues, Uhrmacher et al. (2016) proposed the use of domain-specific languages for the description, specification, and execution of simulation experiments (cf. Section 3.1.1).

When discussing the thorough documentation of experiments, approaches from medicine should be considered as well. Especially in clinical trials but also in medical laboratories in general, standardized protocols and procedures are defined to ensure the reproducibility of conducted experiments and studies. Lazzari (2009) presented a standard protocol for clinical laboratories as a checklist. As one of the considered implementation points, both creation and maintenance of a documentation is proposed. Besides the procedure of the conducted tests and a quality control log, the documentation consists of supplemental documents such as result forms, flow diagrams, and comparison study sheets.

In some parts of medical research, mandatory legal guidelines exist that also define the documentation of studies. As an example, EU regulation No

536/2014 defines the conducting of clinical trials on medicinal products for human use (European Commission, 2014). In this regard, the documentation of the clinical trial must "allow effective supervision" (European Commission, 2014, L 158/7). In an earlier version of the guidelines on *Good Clinical Practice*, a more detailed specification of documentations was provided. It must include "all records, in any form [...] that describe or record the methods, conduct, and/or results of a trial, the factors affecting a trial, and the actions taken" (European Commission, 1996, p. 8). Furthermore, a list of essential documents that are required for conducting clinical trials must be provided. This includes information on the randomization of the trial population and how blinded trials can be decoded. To learn from such approaches and to address the lack of information in experiment protocols in published manuscripts, Soldatova et al. (2008) developed the *EXACT* ontology. Using the presented ontology, biological laboratory protocols can be formalized with predefined experiment actions. Presented actions include information on how chemicals were combined (e.g., mixed or dissolved) or separated (e.g., centrifuged or filtered). The use of this ontology facilitates the generation and publication of reproducible experiment protocols.

In simulation, a lack of documentation can be identified which results in a decreased reproducibility of studies and experiments. Approaches exist for the documentation of simulation studies. Simulation frameworks like NetLogo provide functionalities that automatically generate documentations of specific simulation steps, i.e., spreadsheets of simulation runs or searchconfigs of the included BehaviorSearch plugin. However, such documentations are often limited to specific aspects and do not cover the entire life-cycle of the conducted experiments. Furthermore, general specifications of the documentation process are not provided even though approaches for the standardized documentation of experiments by means of specific guidelines exist in other disciplines.

6.3 Design of Experiments

The two previous sections formally specified simulation models and the research hypotheses. Both components must be provided by the experimenter to conduct Hypothesis-Driven Simulation Studies. The following three sections introduce and specify services that are required for assisting each individual phase of experimentation during the study. This section particularly focuses on services that must be provided to assist the design of experiments. This includes factor screening services to identify important input factors of the model as well as design of experiment services for the efficient definition of factor-level-combinations to be investigated for answering the research question. Furthermore, as the assistance system focuses on analyzing the behavior of stochastic models, the estimation of a sufficient number of replications must be part of the experimental design as well, to ensure statistical certainty of the results.

6.3.1 Factor Screening

Especially when applying simulation to complex models that describe sophisticated systems, the number of input variables might be great. Thus, the execution of the model with all possible factor-level-combinations is often not feasible due to the combinatorial explosion of all potential parametrizations. With respect to the *sparsity-of-effect principle (parsimony principle)*, a full coverage is not necessary as in most systems a small set of factors is sufficient to explain most of the behavior of a system (Kleijnen, 2015). At the same time, it is challenging to identify these relevant factors as well as the necessary factor-level-combinations of the model, which must be simulated to answer the study's research question. For this purpose, the conducting of a *sensitivity analysis* (what-if analysis) is reasonable (Kleijnen, 2010). Just like the method presented in this thesis, sensitivity analysis pursues a black box approach, which allows for investigation and optimization of inaccessible systems. A review of different sensitivity analysis approaches is presented by Iooss and Lemaître (2015).

As a first necessary step towards the intelligent design of simulation experiments, factors must be identified that influence the performance measure the hypothesis makes an assumption about. For this purpose, *factor screening* techniques were developed. The aim of these approaches is to dynamically identify important factors of simulation models with many factors. At the same time, Kleijnen et al. (2003) emphasize that the importance of each factor depends on the experimental frame (domain of the model). This is why the importance of each factor cannot be identified without detailed knowledge about the question or goal that drives the study. It is the experimenter's responsibility to provide information on the model and to define the scenario of interest as accurately as possible.

Kleijnen provides a definition of "importance" in terms of factor screening approaches. He describes the simplest form of importance as factors having an additive effect towards a single response of the model. In this case, the input-output relationship can be described by a first-order polynomial and the importance of each factor is assessed based on the absolute value of its first-order effect (*main effect*; cf. Definition 6.15). Likewise, the least important factors have a main effect which is close or equal to zero. Accordingly, the result of factor screening is a set of important factors as subset of the set of all potential factors a model provides. Preferably, the set is sorted according to each factor's relevance. The cumulated main effect the important factors have on the model's performance measure is considerably higher than the main effect of the remaining input factors. By definition, the cumulated main effect of all input factors is 100% and the observable changes of the performance measure can almost entirely be explained by the effect the input factors of the model have.

Definition 6.15 (Effect of Inputs) *The effect each input and each combination of inputs has on a specific performance measure $P^\star \in P$ can be measured.*

$$\forall p \in P, \ \forall x_i \in X$$

$$\exists \beta_i := \text{ Influence of input } x_i \text{ on performance measure } p$$

$$(\text{individual main effect})$$

$$\exists \beta_{ij} := \text{ Influence of the combination of the inputs } x_i \text{ and } x_j$$

$$\text{on performance measure } p \text{ (group effect).}$$

Consequently it follows:

$$\sum_{i=1}^{n} \beta_i + \sum_{i=1}^{n} \sum_{\substack{j=1 \\ i \neq j}}^{n} \frac{\beta_{ij}}{2} \leq 100$$

with $i, j, n \in \mathbb{N}$, assuming that interactions of three and more factor do not occur.

By quantifying the influence individual factors or combinations of factors have on a performance measure of a model, the factors can be ordered by the impact they have. To this end, a differentiation between *important* and *unimportant factors* can be made using a specific threshold θ (cf. Definition 6.16). This allows for the selection and limitation of factors to be investigated more closely during the study.

Definition 6.16 (Important Factors) *From Definition 6.15 it follows: The inputs can be permuted according to the strength of their effect on a specific performance measure (importance). With b_i being the effect of a single factor β_i or the effect of the interaction of two factors β_{ij}, an order $B = \{b_1, ..., b_{n\frac{n+1}{2}}\}$ can be defined with $|b_1| \geq |b_{i+1}|$ for $i, j = 1, ..., n$, $i \neq j$, and $i, j, n \in \mathbb{N}$.*

With respect to a threshold θ (e.g., 80%), index k that splits B into a set of important factors and a set of unimportant factors can be defined as

$$\sum_{i=1}^{k} b_i \geq \theta \text{ and } \sum_{i=1}^{k-1} b_i < \theta$$

such that the cumulated effect of $b_1, ..., b_k$ exceeds threshold θ with $i, k \in \mathbb{N}$.

Factor screening, as defined and presented by Kleijnen, pursues a black box approach (cf. Definition 6.17). Information on the inner structure of the model, of its states, or the transition between the states, is not required. Instead, these approaches assess the importance of each factor by means of systematic parametrization of and experimentation with the model. They make use of the sequential collection of simulation data, which enables the experimenter to examine the model's observed behavior before designing and executing the next simulation experiment, run, or iteration. More specifically, the factor screening technique presented by Kleijnen (2015) pursues a divide-and-conquer approach to systematically identify the main effects of the most important factors (β_i) or groups of factors (β_{ij}) of a simulation model with respect to a specific performance measure. For this purpose, the extreme scenarios of the model are simulated first. In case the most important factors with the largest main effects have been identified, it might be sufficient to terminate the factor screening process after k of the n factors were investigated.

Definition 6.17 (Factor Screening) *Factor screening is the process FS of determining the effects individual factors and combinations of factors have on a specific performance measure of a simulation model with respect to identifying the most important factors or combinations of factors. The result of a (two factor interaction) factor screening is set B that consists of β_i and β_{ij} for $i, j = 1, ..., k$, $k \leq n$, $i \neq j$, and $i, j \in \mathbb{N}$ (cf. Definition 6.16).*

$$FS\colon (M, X, P) \to B$$

In practice, many approaches for factor screening exist, which can be differentiated by the design of the screening procedure. In discrete-event simulation, the *sequential bifurcation* approach introduced by Bettonvil and Kleijnen (1996) is most commonly used. In addition to sequential bifurcation, Kleijnen (2009) discriminated between four further types of screening designs when introducing competitors to sequential bifurcation: *classic two-level factorial designs, frequency domain experimentation, supersaturated designs*, and *group-screening designs*. What all of the presented approaches have in common is that they pursue black box approaches. While classic *two-level factorial designs* require a large number of parametrizations to be executed (at least $n = k + 1$ with k being the number of model factors), *frequency domain experimentation* factor values are oscillated during the simulation runs and thus their application is more challenging. In *supersaturated designs*, the number of factor-level-combinations is smaller than the number of factors ($n < k$). However, Kleijnen (2009) argued that these designs are not sufficiently efficient as the procedure is not sequential and observations made at runtime cannot be taken into account for optimizing the process. Finally, group-screening designs reduce the number of combinations by summarizing factors in groups. These groups are then executed and evaluated stepwise for determining the main effect of the model's factors. Besides sequential bifurcation, the *Morris method* is an approach from this group of screening designs and as well established in simulation (Morris, 1991).

The Morris method is a *one-factor-at-a-time* screening design whose implementation is simple compared to other factor screening designs (Campolongo et al., 2005). For the application of the approach, the value range of each of

the model's input factors (k) is discretized in a number of levels (l). From
the resulting grid of possible factor-level-combinations (l^k), a subsample
of points is randomly drawn. For each selected design point, the model is
repeatedly executed with the respective parametrizations while the factor
levels are changed one-at-a-time for observing results in the behavior of the
model. This results in a comparatively high number of required executions
of the model. The observations made during the simulation then serve as
a basis for estimating the distribution of *elementary effects* of the model's
factors. The Morris method discriminates between three types of effects:
negligible effects, large linear effects, and *large interaction effects* (Iooss and
Lemaître, 2015).

Due to the high number of required model executions, the sequential
bifurcation approach introduced by Bettonvil and Kleijnen (1996) is most
commonly used for factor screening in discrete-event simulation. In contrast
to Morris's method, sequential bifurcation pursues a sequential divide-and-
conquer approach for estimating the *main effect* of each factor. As a result
of this, observations and findings from each iteration of the algorithm
can be used for optimizing the target-oriented identification of important
factors. Accordingly, sequential bifurcation is more efficient as it requires
fewer executions of the simulation model compared to the Morris method
(Kleijnen, 2009).

For the application of sequential bifurcation, multiple assumptions need
to be met. The first assumption of sequential bifurcation is that the input-
output behavior of a model can be approximated by a metamodel, which
is a first-order polynomial (cf. Definition 6.18). For sequential bifurcation,
Kleijnen defined a metamodel as an *"adequate approximation* of the In-
put/Output (I/O) function that is implicitly determined by the underlying
simulation model" (Kleijnen, 2009, p. 159). For this purpose of defining a
metamodel, each quantitative input variable of the model is standardized
such that only two levels remain. One that results in a *low* output of the
model and one that generates a *high* output. Additionally, first-order polynomial used for the approximation consists of the main effects of each factor
(β_j) as well as an overall effect (β_0). The approximation error is assumed
to be smaller than the effects of the factor and thus is neglected in the
approach.

Definition 6.18 (Metamodel for Sequential Bifurcation)
According to Kleijnen (2015), sequential bifurcation requires that the input-output behavior of the model can be approximated by a metamodel such that a linear combination of each factor's main effect (β) as well as its standardized level (x) estimates the model's output:

$$y = \beta_0 + \beta_1 x_1 + ... + \beta_n x_n \text{ , with } n = |X| \text{ and } n \in \mathbb{N}.$$

The second assumption that has to be met by the model concerns the direction of the factor's influence on the model's output. Bettonvil and Kleijnen (1996) defined, that the effect must be known and non-negative such that each β must be greater or equal to zero (cf. Definition 6.19). Based in this assumption, the minimal output (y_0) of a model can be observed when setting the value of each input factor to 0 (*low value*) and the maximum output (y_k) of the model can be observed when setting the value of each input variable to 1 (*high value*). Thus, as the first step of sequential bifurcation, y_0 and y_k are experimentally gathered to receive an estimate of the main effect β_{0-k}. As the minimal and maximal output of the model are used to calculate β_{0-k}, the respective value must be greater than zero (assuming $y_0 \neq y_k$) and thus is important by definition. To estimate the main effect each factor has or groups of factors have on the model's outputs and to identify the most important factors, the divide-and-conquer approach bifurcation pursues sequentially and systematically sets the values of input factors or groups of input factors to their *low* and *high* values.

The approaches' sequentiality is that after the effect of a group of factors is experimentally estimated, the following iteration splits the group with the highest identified effect into two new groups of factors and estimates their effects. Thus, in a second step, $y_{k/2}$ and accordingly $\beta_{1-k/2}$ as well as $\beta_{k/2-k}$ are determined and the respective importance of each group of factors is assessed. This procedure is then repeated until the most important factors are isolated and identified. An example of a potential resulting search tree is illustrated in Figure 6.11. In this example, β_4, β_8, and β_{12} were identified as most important factors. Together, these three factors explain more than 75% of the model's total effect ($\beta_{4-12} = 91.75$).

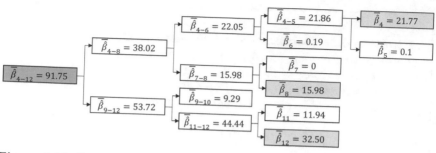

Figure 6.11: Search tree of application of sequential bifurcation (Lorig et al., 2017b).

Definition 6.19 (Sequential Bifurcation) $y_{(j)}$ *is defined as the output of the model, when*

- *factors 1 to j are set to their* high *value and*

- *factors $j + 1$ to k are set to their* low *value.*

Based on this, $\beta_{j'-j}$ with $j > j'$ is defined as the sum of main effects of the factors $j' - j$ and $\bar{\beta}_{j'-j}$ as the average main effect calculated from $n > 1$ replicates with

$$\bar{\beta}_{j'-j} = \frac{\sum_{r=1}^{n} \beta_r}{n} \text{ and } \beta_{j'-j} = \frac{(y_{(j)} - y_{-(j)}) - (y_{(j'-1)} - y_{-(j'-1)})}{4}$$

where $y_{-(j)}$ is the mirror observation of $y_{(j)}$ and $j', j, k, n \in \mathbb{N}$.

Accordingly, $y_{(0)}$ and $y_{(n)}$ with $y_{(0)} < y_{(n)}$ define β_{1-n}, the aggregated main effect.

In practice, it must be assumed that in most models the factors do not independently influence the model's output. Instead, often interactions exist between the factors. Sanchez (2007) illustrated such interactions and respective challenges this results in. Taking the example of the "Capture-the-Flag" game, where two opposing teams try to sneak up to the other team's flag to steal it and escape with it, she pointed out the importance of the obvious factors *stealth* and *speed* (cf. Figure 6.12). Measuring the success of a team based on low and high values for the factors speed and stealth, it can be observed that low speed and low stealth do not lead to success in the game. Likewise, neither high speed and low stealth nor high stealth and low speed will result in a successful capture of the enemies flag. However, the combination of high speed and high stealth makes the team win the game. This implies, that an interaction exists between the two factors. This is not detectable by one-at-a-time factor screening approaches. Even though sequential bifurcation might identify the importance of the group that contains both factors (if they are by chance located in the same group), dividing the group will make the observable effect vanish as the factors are no longer simultaneously set to their high values.

Speed	Stealth	Success?
Low	Low	No
High	Low	No
Low	High	No

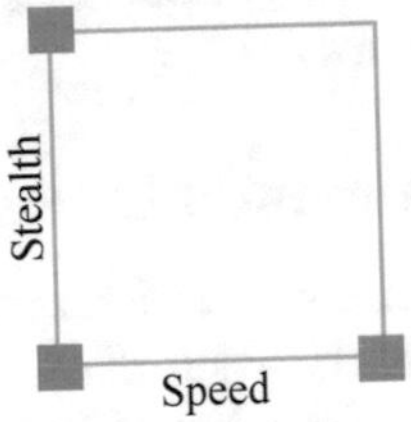

b. One-at-a-time sampling effects

Figure 6.12: Design matrix of a one-at-a-time sampling applied to a *capture the flag* simulation model (Sanchez and Wan, 2012).

Numerous extensions of the approach were proposed to take this and other restrictions of the initial sequential bifurcation approach into account. Some extensions of the sequential bifurcation approach take interactions between factors into account (Wan et al., 2010; Kleijnen, 2015). Examples are *sequential bifurcation for two-factor interactions* or *fold-over designs* (Kleijnen, 2008). As discrete-event simulation and the approach presented in this work focus on stochastic simulations, *Controlled Sequential Bifurcation* must be emphasized which extends sequential bifurcation by hypothesis-testing to control error and power (Wan et al., 2006).

Kleijnen noted, that a major shortcoming of sequential bifurcation is the lack of suitable software (Kleijnen, 2009). Therefore, he encourages the development of software for simplifying the application of sequential bifurcation in simulation experiments. He places especial stress on the sequential context switches between simulations and calculations that are required when applying and conducting sequential bifurcation. Thus, to facilitate the integration of sequential bifurcation in simulation studies, the automated exchange of runtime information between the model and the screening algorithm is reasonable. After initializing sequential bifurcation, its further procedure does not need to be supervised. The algorithms for estimating the main effects are defined and respective simulation runs can be executed automatically based on a parametrization that is defined by sequential bifurcation.

To conclude, factor screening in simulation provides promising approaches for the identification of important factors. Such information regarding the simulation model is required for the intelligent assistance presented here. By this means, the sparsity-of-effects principle can be taken into account. The identification of important factors allows for a more targeted and efficient investigation of the parameter space that influences a specific performance measure of the model.

6.3.2 Experimental Design

After a set of important factors was identified, the next step in a simulation study is the identification of relevant experiments and runs. As described in Section 6.1.2, the number of factors in simulation models is usually too large to cover the entire parameter space when analyzing the behavior of a model in a simulation study. To overcome this issue, the identification of important factors is a first step towards the limitation of the parameter space. However, the number of levels per identified relevant factor might still be too large to cover the entire parameter space and to simulate all resulting factor-level combinations. Furthermore, factors that were not identified as important might still have a minor impact on the performance measure. This is why the systematic and justified selection of one or even multiple levels for each factor is important with respect to the soundness of the study and its results.

Design of experiments comprises approaches (*experimental designs*) for planning scientific experiments. The aim of experimental designs is to facilitate the systematic, efficient, and methodologically sound specification of experiments. In simulation, such techniques can be used for the methodologically-grounded selection of parametrizations that are applied to the model during the study. The definition of experiments depends on both the research hypothesis which ought to be answered by the simulation study as well as the estimated importance of the model's factors. Accordingly, experimental designs provide a sampling of investigated values for all input variables of the model that are not explicitly defined by the hypothesis but are still of importance for the sound observation of the model's behavior. For this purpose, this subsection focuses on the combination as well as the formal specification of experimental designs for answering research questions in Hypothesis-Driven Simulation Studies.

Definition 6.20 (Experimental Design) *An experimental design (ED) is a set (design matrix) that systematically defines all observations (design points) of a model's behavior where*

- $L_1 = (1, ..., l_1)$ *defines the levels of the first factor $x_1 \in X$,*

- $L_2 = (1, ..., l_2)$ *defines the levels of the second factor $x_2 \in X$,*

- $L_k = (1, ..., l_k)$ *defines the levels of the k-th factor $x_k \in X$,*

- $R = (1, ..., n)$ *defines the replications of each design point.*

Thus, for a model with two factors x_1 and x_2 it follows:

- $\forall i = 1, ..., l_1, j = 1, ..., l_2, k = 1, ..., n \ \exists \eta_{i,j,k} \in ED$ *and*

- $|ED| = l_1 \cdot l_2 \cdot n$ *with*

- $l_1, l_2, l_k, i, j, k,$ *and* $n \in \mathbb{N}$.

The parameter space of a model defines the maximum possible number of factor-level-combinations (cf. Definition 6.20). Based on this, experimental designs systematically define those factor-level-combinations, which are applied to the model as parametrizations in a simulation study (*design points*) (Montgomery, 2013). For each input variable (*factor*) x_i of a model M, a set of admissible values (*levels*) $\mathbb{D}_i$ exists (cf. Definition 6.2). The number of levels for the 1st factor $x_1 \in X$ is l_1, for the 2nd factor $x_2 \in X$ it is l_2, and l_k for the kth factor $x_k \in X$. The following definitions refer to *two-factor designs* where only two factors (x_1 and x_2) are processed by the experimental design. When initializing and executing a model with a specific factor-level-combination according to a defined design point $\eta_{i,j} \in ED$, the corresponding observable output (response) Y of model M is defined as y_{ij}. Here, factor x_1 is set to level i and factor x_2 is set to level j with $i = \{1, ..., l_1\}$ and $j = \{1, ..., l_2\}$.

In stochastic simulations, n is the estimated number of required replications for statistical certainty. Accordingly, y_{ijk} is defined as the output Y of model M when factor x_1 is at level i, factor x_2 is at level j for the k-th replication of the parametrization with $i = \{1, ..., l_1\}$, $j = \{1, ..., l_2\}$, and $k = \{1, ..., n\}$. When the same factor-level-combination is simulated multiple times $(n > 1)$, μ_{ij} is the arithmetic mean of all respective y_{ij}, i.e., the mean of the ij-th cell of the design matrix shown in Figure 6.13. Making use of this aggregation of responses for equal parametrizations in probabilistic simulation, experimental designs can be defined by their *means model* (cf. Definition 6.21). For this purpose, the model's response y_{ijk} is defined via a metamodel as the sum of μ_{ij} and a respective error term ϵ_{ijk}. Commonly used experimental designs are the 2^k factorial design or *Latin Hypercube Sampling*.

Definition 6.21 (Model Response) *According   to   Montgomery (2013), the model's responses that are observed based on an experimental design (ED; cf. Definition 6.20) are defined by a* means model *so that for each design point $\eta_{i,j,k} \in ED$ the observed response can be described by*

$$y_{ijk} = \mu_{ij} + \epsilon_{ijk} \begin{cases} i & = 1, ..., l_1 \\ j & = 1, ..., l_2 \\ k & = 1, ..., n \end{cases}$$

with

$$\mu_{ij} = \frac{1}{n} \sum_{k=1}^{n} y_{ijk}$$

and the random error component ϵ_{ijk} for $l_1, l_2, i, j, k, n \in \mathbb{N}$.

Experimental designs are not limited to two factors. For each further factor, the definitions can be extended by the respective factors. Accordingly, *three-factor designs* are a simple extension of two-factor designs by a third factor x_3 (Montgomery, 2013). In this case, the new third factor $x_3 \in X$ consists of l_3 levels and the total number of observations increases to $l_1 \cdot l_2 \cdot l_3 \cdot n$ for probabilistic models. y_{ijmk} is the model's response when factor x_1 is at level i, factor x_2 is at level j, factor x_3 is at level m for the k-th replication of the parametrization with $i = \{1, ..., l_1\}$, $j = \{1, ..., l_2\}$, $m = \{1, ..., l_3\}$, and $k = \{1, ..., n\}$. For more than three factors, the extension of the experimental design is implemented similarly.

	Factor x_2: 1	2	...	l_2
Factor x_1: 1	$y_{111}, y_{112}, ..., y_{11n}$	$y_{121}, y_{122}, ..., y_{12n}$	...	$y_{1b1}, y_{1b2}, ..., y_{1bn}$
2	$y_{211}, y_{212}, ..., y_{21n}$	$y_{221}, y_{222}, ..., y_{22n}$	...	$y_{2b1}, y_{2b2}, ..., y_{2bn}$
...	...	...	...	...
l_1	$y_{a11}, y_{a12}, ..., y_{a1n}$	$y_{a21}, y_{a22}, ..., y_{a2n}$	...	$y_{ab1}, y_{ab2}, ..., y_{abn}$

Figure 6.13: General design matrix and corresponding results for a two-factor factorial design (Montgomery, 2013).

Experimental designs consist of $l_1 \cdot l_2 \cdot ... \cdot n$ independent observations and the order in which the observations are made is not specified. In this regard, Lattner et al. (2011a) presented two fundamental strategies that provide an order in which the observations are made: *replication-based execution* and *parameter configuration-based execution* (cf. Figure 6.14). This is relevant for stochastic simulations. If all required replications per run are executed for each parametrization, the generated results have a high statistical reliability. However, the response surface is investigated gradually and remains incomplete during the execution of this strategy. Another approach is to iteratively simulate one iteration per parametrizations to receive a first vague impression of the shape of the resulting response surface as soon as possible. In this case, the statistical certainty of the results is achieved as multiple iterations (replications) are performed.

The most basic experimental design is the *full factorial design*. As the name implies, the full factorial design consist of all possible factor-level-combinations of a model. This provides highest-confidence results and thus is well suited for analyzing the entire parameter space of a model. Yet, Sanchez and Wan (2012) compared full factorial designs to a brute force approach and emphasize its inefficiency for models with a large number of factors.

In practice and in terms of computational complexity, this is only applicable if the model consists of a small number of input factors and a small number of levels per factor. Hence, in case information on the interaction of a large

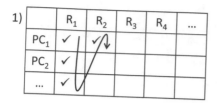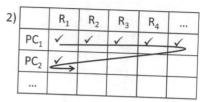

Figure 6.14: Orders for performing simulation runs with different parameter configurations (PC): 1) replication-based execution and 2) parameter configuration-based execution (Lattner et al., 2011a).

number of factors in a more complex model is required, the range of factor levels must be limited. An example of an *fractional factorial design* with limited factor levels is the 2^k *factorial design* where only two levels per factor are considered, i.e., a *low* (-1) and a *high* (+1) value (cf. Definition 6.22). The process of normalizing the levels of each factor to the domain $[-1, 1]$ is referred to as *coding* (cf. Table 6.2) (Natrella, 2012). For the application of this design, and with respect to the quality of the generated results, the type of factors must be considered. While the 2^k design works well with a smaller number of quantitative factors, it is not well-suited for qualitative factors. In case the number of levels is limited ($m \leq 10$), the m^k design can be applied instead (Sanchez and Wan, 2012). Here, m levels are investigated instead of only two levels as in the 2^k design.

Definition 6.22 (Experimental Design: 2^k factorial design)
According to Sanchez and Wan (2012), for two factors x_A and x_B with the low $(-)$ and high $(+)$ levels $\mathbb{D}_{x_A} = \{A^-, A^+\}$ and $\mathbb{D}_{x_B} = \{B^-, B^+\}$, the observations made by a 2^k factorial design

$$y_{ij} \text{ with } i \in \{1, 2\} \text{ and } j \in \{1, 2\}$$

are defined as

$$y_{11} = y_{A^-B^-}, \ y_{12} = y_{A^+B^-}, \ y_{21} = y_{A^-B^+}, \text{ and } y_{22} = y_{A^+B^+}$$

by a $k \times 2^k$ design matrix (cf. Table 6.2).

Considering a model with 10 factors and 10 levels per factor, the increase in efficiency provided by fractional factorial designs can be illustrated. While the uncontrollable amount of $10^{10} = 10{,}000{,}000{,}000$ design points needs to be analyzed in a full factorial design only $2^{10} = 1{,}024$ design points result from a 2^k factorial design. However, considering Sanchez's capture-the-flag example from the previous subsection (cf. Figure 6.12), reducing the parameter space by means of a fractional factorial design might result in a bias perception of the actual shape of the model's response that must be considered as well (Sanchez and Wan, 2012).

Table 6.2: Design matrix of a 2^k factorial design (Sanchez and Wan, 2012).

Design Point	Factor A	Factor B	Response
1	A^-	B^-	y_{11}
2	A^+	B^-	y_{12}
3	A^-	B^+	y_{21}
4	A^+	B^+	y_{22}

It is important to note that the low and high values of a factorial design must not be mistaken with the low and high values of factor screening approaches. In contrast to the factor screening terminology, where low or high is defined by the factor level's impact on the model's behavior, low and high levels in factorial designs represent numerically low and high values of the respective factor. This does not apply for factors whose values are nominally scaled as they cannot be sorted. In this case, low and high levels of the factor must be defined by the experimenter.

To overcome shortcomings in the coverage of the model's response of classical fractional factorial designs like the 2^k factorial design, more advanced designs need to be applied. A widely used and efficient design for models with a large number of factors and levels is the *Latin Hypercube Design* (Hernandez et al., 2012). It was developed with respect to reducing the variance when drawing samples but is also well suited as screening technique (Saliby, 1997). In contrast to 2^k and other m^k factorial designs, the *space-filling properties* of latin hypercube designs must be emphasized. Design points do not cover the model's response like a grid but can randomly cover any point on the entire response of the model. Thus, latin hypercube designs are well suited for visualizations and visual analysis of the model's input-output relations for a low number of dimensions.

For generating a random latin hypercube design, it is assumed that the probability distribution of the random input variables is known (cf. Definition 6.23). As a next step, the range of levels for each input factor of the model is divided into n parts (*stratum*) such that the probability of drawing a random sample from each segment is equal $(1/n)$ (McKay et al., 1979). Finally, a random value of drawn from each stratum which serves as design point. In practice, the selection of each stratum's median value is applied, which again results in a grid-like order of the design points (Hernandez et al., 2012). Based on the random values from or medians of the strata, the design matrix is generated columns-wise for each of the model's factors. For each column, a random permutation of the sampled levels of the respective factor is generated such that the values are randomly assigned to the n design points. Out of n^k potential design points, a latin hypercube design randomly selects a subset of n design points such that only one design-point is selected for each row and column (cf. Figure 6.15). The identification of an admissible design and the resulting optimization problem is related to the mathematical n *queens problem*. However, in this case, diagonals are not part of the search problem.

Definition 6.23 (Experimental Design: Latin Hypercube) *For each of the model's k random factors $x_1, x_2, ..., x_k$, the probability distribution is known. Based on this, the range of possible levels is divided into n intervals (*strata*) of equal probability $(1/n)$. For each factor, one random value is drawn from each interval.*

The design matrix (ED) of a Latin Hypercube Design is then represented by a $(k \times n)$ latin square such that each of the k columns consist of a permutation of the levels that were randomly drawn for the respective factor.

$$ED = \begin{bmatrix} \eta_{11} & \cdots & \eta_{1k} \\ \cdots & \cdots & \cdots \\ \eta_{n1} & \cdots & \eta_{nk} \end{bmatrix}$$

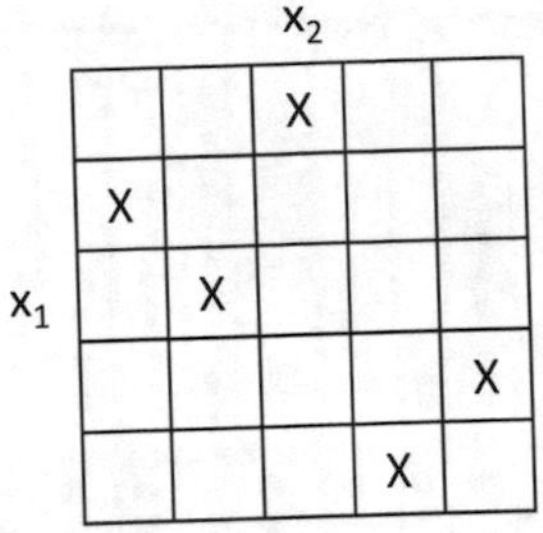

Figure 6.15: Latin hypercube design for two factors and five design points (Matala, 2008).

The result of this process is a $(k \times n)$ design matrix where specific factor levels of each of the k factors are defined for each of the n design points. In total, $(n!)^k$ possible designs exist (Joseph and Hung, 2008). To facilitate the process of generating valid latin hypercube designs, numerous algorithms exist, e.g, the *columnwise-pairwise algorithm* (Park, 1994).

Many helpful designs exist for the specification of simulation experiments. However, the identification and selection of adequate designs is challenging and depends on multiple criteria. To facilitate the determination of a design for a specific application, Sanchez and Wan (2012) presented different criteria for the differentiation of factorial designs and assess common designs accordingly (cf. Figure 6.16). Criteria include the number of factors, discreteness of factors, and the type of factors (e.g., controllable and uncontrollable factors). Especially with respect to the assistance of the design of experiments, a decision support that supports the selection of a well-suited design is valuable.

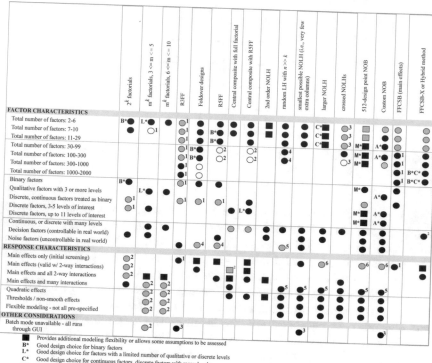

Figure 6.16: Comparison of different factorial designs (Sanchez and Wan, 2012).

6.3.3 Replication Estimation

The two previous steps of the design of experiments included the screening for important factors and the specification of design points for the execution of the model. This thesis focuses on the use of stochastic models for answering research questions by means of simulation studies. Thus, and in contrast to deterministic simulation models, equal parametrizations of the model do not necessarily result in the same observed values of the model's output variables. In contrast, a value from an (unknown) probability distribution is observed. To assess shape and density of this probability distribution and to estimate its mean value, multiple samples with different random number streams need to be drawn from the distribution to achieve statistical certainty. Thus, the required number of replications (*simulation iterations*) must be estimated during the process of a simulation study, i.e., how often the model needs to be executed and how many observations are needed.

In most simulation textbooks, *replication estimation* is part of the output analysis of simulation studies. This is reasonable, as many approaches provide an estimation of whether or not a performed number of simulation iterations is sufficient based on the respective output data (cf. Definition 6.24). In the approach presented in this thesis, the number of replications must be sufficient to draw conclusions while conducting as few simulation iterations as possible to ensure the efficiency of the study. When not conducting a sufficient number of replications, wrong conclusions might be drawn while a too large number of replications is inefficient as hardware capacities are needlessly utilized (Hoad et al., 2007). Thus, the ex post estimation whether or not a specific number of iterations is sufficient or not is not suitable as the system can not respond to it. Likewise, in a black box approach as pursued in this thesis, the estimation of the number of replications before executing the model is challenging due to a lack of information on the model and its behavior. It seems most reasonable to evaluate at runtime whether or not a sufficient number of iterations have been conducted. For this purpose, termination criteria must be defined before executing the model which define the required precision when checking if the number of replications is sufficient. The definition of criteria for replication estimation takes place before conducting the experiments. Hence, related approaches are presented and discussed as part of the design phase.

Definition 6.24 (Replication Estimation) *The required sample size of a simulation is defined as the minimum number (n) of independent replications of a simulation model that need to be executed to estimate the mean (μ) of the underlying probability distribution of an output (y_j) based on the mean value of n observations with a given satisfactory precision d_n.*

In accordance with Law (2014), Hoad et al. (2010a) formulated the underlying problem as follows: The goal of a simulation study is to estimate the mean value (μ) of a model's output (y_j), e.g., the mean waiting time of customers in a queuing model. For this purpose, the model is executed n times with the same parametrization to gather a set of output values $y_1, ..., y_n$ where output y_j is one independent and identically distributed observation of an output's value. For a large number of independent replications (n), it is assumed that the mean of a model's output variable or performance measure is approximately normally distributed. Thus, an increasing number of replications (n) results in the convergence of y_j to a normal distribution.

A statistical standard means for estimating the number of required replications are *confidence intervals*, which make use of this feature of simulation outputs. Other approaches for estimating the sample size of simulation iterations exist as well, e.g., the rule of thumb (Law, 2014) or graphical methods (Robinson, 2004). However, these approaches are highly subjective as the estimation of whether or not a number of replications is sufficient is made based on a user's subjective judgment and not based on objective measures or algorithms. Thus, both reproducibility and comparability of the results are limited. Banks (2014) proposed an automatable method for predicting the number of replications based on a small $(n < 5)$ initial set of observations. Yet, the sample size estimated based on this small dataset's variance might lead to an overestimation or underestimation of the required number of replications. While a response to an underestimation is the conduction of further replications, an overestimation is inefficient as too many replications are executed. Confidence intervals, in contrast, enable the user to specify a *precision* for the mean of the considered output variable. Furthermore, a *significance level* must be stated to define the probability of the sampling error. In this regard, a confidence interval for estimating the mean value of the probability distribution of a simulation model's output variable with a specific precision as defined in Definitions 6.25 and 6.26. To ensure that the precision remains within the defined bounds, an additional number of $kLimit$ iterations is performed when the precision is met.

Definition 6.25 (Confidence Interval) *For independent and identically distributed observations of the value of a model's performance indicator, a $100(1 - \alpha)\%$ confidence interval is defined as*

$$\bar{X}_n \pm t_{n-1,\alpha/2} \cdot \frac{S_n}{\sqrt{n}}$$

with the performance measure's mean $\bar{X}_n$, standard deviation S_n, and the Student t-distribution's quantile $t_{n-1,\alpha/2}$ for $n \in \mathbb{N}$.

Definition 6.26 (Confidence Interval: Precision) *To obtain a satisfactory estimate of the mean value, the precision (d_n) is defined as the percentage deviation of the confidence interval about the cumulative mean*

$$d_n = \frac{100 t_{n-1,\alpha/2} \cdot \frac{S_n}{\sqrt{n}}}{\bar{X}_n}.$$

Two shortcomings of the approach must be taken into account when applying confidence intervals for estimating the required number of replications in simulation studies (Hoad et al., 2007). First, due to a random sequence of similar observations that are all distant from the actual mean (outliers), the precision criterion might be met too early. This results in poor accuracy of the result (Heidelberger and Welch, 1981). In the presented approach, the precision (d_n) of the n-th iteration of the algorithm is defined as the half width of the confidence interval and stated as percentage share of the cumulative mean for easier understanding. According to Robinson (2004, p. 156), the precision "acts as a measure of the narrowness of the interval". With the help of an example, the authors illustrate that the number of required simulation runs increases considerably when decreasing the maximum permissible deviation: 3 replications for $<10\%$ deviation, 6 replications for

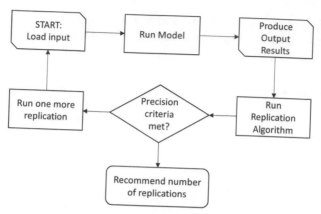

Figure 6.17: Sequence of the confidence interval replications algorithm (Hoad et al., 2007).

<5% deviation, and 12 replications for <3% deviation. Second, a small number of replications in combination with data that is not normally distributed might result in a coverage which is too low. To avoid this issue and to prevent biased results when automating the confidence interval approach for estimating the required sample size in a simulation study, Hoad et al. (2007) introduced the *replications algorithm* (cf. Figure 6.17).

The presented algorithm sequentially defines and executes replications of a specific simulation run until a termination criterion is met. To initialize the algorithm, the experimenter is required to provide values for the *level of precision* as well as for the *significance level* of the confidence interval. However, general standards for required threshold values do not exist and many disciplines defined minimal standard values. According to Hoad et al. (2007), the algorithm executes three replications of the simulation before calculating the confidence interval for the first time. In case the required precision ($d_{required}$) is not met after three initial runs, individual runs are performed until it is met. Once the required precision is met ($Nsol = n$), which might be the result of early and misleading convergence due to outliers, it is reasonable to analyze whether the precision criteria is met permanently and not violated during the following replications. For this purpose, an additional number of $f(kLimit)$ iterations is performed when $d_n \leq d_{required}$. If the precision of all $f(kLimit)$ iterations is less or equal to the required precision, $Nsol$ is defined as minimum required number of replications. A graphical representation of the results is shown in Figure 6.18.

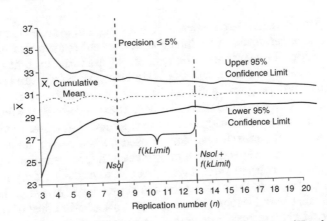

Figure 6.18: Graphical example of the replication algorithm (Hoad et al., 2007).

The shortcoming of the replication algorithm presented by Hoad et al. (2007) is that for some models it might take a long time until the required precision is met. Certainly for simulations where the execution of a single run takes a long time, this is unsatisfactory for the user as the remaining time cannot be assessed. To address this issue, Banks (2014) presented a formula for estimating the number of replications required to achieve a specific precision (cf. Definition 6.27). However, Hoad et al. (2007) concluded that $Nsol$ is not likely to be valid for $n < 30$. Still, as the number of replications increases, this formula provides an increasingly accurate estimate of the remaining number of replications until the precision is met. Another benefit of the presented approach is that its execution does not require human supervision after the definition of the threshold values.

Definition 6.27 (Iterative replication estimation) *According to Banks (2014), the sample size required to reach the desired precision (Nsol) can be estimated based on an estimate of the mean and the standard deviation of a simulation output:*

$$Nsol^* = \left[\frac{100 t_{n-1, \alpha/2} s_n}{\bar{X}_n d_{required}} \right]^2 .$$

This section presented approaches for assisting and automating the design of simulation experiments. This includes the screening for important factors, the application of experimental designs for systematically limiting the investigated parameter space, and the estimation of the required number of replications. With regard to the assistance of the automated conduction of Hypothesis-Driven Simulation Studies, these approaches allow for the identification and specification of required simulation experiments for answering the initial research question. Based on the performance measure, whose behavior under specific circumstances is hypothesized as part of the research question, relevant input factors can be identified and a set of factor-level-combinations can be defined for the experimentation, i.e., individual simulation runs. Furthermore, to ensure statistical reliability of the results for answering the research question, the number of required replications can be estimated automatically as well. This enables the assisted design of experiments that are required to answer the hypothesis.

6.4 Execution of Experiments

In the previous subsection, relevant experiments were designed which are required to decide whether to confirm or refute the study's initial hypothesis. As a next step, these experiments must be executed to observe the behavior of the model.

Experimentation in simulation studies consist of two aspects: the *execution of experiments* as well as the *management of experiments*. According to Maria (1997), important tasks for the *execution of the experiments* include the selection of the run length and the definition of appropriate starting conditions, e.g., the initial amount of customers in a queuing model. Besides the definition of specific starting conditions that require detailed model knowledge and the possibility to modify the model's state, warm-up periods might be required to realistically fill the model (Robinson, 2002). Furthermore, the random number stream used for the execution of the model is important with respect to the comparability and reproducibility of simulation runs (Uhrmacher et al., 2016). In addition to data and the model itself, the execution system (*framework*) is defined as part of the simulation's scenario. It is required to execute the model and to generate its behavior.

Finally, a thorough *management of the experiments* as well as of the generated data is necessary. One or more simulation runs with individual parametrizations of the model are derived from each designed simulation experiment. Each of these simulation runs can be seen as an individual simulation task which combines a scenario, consisting of the model, and a specific parametrization. This allows for the parallelization of the execution of simulation tasks. For this purpose, a central unit, e.g., a queue, is required for the collection and management of these simulation tasks and the respective results.

To facilitate and assist the conducting of experiments in simulation studies, three aspects are considered in this section: simulation frameworks for the execution of the model, the concept of a simulation queue for storing and parallelizing simulation tasks, as well as use and importance of random numbers.

6.4.1 Simulation Framework

As part of the assistance presented in this thesis, the experimenter provides only the model and a respective research question. Thus, for the automated execution of the model, the simulation framework must be part of the assistance, connected to the assistance, or accessible by the assistance (cf. Definition 6.28). This can be achieved by means of suitable wrapper classes or by using (standardized) interfaces that are provided by the frameworks.

Definition 6.28 (Simulation Framework) *The model execution function f (cf. Definition 6.10), which is implemented by model M, is executed by framework F. Accordingly, F generates the model's outputs based on a specific set of inputs and the model's execution function f.*

The simulation framework is accessed, executed, and controlled by the assistance via wrapper classes. An individual wrapper class must be developed for each framework. To execute a model by means of a wrapper class, the framework must at least provide the following interfaces or functionalities:

- *specification or reference of the simulation model to be executed,*

- *specification of the parametrization of the model,*

- *functionalities to start and stop the simulation run,*

- *and an interface to return the outputs of the simulation.*

In this thesis, NetLogo serves as an example framework for the specification and evaluation of the presented approach. It is an established framework that was first released in 1999 and is still maintained (release of version 6.0.4 in June 2018). NetLogo focuses on agent-based simulation, does not require advanced modeling and simulation skills, and still enables the construction of complex models (Abar et al., 2017). The model building is further facilitated by a comprehensive graphical interface that allows for the visualization of both the model execution as well as the evaluation of the results. Hence, it is well-suited for novices as well as experienced users. It is free to use (GNU General Public License) and includes an extensive library of example models from different domains.

NetLogo provides two ways of conducting experiments: with and without using the graphical interface (`headless`). With respect to the automation of simulation studies, the `headless` execution seems more suitable. Neither the assisted operation of the model, e.g., to parameterize the model, nor a graphical illustration of the model's outputs are necessary in such a system. Furthermore, the operation of a graphical interface has a negative impact on the performance of the simulation runs and unnecessarily slows down the execution of the model. Therefore, the headless option of NetLogo (`org.nlogo.headless.Main` class) is well-suited for the conceptualization of the assistance system.

When executing simulations in NetLogo by means of the `headless` option, six arguments can be specified (cf. Definition 6.29). The *model* (the path to the model) is mandatory as well as either the reference to a predefined experiment, which is part of the model or the path to a XML file that defines an experiment. By default, NetLogo does not display or save the outputs generated by the model. Still, they are required to analyze whether or not the hypothesis holds. For this purpose, either the *spreadsheet*, the more detailed *table* option, or both options can be used in case a logging of results was not implemented when building the model. Finally, the `headless` option of NetLogo allows for the definition of the number of CPU threads that shall be utilized by NetLogo to execute model runs in parallel. For the assistance that is specified in this thesis, this option is not relevant. The parallelization of model executions is managed globally by the experiment queue and is not subject to specific parallelization algorithms provided by the simulation frameworks. Thus, this option is set to 1 to disable parallel runs.

Definition 6.29 (Specification of Simulations in NetLogo) *The minimal requirements for the execution of simulations in NetLogo are:*

$$f_{NetLogo} : (model, (setup\text{-}file \oplus experiment),$$
$$(table \lor spreadsheet), threads)$$
$$\rightarrow (table' \lor spreadsheet')$$

with

– *model:* **nlogo** *model that shall be executed,*

one of the inputs

– *setup-file: XML definition of experiment,*

– *experiment: name of predefined experiment in the model,*

optionally one or both outputs

– *table': row-wise data of each run and step, chronologically sorted by the completion of the step (updating table),*

– *spreadsheet': column-wise data of each run, with aggregated and chronological step-wise results (updating spreadsheet),*

and the number of threads which defined how many runs are executed at the same time.

Besides the model, a specification of an experiment is required for conducting simulation runs. In NetLogo, experiments are defined in XML and consist of 4 attributes and 8 different types of elements (cf. Definition 6.30). The structure for specifying experiments in XML is defined by the provided `behaviorspace.dtd` file (cf. Code 6.2). Attributes define basic characteristics of experiments such as its name, in which order the runs are executed, and how the outputs are logged. Furthermore, the number of repetitions is statically defined and applied for each run of the simulation experiments.

Section 6.3.3 outlined the importance of a sufficient number of replications and introduced approaches for individually estimating the required number of replications. Yet, the specification of one sample size for all simulation runs of an experiment is neither efficient nor methodologically reasonable. To ensure the statistical soundness of each runs' results, the sample size of all runs must be equal to the number of replications estimated for the most extensive simulation run. Especially in simulation experiments where the required sample size of the runs varies greatly, this would result in the execution of unnecessary replications.

The decision whether or not to save the values of the output variables after each simulation step depends on both the model and the hypothesis. For example, in some models it is necessary to reset statistical measures after a specific warm-up period to eliminate bias resulting from an unrealistic under-utilization of the model.

Considering the elements for specifying experiments, there must be discrimination between elements to configure and execute the model that require detailed knowledge of the model's structure and elements for specifying the parametrization of the model. With respect to Hypothesis-Driven Simulation Studies, the latter group of elements is most relevant. *Stepped* and *enumerated value sets* define the factor levels that are tested in simulation runs. While stepped value sets define start and end values as well as the stepsize, enumerated value sets define a number of individual values. Furthermore, *time limits* and *exit conditions* can be set as required by the hypothesis.

Definition 6.30 (Specification of Experiments in NetLogo) *In NetLogo, an experiment $exp_{NetLogo}$ is defined by the following attributes*

- *name: unique identifier (name) of the experiment*
- *repetitions: the number of iterations for each simulation run*
- *sequentialRunOrder: whether or not the order of runs is of importance*
- *runMetricsEveryStep: whether or not the values of the output variables are logged after each step*

and elements

- *setup: procedure for initializing the model*
- *go: procedure for starting the simulation*
- *final: procedure which is executed at the end of each run*
- *timeLimit: number of steps before forced termination of simulation*
- *exitCondition: simulation terminates when this expression applies*
- *metric: output variables*
- *steppedValueSet: step-wise values of an input (e.g., 10 to 40 in steps of 5)*
- *enumeratedValueSet: specific values of an input (e.g., 10, 25, and 60).*

Code 6.2: Document type definition of NetLogo experiments (behavior-space.dtd[10]).

```xml
<?xml version='1.0' encoding='us-ascii'?>
<!ELEMENT experiments (experiment*)>
<!ELEMENT experiment (setup?,go?,final?,timeLimit?,
 exitCondition?,metric*,(steppedValueSet|enumeratedValueSet)*)>
<!ATTLIST experiment
 name CDATA ""
 repetitions CDATA "1"
 sequentialRunOrder (true|false) "true"
 runMetricsEveryStep (true|false) "true">

<!ELEMENT setup (#PCDATA)>
<!ELEMENT go (#PCDATA)>
<!ELEMENT final (#PCDATA)>

<!ELEMENT timeLimit EMPTY>
<!ATTLIST timeLimit steps CDATA #REQUIRED >
<!ELEMENT exitCondition (#PCDATA)>
<!ELEMENT metric (#PCDATA)>

<!ELEMENT steppedValueSet EMPTY>
<!ATTLIST steppedValueSet
 variable CDATA #REQUIRED
 first CDATA #REQUIRED
 step CDATA #REQUIRED
 last CDATA #REQUIRED>

<!ELEMENT enumeratedValueSet (value+)>
<!ATTLIST enumeratedValueSet variable CDATA
 #REQUIRED>
<!ELEMENT value EMPTY>
<!ATTLIST value value CDATA #REQUIRED>
```

---

[10]The DTD file that specifies XML experiment setups in NetLogo is part of the NetLogo.jar file that is provided by the NetLogo installer (https://ccl.northwestern.edu/netlogo/download.shtml [Retrieved Jul. 2019]).

An example of an XML definition of an experiment in NetLogo is presented in Code 6.3. The model, based on which this experiment was designed, simulates the spread of a virus in a human population. A certain percentage of a predefined number of people is infected with a virus and infects other people while moving around in an environment. The model can be used to analyze how the density of the population, different levels of infectiousness, chances to recover from the virus, and the timespan between infection and recovery affect the spread of the virus.

Code 6.3: XML specification of a simulation experiment for the NetLogo virus model (Wilensky, 1999).

```
<experiment name="exp1" repetitions="1"
runMetricsEveryStep="false">
<setup>setup</setup>
<go>go</go>
<timeLimit steps="100"/>
<exitCondition>%infected = 100</exitCondition>
<metric>count turtles with [ sick? ]</metric>
<enumeratedValueSet variable="infectiousness">
<value value="50"/>
<value value="60"/>
<value value="70"/>
</enumeratedValueSet>
</experiment>
```

NetLogo experiment `exp1` is specified by this XML file and consists of three simulation runs. Each of the runs is replicated only once. The values of the output variables are gathered after the simulation has terminated and not after each step. Both `setup` and `go` are functions provided by the model to trigger its initialization as well as its execution. A *time limit* of 100 steps implies that the model will at the latest terminate after 100 simulation steps have passed. In case the *exit condition* is met before, the simulation will terminate even though 100 steps were not yet simulated. In the presented experiment, an infection of 100% of the population will also result in the termination of the model as no further infections can occur. However, the model might also terminate independently and while none of the two criteria is met. Possible causes are internal termination criteria such as the eradication of the virus or an error that occurred during the execution of the model. *Metric* defines, which of the model's variables serves as output. The values of this variable are logged after each simulation run or even after every step of the simulation if required. Finally, the *enumerated value set* defines that three different simulation runs are executed and that the model is parametrized with three different values (50, 60, and 70) of the input variable `infectiousness`. The remaining input variables are set to their standard values, which are defined by the model.

Based on an XML description of an experiment and a runnable model, NetLogo executes simulation runs and returns the observed values of the output variables (metrics). Both the spreadsheet and the table format for exporting the outputs of the model save the data as CSV files where each row or column represents the (stepwise) output values of one simulation runs. Aggregation, advanced statistical processing, and interpretation of these results are not part of NetLogo's range of functions. It is limited to the indication of basic minimum, maximum, and mean values of the output variable or variables for each simulation runs. Thus, to draw conclusions from results generated using NetLogo, external tools must be utilized.

To use, integrate, and utilize a simulation framework as part of the simulation assistance, a wrapper class is required (cf. Definition 6.28). In the case of NetLogo, the minimal requirements for the execution of a simulation consist of two mandatory components: a model and a specification of one or many experiments. While the NetLogo model that is required for the simulation study is directly provided by the experimenter, the experiments are specified by the assistance and exist in a framework-independent format. For the use in NetLogo, the wrapper class must first convert these experiments into XML files that correspond to the NetLogo experiment specification standards (cf. Code 6.2). After executing all experiments, the NetLogo framework returns CSV output files that contain all results. All data from these files must be aggregated and converted into a unified format such that they can be processed by the assistance (cf. Figure 6.19).

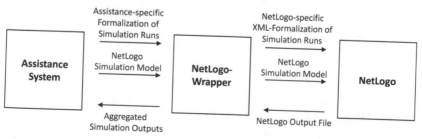

Figure 6.19: Integration of a simulation framework (NetLogo) into the assistance.

The simulation framework is an important component to execute the simulation models, to generate and observe the behavior of the model, and to record values of the output variables for further analyses. Even though some frameworks support the design of simulation experiments, this is no standard functionality of simulation frameworks. To execute experiments and to observe the behavior of the model under specific circumstances, both a runnable simulation model as well as a specification of an experiments must be provided in a format which is determined by the framework. Yet, the step of a simulation study in which experiments are conducted is not limited to the operation of a simulation framework. Especially in experiments where a large number of factor-level-combinations is simulated, the parallelization of simulation runs is reasonable. Even though some frameworks support the parallel execution if simulation runs, the approach presented in this thesis decouples conduction and parallelization of simulation runs by means of a central experiment queue. By this means, model-specific adaptations that allow for the parallelization are not required. With respect to parallel discrete event simulation, the synchronization of the distributed execution of simulation models is challenging so that results correspond to those received during the sequential execution of the model (Fujimoto, 2000).

6.4.2 Scaling and Parallel Execution of Simulation Runs

Simulation frameworks provide functionalities to execute simulation runs based on a specification of an experiment and the corresponding model. In simulation studies, a great number of simulation experiments and runs might be required to answer the initial research question. A reason for this is the large number of factor-level-combinations that results when multiple factors as well as multiple levels per factor must be considered.

Accelerating the efficient execution of simulation experiments is challenging and many common simulation frameworks perform poorly when scaling experiments (Lorig et al., 2015). These shortcomings often cannot be avoided by providing better simulation hardware such as more RAM and CPU cores. To reduce the time that is required to execute a model with all identified parametrizations, parallelization of simulation runs seems reasonable as no model specific adaptations are required. Both technical hardware limitations as well as issues related to the economic inefficiency of upgrading existing hardware can be overcome by this means.

Distributed systems are a possible approach for the parallelization of simulation runs. Yet, for parallelizing simulation runs with distributed simulation systems, queuing mechanisms must be provided to manage and distribute simulation tasks. In this subsection, metrics for measuring how simulation performs in scaled and parallel environments are presented.

When distributing simulation runs to a network of simulation servers, an allocation problem occurs. Usually, both servers and simulation runs differ in their capacities and requirements. Thus, to swiftly execute simulation runs while efficiently utilizing available hardware, criteria for solving the allocation problem are required. *Speedup* and *efficiency* can serve as indicators to compare different hardware configurations with respect to efficiently executing simulation runs (cf. Definition 6.31). Both measures are commonly used to assess the performance of parallel algorithms and systems (Eager et al., 1989). Pawlaszczyk and Strassburger (2009) proposed the application of these measures to quantify the performance of distributed simulations.

Definition 6.31 (Simulation Performance Metrics) *The* speedup *is defined as the ratio between the execution time of a simulation run in serial execution (Z_{serial}) and the execution time of the same simulation run in parallel execution ($Z_{parallel}$) with multiple CPU cores:*

$$speedup = \frac{Z_{serial}}{Z_{parallel}}$$

Based on this, efficiency *is defined as the ratio between the achieved speedup and the number of CPU cores that were provided for the parallel execution:*

$$efficiency = \frac{speedup}{\#CPU\ cores}$$

The *speedup* metric can be calculated when simulation runs are scaled to multiple CPU cores. When doing so, the effect a parallel execution of a simulation model has compared to the serial execution is measured and compared to the time that is required for the single-core execution. In practice, the ideal scenario (a linear speedup of 100%) can hardly be measured due to additional efforts that are required to distribute and coordinate parallelized simulation runs. In theory, values between 0% (doubling the number of CPU cores does not affect the execution time at all) and 100% (doubling the number of CPU cores halves the execution time) are possible. *Efficiency* is based on the speedup and is defined as the ratio between speedup and the number of used CPU cores. Accordingly, it is a measure for the utilization of the provided CPU cores. Negative values are possible as parallelization might also affect the execution time of a simulation run in a negative way.

With respect to the distribution of simulation runs and the efficient utilization of available simulation hardware, the two presented metrics can be used to measure how different simulation models and parametrizations of a model are affected by scaled hardware resources (Lorig et al., 2015). Accordingly, individual simulation tasks can be distributed to appropriate servers in a distributed system. By this means, each simulation run can be assigned to a well-suited server so that unused computation capacities are minimized while considering the potential for acceleration of each simulation task. To generate data for the calculation of the presented metrics, simulation models must be benchmarked using different hardware configurations.

6.4.3 Random Numbers

For the execution of probabilistic models, random numbers are required (cf. Section 2.2.2). It is challenging to generate random numbers from a specific probability distribution in a convenient and efficient way. In this regard, Law (2014) emphasized, that the phrase "generating random variables" is misleading as random variables are defined by probabilistic distributions. Instead, the process of generating random numbers as values of input variables should be referred to "generating random variates". For the purpose of generating a *random number stream*, *random number generators* are used, which produce a deterministic sequence of random numbers (L'Ecuyer, 2012). Yet, not all random number generators are equally useful and L'Ecuyer (2012) argued that results of simulation studies are meaningless in case a poor random number generator was used. Especially with respect to the replication and verification of simulation results, the generation of random variates must comply with methodological requirements. With respect to the sound integration of random number generators, this subsection specifies and discusses the concept of *random numbers* in simulation studies as well as the integration of *random number generators*.

Traditionally, random numbers are generated based on physical probabilistic processes such as throwing a dice, drawing numbers from an urn, or based on radioactive decay (Grimmett and Stirzaker, 2001). Such processes can be used for generating *real random numbers*. However, with respect to simulation studies, the generation of real random numbers is not feasible. For one thing, physical processes cannot be accelerated and they are cost-intensive. For another thing, the exact reproduction of such processes is often not possible unless the drawn random numbers are recorded thoroughly and the record is used for the reproduction of the simulation runs. In this case, an extension of either the model or the simulation is not possible as additional numbers from the same sequence cannot be drawn retrospectively.

To simplify the generation of streams of random variates, the use of *pseudo random numbers* is reasonable. Pseudo random number generators pursue a numerical approach for generating random variates. Just like real random numbers, good pseudo random numbers must fulfill statistical criteria such as *uniformity* and *independence* (L'Ecuyer and Simard, 2007). Yet, in contrast to real random numbers, they are both predictable and reproducible, which makes them well suited for the conduction of simulation experiments. With respect to conducting simulation studies, the benefits of real random numbers do not compensate their shortcomings which is why pseudo random numbers are used in the proposed approach. Furthermore, when referring to "random numbers" and "random number generators" in this thesis, and unless explicitly stated otherwise, the interpretation as pseudo random numbers is implied.

Definition 6.32 (Random Number Generator) *According to L'Ecuyer (1997), a* random number generator *(RNG) is defined by a sequence of* states *from a finite* state space S *with the transition function* $f \colon S \to S$ *and* $s_n = f(s_{n-1})$ *where* n *enumerates the steps with* $n \geq 1$ *and* $n \in \mathbb{N}$. *The initial state* $s_0 \in S$ *is also referred to as* seed *value of the RNG.*

The output of the RNG at step n *is* $u_n = g(s_n)$ *with the output function* $g \colon S \to [0,1]$ *and the output sequence* $\{u_n,\ n \geq 0\}$ *with* $u_n \in [0,1], u_n \in \mathbb{R}$.

As S *is finite, the sequence is periodic with periodic length* p, *where* p *near* $|S|$ *is desirable.*

Formally, a pseudo random number generator is defined by a state (s_n) from a state space (S) as well as a transition function $(f \colon S \to S)$ that calculates the following state based on a given state (cf. Definition 6.32). The initial state (s_0) of a random number generator is also referred to as the *seed value*. This value can be used to exactly reproduce a sequence of random numbers. As the state space of the random number generator is finite and as the transition function is defined for each possible state, the generated sequence of random numbers is periodic, i.e., repetitive and infinite. In this regard, it is desirable that the period length (p) of a random number generator is close or equal to the cardinality of the set of possible states (L'Ecuyer, 1997).

The output of a random number generator is a sequence of numbers in the real interval $[0, 1]$. The numbers of the resulting sequence are referred to as *random numbers*. To assess the quality of random numbers, the aforementioned criteria of *uniformity* and *independence* can be used (L'Ecuyer and Simard, 2007). The uniformity of a sequence of random numbers is given if the generated random numbers are equally distributed over the range of possible values. This can be tested by dividing the interval $[0, 1]$ into k equal groups. The chance, that a generated random number falls into one of these groups should always be $1/k$. A sequence of random numbers is independent if no relation exists between the individual numbers of the sequence. Accordingly, the probability that a random number falls into a specific group is not influenced by other random numbers that were previously drawn. Further tests for assessing the quality of random number generators were developed and published as part of the *diehard* and *dieharder* test suites (Marsaglia, 1997; Brown et al., 2013).

In simulations, random numbers that correspond to these criteria are referred to as *independent and identically distributed random numbers* (Law, 2014). Based on the real interval $[0, 1]$, such random numbers can also be described by a continuous uniform probability distribution ($U(0, 1)$). Yet, for most simulation models, random numbers from $U(0, 1)$ are not sufficient. They require a more advanced distribution of the generated random numbers.

In manufacturing simulations, the time required to assemble a product results from the time of each involved operation. *Normal distributions* are well suited for the representation of the underlying stochastic distribution of manufacturing times. In contrast to this, *exponential probability distribution* are appropriate to represent the time to failure of a machine in a manufacturing system (Biller and Gunes, 2010). Furthermore, a differentiation between *continuous* and *discrete* probability distributions needs to be made (Ross, 2013) (cf. Figure 6.20). While continuous probability distributions can (theoretically) produce any possible value $x \in \mathbb{R}$ within a defined range of values, the amount of observable values is exactly specified and finite for discrete distributions. In the case of manufacturing simulations, where the order quantity of a customer varies between 1 and 10 products, discrete

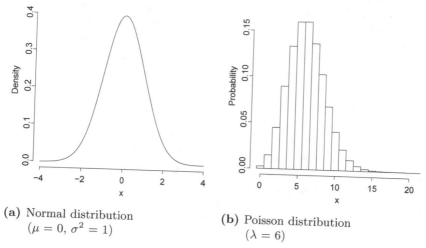

(a) Normal distribution
($\mu = 0$, $\sigma^2 = 1$)

(b) Poisson distribution
($\lambda = 6$)

Figure 6.20: Continuous (normal) and discrete (Poisson) probability distribution.

distributions (e.g., a *Poisson distribution*) can be used as only whole numbers of products exist.

Statistically, a probability distribution is defined by its *probability density* (cf. Definition 6.33). For a specific range of values, the respective *probability density function* specifies relative probability to observe a value from this range. This applies only for continuous random variables where it is nearly impossible to observe one specific value $x \in \mathbb{R}$. Discrete random variables, in contrast, are defined by a countable number of values. Thus, discrete random variables are specified by a *probability mass function* where the exact likelihood to observe value x can be obtained. For many probability distributions, the probability density function or probability mass function is dependent on further parameters which specify the shape of the respective function. The *normal distribution*, as an example for a common continuous probability distribution, is defined by its *mean* (μ) and its *variance* (σ^2). Thus, μ can be utilized to shift the probability density function along the x-axis while σ^2 vertically stretches or compresses the function (cf. Figure 6.21).

Definition 6.33 (Cumulative Distribution Function) *According to Abramowitz and Stegun (1965), the* cumulative distribution function F_X *of random variable X specifies, for a given x, the probability that X will generate a value less or equal to x with*

$$F_x(x) = P(X \leq x).$$

To construct random number generators for each required probability distribution and ensuring that they correspond to the quality criteria of uniformity and independence is challenging. It is more desirable to generate random variates from all required probability distributions based on random numbers from $U(0,1)$ for which the compliance with the criteria can be guaranteed. In simulation studies, the challenge of expressing probabilistic inputs by probability distributions is part of the *simulation input modeling* (Leemis, 1999). *Distribution fitting*, as respective technique, is applied to

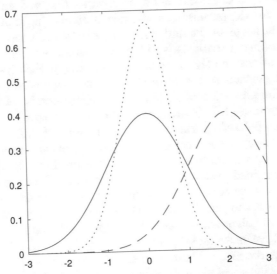

Figure 6.21: Comparison of the shape of the probability density function of normal distributions with $\mu = 0$ and $\sigma^2 = 1$ (solid), $\mu = 2$ and $\sigma^2 = 1$ (dashed), as well as $\mu = 0$ and $\sigma^2 = 0.6$ (dotted).

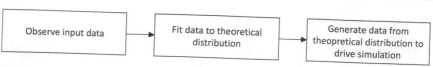

Figure 6.22: The role of theoretical probability distributions (Chung, 2004).

express a set of input data by a suitable probability distribution (Law and McComas, 2003). For the fitting procedure, parameters of common probability distributions, e.g., *Uniform, Lognormal,* or *Beta distribution,* are adjusted such that a satisfactory *goodness-of-fit* is achieved. By this means, well-suited probability distributions as well as respective values for the parameters of the distribution can be identified (cf. Figure 6.22). Collections of probability distributions as the one provided by Leemis and McQueston (2008) can be used for the fitting.

When applying distribution fitting to model more complex input data, e.g., input data that is not curve-, parable-, or line-shaped when plotted, highly sophisticated and uncommon probability distributions must be used in the fitting process. As this process is challenging, Law (2011) emphasized two common pitfalls that must be avoided to ensure the quality of the simulation: simply replacing a distribution by its mean value and using the wrong distribution. For the purpose of distribution fitting, the experimenter must be aware of the shape of the underlying distribution to consider respectively shaped probability distributions. This facilitates the identification of well-suited distributions and the removal of unsuitable probability distributions to reduce the runtime of the algorithm. Either way, it cannot be ensured that any of the selected probability distributions can be modified so that a specific goodness-of-fit is achieved. When comparing the goodness-of-fit of the most suitable parameter configurations of different probability distributions to represent a set of input data, relative scores are stated by commercial software products. Such software products provide a ranking of a set of predefined probability distributions as well as the most suitable parametrizations for each distribution. It is possible that all predefined distributions perform poorly due to the specific shape of the input data's distribution. In this case, one could say that such tools are only able to identify the "least unsuitable" probability distribution. When conducting simulation experiments, variations in the distribution's appropriateness to represent a specific set of input data can result in a model output error (Law, 2011). During the interpretation of the results of an experiment, this error induced by the input distribution needs to be taken into account as well.

Instead of fitting existing distributions, it is more desirable to define individual distributions that adequately represent the underlying dataset regardless of the shape of its distribution. This might be achieved by means of *numerical interpolation*. First, one must be able to model the shape of the input data's distribution as a high-order polynomial, e.g., by using splines or polygonal chains. In this step, it might be reasonable to divide the input data values into x classes and to calculate the relative probabilities that an observed values falls into each class. The resulting probability density function can then for example be interpolated by a polynomial of degree x. To proceed, it is important that the resulting function is normalized and integrates to 1.

As for all probability distributions, the generation of random numbers via a valid random number generator on $U(0, 1)$ is desirable. This can be achieved by means of *inverse transformation sampling* where random numbers are be generated from any probability distribution that is defined via a *cumulative distribution function* ($F_X \colon \mathbb{R} \to [0, 1]$; cf. Definition 6.33). Thus, to enable the generation of random numbers based on an individual probability density function, the corresponding cumulative distribution function is required. For continuous input variables, the cumulative distribution function is defined as the integral of the probability density function. Instead, the cumulative distribution function of the dataset can also be interpolated directly and from the relative probabilities of the defined classes. Based on the cumulative distribution function, the inverse transformation sampling method requires the calculation of the *inverse distribution function* (*quantile function*) such that $Q = F^{-1}$ and $Q \colon [0, 1] \to \mathbb{R}$. This enables the generation of random numbers from the interpolated density function of the underlying input dataset by means of random numbers drawn from $U(0, 1)$. The feasibility of a related approach has been shown for Monte Carlo simulations (Avramidis and Wilson, 1994).

For conducting of Hypothesis-Driven Simulation Studies and especially for the reproduction of results, the appropriate and replicable generation of random numbers is of high relevance. Both the selection of an adequate probability distribution that fits the distribution of the input data with sufficient accuracy as well as the generation of reproducible random number streams are important tasks with respect to conducting sound simulation studies. Thus, the random number service which is required to provide assistance must be capable of two tasks. The first task is the generation of random numbers as required by the model, e.g., by fitting common probability distributions or by generating custom distributions based on provided input data. The second task is the documentation of the generated random number stream. This can be accomplished by a detailed documentation of the random number generator which includes the applied cumulative distribution function as well as the specification and configuration of the underlying $U(0, 1)$ pseudo-random number generator including the used seed value. Alternatively, the list of generated random numbers can be stored. This is more simple than documenting the random number generator. However, the replication of simulation experiments is not possible in case the model has been changed and requires a larger stream of random numbers. An example of a service that allows for both generation and testing of random numbers with respect to simulation studies is the JAMES II add-on presented by Ewald et al. (2008).

6.5 Analysis of Experiments

After the design and execution of all relevant simulation experiments, the analysis of the observed data must be executed with respect to confirming or refuting the underlying research hypothesis is another essential part of the simulation study. To this end, this section specifies services that are required for analyzing simulation output data. Due to the separation of simulation experiments into multiple simulation runs with specific parametrizations of the model as well as the execution of multiple replication of each simulation run, the outputs of the iterations must be reaggregated before they can be analyzed by means of hypothesis testing. When aggregating simulation outputs, incorrect values such as outliers or missing values can occur, e.g., in case the simulation terminated unexpectedly due to an error that took place during runtime. Thus, before aggregating output values, a decision whether or not the output of a simulation iteration is included into the results or whether an output is substituted by another value must be made. Finally, statistical hypothesis testing approaches are be applied for determining whether the aggregated outputs provide sufficient evidence for confirming the initial research hypothesis.

6.5.1 Outliers and Missing Values

After all designed simulation experiments and the respective runs were executed, the generated results must be aggregated and analyzed. By this means, a data basis is generated that allows for the confirmation or refutation of the initial research hypothesis. Law (2008) emphasized that simulation output data must not be treated as abstract numbers. When aggregating simulation results, also the process of data generation need to be taken into account. This is especially important when observing unexpected values (*outliers*) or when values are missing. With respect to outliers, a thorough consideration of the simulation process allows for assessing whether the observed data is legitimate or whether it is a result of simulation or measurement errors. Either way, procedures for handling implausible or missing data points are required. This subsection presents methods for the *identification* as well as for the *handling* of outliers and missing values.

While the identification of missing values is simple, the identification of outliers in simulation output data results requires a definition in what case an observed value is considered as *outlier*. A statistical definition of outliers is provided by Hawkins (1980, p. 1):

> *"the intuitive definition of an outlier would be 'an observation which deviates so much from other observations as to arouse suspicions that it was generated by a different mechanism".*

In this regard, Hawkins (1980) discriminated between *inlying* and *outlying* observations such that the deviation of these values can be perceived as a large gap. Furthermore, he presents two possible mechanisms of drawing samples, which can lead to the observation of outliers. First, if samples are drawn from a distribution with a infinite variance (heavy-tailed distribution), values can be observed that differ greatly from the distributions mean value. Second, if observed data does not originate from a single but from two different distributions. In this case, the *"basic distribution"* is the one that should to be observed and the *"contaminating distribution"* generates outliers (Hawkins, 1980, p. 2).

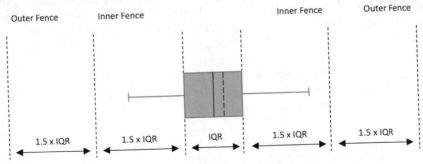

Figure 6.23: Landscape of a boxplot (Mohindra, 2011).

A more specific rule for the identification of outliers is the *1.5×IQR rule*, which is for example applied in boxplots (Moore et al., 2009). The rule makes use of the *interquartile range*, which is defined as the distance between the first and third quartile and in which 50% of the observations around the median fall. For this purpose, an *inner fence* and an *outer fence* are defined each of which each cover an area of 1.5 interquartile ranges starting from the first and third quartile (cf. Figure 6.23) (Schwertman et al., 2004). According to the *1.5×IQR rule*, observed values that lie outside the inner fences are *outliers* (Moore et al., 2009). Some authors distinguish between different types of outliers and refer to observations outside the outer fence as *extreme* or *far out outliers* (Schwertman et al., 2004). For the assisted detection of outliers, the EDAsim approach proposed by Bogon et al. (2012) provides respective functionalities.

In statistics, more advanced techniques for the identification of outliers exist. Those approaches make use of the 1.5×IQR rule for identifying potential candidates for outliers. In a second step, and depending on the number of identified potential outliers, different tests can be applied to verify whether those values are actual outliers. The most common test is *Grubbs' test for outliers*, which can also be iteratively applied for samples with multiple outliers. To apply this test, it must be assumed that the dataset can be approximated by a normal distribution. Outputs of simulation models are not in general identically and normally distributed (Law, 2014). Considering a queuing model of a service counter, the waiting time of a customer depends on the waiting time of the persons that stand in front of him or her. In stochastic simulations, the model is executed multiple times and a specific output is observed in multiple replications. In contrast to multiple observations of an output variable in one simulation iteration, the observations made over different iterations of the model are independent and identically distributed (Law, 2015). However, not all datasets that are independent and identically distributed are also normally distributed (Nakayama, 2008). Thus, to test whether a dataset is normally distributed, adequate tests must be applied first. Examples are the *Shapiro–Wilk test* or the *Kolmogorov–Smirnov test*. Due to its high power, the *Shapiro–Wilk test* should be preferred (Razali et al., 2011).

Definition 6.34 (Outliers) *According to Moore et al. (2009), an observed output of a simulation model is called* potential outlier *or* outlier candidate, *if it lies more than* $1.5 \times IQR$ *outside the first oder third quartile. Whether or not a potential outlier is an outlier can be tested by means of outlier tests (e.g., Grubbs' test), if the sample is normally distributed.*

After successfully identifying missing values and potential outliers, the next step consists of the handling of these data points. In this regard, different procedures were proposed in statistics, which include *imputation* (substitution of values) and *elimination* (removal of values). Imputation aims at replacing outliers or missing values with suitable values whereas elimination removes these data points without substitution. For the imputation of outliers or missing values, different statistical approaches exist such as *mean substitution* and *hot deck imputation* (Hawthorne and Elliott, 2005). After identifying a missing or outlying value, mean substitution calculates the mean value of all remaining valid observations for this variable and uses the calculated value as a substitute. In contrast to this, hot deck substitution selects a similar data records and substitutes the outlier or missing value with a random value from one of the similar datasets. With respect to simulation, a simulation run in which similar results were generated can be used as a basis for the application of hot deck substitution. Yet, approaches that assist or automate the identification and substitution of outliers and missing values in results of simulation studies could not be identified.

Outliers in simulation studies can be compared to survey errors in empirical studies. However, in simulation, the observation of outliers or missing values often result from implementation errors. The removal of such program errors within the model can be difficult due to a lack of skills or if the model is not accessible. Furthermore, ignoring these measured values is also not an option to maintain the statistical accuracy and soundness of the results. Accordingly, approaches for the substitution of outliers or missing values must be applied.

6.5.2 Aggregation of Results

When conducting a simulation study, sets of values of output (Y), intermediate (Y^I), and target variables (Y^T) are generated whose values provide information for answering a hypothesis (cf. Section 6.1.3). With respect to the analysis of the generated results, these values must be first aggregated to allow for the application of hypothesis testing approaches. This subsection presents challenges that occur during the aggregation of simulation outputs. Furthermore, it proposes a methodology to avoiding misinterpretations and the soundness of the results.

Output, intermediate, and target variables consist of three subsets, as all three types of variables may exist on three different levels of the study, i.e., for each experiment, run, and iteration. For example, output variables (Y) are gathered for each iteration of the simulation and can be summarized stepwise for both each run $(\bar{Y})$ and each experiment $(\tilde{Y})$. The same applies for intermediate variables (Y^I) and target variables (Y^T). For each iteration r $(r = 1, ..., u$ and $r \in \mathbb{N})$, a set Y_r is generated that contains aggregated values of the r output variables $\{y_{r1}, ..., y_{rn}\}$. All iterations of a run are executed with the same parametrization, while only the seed value used the generation of the random number stream differs. Thus, the sets of measured values of the output variables can be summarized by means of descriptive statistics, e.g., by determining central tendency and dispersion. By calculating mean and standard deviation of all values that were measured for each output variable over the total number of iterations, the distribution of the output variable can be estimated. The resulting summary of output data of run s $(s = 1, ..., v$ and $s \in \mathbb{N})$ is stored in set $\bar{Y}_s$. Here, each element $\{\bar{Y}_{s1}, ..., \bar{Y}_{sn}\}$ represents the statistical summary μ of each of the n output variable over all u iterations with $\bar{Y}_{si} = \mu(y_{1i}, ..., y_{ui})$ $(i = 1, ..., n$ and $i \in \mathbb{N})$. For each experiment, the set of summarized output values $\tilde{Y}_t$ is determined analogously based on the run data that have been summarized before (cf. Definition 6.35).

Definition 6.35 (Aggregation of Output Variables) *For each execution (iteration) r of the model, a set of output variables Y is observed:*

$$Y_r := (Y_{r1}, ..., Y_{rn}) \text{ from iteration } r \text{ with } r = i, ..., u \text{ and } r \in \mathbb{N}$$

$\bar{Y}_s$ *is a set of aggregated output variables from run s with $s = i, ..., v$ and $s \in \mathbb{N}$.*

$$\bar{Y}_s := (\mu(y_{11}, ..., y_{u1}), ..., \mu(y_{1n}, ..., y_{un})) = (\bar{Y}_{s1}, ..., \bar{Y}_{sn})$$

$\tilde{Y}_t$ *is a set of aggregated output variables from experiment t with $t = i, ..., w$ and $t \in \mathbb{N}$.*

$$\bar{Y}_t := (\mu(\bar{Y}_{11}, ..., \bar{Y}_{v1}), ..., \mu(\bar{Y}_{1n}, ..., \bar{Y}_{vn}))$$

Function μ that is applied for the aggregation of outputs is a statistical function of central tendency, e.g., arithmetic mean.

On each of the 3 layers (iteration, run, and experiment), target variables are defined and calculated by function g such that:

$$g(Y_r) = Y_r^T$$
$$g(\bar{Y}_s) = \bar{Y}_s^T \neq \bar{Y}_s^{'T}$$
$$g(\tilde{Y}_t) = \tilde{Y}_t^T \neq \tilde{Y}_t^{'T}.$$

Like output data, performance measures also exist for all three levels of simulation studies. In contrast to output data, the unreflected summarization of performance measures might lead to misinterpretations. On the iteration level, this phenomenon does not occur as target variables are directly derived from output data of each iteration. However, when summarizing values of output and target variables on run or experiment levels, the order of the performed steps is crucial for the generation of sound results. Intuitively, it seems appropriate to apply the summary function μ to the set of values of each output $\{y_1, ..., y_u\}$ and target variable $\{\bar{y}_1, ..., \bar{y}_v\}$. For the resulting summarized target variables this implies the application of $g(\mu(Y_r))$. In contrast, summarizing output variables first and then applying g for defining new target variables on the next higher level $(\mu(g(Y_r)))$ is also possible. In terms of *functional composition*, the commutativity of $(\mu \circ g)$ is only given by certain functions and under particular circumstances, which is why $(g \circ \mu) = (\mu \circ g)$ can not be assumed without thorough proof. Accordingly, $\tilde{Y}_s^T \neq \tilde{Y}_s'^T$ and $\tilde{Y}_t^T \neq \tilde{Y}_t'^T$ must be assumed where $\tilde{Y}_s'^T$ and $\bar{Y}_s'^T$ describe the set of aggregated outputs where g was applied before μ.

Thus, when applying the concept of target variables to evaluate the performance of simulation runs and experiments, the experimenter needs to be aware of how the target variables are defined and which conclusions the target variables allows for. With regard to the sound aggregation and interpretation of the model's outputs, Figure 6.24 provides an overview of permissible aggregations and transformations of output variables as well as of resulting intermediate and target variables. To facilitate the compliance with these dependencies the assistance is required to determine the correct order of aggregation based on the initial hypothesis. Depending on both the model and the formulated hypothesis on its behavior, a large number of runs and iterations might be required. As this easily results in a great amount of model output data, the assisted aggregation of these outputs is reasonable. This is not only to avoid mistakes made by the experimenter but also to relieve the experimenter of this monotonous task. Depending on the specified performance measure, the assistance can determine how to correctly aggregate generated output data to allow for the application of hypothesis tests.

6.5.3 Hypothesis Testing

With respect to a justified and statistically reliable confirmation or refutation of a hypothesis, *hypothesis testing* approaches are applied. As defined in Section 4.1.1, statistical hypotheses make an assumption about a not fully

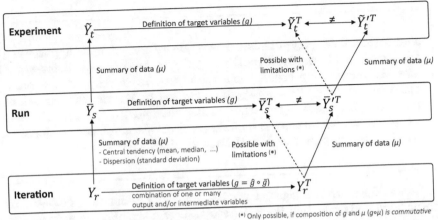

Figure 6.24: Multi-layer dependencies between output and target variables.

known probability distribution of one or many random variables (Moore et al., 2009). Statistical hypothesis tests aim at verifying such hypotheses by providing evidence for or against its validity. Due to the lack of information on the partially or totally unknown probability distribution, such approaches cannot verify hypotheses with absolute certainty. They must make use of a sample drawn from this probability distribution (population) to decide whether or not the hypothesis holds (Hanneman et al., 2013). This approach is referred to as *statistical inference*, where sample data is used to make and confirm propositions about a population, i.e., to draw conclusions about the overall population based on a sample. Inferential statistics stand in contrast to descriptive approaches, which only summarize information from a sample without the aim of deriving a theory.

The assumption made in a statistical hypothesis either focuses on the relationship between two datasets or compares the sample against an idealized dataset. The aim of hypothesis tests is to evaluate whether or not the hypothesized relationship between two datasets exists. Due to the uncertainty regarding the population of the distribution, the existence of the relationship can not be claimed with certainty. Instead, hypothesis tests assess whether the existence of the relationship is *statistically significant*, taking a probability threshold into account to observe a relationship even though it does not exist (Freedman et al., 2007) (cf. Definition 6.36).

Definition 6.36 (Hypothesis Test) *Based on a null hypothesis (H_0) and an alternative hypothesis (H_1), a hypothesis test investigates the relationship between two variables. In this regard, the null hypothesis assumes that no relationship exists between the variables while the alternative hypothesis assumes the opposite. In case the existence of the relationship is unlikely a result of chance, the results are significant with respect to a predefined significance level (α).*

To test for statistical significance, two mutually exclusive hypotheses are formulated and evaluated: the *null hypothesis* and the *alternative hypothesis*. It is necessary that the pair of hypotheses is formulated such that any possible observation is considered by either of the hypotheses. Under the assumption that the null hypothesis holds, i.e., that the hypothesized parameter of the distribution corresponds to the real population, hypothesis tests evaluate whether the probability for the outcome of the examination to be a result of chance is sufficiently small to assume that the alternative hypothesis is valid instead. Most commonly, a probability of ten, five, or one percent (the *significance level*) is assumed to be sufficiently small to reject the null hypothesis in favor of the alternative hypothesis (Moore et al., 2009). However, the selection of a required yet reasonable significance level (p) depends on the respective scientific discipline as well. While some empirical disciplines argue that $p < 0.05$ is sufficient, natural sciences often demand significance levels of 0.01 or even less (Lambdin, 2012). In this case, it is assumed that the observation of the hypothesized relationship is not a result of chance due to its unlikeliness under the assumption that the null hypothesis holds.

A large number of different statistical hypothesis tests exist and identifying an appropriate test for a specific hypothesis is challenging (Haq and Nazir, 2016). Common criteria to characterize and distinguish hypothesis tests include but are not limited to the number of samples, whether or not the samples are independent, and whether a parameter of the distribution or the distribution itself is tested. Additionally, the application of most tests is linked to preconditions that must be met to generate valid results. Both the *one sample t-test* and the *one sample Z-test* can be applied to test for the mean value of a distribution. Either of the tests requires the population to be normally distributed or that the *central limit theorem* applies, i.e., that the sample size is sufficiently large. Yet, while the *one sample t-test* assumes that

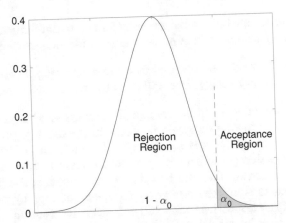

Figure 6.25: Significance level and rejection region in hypothesis testing.

the variance of the population is unknown, knowing about the population's variance is a precondition of the *one sample Z-test* (Montgomery et al., 2010). In summary, the application of statistical hypothesis tests depends on multiple factors such as the content of the hypothesis as well as the assumption of a particular distribution of the population.

The decision which hypothesis test to apply for evaluating the results of a simulation study strongly depends on how the hypothesis is formulated at the beginning of the study. An initial differentiation needs to be made according to the number of parametrizations that are part of the hypothesis. Here, two classes of hypotheses must be distinguished into: hypotheses that make an assumption about the model's behavior under *one parametrization* and hypotheses that make an assumption about how the model's behavior will change between *two or more parametrizations*. As statistical hypotheses tests require a statement about the relationship between two datasets, hypotheses whose parametrization part only consists of one input configuration of the model can not be tested without further information. A reference dataset is required, even though it might be artificial or idealized. Often when a hypothesis is stated with just one parametrization of a model as part of a simulation study, it is implied that the assumed behavior shall be compared to a standard or initial configuration of a model. Here, changes regarding the parametrization of the initial model can either be relative or absolute.

In the following, this difference is illustrated on the basis of a manufacturing simulation. It is assumed that the model's behavior, which is measured via the average processing time, is of interest in a simulation study in dependence of the number of machines that are used in the manufacturing process. A single absolute parametrization of the model could be formulated as follows:

If 17 machines are used in a manufacturing process,
the average processing time will decrease to 145 minutes or less.

The evaluation of whether the change of the number of machines is indeed the causal reason for the observed decrease in the average processing time is not possible based on this hypothesis. Instead, an additional dataset is required containing the average processing time before the number of machines was changed. This can be achieved by providing simulation results from experiments that were executed independently or by providing the mean value of the respective (artificial) reference distribution. Alternatively, the hypothesis can be extended so that a second parametrization is provided as reference value. The same applies, if the observed behavior is stated relatively, e.g., a decrease of the average process time by 10% is assumed, where a reference is required as well.

In contrast to this, a relative parametrization would assume the average processing time will increase or decrease as a result of an increased or decreased number of machines. Such a hypothesis could read as follows:

If the number of machines increases by 2,
the average processing time will decrease by at least 10%.

To apply hypothesis tests, further datasets are required. In this case, the definition of a reference dataset is more crucial with respect to the reproducibility of the results. It must be assumed that an increasing number of machines will not have the same linear effect on the processing time for all possible initial configurations of the model. While an increase from 2 to 4 machines is a 100% increase, the step from 100 to 102 machines is only an increase by 2%. Accordingly, it must be assumed that the average processing time will not decrease equally in both cases. Thus, either a specific reference value or a range of values must be defined along with the hypothesis. The range of values can then be evaluated stepwise from the minimal to the maximal value, e.g., the relative increase of the number of machines by 2 from starting from 10 machines up to a total number of 100 machines in steps of 5. Here, the definition of a more specific and unambiguous hypothesis is reasonable to avoid misinterpretations. This can be achieved by means of FITS (cf. Section 5.1).

For hypotheses whose parametrization part includes two or more configurations of the model, the task of generating reference datasets is less inconvenient. The datasets on which the hypothesis test is applied on are specifically defined and the required simulation runs can be derived directly from the hypothesis. A potential hypothesis with two parametrizations could be:

If the number of machines increases from 15 to 17,
the average processing time will decrease by 10%.

In this example, a dataset where the input variable *number of machines* is set to 15 and another dataset where this variable is set to 17 can be generated by means of simulation and under consideration of the challenges that arise from the segmentation and aggregation of experiments into runs and iterations (cf. Section 4.2.2).

To conclude, the conducting of hypothesis tests is essential for the assessing whether or not a hypothesized relationship between two datasets exists, taking the chance of random observations into account. In terms of simulation studies, hypothesis tests can be used to verify whether or not the behavior of the model that is assumed as part of the hypothesis can be confirmed based on the observed simulation outputs. In this regard, the selection as well as the application of an appropriate hypothesis test is challenging due to limiting preconditions that apply for most hypothesis tests. It is necessary to specify the study's research hypothesis as precisely and as comprehensive as possible such that the compliance with the preconditions of potential tests can be investigated. This includes in particular the statement of a reference scenario or value when only including one parametrization of the model in the hypothesis. FITS, the language that enables the formal specification of hypotheses in simulation studies, can be utilized to facilitate this process.

6.6 Conclusions

This chapter introduced formal specifications of all logical entities that are required for the assistance of Hypothesis-Driven Simulation Studies. In this regard, the focus of this chapter lies on the identification and definition of required functionalities rather than on the selection of specific approaches or methods. The presented entities can be divided into five groups according to the phase of the study they assist or automate. While the simulation model and the research hypothesis affect all phases of the study, other entities can be explicitly assigned to the design, conducting, or analysis of simulation experiments. Figure 6.26 shows all presented entities as well as the interactions between them.

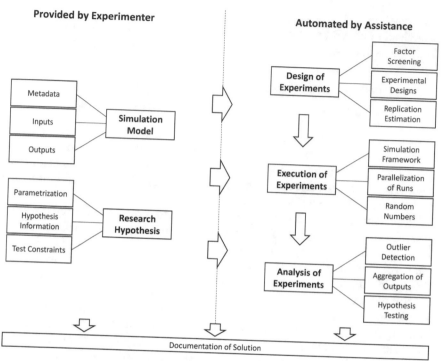

Figure 6.26: Logical entities for assisting Hypothesis-Driven Simulation Studies.

Both the simulation model and the research hypothesis must be provided by the experimenter. Based on these two entities, all necessary steps of the study are planned and conducted by the assistance. To enable the automated processing of these entities, this chapter specified the structure of the required data and information. For the simulation model, this includes metadata for the identification of the model as well as a specification of the inputs and outputs of the model, i.e., data types, range of admissible values, and labels. As the research hypothesis is usually provided by the experimenter in natural language, this chapter presented the machine-readable language *FITS*. It can be used to specify assumptions on the behavior of simulation models such that the assistance can automatically design and execute all experiments that are required to confirm or refute the hypothesis.

In the following steps of the simulation study, the active participation of the experimenter is not required. Instead, the following steps are automated by the presented assistance. Based on the provided hypothesis, this chapter introduced specifications of entities that are necessary to design relevant experiments. This includes the screening for important factors whose impact on the model behavior must be analyzed as well as the application of experimental design for the systematic investigation and limitation of the resulting parameter space. In this thesis, the evaluation of stochastic simulation models is pursued. Thus, it is necessary to estimate the required number of simulation iterations to achieve a desired level of statistical certainty. As a result of this phase of the study, the assistance proposes a limited set of model parametrizations that must be executed to provide evidence for or against the validity of the hypothesis.

Furthermore, this chapter specified entities that are required for the execution of the designed experiment. Most simulation models are developed using particular simulation frameworks. As these frameworks are usually also required for the execution of the model, unified interfaces must be provided such that the assistance can control the framework. In this thesis, the use of wrapper classes is proposed, which convert the designed experiments into a format that can be interpreted by the respective framework. Likewise, outputs that are generated by the framework are transformed to be processed by the assistance. To facilitate the parallelization of simulation runs in distributed systems, this chapter presented measures, which can be used to assess the effect parallelization and scaling has on the execution of the model. Yet, conducting simulation experiments is not limited to the execution and parallelization of given designs. With respect to the reproduction of the generated outputs, the random number stream that was used for the execution of a design is of utmost importance. The focus lies not only on ensuring the quality of the random number generator and the respective random number stream that is provided during the execution of the model must be ensured. Also the configuration of the generator must be documented, which includes the used seed values. In this regard, the automated parametrization, distribution, and execution of simulation models is a typical task for an assistance system.

Finally, the outputs which are observed during the execution of the model must be analyzed to allow for the verification of the study's research hypothesis. For this purpose, this chapter specified entities that are required for analyzing the results of the conducted experiments. Like in empirical studies, the quality of each individual observation of a study must be assessed before applying descriptive statistics for the interpretation of the results. Upon consideration of the outputs, outliers and missing values can be identified and a decision whether to include, substitute, impute, or eliminate respective values needs to be made. After the correction of the dataset, the output values of the simulation runs as well as of the respective iterations must be aggregated. This is done with regard to confirming or refuting the initial research hypothesis by means of statistical hypothesis testing. The results generated by the presented services serve as a basis for the interpretation of the simulation study's outcome. However, this task cannot or not entirely be accomplished by the assistance. Instead, the experimenter is provided with relevant data whose interpretation must take place in accordance with the real world.

The appropriateness of individual approaches or methods strongly depends on the scope of the study which is defined by the model and the corresponding hypothesis. This thesis presents a selection of components that are suitable for the verification of phenomenological hypotheses on the behavior of a simulation models. Yet, as part of future work, the development of mechanisms for the automated selection and combination of required components is desirable.

Part III

Application and Evaluation

7 Case Study: Supply Chain Management

The previous chapters proposed a methodology for Hypothesis-Driven Simulation Studies and specified the assistance of this process. Through this, a methodical frame for the systematic design, execution, and evaluation of simulation studies is provided, which allows for the replicable and reproducible verification of hypotheses on the behavior of simulation models. With respect to the feasibility of the presented approach, its quality must be evaluated first. Most methods and theories that were used for the development of the procedure model were deductively derived from established theories and approaches. It must be assumed that each of these entities has been evaluated and approved. Based on this, the contribution of this thesis lies in the identification as well as the logical combination of the individual entities. To ensure the applicability and suitability of the resulting integrated procedure model, this chapter evaluates the proposed approach in two case studies.

For this purpose of the evaluation, this chapter is structured as follows: First, a scenario is introduced for each case study. This includes the presentation of the used manufacturing simulation model, the definition of reasonable research hypotheses, and the ex-ante analysis of the model's response surface. Subsequently, the presented methodology for conducting Hypothesis-Driven Simulation Studies is applied to the two scenarios. To this end, also a conventional investigation of the model's behavior is conducted, which allows for the comparability of the generated results. Subsequently, the proposed procedure model is applied, the executed steps are presented, assisted design decisions are emphasized, and the results of the simulation study are illustrated.

7.1 Introduction of Simulation Model and Definition of Scenario

In this section, a model and a corresponding scenario are introduced based on which the entire process of Hypothesis-Driven Simulation Studies is applied, to evaluate the assistance presented in the previous chapter of this thesis.

© Springer Fachmedien Wiesbaden GmbH, part of Springer Nature 2019
F. Lorig. *Hypothesis-Driven Simulation Studies,*

With respect to the reproducibility of this evaluation, restrictions that are related to the framework must be considered when selecting a model. In this regard, it is desirable to chose a model which has been developed by means of a free-to-use framework. For the evaluation presented in this chapter, a NetLogo model of a supply chain is selected. Compared to other simulation frameworks, NetLogo is freely available, commonly applied by researchers, and easy to use. Likewise, the selected supply chain model can be accessed via the open NetLogo community repository *Modeling Commons*[11]. In contrast to other models, a supply chain model has numerous advantages, which are beneficial for this evaluation. Supply chains are a standard concept from economics whose operations and procedures are easy to understand. At the same time, effects and phenomena that occur in supply chains are sufficiently sophisticated to be investigated as part of a simulation study. Thus, as a foundation for the following case studies, this section introduces the simulation framework NetLogo as well as the selected supply chain model. Moreover, this section presents scenarios and related research hypotheses for the two case studies.

With respect to the reproducibility of all experiments and respective results that are conducted and generated during the evaluation, two major criteria must be met by the simulation model. First, the simulation model must be available for the public. One possibility is that models are hosted in a public repository for simulation data which does not require the user to login in order to download the model and whose availability is ensured for the near future. Simulation models are often provided via the website of a research group or via cloud services. It often shows that these download options are not persistently available as researchers change universities or institutes, leave the research sector, or files are removed from cloud storages due to inactivity. Second, the simulation framework which was used for the development of the simulation model should also be available freely and without any charges. In this regard, the licensing model of the simulation frameworks as well as the potential for maintenance must be considered. In particular, professional frameworks provide a large number of functionalities which results in high license fees.

7.1.1 NetLogo Simulation Framework

A large number of simulation frameworks was developed during the last decades. Many of these frameworks emerged from scientific research pro-

---

[11]http://modelingcommons.org/ [Retrieved Jul. 2019]

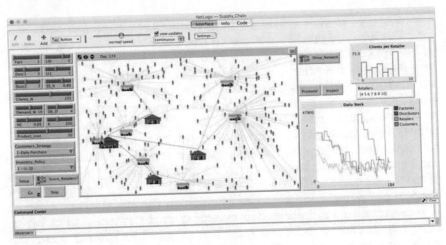

Figure 7.1: User interface of NetLogo (version 6).

jects and were developed by smaller research groups rather than by large companies. Thus, most simulation frameworks are free-to-use and often the sourcecode is available to either verify the correctness of the framework or to extend the framework with respect to specific needs. However, most simulation frameworks are only applicable for specific research domains and detailed knowledge is assumed for the operation of these frameworks. Multi-purpose and domain-independent frameworks that were developed considering the ease of use are often distributed with a commercial background and subject to a payment model, i.e., AnyLogic, Rockwell Arena, Siemens Plant Simulation, or Simio. Considering free-to-use frameworks only, *NetLogo*[12] is a common simulation frameworks. The first version of NetLogo was published by Uri Wilensky in 1999 and currently the 6th major release of NetLogo is available under the GPL licence. As the framework is written in Java, it can be executed on any platform that supports the *Java virtual machine*. The developers describe NetLogo as a "multi-agent programming language and modeling environment for simulating complex phenomena" (Tisue and Wilensky, 2004, p. 2). It can be used in research as well as in education across various disciplines and on different education levels. Therefore, NetLogo is well-suited for the evaluation of the approach presented in this work. It is not limited to specific domains and can be used for the exchange of knowledge between disciplines.

---

[12]http://ccl.northwestern.edu/netlogo/ [Retrieved Jul. 2019]

In NetLogo, models consist of three components: *interface, info,* and *code.* The interface provides a visual representation of the modeled *world* as well as optional controls (cf. Figure 7.1). The model's world is represented by a 2-dimensional grid on which each agent is located. To improve the understanding of the model, agents can be visualized as shapes or icons and relationships between agents can be illustrated as connecting lines. By means of optional control panels, the values of input parameters can be set, events can be triggered, and output values can be observed. If implemented, this facilitates the experimentation with the models as parametrizations can be easily changed to observe the resulting behavior. The *info* section of the model consists of user-defined text fields in which the developer of a model can provide additional information on the model. The developer is encouraged to add information regarding what the model is trying to show, rules the agents follow, what the user might notice when executing the model, or parametrizations the user should try when executing the model. Additionally, technical information should be provided such as a description and explanation of the model's interface, information on how to extend the model, and a reference to netlogo specific features that are utilized by the model. Finally, the developer might reference related models, scientific papers that are related to the model, or a website.

The code section contains the source code of the model and its logics. NetLogo models are written in the *Logo* programming language, which is related to the functional programming language *Lisp.* The language was developed for educational purposes and pursues a procedural approach (Feurzeig, 1969).

NetLogo's stand-alone desktop version as well as the browser-based web version provide access to a model library from which a large amount of sample models from different disciplines. This includes a selection of sample models from natural sciences like Biology, Chemistry, and Mathematics, but also from humanities such as Philosophy and Social Science. Additionally, NetLogo provides the *Modeling Commons Repository* where users can upload their NetLogo models to make them available to the public.

7.1.2 Supply Chain Simulation Model

For the purpose of this evaluation, the "Supply Chain" model by Alvaro Gil is chosen (Gil, 2012). It is available via the modeling commons repository and can be downloaded without the need of a registration. To provide an overview, the model's metadata is presented in Table 7.1.

Table 7.1: Metadata of the supply chain model according to Gil (2012) (part 1/2).

Object	Item	Entry
Identifier	Model Name	Supply Chain
	ID	
	Date of Creation	2012
	Version	1
	Citation	Gil, Alvaro (2012). Artificial supply chain. École Polytechnique de Montréal.
	Initial Model	-
Responsibility	Full Name	Alvaro Gil
	Mail Address	alvaro.gil@polymtl.ca
	Postal Address	École Polytechnique de Montréal, Montréal, Canada
	Affiliation	Department of Mathematics and Industrial Engineering
	Phone	-
Description	Abstract	This model is an artificial market with four types of participants. The model can help students and professionals to understand better the supply chain with a single product, and how simple changes as the promotions, can affect the stocks levels and the demand calculation with a considerable amplitude, which is know as the bullwhip effect.
	Keywords	logictics, supply chain
	Related Work	-
	Related Models	-

Table 7.2: Metadata of the supply chain model according to Gil (2012) (part 2/2).

Object	Item	Entry
Description	Instructions	The user should fix some values and play the model (I recommend at least 720 periods for having some stable results), then collect statistics and play again. Different values will result in different costs and stock levels which can be compared in the analysis and conclusions phase.
Requirements	Platform	NetLogo 5.0
	Operation System	Windows, Mac OS, Linux
	Programming Language	Logo
	Software Requirements	-
	Hardware Requirements	-
	Expertise	-
Files	Model Files	Supply_Chain.nlogo
	Data Files	not required
	Documentation Files	part of the model
	Additional Files	Jama-1.0.2.jar; matrix.jar; Supply Chain.png; table.jar

In its basic form, a *supply chain* consists of a number of independent firms that are involved in the manufacturing of a product. Materials and components that are required for the manufacturing process of the product are processed and passed forward by these firms. The resulting chain of firms, which reaches from raw materials to the final product, is then referred to as supply chain (La Londe and Masters, 1994). Simulation models of supply chain facilitate the comprehension of supply chain processes as they can be used for studying occurring phenomena. This includes an advanced understanding of the effect minor changes of the process have on individual components of the supply chain. These effects often result from slightly changed purchase strategies, which affect the stock levels and demand calculations of other participants and have major impact on the behavior of the entire supply chain.

One of the most common effects in supply chains is the *bullwhip effect* (cf. Figure 7.2). Forrester (1961) first described the delayed reaction of inventories to incoming orders. As a result of this, minor variations in the demand of low-level participants of the supply chain escalate at higher levels and result in major variations and inconsistencies of order and production quantities (Lee et al., 1997). Ultimately, the occurrence of the bullwhip effect leads to an inefficiency of the entire supply chain (Kurbel, 2013).

The supply chain model by Gil was built using NetLogo version 5.0. For the purpose of this thesis, it was upgraded to NetLogo version 6.0 using built-in conversion functionalities. The model describes an artificial market in which goods are traded between four types of participants: *consumers*, *retailers*, *distributors*, and *factories*. Each of the participants purchases and consumes the traded products in accordance with common supply chain mechanisms (cf. Figure 7.3). Customers have a specific demand and purchase products from the retailers following individual stock keeping strategies. This can occur in periodical or irregular intervals depending on when the stock of the customer falls under a specific reorder level. Depending on the quantity of sold products, retailers individually forecast their demand as well and purchase products from distributors. The distributors behave exactly as the retailers and forecast their demand based on the quantity of products requested by the respective retailers. As a last step of the supply chain, factories produce products when their stock falls below a specific level.

In this model, each participant has only one purchase relationship to the next-higher level, i.e., a consumer only purchases from exactly one retailer and a retailers only purchases from exactly one distributor. However, retailers, distributors, and factories can supply products to multiple vendees. By this means, a four-tier supply network emerges in which only a few

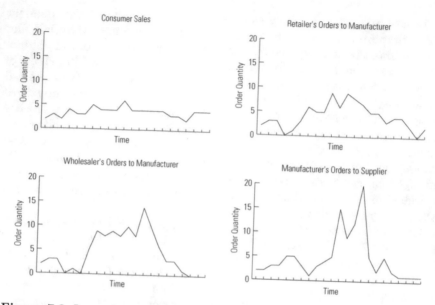

Figure 7.2: Increasing order quantity in supply chains (Lee et al., 1997).

Figure 7.3: Relationships between customers, retailers, distributors, and factories.

central nodes (factories) supply the demand of a large number of consumers via intermediate layers of retailers and distributors. Depending on the number of factories, this supply chain model may consist of multiple disjoint supply networks. When the model is initialized, relationships between the participants are defined with regard to the distance between the participants so that each consumer is linked to its closest retailer et cetera. However, this initial network configuration is subject to change in case of delivery problems during the simulation.

The model implements a step-wise simulation where each step represents one business day (cf. Figure 7.4). To generate the model's behavior, a sequence of tasks is executed for every simulated day. It consists of multiple tasks for each participant in the supply chain. Additionally, the model consist of 14 input parameters, which can be used to configure the circumstances of the supply chain execution such as the number of customers or their purchase strategy (cf. Tables 7.3 and 7.4).

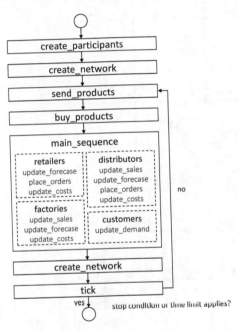

Figure 7.4: Procedure of the NetLogo supply chain simulation model.

Table 7.3: Parameters of the NetLogo supply chain model by Gil (2012) (part 1/2).

Parameter	Description	Min. value	Max. value	Step size	#Possible values
Fact	Factories	1	5	1	5
Distr1	Distributors	#Fact (min. 1)	#Fact * 6 (max. 30)	1	30
Distr2	Retailers	#Distr1 (min. 1)	#Distr1 * 4 (max. 120)	1	120
Clients_N	Customers	#Distr2 (min. 1)	#Distr2 * 50 (max. 600)	1	600
Lt0	Lead time (Distributors)	0	7	1	7
Lt1	Lead time (Retailers)	0	7	1	7

Table 7.4: Parameters of the NetLogo supply chain model by Gil (2012) (part 2/2).

Parameter	Description	Min. value	Max. value	Step size	#Possible values
Demand_W	Mean Demand	5	30	1	26
DS_D	Standard Deviation (Demand)	0	Dem_W / 2 (max. 15)	1	15
HC	Holding cost	0.01	0.1	0.01	10
K	Cost per order	50	400	50	8
Product_cost	Cost per product	5	50	5	10
Customers_Strategy	Purchase strategy of customers	1-Daily Purchase 2-Periodically Purchase	3-Random		3
Inventory_Policy	Inventory strategy of retailers and distributors	1 - (s, Q) 2 - (s, S)	3 - (R, S) 4 - Random		4

The procedure that is implemented by the model follows a static pattern. As a first step of the simulation, the products that were ordered in previous steps of the simulation are delivered by the vendors to the respective vendees (*send_products*). The lead time of distributors ($Lt0$) and retailers ($Lt1$) are equal for all participants and defined via model parameters. In a second step, the customers purchase new products according to their demand and their current stock (*buy_products*). Whether or not a consumer purchases goods on a specific day is determined by its purchase strategy (*Customers_Strategy*). Finally, demand, forecast, and costs are updated for each participant and orders are placed if required (*main_sequence*). Customers only have one task (*update_demand*). They update their demand according to a normal distribution (*Demand_W*) and a corresponding standard deviation (DS_D).

In contrast to customers, retailers, distributors, and factories have multiple tasks. They update their expectations regarding the number of products that will probably be purchased in the next step of the simulation (*update_forecast*). For the purpose of this forecast, they make use of extrapolation and linear regression. At this step, safety values of the stock ($SS\_\%$) are taken into account. In accordance with the forecasted quantities, retailers and distributors determine the optimal order quantity considering holding cost and order cost with respect to their inventory policy (*Inventory_Policy*). The optimal quantity is then calculated using the economic order quantity formula (Harris, 1990). In a next step, orders are placed and costs are updated with respect to the current situation (*place_orders* and *update_costs*). Holding costs are calculated as the product of holding cost (HC), current stock, and product cost (*Product_cost*). Order cost (K) do not have to be calculated as they are provided as model parameter. Accordingly, the total costs results from the sum of both holding and order cost.

To execute the model and to analyze its behavior, the developer recommends the simulation of at least 720 periods (*steps*). This includes a warp-up phase and allows for the observation of unbiased outputs. One period or step of the model corresponds to one business day in the real world. Accordingly, the recommended number of periods is equal to almost two years. In this calculation, the year consist of workdays only. Weekends, holiday seasons, and vacations are not taken into account.

In case simulation experiments are executed with respect to this advice, the developer of the model recommends the observation of the stock levels of the different types of participants. Even though the stock levels differ between the participants, the pattern the stock levels follow are similar and the bullwhip effect can be observed (cf. Figure 7.5).

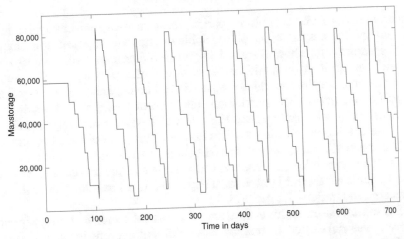

Figure 7.5: Variations in the maximum storage capacity of a factory in the NetLogo supply chain model over 720 days ($Lt0 = 4$, $Lt1 = 4$, $K = 400$, $SS\_\% = 0.7$, $Demand\_W = 30$, $DS\_D = 7$, $HC = 0.1$, $Client\_N = 263$, $Product\_cost = 30$, $random\text{-}seed = 19890206$).

7.1.3 Scenario and Research Hypothesis

To evaluate the proposed procedure model for Hypothesis-Driven Simulation Studies, a scenario as well as a research hypothesis are must be provided by the experimenter in addition to the simulation model. The following two case studies assume an experimenter, which is a researcher in the domain of logistics. Out of many potential disciplines, the choice of logistics seems reasonable for this thesis due to the experience of the work group from which this thesis originates. As part of earlier work, the group participated in the *AssistSim* project, which focused on the automation of simulation studies in logistics (Lattner et al., 2011a). By choosing a logistics context for this evaluation, research questions from this project can be taken up and results can be compared.

The NetLogo manufacturing model that was introduced in Section 7.1.2 can be used to investigate whether and how different factors influence the occurrence and intensity of the bullwhip effect in a four-tier supply chain. By this means, the model can be utilized as a serious game. It enables the user to experience the effect different stock and purchase strategies might have on order quantities of different types of participants in supply chains. However, the presented model can also be used for scientific investigations such as the search for an optimal parametrization with respect to minimizing or maximizing a specific output variable or the investigation how changes of the parameters affect the model's performance measures. An example of such an application could be the attempt of a participant of a supply chain to analyze the maximum required storage capacity. For the purpose of this investigation, the participant might want to simulate how different circumstances affect order quantities and which storage capacity is sufficient to store the traded products. To allow for the generation of sound and reliable results, such questions should be answered by means of a simulation study. This subsection presents a scenario for such a simulation study as well as a testable research hypothesis. They serve as a basis for the evaluation presented in Sections 7.2 and 7.3.

The scenario used in this evaluation assumes that a model of a supply chain process was developed to analyze how different factors influence specific performance measures (cf. Section 7.1.2). For the development of the model, the NetLogo simulation framework was used and verification as well as validations techniques were applied to ensure the model's adequacy with respect to the use in simulation studies. The model is available and executable without the need of further data or applications. It must be initialized and executed with a parametrization that assigns specific values to each of the model's inputs.

A simulation study of a supply chain model likely has a goal that is related to the acquisition of information a decision maker requires to manage existing or plan future scenarios. The simulation model presented in the previous subsection focuses on the observation of the daily stock level of customers, retailers, distributors, and factories. A reasonable goal of a simulation study that examines this model is the investigation of how changes of the model's inputs affect the stock levels of each of the participants. As an indicator for the efficiency of a specific configuration of the model, the maximum stock level in a specific period of time seems to be reasonable. It provides information about the required storage capacity, which is a key variable with respect to cost effectiveness. To this end, a potential research question that was introduced as part of the *AssistSim* is whether a specific storage capacity is sufficient in case of changing circumstances, e.g., increasing volume of orders (cf. Section 5.1.1).

As a goal of a simulation study, it is desirable to understand which circumstances lead to the requirement of large storage capacities to reduce or prevent their occurrence. This is especially relevant for the factory that participates in the supply chain. It must be assumed that fluctuations in demand affect the factory's production volume the most and thus also the required storage capacity. With regard to identifying how different factors influence the storage capacity of the factory, this subsection presents two possible assumptions that can be evaluated by means of a simulation.

The first assumption supposes a direct dependency between the number of customers and the maximum storage capacity. It is formulated so that a stable threshold of the performance measure will not be exceeded in case the value of a defined input remains under a specific level. About the behavior of the remaining inputs of the model, no assumption is made.

> **Assumption 1**: *In the modeled supply chain, a maximum storage capacity of 60,000 units is sufficient for the factory, if the number of customers does not exceed 150.*

The second assumption hypothesizes an interdependency between the values of one of the model's inputs and the defined performance measure. Altering the demand of the customers (*Demand_W*) will systematically affect the maximum storage capacity. Unlike the first assumption, no specific values or dimensions are stated. Instead, *disproportionality* is the only mentioned criterion that specifies the dependency.

> **Assumption 2**: *In the modeled supply chain, the customer demand and the maximum storage capacity required by the factory interdepend so that an increase of the customer demand results in a overproportional increase of the maximum storage capacity per customer.*

Considering the published version of the model, the maximum storage capacity, which is used as performance measure in both assumptions, is not initially provided. However, it can be calculated based on the output *daily stock* as the maximum value returned during the execution of the model. Modifications of the model are not required and accordingly the black box assumption is not violated that is pursued in this thesis.

To enable the systematic and reproducible identification, design, execution, and evaluation of simulation experiments, the formulation of an assumption regarding the behavior of a model is not sufficient. With respect to the method presented in this thesis, a testable hypothesis needs to be specified first (cf. Section 4.1.1). The testability criterion of a hypothesis aims at the indication of specific values for the application of statistical hypothesis testing techniques. Furthermore, the hypothesis must be structured so that one or many premises are logically linked to a conclusion. Following this structure, a hypothesis that is formulated in natural language can be formally specified by means of the FITS language (cf. Section 6.2). This allows for the automated execution of the steps that are required to provide evidence for or against the validity of the initial assumption. Based on the aforementioned assumptions, potential corresponding hypothesis can read as follows:

Hypothesis 1: *If the number of customers increases to 150, the factory's required maximum storage capacity of will be less than 60,000 units.*

Hypothesis 2: *If the average customer's demand increases by 10 units, the required maximum storage capacity of the factory will increase by more than 100 units per customer.*

In contrast to the initial assumptions, hypotheses must be reduced to comprehensible and testable *if-then*-statements. Moreover, specific values have to be provided for the application of hypothesis tests. In this regard, it is also essential that hypotheses are formulated such that the statement can only be true or false. Additionally, sufficient information must be provided to determine in which case the statement is true or false. With respect to the significance of the result, it is essential that the observation of a specific model behavior is unlikely a result of chance. This can only be ensured, in case relevant experiments are properly identified and executed.

It is challenging to identify those parametrizations of the model that must be evaluated by experiments to prove or disprove a research hypothesis. Considering the ranges of admissible values of each of the model's inputs results in a total number of $19,813,248,000,000,000$ (1.98×10^{-16}; 19.8 quadrillion) possible design points that constitute the model's response surface. It is apparent, that the scale of the response surface is too large to allow for the complete analysis of the model's behavior. Accordingly, a limited and more manageable subset of inputs values is specified and considered as scenario. Instead of analyzing different quantities of factories, distributors, and retailers, this chapter only investigates one specific configuration. With respect to the assumptions presented in this section, this enables a more realistic investigation. A decision maker most likely has one specific supply chain configuration in mind when conducting a simulation study. Customer strategy and inventory policy are predetermined as well. In this scenario, customers purchase products on a daily basis and all participants apply the (s,Q) inventory policy (cf. Table 7.5). Finally, the number of customers (*Clients_N*) is further discretized such that the new step size of 25 reduces the amount of possible values from 250 to 15. By this means, a reduction of the parameter space by factor $324,000,000$ is achieved and $61,152,000$ possible design points remain.

Table 7.5: Parameter values of the scenario used for the evaluation.

Parameter	Min. value	Max. value	Step size	#Possible values
Fact	1	1	1	1
Distr1	3	3	1	1
Distr2	7	7	1	1
Clients_N	25	350	25	15
Lt0	0	7	1	7
Lt1	0	7	1	7
SS_%	0.5	0.95	0.5	10
Demand_W	5	30	1	26
DS_D	0	3	1	4
HC	0.01	0.1	0.01	10
K	50	400	50	8
Product_cost	5	50	5	10
Customers_Strategy	1 - Daily Purchase			1
Inventory_Policy	1 - (s, Q)			1

In summary, this subsection limited the parameter space of the presented NetLogo model and presented two assumptions that can be analyzed by means of simulation experiments. Additionally, a potential resulting research hypothesis was specified for each assumption. Each of the two hypotheses formulates the corresponding assumption as an inferential link such that it can be tested by means of statistical approaches. The resulting scenarios are used in the following sections to evaluate the approach presented in this thesis. In this regard, the limitations and reductions are not part of the simulation assistance. Their purpose is to define the scenario of the study as well as the parameter space of the model for the two presented case studies.

7.2 Scenario 1: Maximum Required Storage Capacity

The first scenario presented in this evaluation addresses hypothesis 1 as stated in the previous section. To investigate the hypothesis that the factory's required maximum storage capacity of less than 60,000 units is sufficient if the number of customers (clients) increases to 150, a simulation study is conducted in accordance with the Hypothesis-Driven Simulation Study methodology proposed in Chapter 5. In this section, all steps that are required for confirming or refuting this hypothesis are executed as specified by the assistance, i.e., the design, execution, and analysis of relevant simulation experiments. This section provides detailed insights into how the proposed intelligent assistance can facilitate and control the entire procedure based on the provided hypothesis. Important design decisions are outlined, generated datasets as well as interim results are presented, and hypothesis tests are applied. By this means, the replicability of the conducted simulation study is increased to facilitate the reproduction of the presented results.

The described scenario requires the application of a *one-tailed hypothesis test*, more specifically a *lower-tailed test*, for verification of the formulated assumption. Thus, the null and alternative hypothesis must be formulated as follows. As the investigated assumption states that less than 60,000 units of storage capacity are required, it is defined as an alternative hypothesis. Complementary to this statement, the null hypothesis states that the storage capacity is not sufficient.

$$H_0: \mu \geq 60{,}000 \qquad\qquad H_1: \mu < 60{,}000$$

To initialize the assistance, both an executable model and a respective experiment hypothesis must be provided by the user of the assistance. The first requirement is met, since a simulation model from an open repository is used, which can be executed by the NetLogo simulation framework. Thus, to meet the second requirement, a formalized and testable hypothesis must be generated from the assumption that exists in natural language only. This hypothesis must express both null and alternative hypothesis as defined above. For the formal specification of research hypotheses on the behavior of simulation models, the FITS language was introduced. Transferred to and specified in FITS, a possible formalization of the natural language hypothesis could read as follows:

$$Clients\_N(150) \wedge \#$$
$$\Rightarrow \mu(\text{Maxstorage}) \wedge (H_0(\mu \geq 60{,}000) \vee (H_1(\mu < 60{,}000)) \mid$$
$$\alpha(0.05) \wedge n(d_n \leq 0.05)$$

Unlike the static definition of a sample size, which was presented upon the introduction of FITS, a dynamic replication estimation is applied here as proposed by Hoad et al. (2010a). Accordingly, n is specified as $d_n \leq 0.05$, implying a sample size such that a precision of at least 5% is achieved.

Moreover, the performance measure *Maxstorage* is not provided by the original version of the simulation model. Still, one of the model's outputs represents the factory's storage capacity after each step of the simulation. To derive the maximum storage capacity from this output, the maximum value of the factory's storage capacity output over all simulation steps must be determined as target variable, i.e., Maxstorage = max(storage capacity).

7.2.1 Conventional Investigation of the Model's Behavior

To evaluate whether the results that are generated by the approach proposed in this thesis are plausible and sound, a conventional investigation and discussion of the model's behavior is provided in advance. For this purpose, this section analyzes the influence the selected factors and their ranges of admissible values have on the model's behavior. The investigation is conducted by means of standard features that are provided by NetLogo, i.e., the *BehaviorSearch* tool for exploring the parameter space of a model with heuristic optimization methods.

Parameter Space of the Model

As a first step, an analysis determines whether the observed behavior of the model can be attributed to one or many of the model's inputs or if it is the result of chance. By systematically searching for minima and maxima in the response surface of the simulation model, dependencies between input values and observed model behavior can be identified. Hence, conclusions can be drawn regarding the importance of the inputs with respect to their ability to influence the behavior of the model. The identification of dependencies between factor levels and observed model behavior is valuable to further limit the considered parameter space and to focus on specific areas that provide evidence for or against the initial assumption.

The automated exploration of parameter spaces of simulation models is the primary goal of the *BehaviorSearch*[13] tool. Initially, BehaviorSearch was implemented as a stand-alone tool that enables the application of genetic algorithms and other mathematical optimization techniques for searching parameter-spaces and for approximating or identifying local and global optima. Since NetLogo version 6.0.1, BehaviorSearch is an inherent part of the NetLogo framework and provided upon installation. BehaviorSearch pursues a four-step approach to explore the parameter-space of NetLogo models. First, the user is required to define a measure by which the behavior

---

[13]http://www.behaviorsearch.org/ [Retrieved Jul. 2019]

of the model can be assessed in a quantitative way. This corresponds to the definition of a performance measure as it is required by the presented Hypothesis-Driven Simulation Study approach. Second, admissible values or ranges of values must be specified for each of the model's input parameters. A reasonable size of the parameter-space that is defined during this step is a trade-off between two criteria: *precision* and *computational cost*. Narrow parameter-spaces result in a faster termination of the search algorithm as optima are found more quickly. However, the n-dimensional grid of design points that results from the specified parameter values might not include relevant optima in case the grid cells are too wide. In contrast to this, the specification of a parameter space that consist of a large number of design points might cause the search algorithm to not properly identify optima due to a lack of computational power. As a third step, either one of the four pre-implemented search algorithms (*genetic algorithm, hill climbing, simulated annealing,* or *random search*) can be selected or a custom algorithm can be added. After this step, the exploration of the parameter-space takes place in an automated way and relevant experiments are designed and executed by the BehaviorSearch tool. To accelerate the execution of the experiments, the parallelization of different experiments is reasonable at this step. Finally, the results are presented in tabular form and in different granularities. This includes files that contain the full results of each simulation step and run but also excerpts that only contain the final best results of each run.

The first and second step of the BehaviorSearch procedure are model-specific. For the first step, the definition of a quantitative measure that is utilized to measure the model's behavior, the *maximum storage capacity* is required. Instead of the maximum value, the model only provides the storage capacity of the current time step. Hence, the overall maximum value (MAX_ACROSS_STEPS) must be extracted from the time series of storage capacity data. To define the parameter space in the second step, the range of values that are admissible by definition of the model is chosen. For $Clients\_N$ and $Demand\_W$, the number of admissible values is limited in accordance with the defined scenario to avoid the over representation of these factors (cf. Table 7.5). This results in the adapted search space, which is shown in Table 7.6.

For the third step, the definition and execution of the search algorithm, specific parameters of the search need to be stated (cf. Table 7.7). The inconsiderate definition of some parameter values might result in incorrect results. For example the specification whether the objective of the search algorithm is to maximize or minimize the fitness function or the collection of the performance measure as median, mean, maximum, or minimum across

Table 7.6: Specification of the parameter's search space for BehaviorSearch.

Parameter	Search Space
Fact	[1]
Distr1	[3]
Distr2	[7]
Clients_N	[25 50 75 100 100 125 150 175 200 225 250 275 300 325 350]
SS_%	[0.5 0.55 0.6 0.65 0.7 0.75 0.8 0.85 0.9 0.95]
Lt0	[0 1 2 3 4 5 6 7]
Lt1	[0 1 2 3 4 5 6 7]
Demand_W	[5 7 9 11 13 15 17 19 21 23 25 27 29 30]
DS_D	[0 1 2 3]
HC	[0.01 0.02 0.03 0.04 0.05 0.06 0.07 0.08 0.09 0.1]
K	[50 75 100 125 150 175 200 225 250 275 300 325 350 375 400]
Product_cost	[5 10 15 20 25 30 35 40 45 50]
Customer_Strategy	["1-Daily Purchase"]
Inventory_Policy	["1 - (s, Q)"]

the simulated steps. Other parameters can also bias the results if they are not defined with due regard to simulation principles. Examples are the number of replications per parameter configuration that is evaluated by the search algorithm or the evaluation limit that terminates the search.

BehaviorSearch provides four pre-implemented search algorithms: *standard genetic algorithm, mutation hill climber, simulated annealing,* and *random search* (cf. Table 7.8). Genetic Algorithms adapt the idea of natural selection and make use of historical information to direct the direction of search (Russell et al., 2010). Hill climbing is inspired by the idea of ascending an unknown mountain by searching for the steepest way for each step. In case all possible steps result in a descent, a local maxima was found. This algorithm is well-suited if only one maximum or minimum exists. From a random position, random search samples a random point from the neighborhood of the current position. In case the fitness of the sampled point is better than the current

Table 7.7: Search configuration for BehaviorSearch.

Setting	Value
fitnessMinimized	true
fitnessCollecting	MAX_ACROSS_STEPS
fitnessSamplingReplications	10
fitnessCombineReplications	MEAN
evaluationLimit	300
chromosomeRepresentation	GrayBinaryChromosome

Table 7.8: Configuration of search algorithms supported by BehaviorSearch.

Search Method	Parameters
StandardGeneticAlgorithm (GA)	mutation-rate 0.03 population-size 50 crossover-rate 0.7 population-model generational tournament-size 3
MutationHillClimber (HC)	mutation-rate 0.05 restart-after-stall-count 0
RandomSearch (RS)	not required
SimualtedAnnealing (SA)	initial-temperature 1.0 mutation-rate 0.05 temperature-change-factor 0.99 restart-after-stall-count 0

point's fitness, the algorithm moves to this position. Simulated annealing pursues an approach that is similar to hill climbing, yet, solutions that are worse than the previous one can be accepted. By this means, simulated annealing explores the response surface more extensively. The name is inspired by metallurgy, where materials are annealed to alter their physical properties. All algorithms except random search can be parametrized and modified by the user of Behavior Search. Yet, initial parametrizations are provided for each algorithms so that they can be executed immediately.

For the purpose of this evaluation, all four algorithms are applied and the results are compared. Each algorithm is applied twice, once with the goal of maximizing the fitness and once with the goal of minimizing the fitness. A

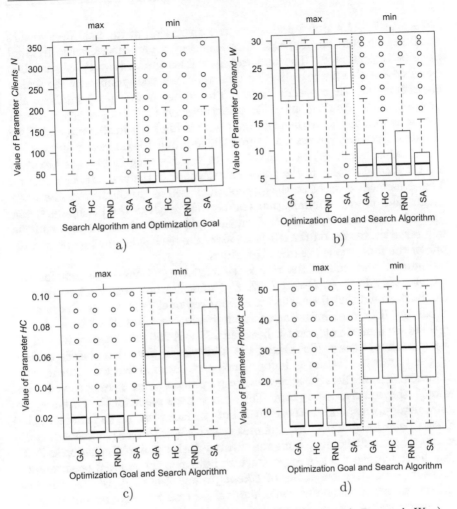

Figure 7.6: Final best values of parameters a) *Client_N*, b) *Demand_W*, c) *HC*, and d) *Product_cost* to minimize and maximize output *Max-stock*.

maximum of 300 models runs, a model step limit of 720 simulation steps, and 10 iterations per parameter configuration are executed. The observed fitness values from each of the 10 iterations are combined by their arithmetic mean.

Figures 7.6, 7.7, and 7.8 visualize the dispersion of the final best results of all search runs as boxplots. For each input parameter, an individual boxplot is presented. The best fitness values found in each of the 1000 executed searches are visualizes by their quartiles and grouped by the search algorithm and the respective goal. The upper and lower bounds of the box represent the 25% and 75% quartile such that 50% of all observed values as well as the median (marked with a line) fall in this interval. The antennas (whisker) represent 1.5 times the interquartile range and outliers are visualized as points (cf. Section 6.5.1). In the following figures, the boxplots are grouped according to the apparent relevance of the respective parameter. The assessment is based on the dispersion as well as the distinctness between maximization and minimization results. For each of the parameters, the maximization results are depicted on the right-hand side of the plot and the minimization results on the left-hand side. On each side, one box represents one of the four applied search algorithms.

Figure 7.6 visualizes the results generated by BehaviorSearch for the parameters *Client_N*, *Demand_W*, *HC*, and *Product_cost*. At first view, it can be detected that the median of all four parameters is very similar or even equal for all four minimization or maximization searches. For *Client_N*, the median for a maximal fitness is between 275 and 300 and between 25 and 50 for a minimal fitness. The size of the whiskers implies that the dispersion of the parameter values is higher during the maximization. During the minimization, outliers for almost every parameter value were observed even though the occurrences are rare. The observations made for the *Demand_W* parameter correspond to those of *Client_N*. However, no variations of the median can be identified for different search algorithms. The median is 25 during the maximization, while the median during the minimization is 7. It can be concluded, that both parameters influence the model's performance measure such that low values of *Client_N* and *Demand_W* result in low output values of the model while high values result in high output values.

The opposite can be observed when analyzing the boxplots of *HC* and *Product_cost*. Here, the relationship between low and high parameter and output values is reversed. Low values of both parameters maximize the output of the model whereas high parameter values minimize the output. Another observation is that parameter values that maximize the output are mostly located at the lower end of the range of possible values, i.e., between 0.01 and 0.02 for *HC* and between 5 and 10 for *Product_cost*. The whiskers are relatively shorter and higher parameter values are only classified as outliers. For the minimization, the median values correspond to the center of the range of possible values (0.06 for *HC* and 30 for *Product_cost*) and the whiskers cover the entire value range. No statement can be made about the importance and influence of these factors.

The boxplots of the remaining parameters are shown in Figures 7.7 and 7.8. It can be noted that the two upper plots, that represent the parameters K and $Lt0$, are similar to those shown in Figure 7.6. High values of both parameters result in a maximization of the model's performance measure and low values result in a minimization. While the lower median of K is between 100 and 125, the higher median is between 300 and 250. For $Lt0$, the minimization median is exactly 1 and the maximization median is equal to 6. For both parameters, the whiskers almost cover the entire range of admissible values.

The boxplots of $Lt1$, $SS\_\%$, and DS_D differ from the other plots. A visual distinction between maximization and minimization searches can hardly be made. None of the median values of the searches is located at the outer parts of the parameter value ranges. Instead, the values of both searches are situated in the middle part of the range of values. Furthermore, the whiskers cover the entire range of admissible values such that no outliers exist. It can be assumed that the parameters $Lt1$, $SS\_\%$, and DS_D do not systematically influence the behavior of the simulation model. However, whether these parameters have a random influence on the performance measure or no influence is subject to further analysis. Likewise, the existence of two- or multi-factor interactions (correlations) cannot be determined based on this first brief analysis and further investigations are required.

The results of this first pre-analysis of the model's parameters show that three of the nine existing model parameters seems to be relevant for the storage capacity that can be observed when executing the model. While *Clients_N* and *Demand_W* have a positive effect of the storage capacity, *Product_cost* has a negative effect. Accordingly, low values of *Product_cost* result in a high storage capacity and vice versa. The models' performance measures of the two presented hypotheses are very similar. The only difference is that the second scenario does not make an assumption on the total storage capacity but on the storage capacity per customer. Hence, it can be assumed that the directions of the factors' effects are similar except for parameter *Client_N* where an inversion of the effect must be expected. As the number of clients is the denominator of the performance measure, an increasing number of clients decreases the value of the performance measure, assuming a constant numerator.

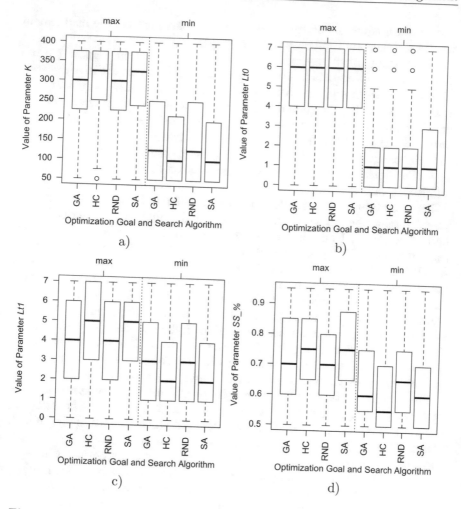

Figure 7.7: Final best values of parameters a) *K*, b) *Lt0*, c) *Lt1*, and d) *SS_%* to minimize and maximize output *Maxstock*.

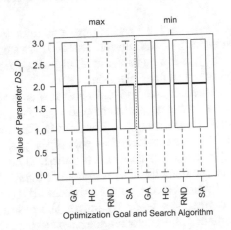

Figure 7.8: Final best values of parameter DS_D to minimize and maximize output *Maxstock*.

Response Surface of the Model

Before applying the assistance for conducting a Hypothesis-Driven Simulation Study, this section investigates the shape of the expected response surface. By this means, those areas of the response surface in which the stated hypothesis is violated can be identified and serve as reference data for the assessment of the results. This allows for a comparison of the evidence provided by the presented approach to the data generated during the pre-analysis and to evaluate the approaches' validity.

Due to spatial limitations, the response surface of the investigated model can only be visualized as a 3D plot. Accordingly, the plots can only contain information regarding how two input parameters of the model influence the specified performance measure with respect to all possible parameter value combinations. In both assumptions presented in Section 7.1.3, the performance measure *maximum required stock level* is used to assess the behavior of the model. Accordingly, the z-axis of the following response surface plots represents the observed value of the model's performance measure. It can be considered as the function value of the model execution function $f(x_1, x_2)$ where x_1 and x_2 are the values of two model inputs. When executing simulation models, specific values need to be assigned to all input parameters. Hence, constant values are applied for all remaining parameters except x_1 and x_2. In this subsection, those constant parameter values are referred to as *low*, *medium*, and *high values*. Unlike the terminology used in factor screening (cf. Section 6.3.1), this does not refer to the impact these values have on the output of the model. Instead, it refers to the region of the value range such that low input values originate from the numerically lower part of the range of admissible values, etc.

Because of the aforementioned visual limitations, a small set of input parameters must be selected to generate and plot the respective response surfaces of the model. Considering the boxplots in Figures 7.6, 7.7, and 7.8 as well as the inputs that are mentioned as part of the presented assumptions, potentially relevant parameters can be identified. The number of clients (*Client_N*) as well as the demand of the clients (*Demand_W*) are subject to the presented assumptions. As the quartiles are relatively smaller compared to the other parameters, the boxplots affirm the assumption that these two parameters influence the performance measure. Furthermore, a clear distinction can be made between the minimization and maximization median values of both parameters. The costs of the product (*Product_cost*) are chosen as a third parameter for the investigation of the model's response surface. It can be assumed, that the price that must be paid for the product has a major influence of the order quantity and accordingly also on the required storage level.

The response surface plots that are presented are arranged as follows: x- and y-axis of the plots consist of the values of the parameters (*Client_N*) and (*Demand_W*). Vertically, on the z-axis, the value of the maximum required storage capacity is plotted. Both product cost and the remaining

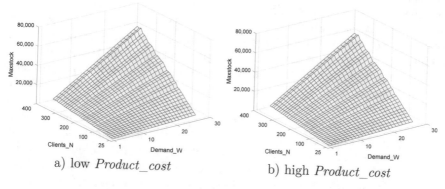

a) low *Product_cost*   b) high *Product_cost*

Figure 7.9: Response surface of interactions between parameters *Clients_N* and *Demand_W* with low and high values of remaining parameters.

parameters have constant values for each plot. Each group of plots that is presented in the remainder of this subsection visualizes a different level of the remaining parameters. The plots summarized in one group only differ in the level of the *Product_cost* parameter. In this regard, low *Product_cost* represent a value of 5, medium cost a value of 25, and high cost a value of 50.

In Figure 7.9, the interactions between the parameters *Client_N* and *Demand_W* are depicted for low values of the remaining parameters. Accordingly, the remaining parameter values are specified such that $SS\_\% = 0.5$, $Lt0 = 0$, $Lt1 = 0$, $DS\_D = 0$, $HC = 0.01$, and $K = 50$. Considering the response surfaces for low and high values of the *Product_cost* parameter, it can be observed that these plots appear identical. Yet, not only the shape of the plots but also the underlying data are equal in these plots. The same applied for medium *Product_cost* even though this plot is not shown. This behavior of the model is plausible, as lead times ($Lt0$ and $Lt1$) do not exist. Thus, forecasting demands is no longer required just like the calculation of the economic order quantity.

Figure 7.10 illustrates the response surface when the values of the remaining parameters are set to medium values, i.e., $SS\_\% = 0.7$, $Lt0 = 3$, $Lt1 = 3$, $DS\_D = 2$, $HC = 0.05$, and $K = 225$. In contrast to the low values presented in Figure 7.9, differences can be observed between the three plots. For one thing, increasing product cost results in a smoother surface even though the number of replications is equal for all three plotted scenarios. For another thing, the plot that visualizes the surface with low product costs shows a steeper surface compared to the two remaining plots. As the lead time is no longer equal to 0, it is plausible that low product costs result in increasing order quantities and thus requirer larger maximum storage capacities of the factory. Additionally, it can be observed that low product costs result in a convex response surface while medium and high product costs shape a concave surface.

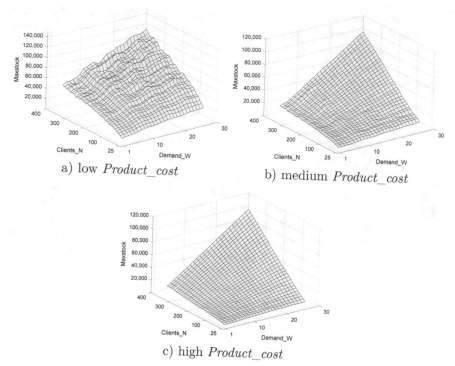

a) low *Product_cost*

b) medium *Product_cost*

c) high *Product_cost*

Figure 7.10: Response surface of interactions between parameters *Clients_N* and *Demand_W* with medium values of remaining parameters.

Finally, in Figure 7.11, the response surface for high values of the remaining parameters is shown. Similar to the plots of the medium values, a smoothing of the surface can be observed as the product costs increase. Furthermore, also a change of the surfaces' shapes can be observed from a convex to a concave shape with increasing product costs.

In summary, it can be stated that the shape of all presented surfaces is similar. The lowest values of the performance measure are observed at the zero point where x- and y-axis meet. The highest values are located the opposite corner where the maximum x and y values are visualized. It can be concluded that both parameters *Clients_N* and *Demand_W* have a positive effect on the performance measure. This applies individually for each of the parameters as well as for the interaction between both parameters. Hence, it must be assumed that the effects of both parameters intensify each other

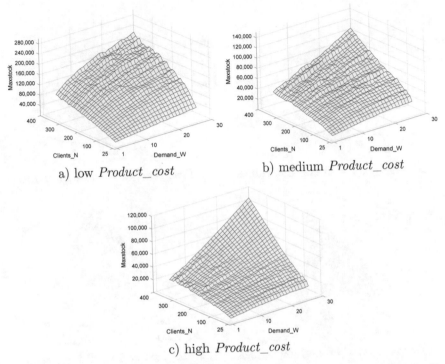

a) low *Product_cost*   b) medium *Product_cost*

c) high *Product_cost*

Figure 7.11: Response surface of interactions between parameters *Clients_N* and *Demand_W* with high values of remaining parameters.

and that the effects of the factors correlate.

It can also be observed that the surface of lower parameter values tend to be convex while the surfaces that results from higher parameter values have a more concave shape. Accordingly, for lower parameter values, the required maximum storage capacity increases quickly as a result of increasing values of *Clients_N* and *Demand_W* and flattens the more the values increase. For higher values of the remaining parameters, a flat ascent of the surface can be observed at first, which increases as the values of *Clients_N* and *Demand_W* increase. With respect to the maximum storage level, it can be stated that the remaining parameters seem to have a positive influence on this performance measure while increasing product costs decrease the maximum required storage capacity. The highest storage capacity values can be observed in Figure 7.11 for low *Product_cost*.

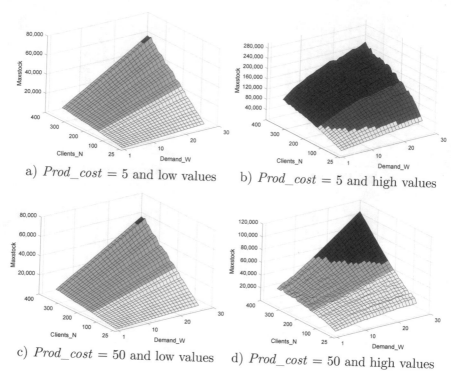

a) $Prod\_cost = 5$ and low values   b) $Prod\_cost = 5$ and high values

c) $Prod\_cost = 50$ and low values   d) $Prod\_cost = 50$ and high values

Figure 7.12: Response surface for $Prod\_cost = 5$ with a) low and b) high values of the remaining parameters and for $Prod\_cost = 50$ with c) low and d) high values of the remaining parameters. Areas in which the maximum storage capacity is over 60,000 are colored in dark gray.

With regard to the two assumptions and the corresponding hypotheses stated in this section, it can be ascertained that a storage capacity of 60,000 is not sufficient if the number of clients increases to 150. In Figure 7.12, those parts of the response surface in which this assumption does not hold are marked in gray, i.e., where the number of clients is greater than 150 and where the required storage capacity is greater than 60,000. In this regard, the area in which the maximum storage capacity requirement is violated is marked in a darker gray while the area in which the number of clients in greater than 150 is colored in a brighter gray. When applying the approach for Hypothesis-Driven Simulation Studies that is proposed in this thesis, the challenge is to correctly identify those areas of the response surface in which the initial assumption is violated and to provide evidence that the hypothesis does not hold.

7.2.2 Design of Experiments

With respect to the design of relevant simulation experiments, a limitation of the considered parameter space is necessary. It is not possible to simulate all potential factor-level combinations in reasonable time. Thus, those inputs must be determined that are varied and tested in simulation experiment. In the parametrization part of the presented formalized hypothesis, a specific value is only provided for the *Clients_N* input parameter. The values of the remaining inputs are summarized under the *ceteris paribus* sign (#). This implies that no specific values are defined for these inputs as part of the hypothesized assumption and that standard values are used instead. According to *sparsity-of-effects principle* (cf. Section 5.1), it is likely that only a small numbers of these factors is of relevance for the observed behavior of the model. Consequently, as a next step, those factors that are important for the investigated performance measure must be identified based on the specified hypothesis.

As a commonly used approach for factor screening, *sequential bifurcation* was introduced and specified in the previous chapter (cf. Section 6.3.1). To apply sequential bifurcation in this scenario, two assumptions must be met. First, a first-order polynomial with noise must be a suitable metamodel for the output of the simulation model. Second, the signs of all main effects must be known and not negative. This refers to the awareness of low and high values for each parameter of the model, which result in a minimization or maximization of observed performance measure of the model. Usually, the model builder can provide such information or at least an educated guess whether parameters have a positive or negative influence on the model's outcome. As part of the assistance, this knowledge cannot be supposed. However, using the BehaviorSearch optimization tool, the direction of each parameter's effect as well as suitable low and high values can be identified (cf. Section 7.2.1). This applies only for quantitative inputs. For the qualitative inputs of the presented model, factor screening cannot be applied. This includes the pursued purchase and inventory strategies as well as the model extension that implements retailer scoring. In the presented scenario, it seems reasonable to set these inputs to constant values and consider them as part of the scenario description. Accordingly, for the application of sequential bifurcation, low, high, and constant values of the model's inputs are defined as shown in Table 7.9.

Table 7.9: Low ($\downarrow$), high ($\uparrow$), and constant values of inputs for factor screening.

ID	Name	Purpose	Value	
-	*Fact*	#Factories	1	
-	*Distr1*	#Distributors	3	
-	*Distr2*	#Retailers	7	
-	*Cust._strat.*	Purchase strat.	1 - daily	
-	*Inv._pol.*	Inventory strat.	1 - (s,Q)	
-	*Score_Retailers*	Score purchase and choose best supplier	false	

ID	Name	Purpose	$\downarrow$	$\uparrow$
1	*Clients_N*	#Clients	25	350
2	*Lt0*	Lead time (Dist.)	0	7
3	*Lt1*	Lead time (Ret.)	0	7
4	*SS_%*	Safety value	.5	.95
5	*Demand_W*	mean(demand)	5	30
6	*DS_D*	σ(demand)	0	15
7	*HC*	Holding cost	.1	.01
8	*K*	Cost per order	50	400
9	*Product_cost*	Cost of product	50	5

To estimate the main effects of each of the model's input parameters, different extensions and modifications of sequential bifurcation were proposed. Standard sequential bifurcation is not capable of estimating effects which result from the correlation of two or more factors. Instead, *foldover designs* must be used for the identification of such effects.

When applying standard sequential bifurcation to a model with n parameters, the output of the model must be analyzed for $n + 1$ different parametrizations. Besides the outputs of the extremes $y_{(0)}$ (all factors set to their low levels) and $y_{(n)}$ (all n factors set to their high levels), sequential bifurcations requires stepwise outputs where the value of one additional factor is set to its high level. Moveover, for the calculation of the foldover design, output values for the respective mirror scenarios are required as well. In the mirror scenarios, all factors that were set to the high levels in the corresponding original scenario are set to their low levels and vice versa. Accordingly, the parametrization and consequently also the output value of the scenario $y_{(0)}$ and the mirror scenario $y_{(9)}^*$ are equal. The same applies for $y_{(9)}$ and $y_{(0)}^*$.

The output values $y_{(0)}$ to $y_{(9)}$ as well as the outputs of the respective mirror scenarios $y_{(0)}^*$ to $y_{(9)}^*$ are presented in Table 7.10. Here, the IDs of the factors correspond to the IDs defined in Table 7.9. Kleijnen (2015) suggested that knowledge of the model and respective assumptions of the potential importance of each factor can be used to presort the factors. By this means, the efficiency of sequential bifurcation can be increased as a large number of unimportant factors can be removed in the first iteration of the algorithm when performing the first separation of the search space. With respect to the goal of this thesis, knowledge of the model's behavior cannot be assumed. Accordingly, a random permutation of the factors is used as a basis for factor screening.

As a first step, the extreme scenarios $y_{(0)}$ and $y_{(9)}$ are simulated to obtain the group effect ($\bar{\beta}_{1-9} = 373,763.32$) of all 9 considered factors. It can be observed, that the values of the outputs increase, the more factors are set to their **high** levels. Likewise, a decrease of the output values can be noticed for the mirror scenarios, where the levels of the factors are stepwise set to their **low** levels. Upon the inclusion of factors 3 (K) and 4 ($Lt0$), no increase of the output values $y_{(3)}$ and $y_{(4)}$ can be perceived and the values remain the same. Based on this observation, it can be assumed that the effect and thus also the importance of these factors with regard to the maximum storage capacity is relatively smaller.

By definition, the sequential bifurcation factor screening approach pursues a *divide and conquer* approach. After the determination of the model's overall effect $\bar{\beta}_{(1-9)}$, the set of factors is divided into two subsets ($\bar{\beta}_{(1-4)}$ and $\bar{\beta}_{(5-9)}$) and the respective effect of each of the resulting sets is estimated. What follows is an iterative process where the group with the largest effect is again divided into two subgroups until the most important factors were identified. The resulting search tree is presented in Figure 7.13. In the figure, factors and groups of factors whose relative effect explains more than 15% of the model's overall effect are colored gray. Applying sequential bifurcation, factors 1, 2, and 8 are identified to be most important. Together, *Demand_W*, *Clients_N*, and *Product_cost* explain more than 75% of the model's overall effect. Moreover, the observation that outputs $y_{(3)}$ and $y_{(4)}$

Table 7.10: Averaged observations $y_{(k)}$ and mirror observations $y^*_{(k)}$ based on 50 replicates (*seed-values* = 19890206-19890255).

	mean (μ)	st. dev. (σ)
$y_{(0)}$	811.98	169.46
$y_{(1)}$	4,835.22	1,007.98
$y_{(2)}$	70,350.00	12,369.32
$y_{(3)}$	70,350.00	12,369.32
$y_{(4)}$	70,350.00	12,369.32
$y_{(5)}$	79,200.38	25,976.23
$y_{(6)}$	176,161.60	59,899.45
$y_{(7)}$	206,118.70	64,723.53
$y_{(8)}$	621,161.40	93,836.59
$y_{(9)}$	748,338.62	108,706.12

	mean (μ)	st. dev. (σ)
$y^*_{(0)}$	748,338.62	108,706.12
$y^*_{(1)}$	240,964.20	48,053.50
$y^*_{(2)}$	53,784.80	10,833.48
$y^*_{(3)}$	23,001.52	6,112.43
$y^*_{(4)}$	21,641.42	9,148.56
$y^*_{(5)}$	6,482.88	3,022.89
$y^*_{(6)}$	2,122.06	601.86
$y^*_{(7)}$	2,788.26	518.75
$y^*_{(8)}$	1,309.48	142.72
$y^*_{(9)}$	811.98	169.46

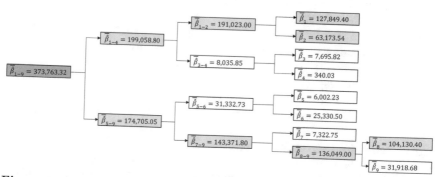

Figure 7.13: Search tree of the sequential bifurcation factor screening. Factors and groups of factors whose relative effect explains more than 15% of the model's overall effect are colored gray.

do not increase when setting the values of the respective inputs to their high levels can be explained such that both factors together have an effect of less than 3%.

According to Kleijnen et al. (2003), the described *divide and conquer* approach allows for the efficient identification of important factors for models with a large number of inputs (>100). This is because groups of unimportant factors are cut off and do not need to be analyzed in detail. The supply chain model that is used for the purpose of this evaluation only consist of 9 factors that are considered as potential important factors. To assess whether factor interactions exist that cannot be taken account of by the chosen foldover design, the application of the step-wise *divide and conquer* approach is reasonable. This allows for the identification of group effects that vanish when splitting groups into smaller subgroups or individual factors. Furthermore, this indicates that the selected design is not capable of correctly identifying the actual effect. Based on the observed output values shown in Table 7.10, the main effects of each factor can be calculated directly. In sum, the individual main effects of each factor presented in Table 7.11 are equal to the estimated overall effect of the model ($\bar{\beta}_{1-9} = 373{,}763.32$). Thus it can be assumed, that the selected foldover design was appropriate for the supply chain model.

The result of the factor screening show that the cumulated main effect of the inputs *Demand_W*, *Clients_N*, and *Product_cost* corresponds to approximately 75% of the model's overall effect. Thus, with respect to

Table 7.11: Average main effects $\bar{\beta}_{(k)}$ of each factor, calculated based on the output values from Table 7.10.

	Factor	$\bar{\beta}_{(k)}$
$\bar{\beta}_{(1)}$	*Demand_W*	127,849.40
$\bar{\beta}_{(2)}$	*Clients_N*	63,173.54
$\bar{\beta}_{(3)}$	*K*	7,695.82
$\bar{\beta}_{(4)}$	*Lt0*	340.03
$\bar{\beta}_{(5)}$	*HC*	6,002.23
$\bar{\beta}_{(6)}$	*Lt1*	25,330.50
$\bar{\beta}_{(7)}$	*DS_D*	7,322.75
$\bar{\beta}_{(8)}$	*Product_cost*	104,130.40
$\bar{\beta}_{(9)}$	*SS_%*	31,918.68

the parsimony principle, *Clients_N* and *Product_cost* should be considered as well when selecting factorial designs for the limitation of the model's parameter space.

In the case study presented here, the response surface of the investigated simulation model is still unknown at this point. Only a small amount of information is available based on the factor screening results. In this regard, Sanchez (2007) proposed the application of *Latin Hypercubes* for models with a large number of factors. Latin Hypercubes are a well suited general-purpose design which allows for a first exploration of a model's response surface. It is well suited for quantitative factors only such as the parameters of the presented simulation model (Deng et al., 2015). In contrast to other designs, Latin Hypercubes have space-filling properties such that a small number of design points can provide first impression of the shape of the response surface.

For this evaluation, the Latin Hypercube Sampling with $k = 9$ factors and $n = 10$ levels is executed. The calculation of a valid design is not trivial as exactly one design point must be identified for each group of possible levels of each factor. To generate a set of design points that corresponds to this constraint, existing software libraries can be used. An example is the *R project* package `lhs`[14] (Carnell, 2018). The provided `randomLHS` function generates a valid set of design points as a $k \times n$ matrix for k variables and n design points. The resulting matrix for a sampling with $k = 9$ factors and $n = 10$ levels is shown in Table 7.12.

Table 7.12: Design points (DP) generated by R Project package `lhs` for $k = 9$ factors and $N = 10$ levels with $seed = 19890206$.

DP	Cl_N	Lt0	Lt1	SS_%	Dem_W	DS_D	HC	K	Prod_c
1	0.7007	0.6613	0.9779	0.3354	0.5914	0.2904	0.4972	0.6756	0.0760
2	0.5425	0.0436	0.5924	0.1785	0.2636	0.4357	0.0868	0.8992	0.4941
3	0.4055	0.7808	0.7683	0.5612	0.8631	0.5870	0.8187	0.5645	0.6796
4	0.9819	0.8830	0.6843	0.2771	0.4499	0.6736	0.1502	0.7515	0.5482
5	0.2127	0.4816	0.3077	0.9600	0.9862	0.7996	0.2810	0.3795	0.2327
6	0.1236	0.5483	0.2828	0.8678	0.0390	0.8868	0.7353	0.2083	0.9859
7	0.0833	0.1712	0.0036	0.7763	0.1097	0.9004	0.3252	0.9614	0.8117
8	0.3638	0.3914	0.8372	0.0799	0.6362	0.1032	0.9091	0.4706	0.1437
9	0.6035	0.2234	0.4026	0.6538	0.7038	0.3183	0.6671	0.1935	0.3688
10	0.8902	0.9570	0.1269	0.4260	0.3400	0.0056	0.5578	0.0545	0.7853

---

[14]https://cran.r-project.org/web/packages/lhs/ [Retrieved Jul. 2019]

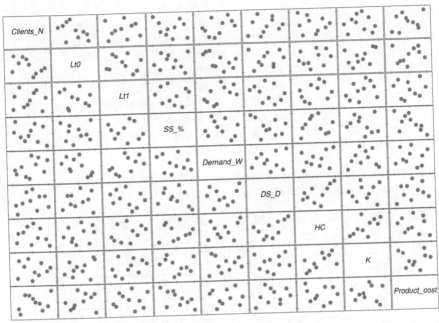

Figure 7.14: Scatterplot matrix for $N = 10$ design points for each of the $k = 9$ controllable parameters of the supply chain model.

To illustrate how the parameter space of the model is covered and that the space-filling properties of Latin Hypercube Sampling apply, all resulting factor-level combinations are visualized in Figure 7.14. The presented *scatterplot matrix* can be read such that each subplot illustrates the considered pairs of values for all possible combinations of two inputs. Accordingly, in this example of nine factors, the scatterplot matrix consists of 81 fields. The diagonal of the matrix is irrelevant, as it shows the same variable on both axes. Furthermore, each subplot appears twice, once below and once above the diagonal, which results in only 36 distinct subplots.

By default, the design points generated by the lhs package are normalized to the interval $[0, 1]$. Considering the model, the interval of admissible values is different for each factor and not equal to $[0, 1]$ (cf. Table 7.5). Accordingly, the generated values must be transformed to correspond to the range of admissible values of each of the model's parameters. Table 7.13 shows the design points that result from the transformation process. For the parameters $SS\_\%$, HC, and $Product\_cost$, the number of admissible values is equal to the number of desired design points. Accordingly, each possible value of these parameters is used in exactly one design point. The number of admissible values of the parameters $Lt0$, $Lt1$, DS_D, and K is smaller than the number of design points. Because of that, certain values must be used in two or more design points. Finally, the range of admissible values of $Clients\_N$ and $Demand\_W$ is larger than the number of design points. Here, 10 equal groups of possible factor levels are defined. As the number of admissible values is not a multiple of the required number of design points, the size of the groups varies.

Table 7.13: Transformation of design points from Table 7.12 to the range of admissible values of each factor.

DP	Cl_N	Lt0	Lt1	SS_%	Dem_W	DS_D	HC	K	Prod_c
1	253	5	7	0.65	20	1	0.05	300	5
2	201	0	4	0.55	12	1	0.01	400	25
3	157	5	5	0.75	27	2	0.09	250	35
4	344	6	5	0.60	16	2	0.02	350	30
5	94	3	2	0.95	30	2	0.03	200	15
6	65	4	2	0.90	6	3	0.08	150	50
7	52	1	0	0.85	8	3	0.04	400	45
8	143	3	6	0.50	21	0	0.10	250	10
9	221	2	3	0.80	23	1	0.07	150	20
10	314	7	1	0.70	14	0	0.06	100	40

To receive a first impression of the shape of the model's response surface, all 10 parametrizations are executed that are defined in Table 7.13. For this evaluation, a sample size of 50 replications is chosen. At this point of the evaluation, a high level of statistical certainty is not of primary relevance. Instead, receiving a first impression of the shape of the response surface and the identification of potentially relevant areas for the verification of the underlying research hypothesis must be achieved. For this purpose, the number of replications is set to a static level ($n = 50$), which is assumed to be sufficiently high to receive unbiased results. The results of the respective simulation runs are presented in Table 7.14.

Due to the space-filling properties of Latin Hypercube Sampling, the generated outputs can be used to gain a first impression on the model's response surface. This is possible, even though only a comparatively small number of design points was simulated. In Figure 7.15, the outputs observed for the 10 defined design points are plotted as black points for all considered

Table 7.14: Simulation outputs: Average *maximum storage capacity* of each design points of the Latin Hypercube Sampling. (random-seed= 19890206 − 19890255 and $n = 50$)

Design Point	Maxstorage	
	Mean	*Standard Deviation*
1	172,904.08	36,818.45
2	24,144.20	128.45
3	47,547.44	3,840.50
4	103,954.10	28,226.55
5	46,482.72	10,786.90
6	5,768.00	1,284.94
7	7,801.90	1,864.89
8	41,219.42	12,150.43
9	53,853.66	2,008.28
10	49,671.02	1,722.84

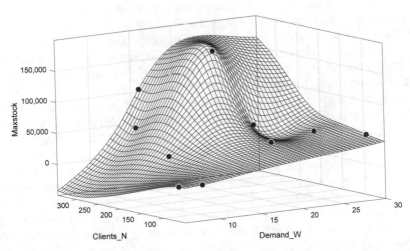

Figure 7.15: Scatterplot of maximum storage capacity for design points from Latin Hypercube Sampling (cf. Table 7.14). The surface is interpolated using *thin plate splines*.

combinations of *Clients_N* and *Demand_W*. To illustrate the response surface that is defined by these observations, *thin plate splines* are used for the interpolation of the resulting surface. Especially for high values of *Clients_N* in combination with low values of *Demand_W*, the randomly generated design points result in a lack of information of these parts of the surface. Due to the steep slope of the surface that is defined by the surrounding measured values, the interpolation algorithm continues this trend in areas where measured data is missing. Thus, the resulting descent of the interpolated surface to negative z values is a result of missing measured values in this area. Considering the logic of the model, such observations cannot be made as a negative storage capacity is not possible. Accordingly, it can be assumed that the storage capacity is close to zero in these areas.

The observed outputs and the interpolated surface suggest that some parts of the parameter space result in a violation of the stated hypothesis. For medium and high factor levels of *Clients_N* and *Demand_W*, maximum storage capacity values of more than 60,000 are observed. This shape of the response surface can be attributed to a potential interaction of these factors. Thus, to analyze whether the study's underlying assumption is indeed violated for medium and high factor levels of *Clients_N* and *Demand_W*, a thorough investigation of this area of the parameter space is required. Likewise, the third important factor (*Product_cost*) that was identified by means of sequential bifurcation factor screening must be investigated. Considering design points with high levels of *Product_cost* where the level of *Clients_N* was high as well, e.g., design points 4 and 10, high maximum storage capacity values can be observed. The same applies for combinations of high levels of *Product_cost* and *Demand_W* (design point 3) or of all three important factors (design point 10).

As a next step, a suitable factorial design must be identified to design simulation experiments with respect to the more detailed investigation of the model's parameter space. To reduce the number of resulting design points and to maintain the efficiency of the simulation study, a larger set of levels must be investigated for each of the important factors. At the same time, the number of analyzed levels should be reduced for less important factors, to avoid a combinatorial explosion of the considered parameter space. In this regard, the focus of the investigation should be on the medium and high levels of the important factors, as implied by the results of the Latin Hypercube Sampling.

With respect to the design of experiments, the level of the *Clients_N* parameter must be held constant during the study as defined by the investigated hypothesis (*Clients_N* = 150). Thus, only the important factors

Demand_W and *Product_cost* are considered for the design of the experiments. The surface interpolated based on the results of the Latin Hypercube Sampling implies, that the response surface of the model has a concave shape (cf. Figure 7.15). Accordingly, it can be assumed that it ascends steadily and that no maxima must be expected in the lower and middle part of the surface. In this regard, the application of a m^k design with $m = 3$ seems sufficient to investigate low, medium, and high levels of the important factors. Defining low and high values for *Demand_W* and *Product_cost* is simple, as the lowest and highest admissible values can be selected. Considering the admissible minimum and maximum values as well as the defined step size of *Demand_W* and *Product_cost*, the definition of a medium value is more challenging, as the exact center of both the value ranges of both parameters is not a whole number and thus by definition not an admissible value. To solve this inaccuracy, the next larger admissible value is selected. For *Demand_W*, 18 is defined as a medium value and for *Product_cost* 30 is defined as a medium value. For the remaining unimportant parameters, a less comprehensive design seems sufficient and thus only two settings of these parameters will be investigated: *all low* and *all high* levels. This results in a total number of 18 design points (simulation runs), that are executed during the simulation study to verify whether or not the stated hypothesis holds (cf. Table 7.15).

After the relevant simulation runs were successfully designed, the required number of replications per simulation run must be determined. Unlike the simulation runs were conducted as part of the Latin Hypercube design, a thorough estimation of the required number of replications is of high relevance here to assess the statistical significance of the generated results. As all 18 simulation runs execute the model with a different parametrization, it must be assumed that the required number of replications is not equal for all runs. Instead, the number of replications must be estimated individually for each parametrization.

In this thesis, confidence intervals are applied for replication estimation. As defined by Hoad et al. (2010a), a *precision criterion* must be met to automatically select the number of replications for a simulation run. The authors define the precision as "the half-width of the confidence interval expressed as a percentage of the cumulative mean of the replications performed" (Hoad et al., 2010a, p. 1634) and recommend a precision of 5%. Unlike other approaches for replication estimation which can be applied before executing the model, e.g., rule of thumb, the selected replication estimation method pursues an a posteriori approach. After the execution of a specific number of simulation runs, the algorithm can determine whether the current number of performed simulation replications is sufficient or whether additional replications are required to reach the desired precision. Accordingly, and even though replication estimation is by definition a *design of experiments* task, it is reasonable to apply the confidence interval approach for replication estimation by Hoad et al. (2010a) during the *conduction of experiments* step of the study. By this means, a more efficient experimentation is enabled as the number of required model executions is reduced.

Table 7.15: Simulation runs that are executed as part of the simulation study.

DP	Cl_N	Dem_W	$Prod\_c$	$Lt0$	$Lt1$	$SS\_\%$	DS_D	HC	K
1	150	5	5	0	0	0.5	0	0.1	50
2	150	18	5	0	0	0.5	0	0.1	50
3	150	30	5	0	0	0.5	0	0.1	50
4	150	5	30	0	0	0.5	0	0.1	50
5	150	18	30	0	0	0.5	0	0.1	50
6	150	30	30	0	0	0.5	0	0.1	50
7	150	5	50	0	0	0.5	0	0.1	50
8	150	18	50	0	0	0.5	0	0.1	50
9	150	30	50	0	0	0.5	0	0.1	50
10	150	5	5	7	7	0.95	3	0.01	400
11	150	18	5	7	7	0.95	3	0.01	400
12	150	30	5	7	7	0.95	3	0.01	400
13	150	5	30	7	7	0.95	3	0.01	400
14	150	18	30	7	7	0.95	3	0.01	400
15	150	30	30	7	7	0.95	3	0.01	400
16	150	5	50	7	7	0.95	3	0.01	400
17	150	18	50	7	7	0.95	3	0.01	400
18	150	30	50	7	7	0.95	3	0.01	400

7.2.3 Conducting of Experiments

In this case study, the simulation framework NetLogo is utilized for the execution of the designed simulation runs. It provides all functionalities that are required to run in on different platforms and its handling does not require detailed simulation knowledge. This subsection discusses different aspects that must be considered during the execution of simulation experiments. This includes the utilization and integration of functionalities that are provided by the framework such as approaches for the parallel execution of simulation runs. Furthermore, it presents techniques for the generation of random variates which are required for the execution of the model as well as the replication estimation which is executed as the model is executed.

For the parallel execution of simulation runs, NetLogo provides its own functionalities. This does not include the multi-thread execution of one simulation run of a model. Instead, NetLogo enables the parallel execution of multiple simulation runs. For this purpose, the `thread` parameter of the `headless` command line instance of NetLogo can be used to configure how many threads of the host system shall be used to execute simulation runs parallel. At this step, the user is able to define any desired number of threads, while the definition of only one thread disables this feature. However, with respect to the physical architecture of the host system, the default setting of one thread per physical processor seems reasonable. This parallelization approach is only promising if multiple simulation runs or iterations of the same parametrization are executed. The execution of a single extensive simulation run cannot be accelerated.

As default pseudorandom number generator, NetLogo implements *Mersenne Twister* (Matsumoto and Nishimura, 1998; NetLogo, 2018). Mersenne twister is one of the most popular pseudorandom number generator for use in simulation due to its large state as well as due to the quality of the generated random variates (L'Ecuyer, 2015). Furthermore, NetLogo's implemented `MersenneTwisterFast` class has the benefit of being 33% faster than the standard Java pseudorandom number generator (`java.util.Random`), according to an own statement.

To initialize a pseudorandom number generator, a seed value is required (cf. Section 6.4.3). By default, a seed value is generated randomly when executing a model in NetLogo. This process is hidden and the experimenter is not informed about the selected seed value. The probabilistic quality of the outputs generated when executing simulation models is not affected by this. However, the reproduction of outputs is challenging as the same sequence of pseudorandom numbers cannot be generated multiple times as the seed value is unknown. To overcome this, specific seed values are defined in for all simulation runs that are executed in the context of this evaluation. The initial seed value chosen is $random - seed = 19890206$ and for each further iteration of the same parameterization of the model, this value is incremented by one.

To generate data that can serve as a basis for the purpose of this evaluation, the 18 defined parametrization are executed in parallel in accordance with the described procedure. At the same time, the replication algorithm is applied to assess whether the number of executed simulation iterations is

Table 7.16: Number of replications for each simulation run (*design point*) with precision $d_n \leq 5\%$ and $kLimit = 4$.

DP	#Replications	Mean	Standard Dev.	Precision (d_n)
1	57	4,895.21	920.02	4.987%
2	57	17657.54	3,317.51	4.985%
3	57	29,141.60	5,526.80	4.985%
4	57	4,895.21	920.02	4.987%
5	57	17,657.54	3,317.51	4.985%
6	57	29,414.60	5,526.80	4.985%
7	57	4,895.21	920,02	4.987%
8	57	17,657.54	3,317.51	4.985%
9	57	29,414.60	5,526.80	4.985%
10	44	132,022.50	21,512.06	4.954%
11	45	291,541.80	48,293.67	4.977%
12	20	408,763.00	42,513.17	4.982%
13	23	68,277.29	7,233.16	4.816%
14	35	157,055.20	21,353.91	4.902%
15	42	224,407.00	34,503.86	4.917%
16	22	59,133.14	6,572.73	4.928%
17	42	132,483.00	20,223.66	4.882%
18	59	162,591.20	31,148.48	4.992%

sufficient. In case the desired precision is not met, the random seed value is incremented by one and an additional iteration of the same parametrization of the model is executed. This procedure is repeated until the specified precision criterion applies.

In Table 7.16, the results of the application of the replications algorithm are presented for each of the defined simulation runs. The desired precision d_n is set to 5% and when the required precision is met $kLimit = 4$ additional replications are executed to evaluate whether the precision criterion remains valid. Considering design points 1-9, it can be observed that the same number of replications ($n = 57$) is suggested. Furthermore, the same mean values occur three times and depending on the level of *Demand_W*. It can be concluded, that for low values of the unimportant factors, the parameter *Product_cost* does not influence the results of the simulation runs.

Yet, differences in the results and in the calculated number of replications can be identified for design points 10-18. The range of suggested replications reaches from 20 replications (design point 12) to 59 replications (design point 18). The step-wise smoothening of the maximum storage capacity's cumulative mean, which is measured in each replication of the model, is visualized in Figure 7.16. In the presented simulation, the desired precision of 5% or less is met after 59 replications.

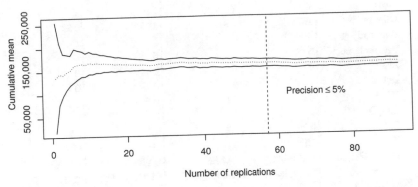

Figure 7.16: Step-wise calculation of the confidence interval for simulation run 18.

NetLogo provides the results of each simulation run in two different ways. Even though the structure and the content of the two output formats differs slightly, most relevant information is provided in both formats. This includes the path of the used model, the name of the executed experiment, the used NetLogo version, the time the experiment was executed, and complete information on each executed run and iteration. The first possible output format are *spreadsheets*. Spreadsheets focus on the analysis and provide an aggregated overview on the results of the experiment. This includes different measures such as minimum, maximum, and final values of each of the model's outputs (cf. Table 7.17). In a second section of the spreadsheet, stepwise run data are provided in detail and for each execution of the model.

As an alternative, the output of the results as *table* is possible. In contrast to spreadsheets, the table output format does not analyze the generated data. Instead, each row of the table consist of the detailed data of a single simulation run or step, depending on the settings defined in NetLogo's behaviorspace. This includes the full parametrization of the model as well as

Table 7.17: Spreadsheet of a NetLogo experiment.

BehaviorSpace results (NetLogo 6.0.2)
Supply_Chain.nlogo
Exp_1
03/06/2018 12:27:14:949 +0100

[run number]	1	2	3	4
random-seed	19890206	19890207	19890208	19890209
Fact	1	1	1	1
Distr1	3	3	3	3
Distr2	7	7	7	7
Clients_N	150	150	150	150
Demand_W	5	5	5	5
Product_cost	5	5	5	5
Lt0	0	0	0	0
Lt1	0	0	0	0
SS_%	0.5	0.5	0.5	0.5
DS_D	0	0	0	0
HC	0.1	0.1	0.1	0.1
K	50	50	50	50
Show_Network	FALSE	FALSE	FALSE	FALSE
Customers _Strategy	"1-Daily P."	"1-Daily P."	"1-Daily P."	"1-Daily P."
Inventory _Policy	"1 - (s, Q)"	"1 - (s, Q)"	"1 - (s, Q)"	"1 - (s, Q)"
[reporter]	wsc_maxstock	wsc_maxstock	wsc_maxstock	wsc_maxstock
[final]	3745	5618	3745	3745
[min]	0	0	0	0
[max]	3745	5618	3745	3745
[steps]	720	720	720	720
[all run data]	wsc_maxstock	wsc_maxstock	wsc_maxstock	wsc_maxstock
	0	0	0	0
	3745	5618	3745	3745
	3745	5618	3745	3745

the values of each output. With respect to human readability, the spreadsheet visualization of the results is preferable. However, for the machine-aided analysis of the outputs, as it is provided by the assistance proposed in this thesis, the table format is preferable.

At this point of the study, all required experiments were designed and successfully executed. It was ensured that the number of performed replication was sufficient to allow for a statistically reliable verification of the study's research hypothesis. Furthermore, simulation data is available in a format that can be automatically processed. In the next step, the generated outputs must be analyzed with respect to confirming or refuting this hypothesis.

7.2.4 Analysis of Experiments

As a final step of the simulation study, the generated results must be analyzed. The goal of this step is to provide sufficient statistical evidence for or against the study's initial research hypothesis. To this end, this subsection reassesses the outputs generated during the execution of the model and substitutes outliers and missing values. Subsequently, the generated output data are aggregated and statistical hypothesis tests are applied to determine whether or not to the stated hypothesis holds.

By this means of outliers detection, the assistance can compensate for potential measuring or modeling errors. As the overall results of the study are affected by this step, it must be documented thoroughly. Such interventions must be considered when interpreting the results of the study. The substitution of outliers is reasonable when deriving recommendations for action as potential bias resulting in inaccuracies can be identified and eliminated. However, in a strict sense, these results no longer represent the original behavior of the simulation model. It is the responsibility of the user of the intelligent assistance to decide on this trade-off in accordance with the hypothesis and to determine whether or not outliers and missing values shall be substituted. Either way, the assistance provides necessary guidance to ensure the generation of reproducible and reliable results.

To detect potential outliers in the set of generated data, it is necessary to determine the interquartile range of each simulation run. For this purpose, the values of the lower and higher quartile are required, i.e., the values that split the highest and lowest 25% of the observed values from the rest of the sorted dataset. The interquartile range is then defined as the middle 50% of values, which is the distance between the lower and higher quartile. Candidates for outliers are defined as observed values that fall outside the lower and higher inner fence. In this regard, the lower inner fence is the quartile which lies 1,5 times the interquartile range outside the lower quartile. The higher inner fence is defined accordingly based on the higher quartile.

Applying this definition to the simulation outputs, the values shown in Table 7.18 are identified as potential outliers. They occur only in 3 of the 18 designed and executed simulation runs. In run 14, two candidates for outliers can be identified, which are the output of replication 8 and 34. Here,

Table 7.18: Potential outliers, that fall outside the upper or lower fence.

DP	replic.	Output value	Median	1.5×IQR	Lower fence	Upper fence
14	8	218,960.00	159,630.00	42,096.38	96,805.88	209,062.90
14	34	213,986.00	159,630.00	42,096.38	96,805.88	209,062.90
15	1	150,102.00	219,533.50	43,740.38	165,907.60	282,548.60
15	8	317,590.00	219,533.50	43,740.38	165,907.60	282,548.60
15	12	272,923.00	219,533.50	43,740.38	165,907.60	282,548.60
15	26	298,337.00	219,533.50	43,740.38	165,907.60	282,548.60
15	34	280,900.00	219,533.50	43,740.38	165,907.60	282,548.60
15	37	275,599.00	219,533.50	43,740.38	165,907.60	282,548.60
15	41	149,232.00	219,533.50	43,740.38	165,907.60	282,548.60
16	7	41,640.00	59,174.50	7,850.63	48,774.12	69,709.12
16	8	75,472.00	59,174.50	7,850.63	48,774.12	69,709.12

the observed values of 218,960 and 213,986 lie outside the upper inner fence (209,062.90). Likewise, the outputs of replications 1, 8, 12, 26, 34, and 37 of run 15 as well as replications 7 and 8 of run 16 are identified as potential outliers. All of these output values fall outside the lower or higher fences.

As a next step after detecting potential outliers, suitable tests must be applied to determine whether or not these values are indeed outliers, e.g., *Grubbs' test for outliers*, which requires the dataset to be normally distributed. The application of the *Shapiro–Wilk test* shows that most results of the 18 simulation runs are *not* normally distributed with a $p - value \leq 0.05$ (cf. Table 7.19). However, for runs 12, 13, 14, 16, and 17, the *Shapiro–Wilk test* reveals $p_{12} = 0.1087$, $p_{13} = 0.7602$, $p_{14} = 0.1779$, $p_{16} = 0.7587$, and $p_{17} = 0.1865$. Using a significance level of 5%, it must be assumed that the outputs of these simulation run are normally distributed. Accordingly, *Grubbs' test for outliers* may not be applied to the results of the remaining runs.

For simulation runs 14 and 16, *Grubbs' test for outliers* can be applied to calculate test static $\hat{G} = 2.4882$ and p-value of 0.2095 for run 14 as well as $\hat{G} = 2.5480$ and p-value of 0.1719 for run 16. Both p-values are not smaller than the significance level $\alpha = 0.05$. Thus, the null hypothesis holds, and the existence of outliers is not confirmed. Still, removing all data points that were identified as potential outliers from the dataset without substitution results in a decrease of the required number of replications. For simulation run 14, the number of required replications, such that a precision of 5% is met, decreases from 35 to 21 replications. For simulation run 16, the number

Table 7.19: P-values of Shapiro-Wilk test of normality applied to the outputs of each simulation run.

DP	p-value	normally distributed?
1	6.33×10^{-11}	not normally distributed
2	6.26×10^{-11}	not normally distributed
3	6.25×10^{-11}	not normally distributed
4	6.33×10^{-11}	not normally distributed
5	6.26×10^{-11}	not normally distributed
6	6.25×10^{-11}	not normally distributed
7	6.33×10^{-11}	not normally distributed
8	6.26×10^{-11}	not normally distributed
9	6.25×10^{-11}	not normally distributed
10	0.0159	not normally distributed
11	0.0037	not normally distributed
12	0.1087	normally distributed
13	0.7602	normally distributed
14	0.1779	normally distributed
15	0.0364	not normally distributed
16	0.7587	normally distributed
17	0.1865	normally distributed
18	0.0291	not normally distributed

of required replications decreases to 7. With and without removing outliers, 22 replications are required.

Another approach for outlier handling that was presented in this thesis is imputation where outliers are substituted by the median value of the dataset. Using the median values from Table 7.18 as substitute, the number of replications can be decreased from 35 to 21 for simulation run 14 as well. For simulation run 16, a decrease from 22 to 7 replications can be identified. These observations are identical to those made when removing outliers without substitution. In this evaluation, outliers are accepted as given by the model and will not be removed or substituted for the further course of the model analysis. Nevertheless, depending on the goal of the analysis, experts might consider substituting them.

After outlying and missing data points were identified and removed or substituted, the observed outputs of the simulation model must be aggregated.

By doing so, a data basis is generated that can be used as a basis for the application of statistical hypothesis tests. The aggregation must be conducted in accordance with the structural components of simulation study, which were presented in Section 4.2.2. At this point of the study, the first and second step of the output aggregation were already performed as part of the runtime replication estimation.

In the scenario presented here, NetLogo is used for the execution of the simulation model. Even though NetLogo enables the implementation of continuous time simulations, most modes implement time-progress in discrete steps. For this purpose, NetLogo provides a tick counter, which can be used for both changing or retrieving the current time in time. By this means, time can be advanced in specific granularities and simulated entities can make decisions dependent on the current simulation time.

This also results in a time-discrete advance of the model's states. Accordingly, the outputs of the model can be measured after every step of the simulation. In NetLogo, the experimenter can decide whether or not outputs are stored for every step of the simulation. In case this option is not selected, the outputs of the model are only observed after the last simulation step. With respect to the aggregation of simulation outputs, NetLogo performs this first task of aggregating the outputs of simulation steps for each simulation iteration. However, warm-up periods of the model cannot be considered when using this build-in functionality of NetLogo. In the scenario presented in here, the warm-up period of the model is part of the scenario definition. A minimum number of 720 ticks are simulated as suggested by the developer of the model to ensure the observation of unbiased results. Furthermore, it can be assumed that the warm-up period does not result in the observation of storage levels that are too high. Instead, in this scenario, the warm-up period is required to generate demand and to fill the storages that are empty at the beginning of the simulation. Summarizing, it is assumed that the simulation of 720 ticks is sufficient to observe unbiased behavior of the model and that the included warm-up period does not bias these observations. Even though NetLogo enables the automated aggregation of the outputs of each simulation step, this functionality cannot be used in the assistance presented here. Instead, all 720 outputs are provided as time series data for each simulation iteration.

As a next step, the data of all simulation iterations must be aggregated for each respective run. In Section 6.5.2, it was emphasized that the order in which this step and the following steps are executed depends on the performance measure and on the fact whether or not the aggregation and target variable function commute with each other. At this point, time series data Y_r is available for each simulation iteration, which consist of 720 data points. They provide information on how the storage capacity changed over time during the execution of the model. By aggregating these datasets, e.g., by calculating the arithmetic mean, the maximum value will be lost and cannot be reconstructed from the resulting mean storage capacity value. Thus, the target variable *maximum storage capacity* (Y_r^T) must be calculated first before aggregating the maximum values of each simulation iteration. All Y_k^T with $k = 1, ..., n$ where n is the required number of replications can then be summarized by their mean value. The resulting $\bar{Y}'^T_k$ value represents the mean maximum storage capacity of a specific simulation run. It consists of the values of all replications that were executed with the same parametrization of the model. The statistical certainty of $\bar{Y}'^T_k$ is given, as the required number of executed replications was calculated by means of confidence intervals.

In this scenario, the composition of functions μ (arithmetic mean) and g (maximum value of output variable *storage capacity*) is not commutative. Bias could result, when calculating the mean storage capacity of each time series first and applying g afterwards. In this case, the maximum of the mean storage capacity is calculated ($\bar{Y}_k^T$). Even though $\bar{Y}_k^T$ is a valid target variable, it does not represent the performance measure, which is part of the hypothesis. Thus, it cannot be used to investigate the model's behavior and to verify the hypothesis.

Finally, the $\bar{Y}'^T_k$ values of each simulation run must be aggregated for each simulation experiment they originated from. In the presented scenario, only one single simulation experiment with a corresponding experiment hypothesis is defined. All 18 defined simulation runs are part of this simulation experiment. With respect to the initial hypothesis, the aggregation of the results of all 18 simulation runs is not reasonable. By generating one aggregated result, the areas of the response surface in which the critical maximum storage capacity of 60,000 units is exceeded will be smoothened. It must be assumed, that this will result in inconclusive results where possible violations of the 60,000 unit limit can no longer be observed. Instead, the aggregation of the results of specific simulation runs seems more reasonable, e.g., only those that were executed with the same levels of the unimportant factors.

To evaluate whether the initial hypothesis holds for each of the designed simulation runs, the statistical significance of the results must be determined. In this scenario, the presented hypothesis makes an assumption about the value of one performance measure. More specifically, the maximum value this performance measure can take is assumed. With respect to statistical hypothesis testing, the relationship between the sample dataset (simulation outputs) and a synthetic dataset is assumed. In this regard, significance implies that it is unlikely to observe the sampled dataset under the assumption that the null hypothesis is true. The null hypothesis assumes that a maximum storage capacity of 60,000 units is not sufficient and will be violated during the simulation. Accordingly, in case a maximum storage capacity of less then 60,000 units is observed, statistical hypothesis testing assesses how likely or unlikely this observation is assuming that 60,000 units are not sufficient. This approach is based on the idea that the observation of a maximum storage capacity of less than 60,000 units is the result of change and does not imply causality.

Considering the initial hypothesis, a *one sample* hypothesis test is required in this scenario. Moreover, as a *less-than* relationship between the datasets is assumed, a *one-tailed* (left-tailed) test is required to assess the statistical significance of the results. The most common hypothesis test that corresponds to these requirements is the *one sample t-test*. It tests, whether the mean of a sample is different from the provided mean of a population. For this scenario, the *rejection region* approach is used instead of the *p-value* approach for determining whether or not the null hypothesis holds. In this approach, a rejection region is defined and H_0 is rejected if the value of the test static falls into this region. For a left-tailed one sample t-test, the rejection region is defined as the interval $(-\infty, -t_{(1-\alpha,n-1)})$. Here, $-t_{(1-\alpha,n-1)}$ is defined as the $1 - \alpha$ quantile of the t-distribution with $n - 1$ degrees of freedom (Freedman et al., 2007). In the presented example, the degrees of freedom are equal to the sample size (number of estimated replications) minus 1.

In Table 7.20, the result of the t-test are shown for each of the 18 simulation runs that were executed as part of this simulation study. To assess the significance of the results, the t-value must be compared to the critical t-value $(-t_{(1-\alpha,n-1)})$. As the required number of replications is estimated for each simulation run, the degrees of freedom differ between the simulation runs. Therefore, the critical t-value must be calculated individually for each simulation run. The resulting critical t-values define rejection regions from $(-\infty, -1, 672)$ to $(-\infty, -1, 729)$. Hence, the null hypothesis that more than 60,000 units of storage capacity are required can be rejected for simulation runs 1 through 9. For runs 10 to 18, the calculated t-value does not fall into the defined interval and accordingly, the null hypothesis cannot be rejected. This implies, that 60,000 units of storage capacity are not sufficient. Only the result of simulation run 16 stands out. Even though the mean storage capacity is lower than 60,000 units (59,133.14), the t-test indicates

Table 7.20: Results of t-test for each design point with $\alpha = 0.05$.

DP	t-value	critical value $-t_{(1-\alpha,n-1)}$	degrees of freedom	p-value	mean	Reject H_0?
1	-452.198	-1.673	56	9.386×10^{-102}	4,895.21	reject
2	-96.361	-1.673	56	3.190×10^{-64}	17,657.54	reject
3	-41.781	-1.673	56	3.327×10^{-44}	29,414.60	reject
4	-452.198	-1.673	56	9.386×10^{-102}	4,895.21	reject
5	-96.361	-1.673	56	3.190×10^{-64}	17,657.54	reject
6	-41.781	-1.673	56	3.327×10^{-44}	29,414.60	reject
7	-452.198	-1.673	56	9.386×10^{-102}	4,895.21	reject
8	-96.361	-1.673	56	3.190×10^{-64}	17,657.54	reject
9	-41.781	-1.673	56	3.327×10^{-44}	29,414.60	reject
10	22.208	-1.681	43	1.000	132,022.50	do not reject
11	32.162	-1.680	44	1.000	291,541.80	do not reject
12	35.845	-1.729	19	1.000	408,763.00	do not reject
13	5.666	-1.717	22	0.999	69,145.04	do not reject
14	25.910	-1.691	34	1.000	158,764.80	do not reject
15	29.605	-1.683	41	1.000	222,598.10	do not reject
16	-0.619	-1.721	21	0.271	59,133.14	do not reject
17	22.356	-1.683	41	1.000	131,524.30	do not reject
18	25.299	-1.672	58	1.000	162,591.20	do not reject

the rejection of the null hypothesis with a significance level of 5%. The probability of observing a mean storage capacity of 59,133.14 units under the assumption that the null hypothesis holds is too high.

To further aggregate the presented results of each simulation run, the scenario of the simulation study must be considered. The underlying hypothesis is formulated from the perspective of a factory that is part of a supply chain. It can be assumed that the results of the simulation study serve as a basis for decision-making processes in the factory. In this regard, the customers' demand is an uncontrollable factor while production costs can be addressed within the company, e.g., by means of business process management such as process improvement. Accordingly, the aggregation of the results with respect to the factor *product_cost* is reasonable and the simulation runs must be aggregated in groups of three, i.e., 1-3, 4-6, 7-9, 10-12, 13-15, and 16-18. The results are presented in Table 7.21.

Table 7.21: Aggregated results of the hypothesis test.

DP	Cl_N	Prod_c	Unimp. factors	Reject H_0?
1-3	150	5	low	reject
4-6	150	30	low	reject
7-9	150	50	low	reject
10-12	150	5	high	do not reject
13-15	150	30	high	do not reject
16-18	150	50	high	do not reject

As a final step of the conducted simulation study, the generated results must be interpreted with respect to the scenario of the study. The factory assumes that a maximum storage capacity of 60,000 units is sufficient to satisfy the demand that occurs in the supply chain. After designing, executing, and analyzing all relevant experiments, it must be concluded that 60,000 units of storage capacity are not sufficient in any case. Even though there are parametrizations of the model which do not exceed this limit, other parametrizations of the model indicate a required storage capacity which lies far above the defined threshold. For low levels of those factors, which were identified as unimportant during the factor screening, a storage capacity of 60,000 units seems to be sufficient. However, for high levels of these factors, an extension of the storage capacity is required. Thus, if an extension of the storage area is not an option, a limitation of the number of clients must be considered. Still, the identification of a maximum number of clients such that the existing storage capacity is sufficient requires the conduction of further simulation studies. In summary, the initial hypothesis of the simulation study cannot be confirmed for the first scenario.

7.3 Scenario 2: Customer Demand and Storage Capacity

Compared to the first scenario, the hypothesis that is stated as part of the second scenario is more sophisticated. The hypothesis presented in scenario 1 makes an assumption about the influence one parameter has on the behavior of the model. Hence, a specific level of the considered parameter is defined as well as a threshold for the performance measure. In contrast to this, the hypothesis presented in the second scenario assumes an interdependency between a parameter of the model and a performance measure such that an increasing customer demand results in a certain increase of the required storage capacity. Instead of an absolute threshold value, the presented hypothesis formulates a relative measure, which describes the relationship between two datapoints. Thus, it is challenging to identify relevant parts of the response surface based on the hypothesis.

When formulated as a statistical hypothesis pair, a more advanced expression is required. Unlike the hypothesis of scenario 1, where only one sample was given, it is not sufficient to assume whether or not the observed mean of a performance measure of lower or higher than the mean of a idealized distribution. In this scenario, two samples must be drawn and the difference between the means of these samples must be assessed. Here, the second sample has to be drawn dependent on the first sample so that the customer demand of the second sample is 10 units lower than the one of the first sample. The mean values of both underlying populations (μ_1 and μ_2) can be used to formulate a hypothesis pair regarding the difference between the two means. As the underlying assumption presumes that the maximum storage capacity per customer will increase by more than 100 units, the alternative hypothesis states that the difference between the the means is greater than 100. Accordingly, the null hypothesis claims the opposite and assumes that the difference is not greater than 100 but less or equal to 100.

$$H_0: \mu_2 - \mu_1 \leq 100 \qquad\qquad H_1: \mu_2 - \mu_1 > 100$$

As a next step, the stated hypotheses must be converted into a machine-readable *FITS* expression. In the statistic hypothesis, a statement is made regarding the difference between the means of two populations. In contrast to scenario 1, two distinct samples are drawn, one from each of the investigated populations. Each population is defined by a different parametrization of the investigated model. To model this in *FITS*, an extension of the language is required so that different parameter sets can be taken into account. While parameter set 1 (*ParSet1*) consists of a wildcard character that represents any possible level of the parameter *Demand_W*, parameter set 2 (*ParSet2*) takes a level which is 10 units higher than the one selected in parameter set 1. By this means, *FITS* can be extended and the increasing demand of the customers can be formally specified. For the remaining parameters, no values are defined, which is why the *ceteris paribus* sign is used in the parametrization part of the hypothesis.

$$\text{ParSet1}(Demand\_W(\text{x})) \land \text{ParSet2}(Demand\_W(\text{x+10})) \land \#$$
$$\Rightarrow \mu_1(\text{Maxstorage/Clients\_N}) \land \mu_2(\text{Maxstorage/Clients\_N}) \land$$
$$(H_0(\mu_2 - \mu_1 \leq 100) \lor (H_1(\mu_2 - \mu_1 > 100)) \mid \alpha(0.05) \land n(d_n \leq 0.05)$$

In the *hypothesis information* part of the *FITS* expression, the difference is quantified between the means of the populations that are defined by the two parametrizations of the model. The measured feature that is used for the calculation of the means is in both cases the maximum storage capacity which is required by the factory (μ_1 and μ_2). Yet, in contrast to scenario 1, the maximum storage capacity is divided by the amount of customers. As the underlying statistical hypothesis assumes that the difference between these two means ($\mu_2 - \mu_1$) is greater than 100 units, null and alternative hypothesis are formulated accordingly in *FITS*. Finally, like in scenario 1, both a significance level and a replication estimation precision of 5% are assumed.

7.3.1 Conventional Investigation of the Model's Behavior

In the second case study, the parameter space of the model does not differ from the parameter space of the first case study. Accordingly, the results that were presented in Section 7.2.1 apply here as well. Yet, the performance measure that is used to investigate the behavior of the model differs between the presented case studies. Instead of the overall maximum storage capacity, the maximum storage capacity per customer is considered. Null and alternative hypothesis are formulated as assumption regarding the difference between the maximum storage capacity per customer of two parametrizations of the model. In contrast to the parameter space, the response surface of the second case study differs and is not equal to the one presented in Section 7.2.1. Hence, in this subsection, the response surface of scenario 2 is investigated to assess the quality of the results of the simulation study. Even though the performance measures differ, the analysis presented in this subsection methodically corresponds to the analysis presented in the previous section.

Based on the analysis of the parameter space presented in Section 7.2.1, it is assumed that *Clients_N* and *Product_cost* are also relevant factors in this scenario. The importance of *Demand_W* is not questioned as this parameter is part of the performance measure.

To generate a data basis for this more advanced performance measure, which is required for plotting the response surface of the investigated model, a modification is necessary of the simulation results from scenario 1. In the previous scenario, the required maximum storage capacity was analyzed for multiple factor level combinations. As a first step, each data points was divided by the number of customers (*Clients_N*) as defined in the corresponding parametrization. By this means, a data basis is generated, which can be used to visualize how different parametrizations of the model systematically affect the maximum storage capacity per customer. However, in the presented scenario the hypothesis assumes a difference between the maximum storage capacity required per customer and thus the difference between the data points in the data set must be calculated. In accordance with the hypothesis, pairs of data points are selected such that the difference between the values of the *Demand_W* parameter is 10 while the values of all other parameters are equal. The resulting response surfaces are presented grouped by the values of the remaining parameters and for different levels of the *Product_cost* parameter.

Figure 7.17 illustrates the surface that results when simulating different parameter combinations of *Clients_N* and *Demand_W*. As the shape of the response surface is equal for low, medium, and high values of *Product_cost*, it

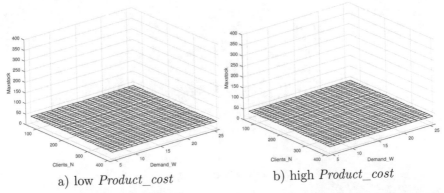

a) low *Product_cost*   b) high *Product_cost*

Figure 7.17: Response surface of interactions between parameters *Clients_N* and *Demand_W* with low values of remaining parameters.

shows only the plots of the extreme values. Furthermore, in this first figure, low values are chosen for all remaining parameters of the model. What can be observed is a surface which is parallel to the x- and y-axis. None of the plotted data points has a z-value which is greater than 50 units. As the surface is flat, it can be concluded that the formulated hypothesis holds for each parametrization of the model in case the less important parameters are assigned low values.

In Figure 7.18, the response surfaces are shown for medium values of the remaining parameters. As the shape of the surfaces differs, the resulting plots for three different levels of *Product_cost* are shown. In contrast to Figure 7.17, a surface which is almost parallel to the x- and y-axis can only be observed for high *Product_cost* as well as for high values of both

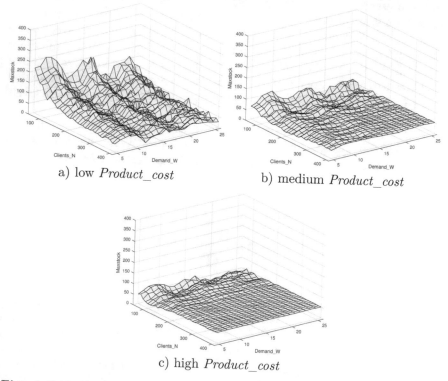

a) low *Product_cost*   b) medium *Product_cost*

c) high *Product_cost*

Figure 7.18: Response surface of interactions between parameters *Clients_N* and *Demand_W* with medium values of remaining parameters.

Clients_N and *Demand_W*. All other parameter configurations result in a convex shape of the response surface. The difference between the required maximum storage capacity per customer is generally higher for lower levels of *Product_cost*. Moreover, an increasing value of *Clients_N* as well as an increasing value of *Demand_W* seem to result in a decreasing difference between the required stock levels per customer. In other words, for a high number of customers and a high initial demand of each customer, an increasing demand results in a proportionally lower increase of the required maximum storage capacity per customer. Based on these observations it can be assumed that a higher number of clients as well as a higher demand of each client weaken the extent of the bullwhip effect.

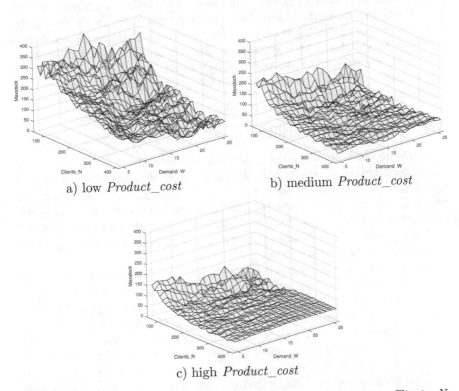

a) low *Product_cost*

b) medium *Product_cost*

c) high *Product_cost*

Figure 7.19: Response surface of interactions between parameters *Clients_N* and *Demand_W* with high values of remaining parameters.

The plots shown in Figure 7.19 correspond to those in Figure 7.18. Yet, for high values of the remaining parameters, the observed effect of the investigated parameters seems to be greater. Especially for medium and high levels of *Product_cost*, those parts of the surface that are parallel to the x- and y-axis are smaller in Figure 7.19. Only a small part of the response surface for high *Product_cost* is even, for high values of *Clients_N* and *Demand_W*. This provides further evidence for the assumption that a high price of the product, a great number of clients, and a high demand of each client weakens the bullwhip effect.

In conclusion, it must be expected that the stated hypothesis cannot be confirmed or refuted for the entire parameter space of the investigated model. Similar to scenario 1, the results of the simulation study that are generated when applying the proposed process of the intelligent assistance most likely consist of multiple design points. For some of these design points, the null hypothesis can be rejected based on the observed behavior of the model. However, for other design points the observed data will not provide sufficient evidence to reject the null hypothesis. In this regard, the interpretation of the results might lead to the discovery that high levels of *Clients_N* and *Product_cost* prevent an increase of the required storage capacity per customer if the demand rises.

7.3.2 Design of Experiments

The following three subsections present the execution of all steps of a Hypothesis-Driven Simulation Study with respect to answering the second hypothesis. The procedure corresponds to the one presented in Section 7.2, where the first scenario was evaluated. To avoid redundancies, all steps, assumptions, and results that are similar or equal in both scenarios will not be repeated in detail. Instead, references are provided to corresponding subsections of the first scenario.

As part of the *design of experiments* step of the first scenario, the limitation of the model's parameter space was discussed. Due to the high number of possible factor-level combinations, the investigation of all potential parametrizations of the model is not feasible. A factor screening approach was applied to determine which factors are of importance for the observed output of the model. By this means, a differentiation can be made between important and unimportant factors. It can be assumed that variations of the level of unimportant factors do not considerably influence the value of the performance measure. Thus, only a greatly reduced number of levels can be investigated for all unimportant factors.

In this thesis, *sequential bifurcation* is presented and used as a method for factor screening. To apply sequential bifurcation, low and high levels must be defined for each of the investigated parameters. Even though the performance measure that is used in this second scenario of the evaluation differs from the one in the first scenario, both performance measures consist of the maximum storage capacity. In the second scenario, the maximum storage capacity is divided by the number of customers. Compared to scenario 1, it can be assumed that this modification of the performance measure does not generally influence the effect the parameters have on the model behavior. Thus, the low and high levels that were defined in scenario 1 (cf. Table 7.9), which are based on results generated with the BehaviorSearch tool, are used in the second scenario as well (cf. Table 7.22). Only the effect of the *Clients_N* parameter might have changed due to the modification of the performance measure. While a positive effect was assumed in scenario 1, where a low level of the *Clients_N* parameter results in a low model output and vice versa, an inverted effect must be assumed for the second scenario. During the calculation of the performance measure, the maximum storage capacity is divided by *Clients_N*. Accordingly, as *Clients_N* is the denominator of the performance measure, low values of *Clients_N* lead to high values of the performance measure and high values of *Clients_N* reduce the overall result. It must be investigated whether the effect a higher value of *Clients_N* has on the numerator of the performance measure (maximum storage capacity) outperforms the effect it has as the denominator of the performance measure.

The application of optimization algorithms seems to be a promising approach for investigating how different levels of the factors influence the output of the model. For this purpose, the *BehaviorSearch* tool is executed with the same configurations that were used in Section 7.2.1 for the new performance measure of scenario 2, i.e., the required maximum storage capacity per customer. In accordance with the recommendations of the model's developer, the model step limit is set to 720 and the maximum storage capacity per customer is measured over all 720 steps. To improve the statistical certainty of the results, 10 sampling replications are conducted and the mean value of these replications is used for further investigations. As no major difference can be identified between the different optimization algorithms, only the standard genetic algorithm is used with the previously presented standard configuration and the gray binary chromosome (cf. Table 7.8).

The factor screening is executed in accordance with the procedure described in Section 7.2.2. Using the low and high values from Table 7.22 results in the observations that are shown in Table 7.23. When all factor are set to

Table 7.22: Low (↓), high (↑), and constant values of inputs for factor screening.

ID	Name	Purpose	Value	
-	*Fact*	#Factories	1	
-	*Distr1*	#Distributors	3	
-	*Distr2*	#Retailers	7	
-	*Cust._strat.*	Purchase strat.	1 - daily	
-	*Inv._pol.*	Inventory strat.	1 - (s,Q)	
-	*Score_Retailers*	Score purchase and choose best supplier	false	

ID	Name	Purpose	↓	↑
1	*Clients_N*	#Clients	350	25
2	*Lt0*	Lead time (Dist.)	0	7
3	*Lt1*	Lead time (Ret.)	0	7
4	*SS_%*	Safety value	.5	.95
5	*Demand_W*	mean(demand)	5	30
6	*DS_D*	σ(demand)	0	15
7	*HC*	Holding cost	.1	.01
8	*K*	Cost per order	50	400
9	*Product_cost*	Cost of product	50	5

their low levels, the minimum effect of the model is $y_{(0)} = 37,50$. In contrast to this, when all factors are set to their high level, $y_{(9)} = 6,235.40$ is the maximum effect of the model. Thus, the resulting group expected effect of all 9 factors is $\bar{\beta}_{1-92} = (y_{(9)} - y_{(0)})/2 = 3,098.95$. Observations $y_{(2)}$ and $y_{(3)}$ are equal. Thus, it can be noted that factor 3 (K) does not influence the behavior of the model in this configuration. Furthermore, the standard deviation of observations $y_{(0)}$ and $y_{(1)}$ is equal to zero. This provides evidence, that the model does not show stochastic behavior for these parametrizations.

As a next step, the main effects of each factor must be estimated to distinguish between important and unimportant factors. For this purpose, the observations and mirror observations from Table 7.23 are used. In contrast to scenario 1, the observations in this table do not always increase

Table 7.23: Averaged observations $y_{(k)}$ and mirror observations $y^*_{(k)}$ based on 50 replicates (*seed-values* = 19890206-19890255).

	mean (μ)	st. dev. (σ)		mean (μ)	st. dev. (σ)
$y_{(0)}$	37.50	0.00	$y^*_{(0)}$	6,235.40	687.06
$y_{(1)}$	225.00	0.00	$y^*_{(1)}$	2,186.90	199.38
$y_{(2)}$	187.31	43.20	$y^*_{(2)}$	846.89	132.17
$y_{(3)}$	187.31	43.20	$y^*_{(3)}$	344.02	65.93
$y_{(4)}$	226.15	63.37	$y^*_{(4)}$	128.25	84.70
$y_{(5)}$	543.68	412.57	$y^*_{(5)}$	45.11	6.50
$y_{(6)}$	2,085.92	143.88	$y^*_{(6)}$	46.29	7.87
$y_{(7)}$	1,859.87	658.91	$y^*_{(7)}$	52.25	4.50
$y_{(8)}$	4,022.80	942.67	$y^*_{(8)}$	37.50	0.00
$y_{(9)}$	6,235.40	687.06	$y^*_{(9)}$	37.50	0.00

when adding factors respectively decrease when removing factors. For mirror observation $y^*_{(2)}$, an increasing mean value can be observed even though less factors are set to their high levels. A possible explanation for this behavior is the existence of a multi-factor interaction such that the first factor correlates with one or multiple other factors. Accordingly, when the level of the first factor is set to its low value, the effect is no longer observable which results in relatively lower output values.

Based on the presented observations, the average main effects of each factor can be calculated (cf. Table 7.24). It is notable, that the $\bar{\beta}$ value of the factor *Clients_N* is strongly negative. Comparing the absolute values of the effects, *Clients_N* has the third largest effect of the model's factors. When applying sequential bifurcation, negative main effects indicate the existence of multi-factor interactions. Yet, in this case, the absolute value of the effect does not provide evidence for the strength of the effect. For *Clients_N*, the existence of such an interaction is reasonable considering the performance measure used in this scenario. All remaining factors have positive or just slightly negative main effects, which are close to zero. Like in the first scenario, the main effects of *Demand_W* (398.67) and *Product_cost* (345.83) are greater than those of the other factors. Thus, *Demand_W*, *Product_cost*, and *Clients_N* are as well considered as *important* factors in this second scenario.

Table 7.24: Average main effects $\bar{\beta}_{(k)}$ of each factor, calculated based on the output values from Table 7.23.

	Factor	$\bar{\beta}_{(k)}$
$\bar{\beta}_{(1)}$	Demand_W	398.67
$\bar{\beta}_{(2)}$	Clients_N	-325.58
$\bar{\beta}_{(3)}$	K	276.53
$\bar{\beta}_{(4)}$	Lt0	38.00
$\bar{\beta}_{(5)}$	HC	164.15
$\bar{\beta}_{(6)}$	Lt1	122.59
$\bar{\beta}_{(7)}$	DS_D	-2.03
$\bar{\beta}_{(8)}$	Product_cost	345.83
$\bar{\beta}_{(9)}$	SS_%	99.99

After identifying those factors that are of major importance for the observed behavior, the more detailed investigation of the model's response surface is the next step of the simulation study. For this purpose, the *Latin Hypercube* general-purpose design is used to explore the unknown shape of the model's response surface at this early stage of the study. As the same model is used in both presented scenarios, the same configuration of the sampling is used, i.e., $k = 9$ factors with $n = 10$ levels. The investigated factor-level combinations are drawn randomly from the 10 defined groups of values. Due to the randomization of the process, it is not necessary to generate new data points and the data points that were generated for scenario 1 are reused (cf. Table 7.25). The space-filling properties of the generated design points were illustrated in Figure 7.14.

The execution of the simulation models with the parametrizations from Table 7.25 leads to the results shown in Table 7.26. Like in scenario 1, interpolation techniques must be applied to approximate the shape of the response surface based on the small number of observed outputs. As *thin plate splines* performed well in scenario 1, the same approach is applied here as well. The resulting interpolated response surface is shown in Figure 7.20.

The shape of the response surface that was presented for the first scenario is similar to the one from this second scenario. For design point 1, the highest output of the model is measured, which results in a maximum in the rear corner of the chart.

Table 7.25: Transformation of design points from Table 7.12 to the range of admissible values of each factor of the second scenario.

DP	Cl_N	Lt0	Lt1	SS_%	Dem_W	DS_D	HC	K	Prod_c
1	253	5	7	0.65	20	1	0.05	300	5
2	201	0	4	0.55	12	1	0.01	400	25
3	157	5	5	0.75	27	2	0.09	250	35
4	344	6	5	0.60	16	2	0.02	350	30
5	94	3	2	0.95	30	2	0.03	200	15
6	65	4	2	0.90	6	3	0.08	150	50
7	52	1	0	0.85	8	3	0.04	400	45
8	143	3	6	0.50	21	0	0.10	250	10
9	221	2	3	0.80	23	1	0.07	150	20
10	314	7	1	0.70	14	0	0.06	100	40

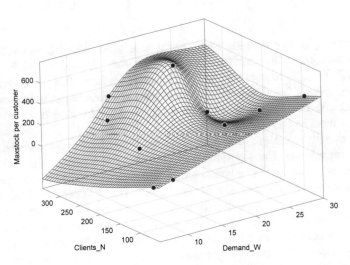

Figure 7.20: Scatterplot of maximum storage capacity per customer for design points from Latin Hypercube Sampling (cf. Table 7.26). Surface interpolated by means of *thin plate splines*.

Table 7.26: Simulation outputs: Average *maximum storage capacity* of each design points of the Latin Hypercube Sampling. ($random - seed =$ $19890206 - 19890255$ and $n = 50$)

Design Point	Maxstorage per customer	
	Mean	*Standard Deviation*
1	683.42	145.53
2	120.12	0.64
3	302.85	24.46
4	302.19	82.05
5	494.50	114.75
6	88.74	19.77
7	150.04	35.86
8	288.25	84.97
9	243.68	9.09
10	158.19	5.49

Moreover, in accordance with scenario 1, a local minimum exists next to this maximum for medium levels of *Clients_N* and for high levels of *Demand_W*. Yet, in contrast to the response surface of the first scenario, it can be observed that the surface of the second scenario ascends for lower levels of *Client_N*. This most likely can be attributed to the modified performance measure used in this scenario.

To properly investigate the model's parameter space to answer the initially stated hypothesis, the simulation of the 16 design points shown in Table 7.27 seems suitable. They represent a compromise between the reduction of the number of executed simulation runs and the coverage of the relevant parameter space. Obviously, the amount of evidence for or against the validity of the hypothesis can be improved by increasing the number of runs and the coverage of the parameter space. However, increasing the number of design points results in a proportional increase of the required runs so that the increased benefit must be traded off against additional efforts.

The presented hypothesis makes an assumption about an increase of the customers' demand by 10 units. Thus, each selected parametrization of the model must be executed for at least two values of *Demand_W* which lie 10 units apart, e.g., *Demand_W* = 5 and *Demand_W* = 15. The range of admissible values of *Demand_W* reaches from 5 to 30 in steps of 1. The design points specified in Table 7.27 cover the lower and upper end of the range of values. This seems sufficient, as the Latin Hypercube Sampling provides evidence for a linear effect the demand has on the storage capacity per customer. Yet, to consider non-linear effects as well, it is possible to specify additional pairs of design points for medium values of $Demand\_W$, e.g., $Demand\_W = 12$ and $Demand\_W = 22$.

Similar to the first case study, confidence intervals are applied for estimating the required number of replications. In contrast to other replication estimation methods, this approach for determining whether or not a specific number of replication is sufficient with respect to a given precision must be applied stepwise during the execution of the simulation runs. Hence, the required number of replications can not be defined during the design phase of the study.

7.3.3 Conducting of Experiments

Similar to the first case study, the simulation framework NetLogo is utilized for the execution of the designed simulation runs. To maintain the comparability of the generated results, the same seed value is chosen for the initial-

Table 7.27: Simulation runs that are executed as part of the simulation study.

DP	Dem_W	$Prod\_c$	Cl_N	$Lt0$	$Lt1$	$SS\_\%$	DS_D	HC	K
1	5	5	350	0	0	0.5	0	0.1	50
2	15	5	350	0	0	0.5	0	0.1	50
3	5	50	350	0	0	0.5	0	0.1	50
4	15	50	350	0	0	0.5	0	0.1	50
5	5	5	25	7	7	0.95	3	0.01	400
6	15	5	25	7	7	0.95	3	0.01	400
7	5	50	25	7	7	0.95	3	0.01	400
8	15	50	25	7	7	0.95	3	0.01	400
9	20	5	350	0	0	0.5	0	0.1	50
10	30	5	350	0	0	0.5	0	0.1	50
11	20	50	350	0	0	0.5	0	0.1	50
12	30	50	350	0	0	0.5	0	0.1	50
13	20	5	25	7	7	0.95	3	0.01	400
14	30	5	25	7	7	0.95	3	0.01	400
15	20	50	25	7	7	0.95	3	0.01	400
16	30	50	25	7	7	0.95	3	0.01	400

ization of the pseudo random number generator ($random$-$seed = 19890206$). As the execution of the model is very similar in both case studies, this subsection focuses in particular on the results of the replication estimation.

As specified during the design phase of the study, the required number of replications is estimated based on the confidence interval approach. The required number of replications of each simulation runs with a precision of $d_n \leq 5\%$ is shown in Table 7.28. Similarities can be observed between the results of all design points where the remaining (unimportant) factors are set to their low levels, i.e., design points 1-4 and 10-13. The replication estimation of these eight design points is equal with 52 replications that are required for all runs. Moreover, it appears that the factor $Product\_cost$ does not influence the behavior of the model for low values of the unimportant factors, even though the factor itself was identified as important factor. The mean values and standard deviations are equal for all pairs of design points in which only the level of $Product\_cost$ is changed and the unimportant factors are set to their low levels.

Table 7.28: Number of replications for each simulation run with precision $d_n \leq 5\%$ and $kLimit = 4$.

DP	#replications	Mean	SD	d_n
1	52	33.41	5.92	4.933%
2	52	100.24	17.76	4.933%
3	52	33.41	5.92	4.933%
4	52	100.24	17.76	4.933%
5	89	2,224.43	524.57	4.968%
6	47	3,520.77	593.10	4.946%
7	118	893.89	243.67	4.970%
8	38	1,451.28	216.91	4.912%
9	52	133.65	23.68	4.933%
10	52	200.48	35.52	4.933%
11	52	133.65	23.68	4.933%
12	52	200.48	35.52	4.933%
13	49	4,108.09	711.08	4.972%
14	53	5,131.96	927.21	4.980%
15	33	1,787.81	248.48	4.928%
16	24	2,442.38	287.36	4.968%

This behavior of the model cannot be observed for high levels of the unimportant factors. In contrast, changing the level of factor *Product_cost* from its low to high value results in a decrease of the output of more than half of its initial value. Likewise, for three of the four pairs of runs, the required number of replications decreases. Only for design points 5 and 7, changing the level of *Product_cost* from 5 to 50 results in an increase of the required number of replications (from 89 to 118). With 118 replications, design point 7 requires the most simulation iterations of all presented simulation runs.

Figure 7.21 shows the step-wise calculation of the confidence interval for simulation run 7. Here, a potential explanation can be observed for the relatively higher number of required replications. After the first three executions of the model, the mean of the performance indicator is 1,024.40. This value lies considerably higher than the final mean of 893.89. Considering the outputs of each execution of the model, the outputs of iterations 1-3 range from 904.00 to 1,112.80. This explains the sudden decrease of the cumulative mean as more iterations are executed. These executions of the model generate lower outputs. For instance, in iteration 19, the maximum storage capacity that is required per customer is only 544.36. Yet, after 118 iterations, the confidence interval reaches a precision which is less or equal to 5.

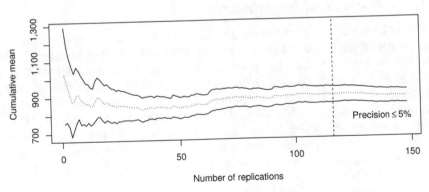

Figure 7.21: Step-wise calculation of the confidence interval for simulation run 7.

To obtain the mean value of the specified performance measure for all 16 simulation runs and with a precision of 5%, a total number of 867 simulations must be conducted during the study. The observed maximum storage capacity ranges from 33.41 to 4,108.09 units per customer. Compared to the results from the application of sequential bifurcation, the minimum storage capacity per customer which was observed for design points 1 and 3 corresponds to the identified minimum effect of the model which was identified by the factor screening. The mean output of the study's experiments is slightly lower, however, this might be the result of stochastic variations. A greater difference can be observed between the maximum from the factor screening and the maximum from the executed simulation runs. While the maximum storage capacity per customer from the factor screening is 6,235.40, the mean output of design points 14 is only 5,131.96, which is approximately 20% less.

In summary, all designed simulation runs were executed and sound model behavior was observed. The outputs generated during the execution of the design matrix confirm the observations from the factor screening. Furthermore, the minimum and maximum effects identified during the factor screening were not obviously violated such that the outputs can be used for the following analyze step of the study. It seems, that a relevant part of the parameter space was investigated and that the outputs from the simulation runs provide a profound data basis for the verification of the study's hypothesis.

7.3.4 Analysis of Experiments

The last step of the experimentation aims at analyzing the data that was generated during the simulation study. After the design and execution of all relevant experiments that provide evidence for or against the validity of the study's hypothesis, this is the third necessary step towards answering hypotheses by means of simulation. In this step of the study, the dataset is tested for outliers. This allows for the identification and substitution of output values that greatly differ from the observed median value. Furthermore, a statistical hypothesis test is applied to investigate whether the study provided sufficient evidence to conform the study's hypothesis or whether it must be refuted.

Table 7.29 shows potential outliers that were identified using the $1.5 \times IQR$ rule. In contrast to the first case study, outliers can be observed in 6 out of the 16 parametrizations. Considering the great number of replications that were required for simulation run 7 as well as the shape of the confidence interval, the results of the outliers analysis provide new insights. Even though the first three outputs that were generated during the execution of simulation run 7 were greater than the final cumulative mean, these

Table 7.29: Potential outliers, that fall outside the upper or lower fence.

DP	replic.	Output value	Median	1.5×IQR	Lower fence	Upper fence
5	53	3,971.20	2,124.40	1,138.80	681.20	3,718.00
7	49	1,509.68	857.00	467.16	251.04	1,496.80
7	65	1,658.80	857.00	467.16	251.04	1,496.80
7	93	1,749.60	857.00	467.16	251.04	1,496.80
8	1	2,000.64	1,436.38	398.57	989.83	1,961.67
8	15	1,970.80	1,436.38	398.57	989.83	1,961.67
13	15	5,846.40	4,100.80	1,207.80	2,485.80	5,706.60
14	15	7,841.60	4,934.40	1,764.60	2,675.40	7,381.00
15	24	2,517.68	1,753.00	400.62	1,256.30	2,324.62

outputs were still considerably lower than the identified outliers. While the cumulative mean of the first three outputs was 1,024.40, this analysis revealed that only values that are greater than 1,496.80 are potential outliers. Thus, it can be concluded that the dispersion of the observed outputs of simulation run 7 is great which is also why a great number of replications is required.

Grubbs' test for outliers can be applied to analyze whether the identified candidates for outliers. As a precondition of this test, the data must originate from a data set which is normally distributed. To test whether a sample comes from a normally distributed population, the *Shapiro-Wilk test* is applied. Table 7.30 shows the results of the *Shapiro-Wilk test* for each of the 16 simulation runs that were conducted in this second case study. Out of the simulation runs in which outliers were identified, only runs 8, 13, and 15 are normally distributed such that *Grubbs' test for outliers* can be applied.

For simulation run 8, the p-value of observation 2,000.64 is 0.1146 and the p-value of observation 1,970.80 is 0.0532. Thus, with a significance threshold of 5%, the null hypothesis that no outliers exist cannot be rejected and it cannot be confirmed that these observations originate from a different population. The same applied for simulation run 13, where observation 5,846.40 can not be classified as an outlier because of the the p-value 0.3642. Only for simulation run 15, the null hypothesis that output 2,517.68 is not an outlier must be rejected due to the p-value 0.0264. Accordingly, it is recommendable to substitute this data point.

As a final step of the analysis of the simulation outputs, a statistical hypothesis test is applied to the data set of each simulation run. In this case study, the *one sample t-test* cannot be used as the investigated hypothesis makes an assumption regarding the difference between the means of two populations. Thus, *Welch's t-test* is applied, which extends the *two sample t-test* for populations with unequal variances. Table 7.31 presents the results for each of the 16 designed simulation runs.

In accordance with the study's hypothesis, the pairs of model parametrizations whose mean outputs are compared only differ in the level of the *Demand_W* factor. Referring to Table 7.27, in which all 16 design points are specified, the eight consecutive pairs of parametrizations can be identified, i.e., design points 1 and 2, 3 and 4, et cetera.

For the application of *Welch's t-test*, two data sets x and y are required that contain independent samples drawn from two different populations. In terms of the conducted simulation study, the data sets consist of the observed outputs from each replication that was executed for the respective simulation run. In Table 7.31, the means of these datasets are referred to as *mean of x* for the mean output of the first data point and *mean of y* for the mean output of the second data point. As it cannot be assumed that

Table 7.30: P-values of Shapiro-Wilk test of normality applied to the outputs of each simulation run.

DP	p-value	normally distributed?
1	8.70×10^{-9}	not normally distributed
2	8.70×10^{-9}	not normally distributed
3	8.70×10^{-9}	not normally distributed
4	8.70×10^{-9}	not normally distributed
5	0.0086	not normally distributed
6	0.5432	normally distributed
7	6.70×10^{-5}	not normally distributed
8	0.0585	normally distributed
9	8.70×10^{-9}	not normally distributed
10	8.70×10^{-9}	not normally distributed
11	8.70×10^{-9}	not normally distributed
12	8.70×10^{-9}	not normally distributed
13	0.3033	normally distributed
14	0.0083	not normally distributed
15	0.4970	normally distributed
16	0.0193	not normally distributed

Table 7.31: Results of *Welch's t-test* for each design point with $\alpha = 0.05$.

DP	t-value	critical value $-t_{(1-\alpha, n-1)}$	degrees of freedom	p-value	mean of x / mean of y	Reject H_0?
1+2	12.776	-1.670	62.195	1.000	33.413 / 100.240	do not reject
3+4	12.776	-1.670	62.195	1.000	33.413 / 100.240	do not reject
5+6	-11.633	-1.663	84.333	1.615×10^{-19}	2,224.431 / 3,520.765	reject
7+8	-10.961	-1.667	69.553	4.175×10^{-17}	893.892 / 1,451.279	reject
9+10	5.603	-1.662	88.856	0.999	133.654 / 200.480	do not reject
11+12	5.603	-1.662	88.856	0.999	133.654 / 200.480	do not reject
13+14	-5.671	-1.661	96.776	7.354×10^{-8}	4,108.088 / 5,131.963	reject
15+16	-7.609	-1.679	45.207	6.240×10^{-10}	1,787.806 / 2,442.383	reject

the variances of both populations are equal, the degrees of freedom must be estimated using the *Welch-Satterthwaite equation* (Satterthwaite, 1941). As in the first case study, the results of the hypothesis test can be evaluated by comparing the t-value to the critical value of the Student's t-distribution or by comparing the p-value to the significance level.

In summary, the assumption that the maximum storage capacity will disproportionately increase by more than 100 units per customer in case the per customer demand increases by 10 units does not apply for all parametrizations of the model. The designed experiments provide evidence, that the hypothesis indeed holds for high levels of the unimportant factors and for a low number of clients. In contrast, for low levels of the unimportant factors and for a great number of clients, this assumption is violated. Here, only a moderate increase of the required per customer storage capacity of less than 100 units per customer can be observed. This can potentially be explained by the greater level of uncertainty which results from a greater number of clients. It is easier to compensate individual fluctuations in demand for a smaller number of clients.

7.4 Conclusions

The goal of this chapter was to evaluate the applicability and appropriateness of the proposed procedure model for Hypothesis-Driven Simulation Studies. To facilitate the practical application of the procedure model, an assistance was specified in this thesis, which logically links existing approaches and techniques with respect to the verification of a given hypothesis. As the applied methods are established and were validated in their respective domains, there is no need to investigate and evaluate the individual appropriateness of these components. Instead, this chapter investigated and assessed whether the combination of these methods is suitable for the systematic generation of knowledge that can be used for the verification of hypotheses by means of simulation. To this end, two case studies were presented in which the assistance was applied to two different scenarios from supply chain management. By this means, evidence was gathered to confirm or refute two hypotheses on the behavior of a simulation model.

The same NetLogo simulation model was used in both case studies. It implements a four-staged supply chain and allows the experimenter to dynamically investigate how stock levels are affected by fluctuations in demand. While the first case study analyzed whether a specific storage capacity threshold is sufficient, the second case study assumed a relationship between an input and an output of the model. For both scenarios, a conventional investigation of the model's parameter space and response surface was provided in advance to assess the results generated during the simulation study. In a second step, the assistance was applied to conduct a study in accordance with the proposed procedure model. Here, the focus lay on the interplay between the individual logical components during the design, execution, and analysis of the relevant experiments with respect to the verification of the hypothesis.

For both case studies, the feasibility and suitability of the approach was confirmed. The design phase consisted of the identification of important factors, the systematic limitation of the parameter space, and the selection of relevant parametrizations based on the formally specified research hypotheses. Subsequently, during the execution phase, the designed runs were conducted by means of the simulation framework under due consideration of the required number of replications. Finally, outliers were identified and substituted in the observed outputs and the outputs were aggregated to allow for the application of statistical hypothesis tests. The results from the conventional investigation of the response surface confirm the results that were generated using the proposed procedure model for Hypothesis-Driven Simulation Studies. Yet, the number of investigated parametrizations is considerably smaller, the efforts of the experimenter are reduced, and the systematics of the applied procedure allow for the thorough documentation of each decision and action that was executed during the study. This is crucial to ensure the replicability and reproducibility of the generated results.

8 Conclusions and Outlook

This thesis addressed the methodological and epistemological shortcomings of simulation studies in the verification of hypotheses on the behavior of a model. Conducting sound studies is challenging as different steps as well as respective methods and techniques must be individually aligned and adapted to answer hypotheses. In this regard, the design, conducting, and analysis of relevant experiments consist of repetitive, yet crucial tasks. These tasks require the thorough and impartial operation of the experimenter to ensure the generation of reliable results. To counteract experimenter bias, which is a threat to the credibility of simulation results, this thesis proposed a concept for conducting and assisting Hypothesis-Driven Simulation Studies. The presented approach is inspired by aviation and clinical trials, where standardized procedures ensure the replicability and reproducibility of study results. Likewise, the assistance introduced by this thesis aims at linking methods and functionalities to facilitate the systematic generation of knowledge in simulation studies. To this end, this thesis lays foundations for the systematic verification of research hypotheses by means of simulation experiments.

This chapter is structured as follows: The first section summarizes the content of this thesis and outlines the contribution this thesis makes for information systems research. Subsequently, the second section provides an outlook and discusses possible directions for future research.

8.1 Summary and Contribution

The introductory chapter of this thesis presented the leading research question, which aims at the development of a methodology to overcome existing challenges in the verification of hypotheses in simulation studies. To address the identified issues, the goal of the remaining chapters was the elaboration of different aspects of this research question.

F. Lorig, *Hypothesis-Driven Simulation Studies,*

In this regard, the first chapter derived five more specific research questions, which represent important milestones towards the conceptualization of Hypothesis-Driven Simulation Studies:

1. What is the current status quo in the application, assistance, and automation of simulation?

2. How can both specification and testing of phenomenological hypotheses be assisted?

3. How can relevant simulation experiments be derived and designed from hypotheses?

4. What is a suitable methodology for conducting Hypothesis-Driven Simulation Studies?

5. How must existing methods, frameworks, and tools be logically linked to provide assistance for the systematic testing of hypotheses in simulation studies?

To answer the first research question, Part 1 of this thesis surveyed relevant literature on foundations of simulation as well as the current state of the art in the application, assistance, and automation of simulation. Chapter 2 provided an overview of the concept of simulation and introduced models and experiments as the two key components. The epistemological challenge of simulation lies in the thorough design of experiments for the systematic investigation of models. Models often consist of parameter spaces that are too large to be investigated completely. Thus, the limitation of the investigated parameter space must be achieved under due consideration of the stated research question to be answered. But also the execution and analysis of experiments must be conducted thoroughly to ensure the generation of replicable and reproducible results. To this end, Chapter 2 investigated methods for the systematic application of simulation in simulation studies.

The sound conduct of simulation studies and the generation of credible results is challenging as the process of a study is sophisticated, error-prone, and time-consuming. To assist the experimentation process and to automate specific steps, Chapter 3 surveyed the current state of the art in the assistance and automation of simulation. This chapter introduced and discussed theoretical as well as practical approaches and methods to facilitate the application of simulation. This included specification languages and guidelines but also toolkits and software frameworks. In summary, a variety of approaches exist that provide a valuable contribution to the assistance and automation of different aspects of simulation. However, most of the presented approaches only address individual steps of simulation studies or neglect hypothesis-driven experimentation. Important design decisions still have to be made by the experimenter, which runs the potential risk of bias. Hence, methodological shortcomings were identified and a research gap was formulated so that research hypotheses can be thoroughly integrated into the process of simulation studies.

To overcome the presented research gap, the second part of this thesis proposed a concept for conducting Hypothesis-Driven Simulation Studies. By this means, research questions 2 to 4 were addressed. Respective requirements for the developed approach were presented in the fourth chapter. To this end, the chapter provided a discussion of the structure of such hypotheses as well as epistemological demands that arise from scientific hypotheses. In a next step, it was evaluated how these requirements are met in practice during the conducting of simulation studies. The status quo of the methodological integration of hypotheses was introduced and structural components were derived that are part of simulation studies. Accordingly, the developed approach must consider the requirements from scientific hypotheses to improve the current integration of hypotheses in simulation studies.

The fifth chapter is the key chapter of this thesis. It addressed the identified methodological shortcomings of simulation studies by proposing an integrated procedure model for the systemized verification of hypotheses on the behavior of simulation models. Based on the scenario of a study, the procedure model assists the specification of phenomenological hypotheses and automates both the design of relevant experiments as well as the aggregation of the generated results. As the resulting process is extensive, and as repetitive tasks might lead to carelessness of the experimenter, it is reasonable to support the execution of the proposed procedure model by means of an assistance system. With respect to the development of such an assistance system, Chapter 5 also specified how existing services can be logically combined to address research question 5 and to facilitate the conducting of Hypothesis-Driven Simulation Studies. Lastly, this chapter presented an abstract architecture for the implementation of an assistance system.

The components that are required for the development of the proposed assistance were formally specified in Chapter 6. Besides a detailed specification of the simulation model as well as the research hypothesis, this chapter introduced services for the design, execution, and analysis of experiments.

To this end, inputs and outputs of all required services were specified and the transformation process was formalized.

The third part of this thesis evaluated the applicability of the proposed approach. As an example of its application, Chapter 7 presented two case studies from the domain of logistics. The NetLogo model that was used for the case studies consists of a four-tiered supply chain and can be applied to investigate both the occurrence and consequences of the bullwhip effect. Based on this model, two fictitious scenarios were presented for conducting simulation studies and two potential resulting research hypotheses were introduced for the application of the proposed approach. To evaluate the plausibility of the generated results, a thorough investigation was conducted in advance of the parameter space that results from each hypothesis. This allowed for the comparison and assessment of the results that were generated during the exemplary application of the procedure model. To further evaluate the feasibility of the proposed approach, all steps and interim results generated by the procedure model are presented in great detail. In summary, the feasibility and applicability of the proposed approach was demonstrated and confirmed.

This thesis lays the foundations for the assisted and hypothesis-driven conducting of simulation studies, with the aim of replicable and reproducible verification of assumptions regarding the behavior of a simulation model. In contrast to existing approaches that only assist single steps of simulation studies or neglect the investigation of specific hypotheses, the hypothesis becomes the key element of the study in the presented approach. By this means, every step and design decision made during the study can be aligned with the hypothesis and contribute to the efficient generation of credible results. In summary, the contributions made by this thesis can be summarized as follows. The proposed approach for conducting Hypothesis-Driven Simulation Studies as well as the presented assistance enable:

- the formal specification of phenomenological hypotheses on the behavior of simulation models,

- the hypothesis-based reduction of the parameter space for the design of relevant experiments,

- the systematic disaggregation of simulation studies into its structural components as well as the reaggregation of the generated results,

- the facilitation and assistance of the process of simulation studies to prevent or reduce the occurrence of experimenter bias,

- and the logical combination of existing services for the automated verification of hypotheses by means of an assistance system.

This thesis does not focus on the development of services for the automation of simulation but on the targeted combination of existing services. The presented architecture for the assistance of simulation studies does not rely on specific services. Instead, the modular architecture of the assistance system allows for the integration of different services that correspond to the specifications presented in Chapter 6. Accordingly, the services presented in this thesis only serve as examples for the respective types of service. They can be individually modified, extended, or exchanged by other suitable methods or techniques.

The presented assistance is beneficial for two groups of users: *practitioners* and *scientists*. Both groups of experimenters impose different requirements on simulation studies. Practitioners often apply simulation to answer specific questions regarding the behavior of a model or compare two or more models in terms of their performance. To thoroughly answer such questions, it might be necessary to execute a large number of parametrizations of the model. This task is monotonous but still has to be carried out with the utmost care to avoid generating false results and drawing incorrect conclusions. The development of an assistance system as proposed in this thesis facilitates this task and allows for a more effortless and simplified execution of simulation experiments.

In contrast to this, scientists apply simulation studies to generate knowledge and to investigate theories. Here, the methodological soundness and the epistemological credibility of the study are of high relevance. The proposed process assistance facilitates the scientific application of simulation as well. As researchers are capable of specifying their hypothesis by means of the introduced *FITS* language, relevant experiments can be derived directly from the question the study aims at answering. This increases both replicability and reproducibility of the generated results, as all steps of the study that are executed by the assistance system are transparent and can easily be documented for publication and further evaluations.

8.2 Outlook and Future Work

Considering the potential for the scientific generation of knowledge this thesis lays foundations for an emerging research topic which requires further efforts in terms of future work. This section presents an outlook of potential future developments and derives prospects for future research that ought to be conducted to further promote the assistance and automation of simulation.

In the past decades, the application of simulation has increased remarkably and experts believe that this development will continue in the future (Yi et al., 2006; Sargent, 2017). Hence, information systems research is under an obligation to facilitate the application of simulation, to ensure the credibility of the generated results, and thus to make simulation available to a greater audience. These goals are addressed by a large number of simulation frameworks, toolkits, and suites, which facilitate various aspects of simulation. However, such softwares provides insufficient guidance for novice experimenters and often does not consider simulation studies as a coherent and rigorous process. To overcome these shortcomings in existing software artifacts, the development of a comprehensive software assistance is advisable from an information systems research perspective.

This thesis provided specifications for necessary services and proposed an abstract architecture for the implementation of an assistance system. Thus, as a next step, it is necessary to implement an information system that corresponds to these requirements. An evaluation must be made whether it is reasonable to extend an existing simulation framework or to implement the assistance system from scratch. With respect to the diffusion and usability of the system it seems reasonable to provide the presented approach as an add-on that can easily be integrated into several existing frameworks. Yet, this intention is accompanied by increased development efforts compared to a stand-alone system. Moreover, a stand-alone system allows for the provision of a central repository for both the execution and storing of results from simulation studies. Individual simulation services that were developed by different researchers and practitioners can be connected to this central repository and dynamically integrated into the process of simulation studies. By this means, the experimenter can flexibly chose between general services that are provided by the assistance system or integrate their own services that correspond to individual needs, e.g., an experimental design or factor screening approach that performs well for a specific model type. In addition to the execution of experiments, a central repository facilitates the documentation, publications, and reproduction of the generated simulation results. A reference to the repository that contains all information on the conducted study can for instance be provided in scientific publications. It enables other researchers to further investigate and reproduce the results or to carry out additional experiments with different parametrizations or hypotheses.

The development of a repository that governs data and results from simulation studies can also improve and facilitate the scientific generation of knowledge. The underlying assumption of a scientific hypotheses might be highly sophisticated. Thus, an assistance system must dynamically adapt the study's process and might even require supplementation with additional services. Considering the abstract architecture that was presented in Chapter 5, the automation of this task can be accomplished by the *simulation experiment assistance*. Based on a suitable knowledge base, the coordinator agent is able to identify potential missing information, which can be dynamically acquired by adjusting the process of the study. For this purpose, approaches from Artificial Intelligence can be applied, such as case based reasoning or machine learning. In doing so, well-suited procedures can be derived from the results of previously conducted studies to answer specific hypotheses. In this regard, a repository for simulation studies can serve as a data base. However, this functionality is not part of the assistance that is presented in this thesis and must be addressed by future work.

Another aspect of future research is the integration of different types of hypotheses. This thesis focused on *phenomenological hypotheses* that make assertions on the *input-output-behavior* of a simulation model. To investigate such hypotheses, it is sufficient to consider the model as a black box whereby no information of the inner structure and mechanisms of the model is available. Yet, Yilmaz et al. (2016) moreover distinguished between *mechanistic hypotheses* and *control hypotheses*. In contrast to *phenomenological hypotheses*, these two types of hypotheses require white box approaches where the mechanisms of the model are known. In particular, the automated assessment of *mechanistic hypotheses* is still a topic of future research. Even though Doud and Yilmaz (2017) proposed the *FASE* framework for the automated analysis of simulation experiments and mechanistic hypotheses, the presented approach does not fully integrate the model. Instead of automatically deriving relevant experiments, *FASE* requires simulation results as inputs for the generation of *Discrete-Time Markov Chains*. To this end, the frameworks does not assist the design and execution of experiments and thus cannot be applied to the conducting of simulation studies.

The discussed perspectives on required future work contribute to further establishing simulation as a tool for practitioners, as method in scientific research, and to cope with future developments. In the years to come, it must be expected that higher requirements will be imposed on simulation studies due to the increasing extent and mechanistic complexity of the investigated models. Thus, the advancement of existing approaches as well as the development of innovative techniques for the assistance of automation of simulation will gain in relevance. Especially with respect to the establishment of simulation as an "epistemological engine of our time" (Tolk et al., 2013b, p. 1154), new methods and techniques in the field of simulation must be developed as individual services so that they can be dynamically combined and integrated into the process of simulation studies. This necessity also corresponds to the vision of Yilmaz et al. (2014), who claimed that the automation of simulation is essential to improve the reproducibility of simulation experiments.

Bibliography

Abar, S., Theodoropoulos, G. K., Lemarinier, P., and O'Hare, G. M. (2017). Agent Based Modelling and Simulation Tools: A Review of the State-Of-Art Software. *Computer Science Review*, 24:13–33.

Abramowitz, M. and Stegun, I. A. (1965). *Handbook of Mathematical Functions*, volume 55. Dover Books on Mathematics.

Achinstein, P. (1990). Hypotheses, Probability, and Waves. *The British Journal for the Philosophy of Science*, 41(1):73–102.

Ahmed, M. D. and Sundaram, D. (2009). Design and Implementation of Scenario Management Systems. In *Encyclopedia of Information Science and Technology*, pages 1030–1039. IGI Global, 2nd edition.

Aigner, M. and Ziegler, G. M. (2014). Buffon's Needle Problem. In *Proofs from THE BOOK*, pages 175–178. Springer, Berlin, Heidelberg.

Alexopoulos, C., Joines, J. A., Kuhl, M. E., Page, E. H., Wainer, G., Tufarolo, J., Chan, V., D'Ambrogio, A., Zacharewicz, G., and Mustafee, N. (2017). History of the Winter Simulation Conference: Modern Period (2008–2017). In *Proceedings of the 2017 Winter Simulation Conference*, WSC '17, pages 100 114, Piscataway, New Jersey. Institute of Electrical and Electronics Engineers, Inc.

Altintas, I., Berkley, C., Jaeger, E., Jones, M., Ludascher, B., and Mock, S. (2004). Kepler: An Extensible System for Design and Execution of Scientific Workflows. In *Proceedings of the 16th International Conference on Scientific and Statistical Database Management*, SSDBM '06, pages 423–424. IEEE.

American Mathematical Society (2010). Announcement of the Fulkerson Prize Committee: 2009 Fulkerson Prizes. *Notices of the American Mathematical Society (AMS)*, 57(11):1475–1476.

Angermann, A., Beuschel, M., Rau, M., and Wohlfarth, U. (2007). *MATLAB - Simulink - Stateflow*. Oldenbourg, München, 5th edition.

© Springer Fachmedien Wiesbaden GmbH, part of Springer Nature 2019
F. Lorig, *Hypothesis-Driven Simulation Studies*,

Armbruster, D., Marthaler, D. E., Ringhofer, C., Kempf, K., and Jo, T.-C. (2006). A Continuum Model for a Re-entrant Factory. *Operations Research*, 54(5):933–950.

Asendorpf, J. B., Conner, M., De Fruyt, F., De Houwer, J., Denissen, J. J., Fiedler, K., Fiedler, S., Funder, D. C., Kliegl, R., and Nosek, B. A. (2013). Replication Is More Than Hitting the Lottery Twice. *European Journal of Personality*, 27(2):138–138.

Atlason, J., Epelman, M. A., and Henderson, S. G. (2008). Optimizing Call Center Staffing Using Simulation and Analytic Center Cutting-Plane Methods. *Management Science*, 54(2):295–309.

Avramidis, A. N. and Wilson, J. R. (1994). A Flexible Method for Estimating Inverse Distribution Functions in Simulation Experiments. *ORSA Journal on Computing*, 6(4):342–355.

Axelrod, R. (1997). Advancing the Art of Simulation in the Social Sciences. In Fandel, G., Trockel, W., Conte, R., Hegselmann, R., and Terna, P., editors, *Simulating Social Phenomena*, volume 456, pages 21–40. Springer, Berlin, Heidelberg.

Balci, O. (1990). Guidelines for Successful Simulation Studies. In Sadowski, R. P., Nance, R. E., and Balci, O., editors, *Proceedings of the 1990 Winter Simulation Conference*, WSC '90, pages 25–32, Piscataway, New Jersey. Institute of Electrical and Electronics Engineers, Inc.

Balci, O. (1998). Verification, Validation, and Testing. In Banks, J., editor, *Handbook of Simulation*, pages 335–393. John Wiley & Sons, Inc., Hoboken, NJ, USA.

Banks, J., editor (1998). *Handbook of Simulation: Principles, Methodology, Advances, Applications, and Practice*. Wiley, Co-published by Engineering & Management Press, New York.

Banks, J. (2000). Introduction to Simulation. In Fishwick, P. A., Kang, K., Joines, J. A., and Barton, R. R., editors, *Proceedings of the 2000 Winter Simulation Conference*, WSC '00, pages 9–16, Piscataway, New Jersey. Institute of Electrical and Electronics Engineers, Inc.

Banks, J. (2014). *Discrete-Event System Simulation*. Always learning. Pearson, Harlow, 5th edition.

Banks, J. and Gibson, R. (1997). Don't Simulate When... 10 Rules for Determining when Simulation Is Not Appropriate. *IIE solutions*, 29(9):30–33.

Barton, R. R. (2013). Designing Simulation Experiments. In Hill, R., Kuhl, M., Pasupathy, R., Kim, S.-H., and Tolk, A., editors, *Proceedings of the 2013 Winter Simulation Conference*, WSC '13, pages 342–353, Piscataway, New Jersey. Institute of Electrical and Electronics Engineers, Inc.

Barton, R. R., Joines, J. A., Morrice, D. J., Page, E. H., Wainer, G., Tufarolo, J., Chan, V., D'Ambrogio, A., Zacharewicz, G., and Mustafee, N. (2017). History of the Winter Simulation Conference: Period of Growth, Consolidation, and Innovation (1993–2007). In *Proceedings of the 2017 Winter Simulation Conference*, WSC '17, pages 87–99, Piscataway, NJ, USA. Institute of Electrical and Electronics Engineers, Inc.

Bates, B. C. (1994). Calibration of the SFB Model Using a Simulated Annealing Approach. *Water Down Under 94: Surface Hydrology and Water Resources Papers; Preprints of Papers*, pages 1–6.

Bauccio, M., editor (1993). *ASM Metals Reference Book*. ASM International, Materials Park, Ohio, 3rd edition.

Beautement, P. and Broenner, C. (2011). *Complexity Demystified: A Guide for Practitioners*. Triarchy Press, Axminster, Devon.

Bednarek, R. and Ulam, F. (1990). *Analogies Between Analogies: The Mathematical Reports of S.M. Ulam and His Los Alamos Collaborators*. University of California Press, Berkley.

Berger, P. D. and Nasr, N. I. (1998). Customer Lifetime Value: Marketing Models and Applications. *Journal of Interactive Marketing*, 12(1):17–30.

Berndt, J. O., Timm, I. J., Krause, J., and Munnich, R. (2017). Toward Hybrid Simulations for Care Demand Forecasting. In Snowdon, J. L., Charnes, J. M., Yücesan, E., and Chen, C.-H., editors, *Proceedings of the 2017 Winter Simulation Conference*, WSC '17, pages 4594–4595, Piscataway, New Jersey. Institute of Electrical and Electronics Engineers, Inc.

Bertossi, L., Hunter, A., and Schaub, T. (2005). Introduction to Inconsistency Tolerance. *Inconsistency Tolerance*, 3300:1–16.

Better, M., Glover, F., and Laguna, M. (2007). Advances in Analytics: Integrating Dynamic Data Mining with Simulation Optimization. *IBM Journal of Research and Development*, 51(3.4):477–487.

Bettonvil, B. and Kleijnen, J. P. C. (1996). Searching for Important Factors in Simulation Models with Many Factors: Sequential Bifurcation. *European Journal of Operational Research*, 96(1):180–194.

Biles, W. E., Kleijnen, J. P. C., van Beers, W. C. M., and van Nieuwenhuyse, I. (2007). Kriging Metamodeling in Constrained Simulation Optimization: An Explorative Study. In Tew, J., Barton, R., Henderson, S., Biller, B., Hsieh, M.-h., and Shortle, J., editors, *Proceedings of the 2007 Winter Simulation Conference*, WSC '07, pages 355–362, Piscataway, New Jersey. Institute of Electrical and Electronics Engineers, Inc.

Biller, B. and Gunes, C. (2010). Introduction to Simulation Input Modeling. In Hugan, J., Yücesan, E., Fu, M., Johansson, B., Jain, S., and Montoya-Torres, J., editors, *Proceedings of the 2010 Winter Simulation Conference*, WSC '10, pages 49–58, Piscataway, New Jersey. Institute of Electrical and Electronics Engineers, Inc.

Birta, L. G. and Arbez, G. (2013). *Modelling and Simulation: Exploring Dynamic System Behaviour*. Simulation foundations, methods and application. Springer, London, 2nd edition.

Bley, H., Franke, C., Wuttke, C. C., and Gross, A. (2000). Automation of Simulation Studies. In *Proceedings of the 2nd CIRP International Seminar on Intelligent Computation in Manufacturing*, ICME 2000, pages 89–94.

Bocciarelli, P., D'Ambrogio, A., Giglio, A., and Gianni, D. (2013). A SAAS-Based Automated Framework to Build and Execute Distributed Simulations from SysML Models. In Hill, R., Kuhl, M., Pasupathy, R., Kim, S.-H., and Tolk, A., editors, *Proceedings of the 2013 Winter Simulation Conference*, WSC '13, pages 1371–1382, Piscataway, New Jersey. Institute of Electrical and Electronics Engineers, Inc.

Bogon, T., Timm, I. J., Jessen, U., Schmitz, M., Wenzel, S., Lattner, A. D., Paraskevopoulos, D., and Spieckermann, S. (2012). Towards Assisted Input and Output Data Analysis in Manufacturing Simulation: The EDASim Approach. In Rose, O., Uhrmacher, A., Rabe, M., Laroque, C., Rasupathy, R., and Himmelspach, J., editors, *Proceedings of the 2012 Winter Simulation Conference*, WSC '12, pages 1–13, Piscataway, New Jersey. Institute of Electrical and Electronics Engineers, Inc.

Bonabeau, E. (2002). Agent-Based Modeling: Methods and Techniques for Simulating Human Systems. *Proceedings of the National Academy of Sciences*, 99(Supplement 3):7280–7287.

Booch, G., Rumbaugh, J., and Jacobson, I. (2005). *The Unified Modeling Language User Guide*. Addison-Wesley, Upper Saddle River, NJ, 2nd edition.

Bossel, H. (2014). *Modeling and Simulation*. Vieweg+Teubner Verlag, Wiesbaden.

Brachner, M. (2015). A Simulation Model to Evaluate an Emergency Response System for Offshore Helicopter Ditches. In Macal, C. M., Rossetti, M. D., Yilmaz, L., Moon, I.-C., Chan, W. K., and Roeder, T., editors, *Proceedings of the 2015 Winter Simulation Conference*, WSC '15, pages 2366–2377, Piscataway, New Jersey. Institute of Electrical and Electronics Engineers, Inc.

Brassel, K.-H. (2001). Flexible Modelling with VSEit, the Versatile Simulation Environment for the Internet. *Journal of Artificial Societies and Social Simulation*, 4(3).

Brazma, A., Hingamp, P., Quackenbush, J., Sherlock, G., Spellman, P., Stoeckert, C., Aach, J., Ansorge, W., Ball, C. A., Causton, H. C., and others (2001). Minimum Information About a Microarray Experiment (MIAME) - Toward Standards for Microarray Data. *Nature genetics*, 29(4):365–371.

Brown, R. G., Eddelbuettel, D., and Bauer, D. (2013). Dieharder: A Random Number Test Suite. https://webhome.phy.duke.edu/~rgb/General/dieharder.php.

Bruce, D. (1997). What Makes a Good Domain-Specific Language? APOSTLE, and Its Approach to Parallel Discrete Event Simulation. In *First ACM SIGPLAN Workshop on Domain-Specific Languages*, ICFP '13, pages 17–35, Illinois, Chicago.

Bulmahn, R. (2009). Aerodynamics of Model Car. https://commons.wikimedia.org/wiki/File:Aerodynamics_of_model_car.jpg.

Byrne, J., Heavey, C., and Byrne, P. (2010). A Review of Web-Based Simulation and Supporting Tools. *Simulation Modelling Practice and Theory*, 18(3):253–276.

Çakırlar, İ., Gürcan, Ö., Dikenelli, O., and Bora, Ş. (2015). RatKit: Repeatable Automated Testing Toolkit for Agent-Based Modeling and Simulation. In Grimaldo, F. and Norling, E., editors, *Multi-Agent-Based Simulation XV*, volume 9002, pages 17–27. Springer International Publishing, Cham.

Campolongo, F., Cariboni, J., Saltelli, A., and Schoutens, W. (2005). Enhancing the Morris Method. In *Proceedings of the 4th International Conference on Sensitivity Analysis of Model Output, SAMO 2004*, pages 369–379.

Carnell, R. (2018). Package 'lhs'. https://cran.r-project.org/web/packages/lhs/lhs.pdf.

Carson, II, J. S. (2004). Introduction to Modeling and Simulation. In Smith, J., Peters, B., Ingalls, R. G., and Rossetti, M., editors, *Proceedings of the 2004 Winter Simulation Conference*, WSC '04, pages 9–16, Piscataway, New Jersey. Institute of Electrical and Electronics Engineers, Inc.

Carter, S. M. and Little, M. (2007). Justifying Knowledge, Justifying Method, Taking Action: Epistemologies, Methodologies, and Methods in Qualitative Research. *Qualitative Health Research*, 17(10):1316–1328.

Casler, M. D. (2015). Fundamentals of Experimental Design: Guidelines for Designing Successful Experiments. *Agronomy Journal*, 107(2):692.

Cayirci, E. and Ghergherehchi, R. (2011). Modeling Cyber Attacks and Their Effects on Decision Process. In White, P., Fu, M., Jain, S., Creasey, R., and Himmelspach, J., editors, *Proceedings of the 2011 Winter Simulation Conference*, WSC '11, pages 2627–2636, Piscataway, New Jersey. Institute of Electrical and Electronics Engineers, Inc.

Centeno, M. A. (1996). An Introduction to Simulation Modeling. In Brunner, D. T., Swain, J. J., Charnes, J. M., and Morrice, D. J., editors, *Proceedings of the 1996 Winter Simulation Conference*, WSC '96, pages 15–22, Piscataway, New Jersey. Institute of Electrical and Electronics Engineers, Inc.

Chockler, H., Kupferman, O., and Vardi, M. (2006). Coverage Metrics for Formal Verification. *International Journal on Software Tools for Technology Transfer*, 8(4-5):373–386.

Chung, C. A. (2004). *Simulation Modeling Handbook: A Practical Approach*. CRC Press, Boca Raton. OCLC: 51967170.

Claeys, F., Vanrolleghem, P. A., and Fritzson, P. (2006). A Generalized Framework for Abstraction and Dynamic Loading of Numerical Solvers. In *Proceedings of 2006 European Modelling and Simulation Symposium*, EMSS 2006, pages 4–6.

Coll-Font, J., Burton, B. M., Tate, J. D., Erem, B., Swenson, D. J., Wang, D., Brooks, D. H., Van Dam, P., and Macleod, R. S. (2014). New Additions to the Toolkit for Forward/Inverse Problems in Electrocardiography Within the SCIrun Problem Solving Environment. In *Comput Cardiol*, volume 41, pages 213–216. IEEE.

Conte, R. and Paolucci, M. (2014). On Agent-Based Modeling and Computational Social Science. *Frontiers in Psychology*, 5(668).

Conway, R. W. and McClain, J. O. (2003). The Conduct of an Effective Simulation Study. *INFORMS Transactions on Education*, 3(3):13–22.

Cortés, P., Muñuzuri, J., Nicolás Ibáñez, J., and Guadix, J. (2007). Simulation of Freight Traffic in the Seville Inland Port. *Simulation Modelling Practice and Theory*, 15(3):256–271.

Cowie, J., Nicol, D., and Ogielski, A. (1999). Modeling the Global Internet. *Computing in Science & Engineering*, 1(1):42–50.

da Silva, A. R. (2015). Model-Driven Engineering: A Survey Supported by the Unified Conceptual Model. *Computer Languages, Systems & Structures*, 43:139–155.

Dalle, O. (2012). On Reproducibility and Traceability of Simulations. In Rose, O., Uhrmacher, A., Rabe, M., Laroque, C., Rasupathy, R., and Himmelspach, J., editors, *Proceedings of the 2012 Winter Simulation Conference*, WSC '12, pages 2763–2774, Piscataway, New Jersey. Institute of Electrical and Electronics Engineers, Inc.

Dallmeyer, J. (2013). *Akteursorientierte multimodale Straßenverkehrssimulation*. Dissertation, Goethe University Frankfurt. Universitätsbibliothek Johann Christian Senckenberg, Frankfurt am Main, Germany.

Dallmeyer, J., Schumann, R., Lattner, A. D., and Timm, I. J. (2015). Don't Go With the Ant Flow: Ant-Inspired Traffic Routing in Urban Environments. *Journal of Intelligent Transportation Systems*, 19(1):78–88.

Dannhauer, M., Brooks, D., Tucker, D., and MacLeod, R. (2012). A Pipeline for the Simulation of Transcranial Direct Current Stimulation for Realistic Human Head Models Using SCIRun/BioMesh3d. In *Proceedings of the 2012 Annual International Conference of the IEEE Engineering in Medicine and Biology Society*, EMBC 2012, pages 5486–5489. IEEE.

Davidsson, P. (2002). Agent Based Social Simulation: A Computer Science View. *Journal of Artificial Societies and Social Simulation*, 5(1).

Davidsson, P., Henesey, L., Ramstedt, L., Törnquist, J., and Wernstedt, F. (2005). An Analysis of Agent-Based Approaches to Transport Logistics. *Transportation Research Part C: Emerging Technologies*, 13(4):255–271.

Davidsson, P. and Verhagen, H. (2013). Types of Simulation. In Edmonds, B. and Meyer, R., editors, *Simulating Social Complexity*, pages 23–36. Springer, Berlin, Heidelberg.

Dekker, L. (1984). Concepts for an Advanced Parallel Simulation Architecture. In Ören, T. I., Zeigler, B. P., and Elzas, M. S., editors, *Simulation and Model-Based Methodologies: An Integrative View*, pages 235–278. Springer, Berlin, Heidelberg.

Deng, X., Hung, Y., and Lin, C. D. (2015). Design for Computer Experiments with Qualitative and Quantitative Factors. *Statistica Sinica*, 25(4):1567–1581.

Dewey, J. (1910a). *How We Think*. D.C. Heath & Co., Boston, New York, Chicago.

Dewey, J. (1910b). Science as Subject-Matter and as Method. *Science*, 31(787):121–127.

Djanatliev, A. and Meier, F. (2016). Hospital Processes Within an Integrated System View: A Hybrid Simulation Approach. In Huschka, T., Chick, S., Jimenez, J., Frazier, P., Roeder, T., Szechtman, R., and Zhou, E., editors, *Proceedings of the 2016 Winter Simulation Conference*, WSC '16, pages 1364–1375, Piscataway, New Jersey. Institute of Electrical and Electronics Engineers, Inc.

Dodig-Crnkovic, G. (2002). Scientific Methods in Computer Science. In *Conference for the Promotion of Research in IT at New Universities and at University Colleges in Sweden*, PROMOTE IT 2002.

Dominka, S., Bröcker, E., and Manzie, C. (2008). A Tool for the Automation of Simulation Studies. In *Proceedings of the 10th International Conference on Computer Modeling and Simulation*, ICCMS 2008, pages 169–174. IEEE.

Doud, K. and Yilmaz, L. (2017). A Framework for Formal Automated Analysis of Simulation Experiments using Probabilistic Model Checking. In Page, E. H., Wainer, G., Tufarolo, J., Chan, V., D'Ambrogio, A., Zacharewicz, G., and Mustafee, N., editors, *Proceedings of the 2017 Winter Simulation Confernece*, WSC '17, pages 1312–1323, Piscataway, New Jersey. Institute of Electrical and Electronics Engineers, Inc.

Eager, D., Zahorjan, J., and Lazowska, E. (1989). Speedup Versus Efficiency in Parallel Systems. *IEEE Transactions on Computers*, 38(3):408–423.

Epstein, J. M. (2006). *Generative Social Science: Studies in Agent-Based Computational Modeling*. Princeton studies in complexity. Princeton University Press, Princeton.

European Commission (1996). Good Clinical Practice (ICH E6: Good Clinical Practice: Consolidated guideline). https://ec.europa.eu/health/sites/health/files/files/eudralex/vol-10/3cc1aen_en.pdf.

European Commission (2014). Regulation No. 536/2014 of the European Parliament and of the Council of 16 April 2014 on Clinical Trials on Medicinal Products for Human Use, and Repealing Directive (2001/20/Ec).

Ewald, R. (2012). *Automatic Algorithm Selection for Complex Simulation Problems*. Vieweg+Teubner Verlag, Wiesbaden.

Ewald, R., Rossel, J., Himmelspach, J., and Uhrmacher, A. M. (2008). A Plug-In-Based Architecture for Random Number Generation in Simulation Systems. In Jefferson, T., Fowler, J., Mason, S., Hill, R., Moench, L., and Rose, O., editors, *Proceedings of the 2008 Winter Simulation Conference*, WSC '08, pages 836–844, Piscataway, New Jersey. Institute of Electrical and Electronics Engineers, Inc.

Ewald, R. and Uhrmacher, A. M. (2014). SESSL: A Domain-Specific Language for Simulation Experiments. *ACM Transactions on Modeling and Computer Simulation*, 24(2):1–25.

Feurzeig, W. (1969). Programming-Languages as a Conceptual Framework for Teaching Mathematics. Final Report on the First Fifteen Months of the LOGO Project.

Fishman, G. S. (1968). Estimating Reliability in Simulation Experiments. In Reitman, J. and Ockene, A., editors, *Proceedings of the 1968 Winter Simulation Conference*, WSC '68, pages 6–10, Piscataway, New Jersey. Institute of Electrical and Electronics Engineers, Inc.

Fishwick, P. A. (1997). Computer Simulation: Growth Through Extension. *Transactions of the Society for Computer Simulation*, 14(1):13–24.

Flanagan, P. D., Currier, J. B., and Willis, K. E. (1973). Simulation in the Design of Automated Air Traffic Control Functions. In Sussman, J. and Hoggatt, A. C., editors, *Proceedings of the 1973 Winter Simulation Conference*, WSC '73, pages 449–462, Piscataway, New Jersey. Institute of Electrical and Electronics Engineers, Inc.

Floore, T. E. and Gilman, G. H. (2011). Design and Capabilities of an Enhanced Naval Mine Warfare Simulation Framework. In White, P., Fu, M., Jain, S., Creasey, R., and Himmelspach, J., editors, *Proceedings of the 2011 Winter Simulation Conference*, WSC '11, pages 2607–2613, Piscataway, New Jersey. Institute of Electrical and Electronics Engineers, Inc.

Forrester, J. W. (1961). *Industrial Dynamics*. MIT Press, Cambridge, Massachusetts.

Frank, A. L. (1968). The Use of Experimental Design Techniques in Simulation. In Reitman, J. and Ockene, A., editors, *Proceedings of the 1968 Winter Simulation Conference*, WSC '68, pages 11–12, Piscataway, New Jersey. Institute of Electrical and Electronics Engineers, Inc.

Frankfurter, G. M. and Horwitz, B. (1971). Earnings per Share, Debt Financing Costs and Debt Composition – A Simulation Model. In Arten, M. and Sussman, J., editors, *Proceedings of the 1971 Winter Simulation Conference*, WSC '71, pages 341–357, Piscataway, New Jersey. Institute of Electrical and Electronics Engineers, Inc.

Freedman, D., Pisani, R., and Purves, R. (2007). *Statistics*. W.W. Norton & Co, New York, 4th edition. OCLC: ocm76142955.

Freire, J., Bonnet, P., and Shasha, D. (2012). Computational Reproducibility: State-Of-The-Art, Challenges, and Database Research Opportunities. In *Proceedings of the 2012 ACM SIGMOD International Conference on Management of Data*, SIGMOD/PODS '12, pages 593–596. ACM Press.

Friedman, L. W. (1996). *Simulation Metamodel*. Springer US, Boston.

Fritzson, P. and Engelson, V. (1998). Modelica – A Unified Object-Oriented Language for System Modeling and Simulation. In Goos, G., Hartmanis, J., van Leeuwen, J., and Jul, E., editors, *Proceedings of the 1998 European Conference on Object-Oriented Programming*, volume 1445 of *ECOOP '98*, pages 67–90, Berlin, Heidelberg. Springer.

Fujimoto, R. M. (1990). Parallel Discrete Event Simulation. *Communications of the ACM*, 33(10):30–53.

Fujimoto, R. M. (2000). *Parallel and Distribution Simulation Systems*. Wiley, New York.

Gamma, E., editor (1995). *Design Patterns: Elements of Reusable Object-Oriented Software*. Addison-Wesley professional computing series. Addison-Wesley, Reading, Massachusetts.

Giere, R. N. (1997). *Understanding Scientific Reasoning*. Harcourt, Brace, Jovanovich, Fort Worth, 4th edition.

Gil, A. (2012). Artificial Supply Chain. http://modelingcommons.org/browse/one_model/3378.

Gilbert, G. N. and Troitzsch, K. G. (2005). *Simulation for the Social Scientist*. Open University Press, Maidenhead, England, 2nd edition.

Gilchrist, W. G. (2000). *Statistical Modelling with Quantile Functions*. Chapman & Hall/CRC, Boca Raton, Fla.

Goble, C. A., Bhagat, J., Aleksejevs, S., Cruickshank, D., Michaelides, D., Newman, D., Borkum, M., Bechhofer, S., Roos, M., Li, P., and De Roure, D. (2010). myExperiment: A Repository and Social Network for the Sharing of Bioinformatics Workflows. *Nucleic Acids Research*, 38(Web Server issue):W677–W682.

Gogg, T. J. and Mott, J. R. (1993). Introduction to Simulation. In Russell, E. C., Biles, W. E., Evans, G. W., and Mollaghasemi, M., editors, *Proceedings of the 1993 Winter Simulation Conference*, WSC '93, pages 9–17,

Piscataway, New Jersey. Institute of Electrical and Electronics Engineers, Inc.

Goldsman, D., Nance, R. E., and Wilson, J. R. (2010). A Brief History of Simulation Revisited. In Hugan, J., Yücesan, E., Fu, M., Johansson, B., Jain, S., and Montoya-Torres, J., editors, *Proceedings of the 2010 Winter Simulation Conference*, WSC '10, pages 567–574, Piscataway, New Jersey. Institute of Electrical and Electronics Engineers, Inc.

Goldstine, H. H. and Goldstine, A. (1946). The Electronic Numerical Integrator and Computer (ENIAC). *Mathematical Tables and Other Aids to Computation*, 2(15):97.

Gooding, D. W. (1990). *Experiment and the Making of Meaning: Human Agency in Scientific Observation and Experiment*. Springer Netherlands, Dordrecht.

Gordon, G. (1978). *System Simulation*. Prentice-Hall, Englewood Cliffs, New Jersey, 2nd edition.

Gordon, G. (1981). The Development of the General Purpose Simulation System (GPSS). In *ACM SIGPLAN Notices - Special Issue: History of Programming Languages Conference*, pages 403–426, New York. ACM Press.

Greasley, A. (2003). Using Business-Process Simulation Within a Business-Process Reengineering Approach. *Business Process Management Journal*, 9(4):408–420.

Griffin, T., Petrovic, S., Poplawski, A., and Premore, B. (2002). SOS: Scripts for Organizing'Speriments. http://ssfnet.org/sos/index.html.

Grimm, V., Berger, U., Bastiansen, F., Eliassen, S., Ginot, V., Giske, J., Goss-Custard, J., Grand, T., Heinz, S. K., Huse, G., Huth, A., Jepsen, J. U., Jørgensen, C., Mooij, W. M., Müller, B., Pe'er, G., Piou, C., Railsback, S. F., Robbins, A. M., Robbins, M. M., Rossmanith, E., Rüger, N., Strand, E., Souissi, S., Stillman, R. A., Vabø, R., Visser, U., and DeAngelis, D. L. (2006). A Standard Protocol for Describing Individual-Based and Agent-Based Models. *Ecological Modelling*, 198(1-2):115–126.

Grimmett, G. and Stirzaker, D. (2001). *Probability and Random Processes*. Oxford University Press, Oxford, 3rd edition.

Grove, W. M. and Menton, W. H. (2015). Hypothetico-Deductive Model. In Cautin, R. L. and Lilienfeld, S. O., editors, *The Encyclopedia of Clinical Psychology*, pages 1–3. John Wiley & Sons, Inc., Hoboken, NJ, USA.

Grüne-Yanoff, T. (2009). The Explanatory Potential of Artificial Societies. *Synthese*, 169(3):539–555.

Grüne-Yanoff, T. and Weirich, P. (2010). The Philosophy and Epistemology of Simulation: A Review. *Simulation & Gaming*, 41(1):20–50.

Gürcan, Ö., Dikenelli, O., and Bernon, C. (2013). A Generic Testing Framework for Agent-Based Simulation Models. *Journal of Simulation*, 7(3):183–201.

Haig, B. D. (1995). Grounded Theory as Scientific Method. *The Philosophy of Education*, 28(1):1–11.

Hales, T. (2005). A Proof of the Kepler Conjecture. *Annals of Mathematics*, 162(3):1065–1185.

Hallagan, A. (2011). *The Design of XML-Based Model and Experiment Description Languages for Network Simulation*. Undergraduate Honors Theses, 43, Bucknell University. Lewisburg, Pennsylvania.

Hanneman, R., Kposowa, A. J., and Riddle, M. (2013). *Basic Statistics for Social Research*. Jossey-Bass, San Francisco, CA, 1st edition.

Haq, I. and Nazir, A. (2016). Which Statistical Hypothesis Test Should I Apply? a Simple Guide for Beginners. *International Journal of Preventive Medicine*, 7(1):81.

Hare, M. and Deadman, P. (2004). Further Towards a Taxonomy of Agent-Based Simulation Models in Environmental Management. *Mathematics and Computers in Simulation*, 64(1):25–40.

Harrell, C., Ghosh, B. K., and Bowden, R. (2012). *Simulation Using ProModel*. McGraw-Hill, New York, 3rd edition.

Harris, F. W. (1990). How Many Parts to Make at Once. *Operations Research*, 38(6):947–950.

Hawkins, D. M. (1980). *Identification of Outliers*. Monographs on Statistics and Applied Probability. Springer.

Hawthorne, G. and Elliott, P. (2005). Imputing Cross-Sectional Missing Data: Comparison of Common Techniques. *Australian & New Zealand Journal of Psychiatry*, 39(7):583–590.

Heidelberger, P. and Welch, P. D. (1981). A Spectral Method for Confidence Interval Generation and Run Length Control in Simulations. *Communications of the ACM*, 24(4):233–245.

Henesey, L. E. (2006). *Multi-Agent Systems for Container Terminal Management.* PhD thesis, Blekinge Institute of Technology, Karlskrona.

Hernandez, A. S., Lucas, T. W., and Sanchez, P. J. (2012). Selecting Random Latin Hypercube Dimensions and Designs Through Estimation of Maximum Absolute Pairwise Correlation. In Rose, O., Uhrmacher, A., Rabe, M., Laroque, C., Rasupathy, R., and Himmelspach, J., editors, *Proceedings of the 2012 Winter Simulation Conference*, WSC '12, pages 1–12, Piscataway, New Jersey. Institute of Electrical and Electronics Engineers, Inc.

Hevner, A. R., March, S. T., Park, J., and Ram, S. (2004). Design Science in Information Systems Research. *MIS Quarterly*, 28(1):75.

Highland, H. J. (1977). Review of "Theory of Modeling and Simulation, by Bernard P. Zeigler". *ACM SIGSIM Simulation Digest*, 8(3):4.

Highland, H. J. (1979). A Taxonomy Approach to Simulation Model Documentation. *ACM SIGSIM Simulation Digest*, 10(3):19–23.

Himmelspach, J. (2007). *Konzeption, Realisierung und Verwendung eines allgemeinen Modellierungs-, Simulations-und Experimentiersystems: Entwicklung und Evaluation effizienter Simulationsalgorithmen.* Informatik. Sierke.

Himmelspach, J. and Uhrmacher, A. M. (2007). Plug'n Simulate. In *Proceedings of the 40th Annual Simulation Symposium*, ANSS '07, pages 137–143. IEEE.

Himmelspach, J. and Uhrmacher, A. M. (2009). The JAMES II Framework for Modeling and Simulation. In *Proceedings of the 2009 International Workshop on High Performance Computational Systems Biology*, HiBi '09, pages 101–102. IEEE.

Hoad, K., Robinson, S., and Davies, R. (2007). Automating DES Output Analysis: How Many Replications to Run. In Tew, J., Barton, R., Henderson, S., Biller, B., Hsieh, M.-h., and Shortle, J., editors, *Proceedings of the 2007 Winter Simulation Conference*, WSC '07, pages 505–512, Piscataway, New Jersey. Institute of Electrical and Electronics Engineers, Inc.

Hoad, K., Robinson, S., and Davies, R. (2010a). Automated Selection of the Number of Replications for a Discrete-Event Simulation. *Journal of the Operational Research Society*, 61(11):1632–1644.

Hoad, K., Robinson, S., and Davies, R. (2010b). Automating Warm-Up Length Estimation. *Journal of the Operational Research Society*, 61(9):1389–1403.

Hofmann, M. A. (2016). Null Hypothesis Significance Testing in Simulation. In Huschka, T., Chick, S., Jimenez, J., Frazier, P., Roeder, T., Szechtman, R., and Zhou, E., editors, *Proceedings of the 2016 Winter Simulation Conference*, WSC '16, pages 522–533, Piscataway, New Jersey. Institute of Electrical and Electronics Engineers, Inc.

Huang, E., Ramamurthy, R., and McGinnis, L. F. (2007). System and Simulation Modeling Using SysML. In Tew, J., Barton, R., Henderson, S., Biller, B., Hsieh, M.-h., and Shortle, J., editors, *Proceedings of the 2007 Winter Simulation Conference*, WSC '07, pages 796–803, Piscataway, New Jersey. Institute of Electrical and Electronics Engineers, Inc.

Huang, Y., Seck, M. D., and Verbraeck, A. (2011). From Data to Simulation Models: Component-based Model Generation with a Data-driven Approach. In White, P., Fu, M., Jain, S., Creasey, R., and Himmelspach, J., editors, *Proceedings of the 2011 Winter Simulation Conference*, WSC '11, pages 3724–3734, Piscataway, New Jersey. Institute of Electrical and Electronics Engineers, Inc.

Hucka, M., Finney, A., Sauro, H. M., Bolouri, H., Doyle, J. C., Kitano, H., and the rest of the SBML Forum:, Arkin, A. P., Bornstein, B. J., Bray, D., Cornish-Bowden, A., Cuellar, A. A., Dronov, S., Gilles, E. D., Ginkel, M., Gor, V., Goryanin, I. I., Hedley, W. J., Hodgman, T. C., Hofmeyr, J.-H., Hunter, P. J., Juty, N. S., Kasberger, J. L., Kremling, A., Kummer, U., Le Novere, N., Loew, L. M., Lucio, D., Mendes, P., Minch, E., Mjolsness, E. D., Nakayama, Y., Nelson, M. R., Nielsen, P. F., Sakurada, T., Schaff, J. C., Shapiro, B. E., Shimizu, T. S., Spence, H. D., Stelling, J., Takahashi, K., Tomita, M., Wagner, J., and Wang, J. (2003). The Systems Biology

Markup Language (SBML): A Medium for Representation and Exchange of Biochemical Network Models. *Bioinformatics*, 19(4):524–531.

Hudert, S., Niemann, C., and Eymann, T. (2010). On Computer Simulation as a Component in Information Systems Research. In Hutchison, D., Kanade, T., Kittler, J., Kleinberg, J. M., Mattern, F., Mitchell, J. C., Naor, M., Nierstrasz, O., Pandu Rangan, C., Steffen, B., Sudan, M., Terzopoulos, D., Tygar, D., Vardi, M. Y., Weikum, G., Winter, R., Zhao, J. L., and Aier, S., editors, *Global Perspectives on Design Science Research*, volume 6105, pages 167–179. Springer, Berlin, Heidenberg.

Hurley, P. J. (2012). *A Concise Introduction to Logic*. Wadsworth Cengage Learning, Boston, MA, 11th edition.

Hussain, T. S., Tiberio, L., and VanderZee, E. (2015). Hierarchical, Extensible Search-Based Framework for Airlift and Sealift Scheduling Using Discrete Event Simulation. In Macal, C. M., Rossetti, M. D., Yilmaz, L., Moon, I.-C., Chan, W. K., and Roeder, T., editors, *Proceedings of the 2015 Winter Simulation Conference*, WSC '15, pages 2342–2353, Piscataway, New Jersey. Institute of Electrical and Electronics Engineers, Inc.

Hylands, C., Lee, E. A., Liu, J., Liu, X., Neuendorffer, S., Xiong, Y., and Zheng, H. (2003). Heterogeneous Concurrent Modeling and Design in Java (Volume 1: Introduction to Ptolemy II). Technical Report No. UCB/EECS-2008-28, https://www2.eecs.berkeley.edu/Pubs/TechRpts/2008/EECS-2008-28.html.

Iannone, F. (2012). The Private and Social Cost Efficiency of Port Hinterland Container Distribution Through a Regional Logistics System. *Transportation Research Part A: Policy and Practice*, 46(9):1424–1448.

Iooss, B. and Lemaître, P. (2015). A Review on Global Sensitivity Analysis Methods. In Dellino, G. and Meloni, C., editors, *Uncertainty Management in Simulation-Optimization of Complex Systems*, volume 59, pages 101–122. Springer US, Boston, MA.

Jansen-Vullers, M. and Netjes, M. (2006). Business Process Simulation – A Tool Survey. In *Workshop and Tutorial on Practical Use of Coloured Petri Nets and the CPN Tools*, volume 38, pages 1–20, Aarhus, Denmark.

Janssen, M. A., Alessa, L. N., Barton, M., Bergin, S., and Lee, A. (2008). Towards a Community Framework for Agent-Based Modelling. *Journal of Artificial Societies and Social Simulation*, 11(2):6.

Johnson, C., Parker, S., and Weinstein, D. (2000). Large-Scale Computational Science Applications Using the Scirun Problem Solving Environment. In *Proceedings of Supercomputing 2000*, ICS '12, pages 263–270. IEEE.

Joseph, V. R. and Hung, Y. (2008). Orthogonal-Maximin Latin Hypercube Designs. *Statistica Sinica*, 18(1):171–186.

Kasaie, P. and Kelton, W. D. (2015). Guidelines for Design and Analysis in Agent-Based Simulation Studies. In Macal, C. M., Rossetti, M. D., Yilmaz, L., Moon, I.-C., Chan, W. K., and Roeder, T., editors, *Proceedings of the 2015 Winter Simulation Conference*, WSC '15, pages 183–193, Piscataway, New Jersey. Institute of Electrical and Electronics Engineers, Inc.

Kelton, W. D. and Barton, R. R. (2003). Experimental Design for Simulation: Experimental Design for Simulation. In Ferrin, D., Morrice, D. J., Sanchez, P. J., and Chick, S., editors, *Proceedings of the 2003 Winter Simulation Conference*, WSC '03, pages 59–65, Piscataway, New Jersey. Institute of Electrical and Electronics Engineers, Inc.

Kenna, C. J. (2008). *An Experiment Design Framework for the Simulator of Wireless Ad Hoc Networks*. Undergraduate Honors Theses, Bucknell University. Lewisburg, Pennsylvania.

Kennedy, O. G. (1973). The Use of Computer Simulation in Health Care Facility Design. In Sussman, J. and Hoggatt, A. C., editors, *Proceedings of the 1973 Winter Simulation Conference*, WSC '73, pages 172–198, Piscataway, New Jersey. Institute of Electrical and Electronics Engineers, Inc.

Kettinger, W. J., Teng, J. T. C., and Guha, S. (1997). Business Process Change: A Study of Methodologies, Techniques, and Tools. *MIS Quarterly*, 21(1):55.

Khabsa, M. and Giles, C. L. (2014). The Number of Scholarly Documents on the Public Web. *PLoS ONE*, 9(5):e93949.

Kiviat, P. J., Villanueva, R., and Markowitz, H. M. (1968). *The SIMSCRIPT II Programming Language*. Prentice-Hall.

Kleijnen, J. P. C. (1995). Verification and Validation of Simulation Models. *European Journal of Operational Research*, 82(1):145–162.

Kleijnen, J. P. C. (1998). Experimental Design for Sensitivity Analysis, Optimization, and Validation of Simulation Models. In Banks, J., editor, *Handbook of Simulation*, pages 173–223. John Wiley & Sons, Inc., Hoboken, NJ, USA.

Kleijnen, J. P. C. (2001). Comments on M.C. Kennedy & A. O'Hagan: "Bayesian Calibration of Computer Models". *Journal of the Royal Statistical Society*, 63(3):464–464.

Kleijnen, J. P. C. (2005a). An Overview of the Design and Analysis of Simulation Experiments for Sensitivity Analysis. *European Journal of Operational Research*, 164(2):287–300.

Kleijnen, J. P. C. (2005b). Supply Chain Simulation Tools and Techniques: A Survey. *International Journal of Simulation and Process Modelling*, 1(1/2):82.

Kleijnen, J. P. C. (2008). Design Of Experiments: Overview. In Jefferson, T., Fowler, J., Mason, S., Hill, R., Moench, L., and Rose, O., editors, *Proceedings of the 2008 Winter Simulation Conference*, WSC '08, pages 479–488, Piscataway, New Jersey. Institute of Electrical and Electronics Engineers, Inc.

Kleijnen, J. P. C. (2009). Factor Screening in Simulation Experiments: Review of Sequential Bifurcation. In Alexopoulos, C., Goldsman, D., and Wilson, J. R., editors, *Advancing the Frontiers of Simulation*, volume 133, pages 153–167. Springer US, Boston, MA.

Kleijnen, J. P. C. (2010). Sensitivity Analysis of Simulation Models: An Overview. *Procedia - Social and Behavioral Sciences*, 2(6):7585–7586.

Kleijnen, J. P. C. (2015). *Design and Analysis of Simulation Experiments*. Number 230 in International series in operations research & management science. Springer, Cham, 2nd edition.

Kleijnen, J. P. C., Bettonvil, B. W., and Persson, F. (2003). Finding the Important Factors in Large Discrete-Event Simulation: Sequential Bifurcation and its Applications. Technical report, Tilburg University, Netherlands.

Kleijnen, J. P. C., Sanchez, S. M., Lucas, T. W., and Cioppa, T. M. (2005). State-of-the-Art Review: A User's Guide to the Brave New World of Designing Simulation Experiments. *INFORMS Journal on Computing*, 17(3):263–289.

Köhn, D. and Le Novère, N. (2008). SED-ML – An XML Format for the Implementation of the MIASE Guidelines. In Hutchison, D., Kanade, T., Kittler, J., Kleinberg, J. M., Mattern, F., Mitchell, J. C., Naor, M., Nierstrasz, O., Pandu Rangan, C., Steffen, B., Sudan, M., Terzopoulos, D., Tygar, D., Vardi, M. Y., Weikum, G., Heiner, M., and Uhrmacher, A. M., editors, *Computational Methods in Systems Biology*, volume 5307, pages 176–190. Springer, Berlin, Heidelberg.

Kravari, K. and Bassiliades, N. (2015). A Survey of Agent Platforms. *Journal of Artificial Societies and Social Simulation*, 18(1).

Król, D., Wrzeszcz, M., Kryza, B., Dutka, L., and Kitowski, J. (2013). Massively Scalable Platform for Data Farming Supporting Heterogeneous Infrastructure. In *The Fourth International Conference on Cloud Computing, GRIDs, and Virtualization, IARIA Cloud Computing*, CLOUD COMPUTING 2013, pages 144–149. IARIA.

Kuhn, W. (2006). Digital Factory - Simulation Enhancing the Product and Production Engineering Process. In Nicol, D., Fujimoto, R., Lawson, B., Liu, J., Perrone, F., and Wieland, F., editors, *Proceedings of the 2006 Winter Simulation Conference*, WSC '06, pages 1899–1906, Piscataway, New Jersey. Institute of Electrical and Electronics Engineers, Inc.

Kurbel, K. (2013). *Enterprise Resource Planning and Supply Chain Management: Functions, Business Processes and Software for Manufacturing Companies*. Springer, Heidelberg.

Kurkowski, S., Camp, T., and Colagrosso, M. (2005). MANET Simulation Studies: The Incredibles. *ACM SIGMOBILE Mobile Computing and Communications Review*, 9(4):50.

La Londe, B. J. and Masters, J. M. (1994). Emerging Logistics Strategies: Blueprints for the Next Century. *International Journal of Physical Distribution & Logistics Management*, 24(7):35–47.

Lambdin, C. (2012). Significance Tests as Sorcery: Science Is Empirical – Significance Tests Are Not. *Theory & Psychology*, 22(1):67–90.

Lattner, A., Pitsch, H., Timm, I., Spieckermann, S., and Wenzel, S. (2011a). AssistSim - Towards Automation of Simulation Studies in Logistics. *Simulation Notes Europe*, 21:119–128.

Lattner, A. D. (2013). Towards Automation of Simulation Studies: Artificial Intelligence Methodologies for the Control and Analysis of Simulation Experiments. *KI - Künstliche Intelligenz*, 27(3):287–290.

Lattner, A. D., Bogon, T., and Timm, I. J. (2011b). An Approach to Significance Estimation for Simulation Studies. In *Proceedings of the 3rd International Conference on Agents and Artificial Intelligence*, ICAART 2011, pages 177–186.

Lattner, A. D., Dallmeyer, J., and Timm, I. J. (2011c). Learning Dynamic Adaptation Strategies in Agent-Based Traffic Simulation Experiments. In *Proceedings of the 9th German Conference on Multiagent System Technologies*, MATES '11, pages 77–88, Berlin, Heidelberg. Springer.

Law, A. (2003). How to Conduct a Successful Simulation Study. In Ferrin, D., Morrice, D. J., Sanchez, P. J., and Chick, S., editors, *Proceedings of the 2003 Winter Simulation Conference*, WSC '03, pages 66–70, Piscataway, New Jersey. Institute of Electrical and Electronics Engineers, Inc.

Law, A. and McComas, M. (1991). Secrets of Successful Simulation Studies. In Kelton, W. D., Clark, G. M., and Nelson, B. L., editors, *Proceedings of the 1991 Winter Simulation Conference*, WSC '91, pages 21–27, Piscataway, New Jersey. Institute of Electrical and Electronics Engineers, Inc.

Law, A. M. (2008). How to Build Valid and Credible Simulation Models. In Jefferson, T., Fowler, J., Mason, S., Hill, R., Moench, L., and Rose, O., editors, *Proceedings of the 2008 Winter Simulation Conference*, WSC '08, pages 39–47, Piscataway, New Jersey. Institute of Electrical and Electronics Engineers, Inc.

Law, A. M. (2011). How the ExpertFit Distribution-Fitting Software Can Make Your Simulation Models More Valid. In White, P., Fu, M., Jain, S., Creasey, R., and Himmelspach, J., editors, *Proceedings of the 2011 Winter Simulation Conference*, WSC '11, pages 63–69, Piscataway, New Jersey. Institute of Electrical and Electronics Engineers, Inc.

Law, A. M. (2014). *Simulation Modeling and Analysis*. McGraw-Hill series in industrial engineering and management science. McGraw-Hill, Dubuque, 5th edition.

Law, A. M. (2015). Statistical Analysis of Simulation Output Data: The Practical State of the Art. In Macal, C. M., Rossetti, M. D., Yilmaz, L., Moon, I.-C., Chan, W. K., and Roeder, T., editors, *Proceedings of the 2015*

Winter Simulation Conference, WSC '15, pages 1810–1819, Piscataway, New Jersey. Institute of Electrical and Electronics Engineers, Inc.

Law, A. M. and McComas, M. G. (1998). Simulation of Manufacturing Systems. In Carson, J. S., Manivannan, M. S., Medeiros, D. J., and Watson, E. F., editors, *Proceedings of the 1998 Winter Simulation Conference*, WSC '98, pages 49–52, Piscataway, New Jersey. Institute of Electrical and Electronics Engineers, Inc.

Law, A. M. and McComas, M. G. (2003). ExpertFit Distribution-Fitting Software: How the ExpertFit Distribution-Fitting Software Can Make Your Simulation Models More Valid. In Ferrin, D., Morrice, D. J., Sanchez, P. J., and Chick, S., editors, *Proceedings of the 2003 Winter Simulation Conference*, WSC '03, pages 169–174, Piscataway, New Jersey. Institute of Electrical and Electronics Engineers, Inc.

Lazzari, M. A. (2009). Developing a Standard Protocol for the Introduction of New Testing Into a Clinical Laboratory. *Laboratory Medicine*, 40(7):389–393.

L'Ecuyer, P. (1990). Random Numbers for Simulation. *Communications of the ACM*, 33(10):85–97.

L'Ecuyer, P. (1997). Uniform Random Number Generators: A Review. In Withers, D. H., Nelson, B. L., Andradóttir, S., and Healy, K. J., editors, *Proceedings of the 1997 Winter Simulation Conference*, WSC '97, pages 127–134, Piscataway, New Jersey. Institute of Electrical and Electronics Engineers, Inc.

L'Ecuyer, P. (2012). Random Number Generation. In Gentle, J. E., Härdle, W. K., and Mori, Y., editors, *Handbook of Computational Statistics*, pages 35–71. Springer, Berlin, Heidelberg.

L'Ecuyer, P. (2015). Random Number Generation with Multiple Streams for Sequential and Parallel Computing. In Macal, C. M., Rossetti, M. D., Yilmaz, L., Moon, I.-C., Chan, W. K., and Roeder, T., editors, *Proceedings of the 2015 Winter Simulation Conference*, WSC '15, pages 31–44, Piscataway, New Jersey. Institute of Electrical and Electronics Engineers, Inc.

L'Ecuyer, P. and Simard, R. (2007). TestU01: A C Library for Empirical Testing of Random Number Generators. *ACM Transactions on Mathematical Software*, 33(4):22.

Lee, A. T. (2005). *Flight Simulation: Virtual Environments in Aviation*. Routledge.

Lee, H. L., Padmanabhan, V., and Whang, S. (1997). The Bullwhip Effect in Supply Chains. *Sloan management review*, 38(3):93.

Leemis, L. (1999). Simulation Input Modeling. In Sturrock, D. T., Evans, G. W., Farrington, P. A., and Nemhard, H. B., editors, *Proceedings of the 1999 Winter Simulation Conference*, volume 1 of *WSC '99*, pages 14–23, Piscataway, New Jersey. Institute of Electrical and Electronics Engineers, Inc.

Leemis, L. M. and McQueston, J. T. (2008). Univariate Distribution Relationships. *The American Statistician*, 62(1):45–53.

Lehmann, E. L. and Romano, J. P. (2005). *Testing Statistical Hypotheses*. Springer texts in statistics. Springer, New York, 3rd edition.

LeNovère, N., Finney, A., Hucka, M., Bhalla, U. S., Campagne, F., Collado-Vides, J., Crampin, E. J., Halstead, M., Klipp, E., Mendes, P., Nielsen, P., Sauro, H., Shapiro, B., Snoep, J. L., Spence, H. D., and Wanner, B. L. (2005). Minimum Information Requested in the Annotation of Biochemical Models (MIRIAM). *Nature Biotechnology*, 23(12):1509–1515.

Leye, S. and Uhrmacher, A. M. (2012). GUISE – A Tool for GUIding Simulation Experiments. In Rose, O., Uhrmacher, A., Rabe, M., Laroque, C., Rasupathy, R., and Himmelspach, J., editors, *Proceedings of the 2012 Winter Simulation Conference*, WSC '12, page 132, Piscataway, New Jersey. Institute of Electrical and Electronics Engineers, Inc.

Liang, J., Lin, Z., and Ma, Y. (2012). OF-NEDL: An Openflow Networking Experiment Description Language Based on XML. In *Proceedings of the 2012 International Conference on Web Information Systems and Mining*, WISM 2012, pages 686–697, Berlin, Heidelberg. Springer.

Liu, J., Perrone, L. F., Nicol, D. M., Liljenstam, M., Elliott, C., and Pearson, D. (2001). Simulation Modeling of Large-Scale Ad-Hoc Sensor Networks. In *European Simulation Interoperability Workshop*, volume 200 of *SIWS '01*.

Llodrà, J., Lladó, C. M., Puigjaner, R., and Smith, C. U. (2011). FORGE: Friendly Output to Results Generator Engine. In *Proceedings of the 2nd ACM/SPEC International Conference on Performance engineering*, ICPE 2011, pages 423–424. ACM Press.

Lorig, F., Becker, C. A., and Timm, I. J. (2017a). Formal Specification of Hypotheses for Assisting Computer Simulation Studies. In *Proceedings of the Symposium on Theory of Modeling & Simulation*, TMS/DEVS '17, pages 18:1–18:12. Society for Computer Simulation International.

Lorig, F., Dammenhayn, N., Müller, D.-J., and Timm, I. J. (2015). Measuring and Comparing Scalability of Agent-Based Simulation Frameworks. In Müller, J. P., Ketter, W., Kaminka, G., Wagner, G., and Bulling, N., editors, *Multiagent System Technologies*, pages 42–60. Springer International Publishing, Cham.

Lorig, F., Lebherz, D. S., Berndt, J. O., and Timm, I. J. (2017b). Hypothesis-driven Experiment Design in Computer Simulation Studies. In Snowdon, J. L., Charnes, J. M., Yücesan, E., and Chen, C.-H., editors, *Proceedings of the 2017 Winter Simulation Conference*, WSC '17, pages 1360–1371, Piscataway, New Jersey. Institute of Electrical and Electronics Engineers, Inc.

Lorig, F., Reuter, L., Zolitschka, J.-F., Timm, I. J., Emmerling, C., and Udelhoven, T. (2016). An Agent-Based Approach for Simulating Transformation Processes of Socio-Ecological Systems as Serious Game. *Interaction Design and Architecture(s) Journal (IxD&A)*, 31(Winter 2016):98–114.

Lorscheid, I., Heine, B.-O., and Meyer, M. (2012). Opening the 'Black Box' of Simulations: Increased Transparency and Effective Communication Through the Systematic Design of Experiments. *Computational and Mathematical Organization Theory*, 18(1):22–62.

Lutz, R. (2011). IEEE Recommended Practice for Distributed Simulation Engineering and Execution Process (DSEEP). https://standards.ieee.org/findstds/standard/1730-2010.html.

Maes, P. (1994). Agents That Reduce Work and Information Overload. *Communications of the ACM*, 37(7):30–40.

Malsch, T. and Schulz-Schaeffer, I. (2007). Socionics: Sociological Concepts for Social Systems of Artificial (and Human) Agents. *Journal of Artificial Societies and Social Simulation*, 10(1):11.

Manicas, P. (2011). American Social Science: The Irrelevance of Pragmatism. *European Journal of Pragmatism and American Philosophy*, III(2):1–23.

Maria, A. (1997). Introduction to Modeling and Simulation. In Withers,
D. H., Nelson, B. L., Andradóttir, S., and Healy, K. J., editors, *Proceed-
ings of the 1997 Winter Simulation Conference*, WSC '97, pages 7–13,
Piscataway, New Jersey. Institute of Electrical and Electronics Engineers,
Inc.

Marsaglia, G. (1997). Diehard Battery of Tests of Randomness. https://web.archive.org/web/20160125103112/http://stat.fsu.edu/pub/diehard/.

Matala, A. (2008). Sample Size Requirement for Monte Carlo Simulations
Using Latin Hypercube Sampling. Technical Report 60968, Department of
Engineering, Physics and Mathematics, Helsinki University of Technology.

Matsumoto, M. and Nishimura, T. (1998). Mersenne Twister: A 623-
Dimensionally Equidistributed Uniform Pseudo-Random Number Generator. *ACM Transactions on Modeling and Computer Simulation*, 8(1):3–30.

Mattila, V., Virtanen, K., Muttilainen, L., Jylha, J., and Vaisanen, V.
(2014). Optimizing Locations of Decoys for Protecting Surface-Based
Radar Against Anti-Radiation Missile with Multi-Objective Ranking and
Selection. In Buckley, S. J., Miller, J. A., Tolk, A., Yilmaz, L., Diallo, S. Y.,
and Ryzhov, I. O., editors, *Proceedings of the 2014 Winter Simulation
Conference*, WSC '14, pages 2319–2330, Piscataway, New Jersey. Institute
of Electrical and Electronics Engineers, Inc.

McKay, M. D., Beckman, R. J., and Conover, W. J. (1979). Comparison of
Three Methods for Selecting Values of Input Variables in the Analysis of
Output from a Computer Code. *Technometrics*, 21(2):239–245.

McKeown, N., Anderson, T., Balakrishnan, H., Parulkar, G., Peterson, L.,
Rexford, J., Shenker, S., and Turner, J. (2008). OpenFlow: Enabling
Innovation in Campus Networks. *ACM SIGCOMM Computer Commu-
nication Review*, 38(2):69.

Meléndez-Colom, E. C. (2001). Special Report: Metadata Standards for Simulation Data / Models. *Information Management News-
letter of the Long Term Ecological Research Network*, Fall 2001.
http://databits.lternet.edu/issues/283.

Melia, M., Llado, C. M., Smith, C. U., and Puigjaner, R. (2008). Experimentation and Output Interchange for Petri Net Models. In *Proceedings
of the 7th International Workshop on Software and Performance*, WOSP
'08, pages 133–138, New York, NY, USA. ACM Press.

Mihram, G. A. (1973). Simulation: Methodology for the System Sciences. In Sussman, J. and Hoggatt, A. C., editors, *Proceedings of the 1973 Winter Simulation Conference*, WSC '73, pages 712–714, Piscataway, New Jersey. Institute of Electrical and Electronics Engineers, Inc.

Mill, J. S. (1872). *A System of Logic, Ratiocinative and Inductive, Being a Connected View of the Principles of Evidence, and the Methods of Scientific Investigation*, volume 2. Longmans, Green, Reader, and Dyer, London, 8th edition.

Mill, J. S. (1882). *A System of Logic, Ratiocinative and Inductive, Being a Connected View of the Principles of Evidence, and the Methods of Scientific Investigation*, volume 1. Harper & Brothers, Publishers, Franklin Square, London, 8th edition.

Mohindra, A. (2011). Deeper into Box Plots. The Nelson Touch Blog, https://nelsontouchconsulting.wordpress.com/2011/01/17/deeper-into-box-plots/.

Mönch, L., Rose, O., and Sturm, R. (2003). A Simulation Framework for the Performance Assessment of Shop-Floor Control Systems. *SIMULATION*, 79(3):163–170.

Montgomery, D. C. (2013). *Design and Analysis of Experiments*. John Wiley & Sons, Inc, Hoboken, NJ, 8th edition.

Montgomery, D. C., Runger, G. C., and Hubele, N. F. (2010). *Engineering Statistics*. Wiley, Hoboken, N.J.

Moore, D. S., McCabe, G. P., and Craig, B. A. (2009). *Introduction to the Practice of Statistics*. W.H. Freeman, New York, 6th edition.

Morris, M. D. (1991). Factorial Sampling Plans for Preliminary Computational Experiments. *Technometrics*, 33(2):161.

Morris, M. D. (2006). An Overview of Group Factor Screening. In *Screening: Methods for Experimentation in Industry, Drug Discovery and Genetics*, pages 191–206. Springer, New York.

Mowen, M. M. (2013). *Cornerstones of Managerial Accounting*. South-Western/Cengage Learning, Mason, OH, 5th edition.

Münnich, R. and Rässler, S. (2005). PRIMA: A New Multiple Imputation Procedure for Binary Variables. *Journal of Official Statistics*, 21(2):325.

Musselman, K. J. (1994). Guidelines for Simulation Project Success. In Sadowski, D. A., Seila, A. F., Tew, J. D., and Manivannan, S., editors, *Proceedings of the 1994 Winter Simulation Conference*, WSC '94, pages 88–95, Piscataway, New Jersey. Institute of Electrical and Electronics Engineers, Inc.

Nakayama, M. K. (2008). Statistical Analysis of Simulation Output. In Jefferson, T., Fowler, J., Mason, S., Hill, R., Moench, L., and Rose, O., editors, *Proceedings of the 2008 Winter Simulation Conference*, WSC '08, pages 62–72, Piscataway, New Jersey. Institute of Electrical and Electronics Engineers, Inc.

Nance, R. E. (1993). A History of Discrete Event Simulation Programming Languages. *ACM SIGPLAN Notices*, 28(3):149–175.

Nance, R. E. and Sargent, R. G. (2002). Perspectives on the Evolution of Simulation. *Operations Research*, 50(1):161–172.

Natrella, M. (2012). A Glossary of DOE Terminology. *NIST/SEMATECH e-Handbook of Statistical Methods*. https://www.itl.nist.gov/div898/handbook/pri/section7/pri7.htm.

Nelson, B. L. (2010). *Stochastic Modeling: Analysis & Simulation*. Dover books on mathematics. Dover Publications, Mineola, N.Y, dover edition.

NetLogo (2018). NetLogo User Manual Version 6.0.4 (org.nlogo.api MersenneTwisterFast). http://ccl.northwestern.edu/netlogo/docs/scaladoc/org/nlogo/api/MersenneTwisterFast.html.

Nikolai, C. and Madey, G. (2009). Tools of the Trade: A Survey of Various Agent Based Modeling Platforms. *Journal of Artificial Societies and Social Simulation*, 12(2):2.

Oinn, T., Addis, M., Ferris, J., Marvin, D., Senger, M., Greenwood, M., Carver, T., Glover, K., Pocock, M. R., Wipat, A., and Li, P. (2004). Taverna: A Tool for the Composition and Enactment of Bioinformatics Workflows. *Bioinformatics*, 20(17):3045–3054.

Österle, H., Becker, J., Frank, U., Hess, T., Karagiannis, D., Krcmar, H., Loos, P., Mertens, P., Oberweis, A., and Sinz, E. J. (2011). Memorandum on Design-Oriented Information Systems Research. *European Journal of Information Systems*, 20(1):7–10.

Özgün, O. and Barlas, Y. (2009). Discrete vs. Continuous Simulation: When Does It Matter? In *Proceedings of the 27th International Conference of the System Dynamics Society*, pages 1–22.

Ozik, J., Collier, N. T., Murphy, J. T., and North, M. J. (2013). The ReLogo Agent-Based Modeling Language. In Hill, R., Kuhl, M., Pasupathy, R., Kim, S.-H., and Tolk, A., editors, *Proceedings of the 2013 Winter Simulation Conference*, WSC '13, pages 1560–1568, Piscataway, New Jersey. Institute of Electrical and Electronics Engineers, Inc.

Park, J.-S. (1994). Optimal Latin-Hypercube Designs for Computer Experiments. *Journal of Statistical Planning and Inference*, 39(1):95–111.

Parmenter, D. (2015). *Key Performance Indicators: Developing, Implementing, and Using Winning KPIs*. Wiley, Hoboken, New Jersey, 3rd edition.

Pawlaszczyk, D. and Strassburger, S. (2009). Scalability in Distributed Simulations of Agent-Based Models. In Dunkin, A., Ingalls, R., Yücesan, E., Rossetti, M., Hill, R., and Johansson, B., editors, *Proceedings of the 2009 Winter Simulation Confernece*, WSC '09, pages 1189–1200, Piscataway, New Jersey. Institute of Electrical and Electronics Engineers, Inc.

Pawlewski, P. and Borucki, J. (2011). "Green" Possibilities of Simulation Software for Production and Logistics: A Survey. In Golinska, P., Fertsch, M., and Marx-Gómez, J., editors, *Information Technologies in Environmental Engineering*, volume 3, pages 675–688. Springer, Berlin, Heidelberg.

Peak, R. S., Burkhart, R. M., Friedenthal, S. A., Wilson, M. W., Bajaj, M., and Kim, I. (2007). Simulation-Based Design Using SysML Part 1: A Parametrics Primer. *INCOSE International Symposium*, 17(1):1516–1535.

Pearson, K. (1900). *The Grammar of Science*. Adam & Charles Black, London, 2nd edition.

Pegden, C. D., Shannon, R. E., and Sadowski, R. P. (1995). *Introduction to Simulation Using SIMAN*. McGraw-Hill, New York, 2nd edition.

Peng, D. (2017). *Reusing Simulation Experiments for Model Composition and Extension*. Dissertation. Univerity of Rostock, Germany.

Perrone, L. F., Main, C. S., and Ward, B. C. (2012). SAFE: Simulation Automation Framework for Experiments. In Rose, O., Uhrmacher, A., Rabe, M., Laroque, C., Rasupathy, R., and Himmelspach, J., editors, *Proceedings of the 2012 Winter Simulation Conference*, WSC '12, pages 1–12, Piscataway, New Jersey. Institute of Electrical and Electronics Engineers, Inc.

Petty, M. D. (2009). Verification and Validation. In Sokolowski, J. A. and Banks, C. M., editors, *Principles of Modeling and Simulation*, pages 121–149. John Wiley & Sons, Inc., Hoboken, NJ, USA.

Popper, K. R. (2002). *The Logic of Scientific Discovery*. Routledge classics. Routledge, London.

Pritsker, A. A. B. and O'Reilly, J. J. (1999). *Simulation with Visual SLAM and AweSim*. Wiley, New York, 2nd edition.

Rabe, M., Spieckermann, S., and Wenzel, S. (2008). A New Procedure Model for Verification and Validation in Production and Logistics Simulation. In Jefferson, T., Fowler, J., Mason, S., Hill, R., Moench, L., and Rose, O., editors, *Proceedings of the 2008 Winter Simulation Conference*, WSC '08, pages 1717–1726, Piscataway, New Jersey. Institute of Electrical and Electronics Engineers, Inc.

Railsback, S. F., Lytinen, S. L., and Jackson, S. K. (2006). Agent-Based Simulation Platforms: Review and Development Recommendations. *SIMULATION*, 82(9):609–623.

Raychaudhuri, S. (2008). Introduction to Monte Carlo Simulation. In Jefferson, T., Fowler, J., Mason, S., Hill, R., Moench, L., and Rose, O., editors, *Proceedings of the 2008 Winter Simulation Conference*, WSC '08, pages 91–100, Piscataway, New Jersey. Institute of Electrical and Electronics Engineers, Inc.

Razali, N. M., Wah, Y. B., and others (2011). Power Comparisons of Shapiro-Wilk, Kolmogorov-Smirnov, Lilliefors and Anderson-Darling Tests. *Journal of statistical modeling and analytics*, 2(1):21–33.

Recker, J. (2013). *Scientific Research in Information Systems: A Beginner's Guide*. Progress in IS. Springer, Berlin Heidelberg New York Dobrecht London. OCLC: 812383075.

Repko, A. F., Szostak, R., and Buchberger, M. P. (2017). *Introduction to Interdisciplinary Studies*. Sage, Los Angeles, 2nd edition.

Richiardi, M. G., Leombruni, R., Saam, N. J., and Sonnessa, M. (2006). A Common Protocol for Agent-Based Social Simulation. *Journal of Artificial Societies and Social Simulation*, 9(1):16–31.

Riley, G. and Pekley, J. (2011). An XML Experiment Description Language for ns-3. In *Proceedings of the 4th International ICST Conference on Simulation Tools and Techniques*, SIMUTools '11, pages 447–453, Brussels, Belgium. ICST (Institute for Computer Sciences, Social-Informatics and Telecommunications Engineering).

Riley, G. F. and Henderson, T. R. (2010). The ns-3 Network Simulator. In Wehrle, K., Güneş, M., and Gross, J., editors, *Modeling and Tools for Network Simulation*, pages 15–34. Springer, Berlin, Heidelberg.

Robinson, S. (2002). A Statistical Process Control Approach for Estimating the Warm-Up Period. In Snowdon, J. L., Charnes, J. M., Yücesan, E., and Chen, C.-H., editors, *Proceedings of the 2002 Winter Simulation Conference*, volume 1 of *WSC '02*, pages 439–446, Piscataway, New Jersey. Institute of Electrical and Electronics Engineers, Inc.

Robinson, S. (2004). *Simulation: The Practice of Model Development and Use*. John Wiley & Sons, Ltd, Hoboken, NJ.

Ross, S. M. (2013). *Simulation*. Academic Press, Amsterdam, 5th edition.

Rossetti, M. D. (2016). *Simulation Modeling and Arena*. John Wiley & Sons, Inc, Hoboken, New Jersey, 2nd edition.

Russell, S. J., Norvig, P., and Davis, E. (2010). *Artificial Intelligence: A Modern Approach*. Prentice Hall series in artificial intelligence. Prentice-Hall, Upper Saddle River, 3rd edition.

Rybacki, S. (2016). *Towards Reproducible Simulation Studies with JAMES II*. Dissertation. University of Rostock, Germany.

Sadowski, R. P. (1992). Selling Simulation and Simulation Results. In Crain, R. C., Wilson, J. R., Swain, J. J., and Goldsman, D., editors, *Proceedings of the 1992 Winter Simulation Conference*, WSC '92, pages 122–125, Piscataway, New Jersey. Institute of Electrical and Electronics Engineers, Inc.

Saliby, E. (1997). Descriptive Sampling: An Improvement over Latin Hypercube Sampling. In Withers, D. H., Nelson, B. L., Andradóttir, S., and Healy, K. J., editors, *Proceedings of the 1997 Winter Simulation Conference*, WSC '97, pages 230–233, Piscataway, New Jersey. Institute of Electrical and Electronics Engineers, Inc.

Sanchez, S. (2007). Work Smarter, Not Harder: Guidelines for Designing Simulation Experiments. In Tew, J., Barton, R., Henderson, S., Biller, B., Hsieh, M.-h., and Shortle, J., editors, *Proceedings of the 2007 Winter Simulation Conference*, WSC '07, pages 84–94, Piscataway, New Jersey. Institute of Electrical and Electronics Engineers, Inc.

Sanchez, S. and Lucas, T. (2002). Exploring the World of Agent-Based Simulations: Simple Models, Complex Analyses. In Snowdon, J. L., Charnes, J. M., Yücesan, E., and Chen, C.-H., editors, *Proceedings of the 2002 Winter Simulation Conference*, WSC '02, pages 116–126, Piscataway, New Jersey. Institute of Electrical and Electronics Engineers, Inc.

Sanchez, S. and Wan, H. (2012). Work Smarter, Not Harder: A Tutorial on Designing and Conducting Simulation Experiments. In Rose, O., Uhrmacher, A., Rabe, M., Laroque, C., Rasupathy, R., and Himmelspach, J., editors, *Proceedings of the 2012 Winter Simulation Conference*, WSC '12, pages 1–15, Piscataway, New Jersey. Institute of Electrical and Electronics Engineers, Inc.

Sargent, R. (2013). Verification and Validation of Simulation Models. *Journal of Simulation*, 7(1):12–24.

Sargent, R. (2017). A Perspective on Fifty-Five Years of the Evolution of Scientific Respect for Simulation. In Snowdon, J. L., Charnes, J. M., Yücesan, E., and Chen, C.-H., editors, *Proceedings of the 2017 Winter Simulation Conference*, WSC '17, pages 3–15, Piscataway, New Jersey. Institute of Electrical and Electronics Engineers, Inc.

Sargent, R. G., Page, E. H., Wainer, G., Tufarolo, J., Chan, V., D'Ambrogio, A., Zacharewicz, G., and Mustafee, N. (2017). History of the Winter Simulation Conference: Coming-of-Age Period (1983–1992). In *Proceedings of the 2017 Winter Simulation Conference*, WSC '17, pages 82–86, Piscataway, New Jersey. Institute of Electrical and Electronics Engineers, Inc.

Satterthwaite, F. E. (1941). Synthesis of Variance. *Psychometrika*, 6(5):309–316.

Sawyer, J. T. and Brann, D. M. (2009). How to Test Your Models More Effectively: Applying Agile and Automated Techniques to Simulation Testing. In Dunkin, A., Ingalls, R., Yücesan, E., Rossetti, M., Hill, R., and Johansson, B., editors, *Proceedings of the 2009 Winter Simulation Confernece*, WSC '09, pages 968–978, Piscataway, New Jersey. Institute of Electrical and Electronics Engineers, Inc.

SC-135 (2014). Environmental Conditions and Test Procedures for Airborne Equipment (DO-160 G). https://www.rtca.org/content/sc-135.

Schepers, R., Minning, T., Moog, Y., and Timm, I. J. (2014). Towards Simulation of Business Processes – Transforming BPMN Models to Enterprise Dynamics Models. In *Proceedings of the Fourth International Symposium on Business Modeling and Software Design - Volume 1: BMSD*, BMSD 2014, pages 159–165. SCITEPRESS - Science and and Technology Publications.

Schmidt, D. C. (2006). Model-Driven Engineering. *IEEE Computer*, 39(2):25–31.

Schmidt, J. W. (1984). Introduction to Simulation. In Pooch, U. W., Pegden, C. D., and Sheppard, S., editors, *Proceedings of the 1984 Winter Simulation Confernece*, WSC '84, pages 64–73, Piscataway, New Jersey. Institute of Electrical and Electronics Engineers, Inc.

Schonherr, O. and Rose, O. (2009). First Steps Towards a General SysML Model for Discrete Processes in Production Systems. In Dunkin, A., Ingalls, R., Yücesan, E., Rossetti, M., Hill, R., and Johansson, B., editors, *Proceedings of the 2009 Winter Simulation Confernece*, WSC '09, pages 1711–1718, Piscataway, New Jersey. Institute of Electrical and Electronics Engineers, Inc.

Schützel, J., Peng, D., Uhrmacher, A. M., and Perrone, L. F. (2014). Perspectives on Languages for Specifying Simulation Experiments. In Buckley, S. J., Miller, J. A., Tolk, A., Yilmaz, L., Diallo, S. Y., and Ryzhov, I. O., editors, *Proceedings of the 2014 Winter Simulation Conference*, WSC '14, pages 2836–2847, Piscataway, New Jersey. Institute of Electrical and Electronics Engineers, Inc.

Schwertman, N. C., Owens, M. A., and Adnan, R. (2004). A Simple More General Boxplot Method for Identifying Outliers. *Computational Statistics & Data Analysis*, 47(1):165–174.

Shannon, R. E. (1975). *Systems Simulation: The Art and Science.* Prentice-Hall, Englewood Cliffs.

Shannon, R. E. (1998). Introduction to the Art and Science of Simulation. In Carson, J. S., Manivannan, M. S., Medeiros, D. J., and Watson, E. F., editors, *Proceedings of the 1998 Winter Simulation Conference,* WSC '98, pages 7–14, Piscataway, New Jersey. Institute of Electrical and Electronics Engineers, Inc.

Shi, W., Shang, J., and Zhigang, Z. (2016). Simulation Screening and False Discovery Rate Control for Both Main and Interaction Effects. In Huschka, T., Chick, S., Jimenez, J., Frazier, P., Roeder, T., Szechtman, R., and Zhou, E., editors, *Proceedings of the 2016 Winter Simulation Conference,* WSC '16, pages 512–521, Piscataway, New Jersey. Institute of Electrical and Electronics Engineers, Inc.

Simon, R. (1989). Optimal Two-Stage Designs for Phase II Clinical Trials. *Controlled Clinical Trials,* 10(1):1–10.

Smith, C. and Llado, C. (2004). Performance Model Interchange Format (PMIF 2.0): Xml Definition and Implementation. In *Proceedings of the First International Conference on the Quantitative Evaluation of Systems,* QEST 2004, pages 38–47. IEEE.

Smith, C. U., Lladó, C. M., and Puigjaner, R. (2010). Performance Model Interchange Format (PMIF 2): A Comprehensive Approach to Queueing Network Model Interoperability. *Performance Evaluation,* 67(7):548–568.

Smith, C. U., Lladó, C. M., and Puigjaner, R. (2011). Model Interchange Format Specifications for Experiments, Output and Results. *The Computer Journal,* 54(5):674–690.

Smith, C. U., Lladó, C. M., Puigjaner, R., and Williams, L. G. (2007). Interchange Formats for Performance Models: Experimentation and Ouput. In *Proceedings of the Fourth International Conference on the Quantitative Evaluation of Systems,* QEST 2007, pages 91–100. IEEE.

Smith, E. R. and Conrey, F. R. (2007). Agent-Based Modeling: A New Approach for Theory Building in Social Psychology. *Personality and Social Psychology Review,* 11(1):87–104.

Smith, L. P., Butterworth, E., Bassingthwaighte, J. B., and Sauro, H. M. (2014). SBML and CellML Translation in Antimony and JSim. *Bioinformatics,* 30(7):903–907.

Smith, M. K., Moodie, S. L., Bizzotto, R., Blaudez, E., Borella, E., Carrara, L., Chan, P., Chenel, M., Comets, E., Gieschke, R., Harling, K., Harnisch, L., Hartung, N., Hooker, A. C., Karlsson, M. O., Kaye, R., Kloft, C., Kokash, N., Lavielle, M., Lestini, G., Magni, P., Mari, A., Mentré, F., Muselle, C., Nordgren, R., Nyberg, H. B., Parra-Guillén, Z. P., Pasotti, L., Rode-Kristensen, N., Sardu, M. L., Smith, G. R., Swat, M. J., Terranova, N., Yngman, G., Yvon, F., Holford, N., and on behalf of the DDMoRe consortium (2017). Model Description Language (MDL): A Standard for Modeling and Simulation: Model Description Language (MDL). *CPT: Pharmacometrics & Systems Pharmacology*, 6(10):647–650.

Sokolowski, J. A. and Banks, C. M. (2009). *Modeling and Simulation for Analyzing Global Events*. Wiley, Hoboken, New Jersey.

Soldatova, L. N., Aubrey, W., King, R. D., and Clare, A. (2008). The EXACT Description of Biomedical Protocols. *Bioinformatics*, 24(13):i295–i303.

Steiger, N. M. and Wilson, J. R. (2002). An Improved Batch Means Procedure for Simulation Output Analysis. *Management Science*, 48(12):1569–1586.

Storey, I. C. and Allan, A. (2014). *A Guide to Ancient Greek Drama*. Blackwell Guides to classical literature. Wiley, Malden, MA, 2nd edition.

Taniguchi, E. and Shimamoto, H. (2004). Intelligent Transportation System Based Dynamic Vehicle Routing and Scheduling with Variable Travel Times. *Transportation Research Part C: Emerging Technologies*, 12(3-4):235–250.

Taylor, B. N. and Kuyatt, C. E. (1994). *NIST Technical Note 1297: Guidelines for Evaluating and Expressing the Uncertainty of NIST Measurement Results*. NIST (United States Department of Commerce Technology Administration - National Institute of Standards and Technology). https://www.nist.gov/sites/default/files/documents/2017/05/09/tn1297s.pdf.

Taylor, C. F., Field, D., Sansone, S.-A., Aerts, J., Apweiler, R., Ashburner, M., Ball, C. A., Binz, P.-A., Bogue, M., Booth, T., Brazma, A., Brinkman, R. R., Michael Clark, A., Deutsch, E. W., Fiehn, O., Fostel, J., Ghazal, P., Gibson, F., Gray, T., Grimes, G., Hancock, J. M., Hardy, N. W., Hermjakob, H., Julian, R. K., Kane, M., Kettner, C., Kinsinger, C., Kolker, E., Kuiper, M., Novère, N. L., Leebens-Mack, J., Lewis, S. E., Lord, P., Mallon, A.-M., Marthandan, N., Masuya, H., McNally, R., Mehrle, A., Morrison, N., Orchard, S., Quackenbush, J., Reecy, J. M., Robertson,

D. G., Rocca-Serra, P., Rodriguez, H., Rosenfelder, H., Santoyo-Lopez, J., Scheuermann, R. H., Schober, D., Smith, B., Snape, J., Stoeckert, C. J., Tipton, K., Sterk, P., Untergasser, A., Vandesompele, J., and Wiemann, S. (2008). Promoting Coherent Minimum Reporting Guidelines for Biological and Biomedical Investigations: The MIBBI Project. *Nature Biotechnology*, 26(8):889–896.

Taylor, I. J. (2011). *Workflows for eScience: Scientific Workflows for Grids*. Springer, London.

Teran-Somohano, A., Dayibas, O., Yilmaz, L., and Smith, A. (2014). Toward a Model-Driven Engineering Framework for Reproducible Simulation Experiment Lifecycle Management. In Buckley, S. J., Miller, J. A., Tolk, A., Yilmaz, L., Diallo, S. Y., and Ryzhov, I. O., editors, *Proceedings of the 2014 Winter Simulation Conference*, WSC '14, pages 2726–2737, Piscataway, New Jersey. Institute of Electrical and Electronics Engineers, Inc.

Teran-Somohano, A., Smith, A. E., Ledet, J., Yilmaz, L., and Oguztuzun, H. (2015). A Model-Driven Engineering Approach to Simulation Experiment Design and Execution. In Macal, C. M., Rossetti, M. D., Yilmaz, L., Moon, I.-C., Chan, W. K., and Roeder, T., editors, *Proceedings of the 2015 Winter Simulation Conference*, WSC '15, pages 2632–2643, Piscataway, New Jersey. Institute of Electrical and Electronics Engineers, Inc.

Tesfatsion, L. (2003). Agent-Based Computational Economics: Modeling Economies as Complex Adaptive Systems. *Information Sciences*, 149(4):262–268.

Thiers, G. and McGinnis, L. (2011). Logistics Systems Modeling and Simulation. In White, P., Fu, M., Jain, S., Creasey, R., and Himmelspach, J., editors, *Proceedings of the 2011 Winter Simulation Conference*, WSC '11, pages 1531–1541, Piscataway, New Jersey. Institute of Electrical and Electronics Engineers, Inc.

Tichy, W. (1998). Should Computer Scientists Experiment More? *Computer*, 31(5):32–40.

Tietjen, G. L. (1986). *A Topical Dictionary of Statistics*. Springer US. OCLC: 968505904.

Timm, I. and Pawlaszczyk, D. (2005). Large scale multiagent simulation on the grid. In *2005 IEEE International Symposium on Cluster Computing and the Grid*, CCGRID '05, pages 334–341. IEEE.

Timm, I. J., Bogon, T., Lattner, A. D., and Schumann, R. (2008). Teaching Distributed Artificial Intelligence with RoboRally. In Bergmann, R., Lindemann, G., Kirn, S., and Pěchouček, M., editors, *Multiagent System Technologies*, volume 5244 of *MATES '08*, pages 171–182, Berlin, Heidelberg. Springer.

Timm, I. J. and Lorig, F. (2015). A Survey on Methodological Aspects of Computer Simulation as Research Technique. In Macal, C. M., Rossetti, M. D., Yilmaz, L., Moon, I.-C., Chan, W. K., and Roeder, T., editors, *Proceedings of the 2015 Winter Simulation Conference*, WSC '15, pages 2704–2715, Piscataway, New Jersey. Institute of Electrical and Electronics Engineers, Inc.

Tisue, S. and Wilensky, U. (2004). NetLogo: Design and Implementation of a Multi-Agent Modeling Environment. In *Proceedings of the Agent 2004 Conference on Social Dynamics: Interaction, Reflexivity and Emergence*, volume 2004 of *Agent 2004*, pages 7–9.

Tobias, R. and Hofmann, C. (2004). Evaluation of Free Java-Libraries for Social-Scientific Agent Based Simulation. *Journal of Artificial Societies and Social Simulation*, 7(1):6.

Tolk, A. (2015). Learning Something Right from Models That Are Wrong: Epistemology of Simulation. In Yilmaz, L., editor, *Concepts and Methodologies for Modeling and Simulation*, pages 87–106. Springer International Publishing, Cham.

Tolk, A. (2017a). Bias Ex Silico: Observations on Simulationist's Regress. In *Proceedings of the 50th Annual Simulation Symposium*, ANSS '17, pages 15:1–15:9. Society for Computer Simulation International.

Tolk, A. (2017b). Code of Ethics. In Tolk, A. and Oren, T., editors, *The Profession of Modeling and Simulation*, pages 35–52. John Wiley & Sons, Inc., Hoboken, NJ, USA.

Tolk, A., Diallo, S. Y., Padilla, J. J., and Herencia-Zapana, H. (2013a). Reference Modelling in Support of M&S – Foundations and Applications. *Journal of Simulation*, 7(2):69–82.

Tolk, A., Heath, B. L., Ihrig, M., Padilla, J. J., Page, E. H., Suarez, E. D., Szabo, C., Weirich, P., and Yilmaz, L. (2013b). Epistemology of Modeling and Simulation. In Hill, R., Kuhl, M., Pasupathy, R., Kim, S.-H., and Tolk, A., editors, *Proceedings of the 2013 Winter Simulation Conference*,

WSC '13, pages 1152–1166, Piscataway, New Jersey. Institute of Electrical and Electronics Engineers, Inc.

Turnitsa, C. and Tolk, A. (2008). Knowledge Representation and the Dimensions of a Multi-Model Relationship. In Jefferson, T., Fowler, J., Mason, S., Hill, R., Moench, L., and Rose, O., editors, *Proceedings of the 2008 Winter Simulation Conference*, WSC '08, pages 1148–1156, Piscataway, New Jersey. Institute of Electrical and Electronics Engineers, Inc.

Uhrmacher, A. M. (2012). Seven Pitfalls in Modeling and Simulation Research. In Rose, O., Uhrmacher, A., Rabe, M., Laroque, C., Rasupathy, R., and Himmelspach, J., editors, *Proceedings of the 2012 Winter Simulation Conference*, WSC '12, pages 1–12, Piscataway, New Jersey. Institute of Electrical and Electronics Engineers, Inc.

Uhrmacher, A. M., Brailsford, S., Liu, J., Rabe, M., and Tolk, A. (2016). Panel – Reproducible Research in Discrete Event Simulation – A Must or Rather a Maybe? In Huschka, T., Chick, S., Jimenez, J., Frazier, P., Roeder, T., Szechtman, R., and Zhou, E., editors, *Proceedings of the 2016 Winter Simulation Conference*, WSC '16, pages 1301–1315, Piscataway, New Jersey. Institute of Electrical and Electronics Engineers, Inc.

Vallverdú, J. (2014). What are Simulations? An Epistemological Approach. *Procedia Technology*, 13:6–15.

van den Berg, R., Lefeber, E., and Rooda, K. (2008). Modeling and Control of a Manufacturing Flow Line Using Partial Differential Equations. *IEEE Transactions on Control Systems Technology*, 16(1):130–136.

van der Aalst, W. M. P., Nakatumba, J., Rozinat, A., and Russell, N. (2010). Business Process Simulation. In Brocke, J. v. and Rosemann, M., editors, *Handbook on Business Process Management 1*, pages 313–338. Springer, Berlin, Heidelberg.

van Deursen, A., Klint, P., and Visser, J. (2000). Domain-Specific Languages: An Annotated Bibliography. *ACM Sigplan Notices*, 35(6):26–36.

VDI (2016). VDI Standard 3633 (ICS 03.100.10). www.vdi.de/3633.

Veziridis, S., Karampelas, P., and Lekea, I. (2017). Learn by Playing: A Serious War Game Simulation for Teaching Military Ethics. In *Proceedings of the 2017 IEEE Global Engineering Education Conference*, EDUCON, pages 920–925. IEEE.

Vincent, S. (1998). Input Data Analysis. In Banks, J., editor, *Handbook of Simulation*, pages 53–91. John Wiley & Sons, Inc., Hoboken, NJ, USA.

von Bertalanffy, L. (1968). *General System Theory – Foundations, Development, Applications*. George Braziller, New York.

Wagner, G., Nicolae, O., and Werner, J. (2009). Extending Discrete Event Simulation by Adding an Activity Concept for Business Process Modeling and Simulation. In Dunkin, A., Ingalls, R., Yücesan, E., Rossetti, M., Hill, R., and Johansson, B., editors, *Proceedings of the 2009 Winter Simulation Confernece*, WSC '09, pages 2951–2962, Piscataway, New Jersey. Institute of Electrical and Electronics Engineers, Inc.

Wagner, T., Schwenke, C., Kabitzsch, K., and Schneider, G. (2013). Automated Planning, Execution and Evaluation of Simulation Experiments of Semiconductor AMHS. In Hill, R., Kuhl, M., Pasupathy, R., Kim, S.-H., and Tolk, A., editors, *Proceedings of the 2013 Winter Simulation Conference*, WSC '13, pages 3891–3904, Piscataway, New Jersey. Institute of Electrical and Electronics Engineers, Inc.

Wainer, G. A., Al-Zoubi, K., Hill, D. R., Mittal, S., Martín, J. L. R., Sarjoughian, H., Touraille, L., Traoré, M. K., and Zeigler, B. P. (2011). An Introduction to DEVS Standardization: Theory anbd Applications. In *Discrete-Event Modeling and Simulation: Theory and Applications*, pages 393 – 426. CRC Press, Boca Raton.

Waltemath, D., Adams, R., Beard, D. A., Bergmann, F. T., Bhalla, U. S., Britten, R., Chelliah, V., Cooling, M. T., Cooper, J., Crampin, E. J., Garny, A., Hoops, S., Hucka, M., Hunter, P., Klipp, E., Laibe, C., Miller, A. K., Moraru, I., Nickerson, D., Nielsen, P., Nikolski, M., Sahle, S., Sauro, H. M., Schmidt, H., Snoep, J. L., Tolle, D., Wolkenhauer, O., and Le Novère, N. (2011). Minimum Information About a Simulation Experiment (MIASE). *PLoS Computational Biology*, 7(4):e1001122.

Waltz, D. and Buchanan, B. G. (2009). Automating Science. *Science*, 324(5923):43–44.

Wan, H., Ankenman, B. E., and Nelson, B. L. (2006). Controlled Sequential Bifurcation: A New Factor-Screening Method for Discrete-Event Simulation. *Operations Research*, 54(4):743–755.

Wan, H., Ankenman, B. E., and Nelson, B. L. (2010). Improving the Efficiency and Efficacy of Controlled Sequential Bifurcation for Simulation Factor Screening. *INFORMS Journal on Computing*, 22(3):482–492.

Wenzel, S., Jessen, U., and Bernhard, J. (2005). Classifications and Conventions Structure the Handling of Models Within the Digital Factory. *Computers in Industry*, 56(4):334–346.

Whewell, W. (1847). *The Philosophy of the Inductive Sciences, Founded Upon Their History*, volume 2. Jhon W. Parker, West Strand, London.

Wilensky, U. (1999). *NetLogo*. Evanston, IL: Center for connected learning and computer-based modeling, Northwestern University. http://ccl.northwestern.edu/netlogo/.

Wilson, E. B. (1990). *An Introduction to Scientific Research*. Dover Publications, New York.

Wilson, J. R., Brunner, D. T., and Swain, J. J. (1996). The Winter Simulation Conference: The Premier Forum on Simulation Practice and Theory. *ACM SIGSIM Simulation Digest*, 25(3):6–10.

Wimpey, B. J., Lennon, C., and Fields, M. A. (2015). Detecting Team Behavior Using Focus of Attention. In Macal, C. M., Rossetti, M. D., Yilmaz, L., Moon, I.-C., Chan, W. K., and Roeder, T., editors, *Proceedings of the 2015 Winter Simulation Conference*, WSC '15, pages 2378–2387, Piscataway, New Jersey. Institute of Electrical and Electronics Engineers, Inc.

Winsberg, E. B. (2010). *Science in the Age of Computer Simulation*. The University of Chicago Press, Chicago.

Winsberg, E. B. (2015). Computer Simulations in Science. In Zalta, E. N., editor, *The Stanford Encyclopedia of Philosophy*. Metaphysics Research Lab, Stanford University, summer 2018 edition. https://plato.stanford.edu/archives/sum2018/entries/simulations-science/.

Wohlin, C. (2014). Guidelines for Snowballing in Systematic Literature Studies and a Replication in Software Engineering. In *Proceedings of the 18th International Conference on Evaluation and Assessment in Software Engineering*, EASE '14, pages 1–10. ACM Press.

Yi, J., Eeckhout, L., Lilja, D., Calder, B., John, L., and Smith, J. (2006). The Future of Simulation: A Field of Dreams. *Computer*, 39(11):22–29.

Yilmaz, L. (2015). Toward Agent-Supported and Agent-Monitored Model-Driven Simulation Engineering. In Yilmaz, L., editor, *Concepts and Methodologies for Modeling and Simulation*, pages 3–18. Springer International Publishing, Cham.

Yilmaz, L., Chakladar, S., and Doud, K. (2016). The Goal-Hypothesis-Experiment Framework: A Generative Cognitive Domain Architecture for Simulation Experiment Management. In Huschka, T., Chick, S., Jimenez, J., Frazier, P., Roeder, T., Szechtman, R., and Zhou, E., editors, *Proceedings of the 2016 Winter Simulation Conference*, WSC '16, pages 1001–1012, Piscataway, New Jersey. Institute of Electrical and Electronics Engineers, Inc.

Yilmaz, L., Chakladar, S., Doud, K., Smith, A. E., Teran-Somohano, A., Oguztuzun, H., Cam, S., Dayibas, O., and Gorur, B. K. (2017). Models as Self-Aware Cognitive Agents and Adaptive Mediators for Model-Driven Science. In Page, E. H., Wainer, G., Tufarolo, J., Chan, V., D'Ambrogio, A., Zacharewicz, G., and Mustafee, N., editors, *Proceedings of the 2017 Winter Simulation Conference*, WSC '17, pages 1300–1311, Piscataway, New Jersey. Institute of Electrical and Electronics Engineers, Inc.

Yilmaz, L., Taylor, S. J. E., Fujimoto, R., and Darema, F. (2014). Panel: The Future of Research in Modeling & Simulation. In Buckley, S. J., Miller, J. A., Tolk, A., Yilmaz, L., Diallo, S. Y., and Ryzhov, I. O., editors, *Proceedings of the 2014 Winter Simulation Conference*, WSC '14, pages 2797–2811, Piscataway, New Jersey. Institute of Electrical and Electronics Engineers, Inc.

Zack, N. (2010). *The Handy Philosophy Answer Book*. The Handy Answer Book Series. Visible Ink Press, Detroit. OCLC: ocn456840520.

Zeigler, B. P. (2016). DEVS: Past, Present, Future. https://devs-network.org/sites/devs-network.org/files/images/files/DEVSPastPresentFuture.pdf.

Zeigler, B. P., Praehofer, H., and Kim, T. G. (2000). *Theory of Modeling and Simulation: Integrating Discrete Event and Continuous Complex Dynamic Systems*. Academic Press, San Diego, 2nd edition.

Index

© Springer Fachmedien Wiesbaden GmbH, part of Springer Nature 2019
F. Lorig, *Hypothesis-Driven Simulation Studies*,

Printed in the United States
By Bookmasters